AT PEACE
AND UNAFRAID

AT PEACE AND UNAFRAID

PUBLIC ORDER, SECURITY, AND THE WISDOM OF THE CROSS

Edited by Duane K. Friesen
and Gerald W. Schlabach

Herald Press

Scottdale, Pennsylvania
Waterloo, Ontario

Library of Congress Cataloging-in-Publication Data
At peace and unafraid : public order, security, and the wisdom of the
cross / edited by Duane K. Friesen and Gerald W. Schlabach.
  p. cm.
 Includes bibliographical references.
 ISBN 0-8361-9308-3 (pbk. : alk. paper)
 1. Peace—Religious aspects—Mennonites. 2. Nonviolence—
Religious aspects—Mennonites. 3. National security—Religious
aspects—Mennonites. 4. Christian ethics—Mennonite authors.
5. Mennonites—Doctrines. I. Friesen, Duane K. II. Schlabach,
Gerald.
 BX8128.P4A8 2005
 261.8'3—dc22

                                    2005025973

AT PEACE AND UNAFRAID
Copyright © 2005 by Herald Press, Scottdale, Pa. 15683
   Published simultaneously in Canada by Herald Press,
   Waterloo, Ont. N2L 6H7. All rights reserved
Library of Congress Catalog Card Number: 2005025973
International Standard Book Number: 0-8361-9308-3
Printed in the United States of America
Book design by Sandra Johnson
Cover by Cathleen Benberg, A Distant Wind

12 11 10 09 08 07 06 05   10 9 8 7 6 5 4 3 2 1

To order or request information, please call
1-800-759-4447 (individuals); 1-800-245-7894 (trade).
Web site: www.heraldpress.com

for our children,
and "their" children too

CONTENTS

**PART II: Seeking the Welfare of the City: Essays on Public
Peace, Justice, and Order**

Section A: A Church Perspective on Security, Safety, and the
Common Good

Section D: Practicing Wisdom in Public Systems

CONCLUSION

FOREWORD

"Look at this pitcher." Ricardo Esquivia lifted a pitcher of water from the table in front of him. "The water in the pitcher represents peace. But it needs some kind of structure to hold it. That structure is 'institutionality' (*institucionalidad*). There can be different shapes to the pitcher, but we need something, some structure, in order for the water to be usable."

Esquivia was speaking with the Mennonite Central Committee (MCC) Peace Committee, a group that meets twice each year to reflect on issues of peace and justice that arise in the international programs of MCC. As a Mennonite from Colombia, he was discussing the work of the church in a context marked by violence and oppression. For him, the key was "institutionality." The Spanish word *institucionalidad* sometimes applies to bureaucracy. But for Esquivia, it signified the structures that a society needs to allow everyone to flourish as they live lives of dignity.

Esquivia also asked the committee to look at the pitcher to see whether it was appropriately designed, whether it was clean and uncorrupted. Order, though absolutely indispensable, can be corrupt and oppressive. Even so, this possibility does not diminish the need for good order. Institutionality represents the order that makes people secure. In Colombia, where the government resorts to violence and armed groups compete for territory and income, and where ordinary people become pawns in the search for power, the need for order is all the more acute, but it must be the right kind of order. The church, said Esquivia, should be part of helping to build good order.

Many Mennonites live in countries where people long for

order. What they long for is not an order built on violent, military force, but on collective responsibility—the net of institutions in a society that ensures safety and well-being. Our brothers and sisters in such contexts ask, "What is the role of the church in a society that needs such order? What does loving our neighbor and our enemy have to do with how our communities are ordered? How do we build security without relying on violent force?"

Questions about order and safety were also on the agenda of many Mennonite and Brethren in Christ church members in the United States and Canada in the weeks following the September 11, 2001, attacks in New York, Washington, D.C., and Pennsylvania. When many persons in these societies impulsively, often unreflectively, assumed that only violent force could provide protection and security, they were discouraging creative imagination or even shutting it down. The fear this event created in average people, especially in the United States, was almost palpable. In public meetings, sports events, and community gatherings people talked and shared their mutual anxiety. When war soon started in Afghanistan—and then again in Iraq—neighbors, friends, and family got caught up in military service, and new fears ignited in peoples' lives. In this context, Mennonites and Brethren in Christ struggled just to think about, let alone to present, alternatives.

Contexts of chaos and disorder. Contexts of fear and insecurity. These are background for this book. As MCC's Peace Committee reflected on the challenges and questions they raise, its sense was that Anabaptist theology has not traditionally worked to answer them. Questions about our Christian responsibility for the wider society are certainly not unknown to Anabaptist-Mennonite peace theology. But to demonstrate Christ-like love for our neighbors and our enemies has rightly taken priority over calls to "responsibility," which so often imply a willingness to dominate others, with recourse to violence if necessary, in ways that are hardly Christ-like. The challenge that contexts of disorder and insecurity pose, however, is this: Christ-like love itself must yearn for neighbor, stranger, and enemy alike to live in safety, "at peace and unafraid." What's more, the very practices that put love into operation often rely on systems of order and conditions of security.

In practical ways, Mennonites have certainly shaped the communities in which they live. So questions of right ordering have not been absent. But we have not generally applied ourselves to think through the church's role or the Christian's role in building right and just order for the wider society beyond the church, beyond the beloved community. Perhaps this results from the sense that Mennonites have of being a small, marginal, or separated group that does not concern itself with the wider good. Perhaps it is because of a fear that such questions would take us too far away from nonresistance or pacifism. While we can find in our history many examples of involvement that worked for the good of those around us, these have tended to be individual rather than systemic. Only too rarely have we struggled theologically with what it means to work for a larger good—for order and safety—in ways consistent with our calling to follow the Prince of Peace.

At the same time, some members of our churches are involved in society's systems of ordering and security. Teachers, social workers, entrepreneurs, lawyers, managers, police, or probation officers—they face practical decisions that require them to apply their faith. For many, the theology they receive from church does not reach into their workplaces, and the questions they encounter from work seem not to connect at church.

As the MCC Peace Committee explored this complex of questions, it felt that simply to develop a study-guide, produce an educational DVD, or hold one more conference would not be enough. We faced a large issue, one that would benefit from a more concentrated study, research, and consultation effort. The question of how our peace theology relates to and takes into account the challenges of order and security is wide-ranging and we would benefit from a sustained conversation over time.

The committee therefore designed a two-year study project, called simply "The MCC Peace Theology Project." It began in January 2003 and continued through December 2004.

During this period of time, the project benefited from the part-time support of five researchers: Duane Friesen (Bethel College), Lydia Harder (Toronto Mennonite Theology Centre), Robert Charles (Mennonite Mission Network), Pamela Leach (Canadian Mennonite University), and Gerald Schlabach (University of St. Thomas). Friesen, Harder, and Schlabach were also members of the MCC Peace Committee and therefore involved in designing the scope and focus of this two-year process of study, research, and consultation. We (Judy Zimmerman Herr and Robert Herr) also participated in this research effort, providing logistic and coordination support.

Along with the work of this team, the project sponsored five regional consultations and one international conference. The regional consultations functioned as "hearings" to seek the comment and participation of as wide a spectrum of Mennonite and Brethren in Christ church members as could be managed in this short time, with limited resources. These consultations took place in Toronto, Ontario; Winnipeg, Manitoba; N. Newton, Kansas; Harrisonburg, Virginia; and Goshen/Elkhart, Indiana. Each of these consultations brought together between thirty and sixty people—social workers, lawyers, school teachers, police officers, theologians, civil servants, historians, members of local government, and many others whose work placed them in the midst of supporting and providing the kinds of ordering systems that this project aimed to reflect upon. A final international conference took place at the MCC offices in Akron, Pennsylvania. The material in this volume comes from the presentations at this conference.

Through the course of this two-year period of consultation, two core themes came to the fore. One was a sense of affirmation for this process—the oft-repeated comment that our theology needs to both speak to and be informed by the context of our lives. Whenever an explicit process of back-and-forth counsel takes place, our lives benefit. A second was a caution. Will we be able to hold to a tradition of commitment to the peaceable witness of the gospel, to our historic peace stance? As we focus on today's experience, will we be able to keep in mind the extensive experience of those who have come before us?

This is of course a permanent tension, and it remained at the core of this two-year process. On the one hand stand those who feel that the church does not adequately acknowledge or support their work, because it does not fit into categories that Anabaptists have traditionally seen as part of the peaceable witness of the gospel. Certainly, in the extreme, this lament came from Mennonite or Brethren in Christ church members who are working as police officers or prison wardens. On the other hand stand historians and theologians, guardians of the tradition, who sometimes expressed their discomfort with the direction of this project's discussions with passion and intensity.

The chapters of this book reflect what we heard during the two years of study and reflection. They represent the content of the international conference that closed this process, but also reflect the discussions that took place in the regional consultations. In some cases, they propose directions to take or ideas to hold on to. Most suggest the need to look carefully at the societies in which we live, and the need for the church to participate consciously in those structures that make life possible.

In its theological reflection, the church dare not treat what Ricardo Esquivia calls "institutionality" as an afterthought. Certainly we must continue to focus on the peaceable witness of the gospel in light of the cross of Christ. But if we are to connect this focus to the call to love both neighbor and enemy we must attend far more deliberately and earlier in our theological reflection to the structures that make a loving witness possible.

It is clear that neither the study project nor this volume have brought this conversation to a final conclusion. In many ways, as we progressed through various meetings and discussions, we felt as though we were only opening up more issues and questions. Questions about the role of Christians in shaping society will never go away. Christians who resolve to live as peacemakers will continue to struggle with the need for order, wondering whether we can envision structures for order and security that do not rely on violence. This project has collected some new experience and this book offers some new thinking, but these will undoubtedly prove merely to be steps along the way.

In the course of our discussions, we also heard suggestions for other resources that MCC and its supporting churches need if they are to continue the conversation. These include a collection of stories that illustrate how church members are working at the right kind of order in their settings. What are we learning, as we seek to live out our faith in the public arena? We heard encouragement for studies that could focus Sunday school class discussion on these topics in our congregations. We heard calls for additional meetings, for discussing these issues with others who we were not able to meet over the course of these two years.

Clearly this project was only the tip of the iceberg, only a small sample of the thinking and conversations that could and should continue as we work together at discernment in our churches. Our hope is that this beginning can help to spark others to begin talking and working on these issues, with no assumption that this book or any of us will have said the last word. A central tenet of Anabaptist-Mennonite theology holds the church to be the locus of ethical discernment; it is our prayer that this small effort at such discernment may encourage others to follow.

So many people participated in this process that it is not possible to do more here than begin a list. However, we want to especially note with thanks Duane Friesen, Lydia Harder, Robert Charles, Pamela Leach, and Gerald Schlabach who gave much time, both to the work involved and the travel it required. Their commitment was the core that kept this process going. Our thanks also go to those who hosted the five consultations: the Toronto United Mennonite Church, MCC Canada Offices in Winnipeg, Bethel College (Kansas), Eastern Mennonite University, MCC Great Lakes staff, and the Associated Mennonite Biblical Seminary. Special thanks must go to Esther O'Hara who oversaw the logistical details of the final conference. At the final conference several came from distant places to share with us from the life of Mennonite churches beyond the United States and Canada. We were pleased to have with us Paulus Widjaja from Indonesia, Alix Lozano from Colombia, Fernando Enns from Germany, Alfred Neufeld from Paraguay, and Judith Gardiner from London. Their presence and comments reminded us that the issues that concern us are shared by many others within the larger global family of Mennonite and Brethren in Christ churches. Lastly, we are very appreciative of the financial support we received from a number of organizations who saw what this project aimed to do and supported it. We especially note the support received from the Mennonite Foundation of Canada, the Schowalter Foundation, the Frank Epp Memorial Fund, the MCC Executive Office, and the MCC Peace Office. Without this support we would not have been able to travel, invite people to gather, process difficult issues, and publish this book. To all these, we offer a heartfelt thanks.

Robert Herr
Judy Zimmerman Herr
MCC Peace Office
September 2005

INTRODUCTION

TRACING THE GRAIN OF THE UNIVERSE: PROJECT OVERVIEW

Gerald W. Schlabach
on behalf of MCC Peace Theology Project team

If God's saving purpose is to heal estranged humanity so that all can live under their vine and fig tree at peace and unafraid of harm, and if the nonviolent "wisdom of the cross" runs with "the grain of the universe" even now, then as peacemakers committed to the way of Jesus Christ, Mennonites should be prepared to take up problems of security and participate in wider ecumenical, national, and international conversations about them. *Are we?*

This question is at the hub of the project that has resulted in the present book. "Preparation" happens in multiple ways, so by implication the hub question connects to at least three spoke questions:

- Is "security" and the ordering of human society a legitimate theological concern for Mennonites in the first place?
- What theoretical resources must we gather in order to contest standard but dubious meanings of "security"?
- What practical resources must we develop in order to work for true human security in nonviolent ways?

These questions have arisen for various reasons:

1. The September 11 attacks suddenly heightened many people's sense of insecurity and prompted policies that have made still others feel insecure around the world. People in our churches shared this insecurity and found themselves caught up in heated, even desperate, debates about how national and international policy makers should respond. The challenge of nonviolent witness in this context has been a presenting issue for this project, but many other issues are before us also.

2. Mennonite Central Committee (MCC) has decades of experience working in conflict zones and in the context of failed states. Long before 9/11, the MCC Peace Committee, which advises the organization's international programs and commissioned this project, had regularly taken up related ethical challenges. How, for example, should Christian pacifists respond in situations of egregious human rights abuse? Situations of this sort prompt Christians in other traditions to call for military forms of "humanitarian intervention." Peacemaking in such situations often requires nonviolent practitioners to cease taking for granted the conditions, structures, and governance that make for the ordering of human society in life-giving ways.

3. Both in North America and in young churches emerging around the world, Mennonite communities have a mixed record at best of providing pastoral guidance for church members whose commitment to service leads them into positions of governance. Governance, after all, is a pervasive human activity. Certainly it includes governmental roles, and the small but growing number of Mennonites who work in civil government are asking for guidance from their church communities. But governance also includes all the institutions of a community, including management, entrepreneurship, social service, legal professions, and leadership roles in the church itself. Mennonites living out their Christian vocations in some of these settings report receiving scarcely more support, understanding, and guidance than those at work in the state.

To inquire into the conditions and structures that order and secure life-giving human relationships is to open up a wide field of inquiry and wide-ranging conversation. The research team that took a lead in the MCC Peace Theology Project drew not only on the disciplines of theology, biblical studies, and Christian ethics, but on social and political science. As the team held consultations in six Canadian and U.S. locations in 2003 and 2004, participants included theologians, historians, lawyers, civic officials, peace activists, conflict transformation practitioners, MCC workers, overseas partners, and more. The three chapters by project team members Duane Friesen, Lydia Harder, and Pamela Leach, which appear in Part I of the present book and that articulate the project's core findings, all passed through multiple drafts as they drew on these interdisciplinary conversations.

As a guide to this wide-ranging conversation and its results, therefore, the present chapter attempts to chart the logical flow of the project's inquiry and findings. In doing so, it draws out major themes from the chapters in Part I by Friesen, Harder, and Leach. It also cross-references these with themes that emerge from the chapters in Part II, which were all part of a conference held at MCC headquarters in Akron, Pennsylvania, in August 2004 on the theme of "Seeking the Welfare of the City: Public Peace, Justice, and Order."

From its inception through its multiple consultations through the communal effort that climaxes in the publication of this book, the MCC Peace Theology Project has practiced a "believers church" approach to theological inquiry. Key to that approach are discipleship and community discernment. Discipleship requires that Christian faith be embodied in living practices as the church makes its way through history. Discernment insists that faith and practice remain subject to continual testing as the community of disciples finds the Lord leading them, along their historical journey, into new challenges.

While this project has issued in conversations that have ranged widely in many directions, therefore, one may chart its flow in much the same way that Latin American theologians have identified a "hermeneutical" circle of "praxis," in which the continuing practice of faith

- leads to new questions, which
- lead to fresh reflection on scripture and theology, which
- leads to a new synthesis by which we better comprehend the faith, which
- issues in freshly invigorated and more coherent practice, which takes us back around the circle, not leaving us unchanged but inviting us to ever-deeper faithfulness.

Each of the following themes represents an emerging conclusion from our project. Yet each one also invites further inquiry and discernment. Likewise, in the ongoing back-and-forth between theology and practice, each theme in some way leads to the next. Every faith conviction leads to fresh questions about how to live it out through concrete peacemaking practices, and every faithful practice invites deeper examination of peace theology, until we come full circle. Thus, even when this project has posed what seem to be new and uncomfortable questions, none are strictly alien questions imposed from outside the Anabaptist-Mennonite tradition but instead arise from conscientiously seeking to be faithful to it and, above all, to our Lord Jesus Christ.

1. *MCC's own work attempting to follow Christ faithfully and put love of neighbor into practice would be enough to raise the issue of security, even without the need to address challenges that have come in the wake of 9/11.* Mennonites serving with both mission boards and MCC had decades of experience working in Somalia, for example, when the utter collapse of its centralized government in the early 1990s forced difficult ethical questions upon them about how to serve "in the name of Christ" in the context of a failed state. MCC workers in Bosnia in the mid-1990s experienced the social chaos that came when irregular para-military forces provided only a meager semblance of gov-

ernment; after NATO intervened militarily to impose order and thwart the genocide of "ethnic cleansing," MCC workers had to admit that this proved helpful for their work. And they had to reflect theologically on the implications of this admission. Currently, in 2005, the government of Congo barely functions outside the capital city of Kinshasa. Some members of Mennonite and Mennonite Brethren churches in Congo have been invited to government positions. Congolese Mennonites are exploring how they can be involved in advocating for good governance, and how to offer their service as nonviolent Christians within the precarious Congolese state.

The biblical vision of *shalom* includes safety and freedom from harm. Everyone sits under his or her vine and fig tree, unafraid and rescued from enemies, while love of neighbor implies some kind of obligation to protect others from harm (Friesen, pp. 41-42, 49). If Mennonite theology has tended to separate its proper emphasis on prophetic critique of violence and injustice from the ordinary work of tending creation in order to shape dependable patterns of relationship ("the rule of law," peaceable "ordering," "infrastructure"), that may result more from the dualistic tendencies of modernity than from biblical theology (Harder, pp. 120, 144, 147). In any case, overseas partners such as Ricardo Esquivia of the Colombia Mennonite Church urge us not to ignore the role of what he calls *institucionalidad* in the work of conflict transformation and peacemaking. For however the U.S. government and Colombian elites, for example, may appeal to "law and order" or "security" in order to promote unjust policies, Colombian society actually suffers from too little order and a too-weak rule of law. Nonviolent peacemakers must help to re-knit the social bonds and civic community that bring true law and order.

Alix Lozano of Colombia, Paulus Widjaja of Indonesia, and Alfred Neufeld of Paraguay show Mennonite Christians around the world responding to the challenges of disorder and insecurity in various ways. The fact that the social situation in a country such as Colombia cries out for true order and human security based on the rule of law and the participation of civil society certainly does not mean the state should be the focus of the church's efforts. As Lozano describes the work of Colombian Mennonites in chapter thirteen, it clearly counters government policies that favor military solutions and inequitable economic development more often than cooperation with the government. Cooperative efforts most often attempt to fill gaps in government programs, while the church's social outreach aims generally at strengthening civil society within the shell of the state.

In Indonesia, some Christians are aggressively seeking to "enter the palace" as Joseph once did in Egypt, in order to dominate the government of a nation with the largest Muslim population in the world. But this only complicates the work of Muslim-Christian dialogue and reconciliation that Widjaja describes in chapter eleven. Still, in chapter nine Alfred Neufeld's account of current Mennonite experience in Paraguay provides an intriguing case study in the possibilities for conscientious Mennonite participation in government. In 2003 the new Paraguayan president invited five Mennonite professionals and entrepreneurs from the Asunción Mennonite Church into his cabinet in hopes that their non-partisan expertise would help him fight government corruption. After careful discernment with a pastoral team and the creation of ongoing accountability structures, they accepted.

Though the societies of Europe and North America may be known as "developed nations," Mennonites and Brethren in Christ there can hardly take for granted the social structures that provide order and security to their lives. Despite his longstanding activism and teaching in opposition to what he considers the imperialistic policies of the United States, Ted Grimsrud argues in chapter fourteen that Anabaptist Christians can hold values and engage in practices that are quite compatible with their theology in U.S. traditions of participatory democracy. Grimsrud distinguishes between two stories that have shaped American culture—an "Empire Story" and a "Democracy Story"—and calls on Anabaptist Christians to "participate fully in the democratic conversation of the American civic nation" without watering down their faith convictions. In any case, security issues can sometimes press even more closely to home. Struggling with how to be a truly "inclusive church" when people who have sexually offended against children wish to join the church, Canadian pastor Carol Penner outlines in chapter seven how she and other pastors have worked very deliberately with both their congregations and parole officers in order to insure the safety of children.

2. *The contested meaning of "security" underscores that theology, ideas, and worldview matter greatly, for they shape the assumptions by which we interpret reality and act in response to insecurity.* Most Christians accept an "ontology of violence" that views public order as necessarily dependent on violent force and that underlies most social and political theory; sharing such assumptions has often kept Mennonites from addressing questions of security and public order (Friesen, pp. 48-49). The biblical narrative in which God calls out a people to be a blessing to all nations, and to overcome evil according to the nonviolent cross of Jesus Christ that stands as the revealing climax of that narrative, should lead Christians to read the world according to a different ontology (Friesen, pp. 49-50).

The Bible's wisdom motif provides an instructive precedent for developing forms of "middle discourse" that identify common patterns to God's creative work, saving work, and providential work in history, thus linking specifically Christian convictions with the sense of "reality" we access through empirical data, social theory, reason, and experience (Harder, pp. 123, 149). Mennonites can mine the biblical theme of wisdom without losing their Christocentric ethic because the Bible itself affirms that Jesus Christ is Wisdom embodied and thus challenges unredeemed "common sense" readings of reality with the wisdom of the cross (Harder, pp. 124, 128, 130-33, 138, 146). Pamela Leach demonstrates that this is both possible and fruitful through an extended case study using the tools of social science to demonstrate both the shortcomings of post-9/11 "national security" policies and the opportunities for nonviolent witness oriented toward the conditions that in reality make for peace and human security.

Sometimes addressing the implications of 9/11 and sometimes addressing other contexts of insecurity, a number of other authors join in contesting standard accounts of the sources for both insecurity and security. In chapter six, Daryl Byler and Lisa Schirch take an "Anabaptist lens" to the post-9/11 challenges of terrorism that prompt most Americans to look for military solutions. Their goal is to act as "strategic doves" who are as wise as "serpents" and as realistic as "hawks" claim to be, by identifying "practical strategies for building a secure world" even while drawing on nonviolent peace theology. To do so they critically examine the cultural assumptions that lead so many to believe that a war on terrorism will make them secure.

This is not to dismiss the fear, insecurity, and suffering of neighbors and fellow citizens in society. Taking the experience of trauma victims seriously is one resource for finding more adequate understandings of security, according to Byler and Schirch. Pam Nath continues this argument in chapter eight, as she draws on psychological studies based on interviews with survivors of violence. At least some forms of risky interdependence and vulnerability actually make human beings stronger and more secure, argue all of these authors. Perfect invulnerability based on complete control is not "realistic" at all but a deep though pervasive illusion. On the way to greater security it is actually more realistic to take risks that build trust through the vulnerability of interdependent relationships, rather than to take the risks that come with illusory attempts to control our human fate through violence and threat. This confirms the wisdom of the cross.

To make such arguments is already to engage in the "middle discourse" of which Friesen and Harder write. A number of other writers either practice or comment on such discourse—Leach, Enns, Widjaja, Grimsrud, Gardiner, Rempel, Gingerich, and Schlabach. But perhaps the most striking example is Alain Epp Weaver's chapter twelve on peacemaking efforts and prospects in Palestine-Israel. Firmly grounded in Christian theology, Epp Weaver finds ways to translate his faith commitments into language and motifs accessible to thinkers and policymakers in both Jewish and Muslim communities.

3. *Theology and social theory are not enough, however; Mennonites and other pacifist Christians need to discover, anticipate, and forge concrete social practices if they expect to take on the question of security.* The biblical narrative itself, as Mennonites understand it, requires embodiment through the social structure of the church according to "the politics of Jesus," which in turn gives rise to social practices that are translatable beyond the church, through actions of witness and the language of wisdom. "Just Peacemaking" theory and practices are a contemporary example (see Friesen's numerous references between pp. 58 and 75).

Still, Mennonite theologians sometimes demonstrate a certain distrust of practitioners, celebrating their work when it vindicates Mennonite theology but writing its lessons off to "acculturation" when those lessons pose uncomfortable challenges (cf. Harder pp. 117, 119-22). For example, the practice of conflict transformation as developed at Eastern Mennonite University suggests that the best work of mediation and peacebuilding may well produce a climate of improved trust yet still require sanctions and structures of enforcement to take hold. The "wise" practices of Abigail, Joseph, Esther, Daniel, and Paul in the Bible (Harder, pp. 126, 139-46) have their equally messy, ambiguous, yet revealing counterparts in the experiences of Mennonite lawyers, social workers, civic officials, and church administrators today. In all eras, after all, wisdom requires acting skillfully and shrewdly in situations that would not require witness or redemption if they did not also present temptations of idolatry and misuse of power (cf. Harder, p. 145).

To dismiss such experiences is to miss opportunities to trace how "the wisdom of the cross" runs "with the grain of the universe." A Mennonite prison warden in Canada, for example, shared his experiences at one consultation. He finds that to respect the dignity and encourage the resourcefulness of inmates does far more to maintain a secure and orderly prison than fearful threats of physical force. Our project team has but barely begun to gather the anecdotes, case studies, and empirical evidence of nonviolent patterns of human ordering and security needed to contest dominant conceptions of security in word and, more importantly, to extend practices of nonviolent ordering more widely in deed.

Still, a number of authors in this book draw upon a growing body of empirical evidence as they move to make concrete proposals for alternative security policies. Project team member Duane Friesen closes chapter two with an extensive catalogue of nonviolent peacemaking practices that have human security in view. Informed by his earlier work developing the theory and practice of "Just Peacemaking," Friesen further extends its practices in light of new challenges. He also makes careful distinctions between shalom practices that are fully compatible with the nonviolent ethic of Jesus and those by which peacemakers may press non-pacifist policymakers toward less violent responses even when leaders are unwilling to renounce recourse to violent sanctions. Similarly, in chapter twenty, Lisa Schirch and Daryl Byler follow up their earlier chapter on becoming "strategic doves" with an extensive set of specific strategy proposals for national and international leaders.

In chapter sixteen, theologian and church historian John Rempel articulates some of the anxiety to which Lydia Harder had referred, concerning the possibility that Mennonite practitioners who contribute to the ordering of society will simply accelerate a process of acculturation by which Mennonites will abandon their very peace theology. According to Rempel, earlier generations of Mennonites in Europe often failed to maintain a distinctively nonviolent identity once they abandoned a sectarian posture in the name of contributing to the well-being of society. Yet Rempel has been a practitioner himself, having served for many years as MCC's representative at the United Nations. He thus searches Anabaptist-Mennonite history for more hopeful precedents and finds one in the sixteenth century Anabaptist leader and civil engineer Pilgram Marpeck of Strassburg. But perhaps Judith Gardiner is a modern-day Marpeck. In chapter seventeen Gardiner tells of holding together an Anabaptist-Mennonite theology that is skeptical of any politics other than the church's own "politics of Jesus" with her work as an elected local politician in one of the poorest neighborhoods of East London. Commitment to the poor has simply gotten her "stuck in," and she is convinced that Anabaptist-Mennonite values and practices can contribute much to the political process.

4. As much of this already implies, *we dare not fear to ask what works or to inquire into how the world works, for faithfulness to an ethic of discipleship itself includes attention to that which will effectively realize love of neighbor, reconciliation with enemies, and the security that comes through right relationship with both.* Other Christian traditions introduce such empirical data into their moral discernment under the rubric of "natural law," but risk setting up "nature" as an autonomous source of moral authority that ends up trumping the authority of Jesus. Peace theology needs a functional equivalent to "natural law" that is more Christocentric, more biblical, and less likely to elevate unredeemed conventional "wisdom" above the wisdom of the cross.

Our project's turn to biblical wisdom provides one way of doing this. But to appropriate biblical wisdom faithfully, we must in fact be truly wise. That is, we must follow Harder's lead in noting how the practices of the wise throughout the Bible involve patient trust in God's providential timing, risk, vulnerability on behalf of others' security, and a willingness to subvert conventional wisdom. Above all, we must remember that all of these find their fulfillment in Jesus Christ, the embodiment of wisdom.

Since wisdom is the Bible's own "middle discourse" for translating between narratives and cultures, as well as between the prophetic and the worldly, our project has sometimes collated this approach with John H. Yoder's use of "middle axioms," his notion of bilingual translation between moral systems, and above all his ontologically stronger claim that "the cross runs with the grain of the universe." Friesen offers a solid argument that instrumental reasoning about what is in fact effective has a place "within a deeper and more profound commitment to an ethic of discipleship that includes love of the enemy whom we may be tempted to kill" (Friesen, p. 50).

If we are mapping the flow of our project's inquiry and discussion, however, a final observation is worth making: This last point turns out to complete a feedback loop or "hermeneutical circle" flowing back into the first points. We should thus expect to continue gathering empirical data not only to argue that the cross runs with the grain of the universe but to enrich the peace theology by which we speak *both* of cross *and* of universe.

In chapter five, Mary Schertz draws on the New Testament witness to show why this is both necessary and possible. God's passionate love is for the world, as none less than the famous text of John 3:16 should have reminded us all along. "We must relinquish notions of the world as a soulless wasteland. The world, including our communities and our nations, is exactly what God is in love with." And though we are not called to be God's agents executing the fury that is integral to God's passionate love, we are called to be partners in God's work in all creation.

As already mentioned, chapters in Part I by Friesen and Leach, as well as chapters in Part II by Schirch and Byler, all give extensive attention to what actually "works" to build more secure communities, societies, and international systems. Even though this inquiry grows directly from the discipleship practices by which Christians in the Anabaptist tradition have sought faithfully to live out love of neighbor and enemy, it also invites them to continue testing and deepening their peace theology.

Just here, in other words, a feedback loop kicks in. Tim Wichert reminds his readers in chapter fifteen, for example, that while Mennonites may have certain reservations about using "rights" language, human rights discourse and advocacy has become integral to the international legal system, thus constituting "one of the most significant, nonviolent, 'political' contributions to public peace, justice, and order in the past fifty years." In chapter eighteen, Jeff Gingerich asks what we actually know about the sociological dynamics both of traditional policing and of recent efforts to encourage what is known as "community policing." On the one hand, Gingerich would like to break the "uneasy silence" among peace churches about their own attitudes toward policing. On the other hand, his goal is to "begin a discussion on the possibilities for a nonviolent community order that relies less upon a traditional armed police force." In chapter nineteen, Schlabach also presses peace churches to clarify their ethical stance toward policing, along with the ways it may differ from their ethical stance toward war. He presses just war churches to do the same, however, in order to explore areas of ecumenical convergence that reduce support for militarism. Meeting these challenges would not necessarily require peace churches to abandon their pacifism, but would require them to reinvigorate the processes of vocational testing and accountability for all members involved in ordering and governance.

In chapter ten Fernando Enns demonstrates that a willingness to take up the challenges of human security in conversation with Christians of other traditions can yield fruit and extend the peace church witness. Writing from years of experience as a German Mennonite representative on the central committee of the World Council of Churches, Enns reports on ways that historic peace church participation has "reshaped the debate" in ecumenical circles on issues of war, peace, terrorism, and international security. Mennonites and other peace churches need not subscribe to "revised just war theory," nor give in to "the temptation of theological legitimization for the use of violence," he writes. But "every tradition needs to be challenged." Mennonites thus must make "a firm commitment to engage in theological and ethical debate." And they must "prove that their beliefs have something to contribute to the 'real challenges' of the 'real world.'"

Indeed, that is the conviction, finding, and continuing task that this book represents.

PART I

IN SEARCH OF SECURITY:
WISDOM AND THE GOSPEL OF PEACE

—2—

IN SEARCH OF SECURITY: A THEOLOGY AND ETHIC OF PEACE AND PUBLIC ORDER

Duane K. Friesen

The disorder of injustice and of violence threatens human life and dignity in our world. This we all know. Our challenge is to respond in ways that do not simply continue cycles of injustice and violence. As we address that challenge we must humbly acknowledge our uncertainty. We are indeed in search of security. Given human sin and imperfection, how can we live humanely in the face of our vulnerability? Our task is to identify theological foundations for an authentic and enduring security.

This essay will lay out a Christian theological and ethical framework for thinking about questions of security and public order. Part I identifies four foundational theological assumptions: a security grounded in a fundamental trust in God; a narrative that defines Christian identity; a rich, thick Christology to guide practice; and a view of security and public order within a larger biblical vision of shalom. Part II describes the challenges and questions that our contemporary context poses to the church. Within the overarching contexts of empire and globalization, churches face complex issues in their work "on the ground." Issues of public order and security, after all, profoundly affect the human needs they seek to address with Christian compassion. Part III seeks to clarify critical theological and ethical issues: whether violence is "necessary" in the establishment of public order; whether engagement of issues of public order leads to the temptation of "Constantinianism"; what we mean by public order; how to distinguish between coercive force and lethal violence; and how to project a multilingual Christian witness. Finally, Part IV demonstrates how the "rubber hits the road." It charts connections between these theological and ethical reflections, and realistic peacemaking practices that are actually making a difference without perpetuating cycles of violence. Empirical evidence lends credibility to our theological claims and ethical analysis. For a growing body of evidence shows that nonviolent alternatives to public order and security are not mere pipe dreams but are realistic approaches that people are practicing all over the world.

FOUR THEOLOGICAL ASSUMPTIONS

A. Our security is ultimately dependent on God.

We humans are not ultimately the engineers and managers of our own security. Human strategic planning can offer only an illusory security when it reflects an arrogance and pride in our own wisdom and power, as if we humans, not God, were the center of the universe. While trust in God does not mean that humans can eschew responsibility for how we conduct our lives, the ultimate ground of security is a fundamental trust in God. The Hebrew word in the Bible that is often translated as safety or security also means "trust" or "confidence." Isaiah 12:2 illustrates this connection: "I will trust, and will not be afraid" (NRSV).

The Psalms and the Hebrew prophets remind us repeatedly that security rests not in us but in God's providential care. The prophets criticized the kings of Israel who relied on military strategy instead of trusting God. Hosea said: "I will have pity on the house of Judah, and I will save them by the Lord their God; I will not save them by bow, or by the sword, or by war, or by horses, or by horsemen" (Hos 1:7). Isaiah criticized those who "trust in chariots because they are many and in horsemen because they are very strong, but do not look to the Holy One of Israel or consult the Lord! . . . The Egyptians are human, and not God: their horses are flesh and not Spirit" (Isa 31:1, 3). The word of the Lord to Zerubabel was: "Not by might, nor by power, but by my Spirit" (Zech 4:6).

Bondage to fear enslaves us. Following the terrorist attacks of September 11, 2001, we saw this fear and insecurity drive many to seek security in human strategic planning and military power. Americans have embarked upon a journey that is sucking us into a bottomless pit. Enslaved to fear, we need to be liberated in order to approach the difficult issues of security with wisdom and calm. The words of the Apostle Paul speak to our time:

> I am convinced that neither death, nor life, nor angels, nor rulers nor things present, nor things to come, nor power, nor height, nor depth, nor anything else in all creation, will be able to separate us from the love of God in Christ Jesus our Lord (Rom 8:35-39).

First John summarizes the basis of our security in one simple but profound sentence: "Perfect love casts out fear" (1 John 4:18).

B. The Christian narrative is formative.

The narrative that shapes our basic identity as Christians is the one by which God calls a people (beginning with Abraham) to be a blessing among the nations. The center of the church's loyalty is Jesus Christ, Lord of history and model of discipleship. The most important question Christians must ask is what "story" or narrative describes the lives we ought to live. In practice, the three most important identities that shape the lives of most North American Christians are family, work, and national identity. We often accept the responsibilities of these three identities uncritically, without placing them within a larger and more comprehensive narrative framework that defines our identity as Christians. Christians have a rich biblical narrative that makes the life, teachings, death, and resurrection of

Jesus Christ central to their identity. And most importantly, this narrative is especially significant and powerful when "bodied" in a social structure, the church. This narrative embodiment is what John Howard Yoder called "the politics of Jesus."

C. We need a rich, "thick" picture of Jesus Christ.

Christians need an orienting center for their lives and a guide for practice that is grounded in a rich, thick description of Jesus Christ. The Christology of many in North America is impotent because so many bypass the life and teachings of Jesus. The Apostles' Creed, for example, jumps from Jesus's birth to his death. "Jesus died to save us from our sins" is the doctrine of salvation for many. This formula abstracts the atonement from Jesus's prophetic engagement with the powers, which provoked his crucifixion. Some reduce the Christian faith to general vague principles like love, again abstracted from the radical teachings and practices of Jesus in his historical context.

A deeper understanding of Jesus helps us see the "end" or the "goal" (the teleology) that commitment to Christ entails. Jesus Christ is God's anointed one (Messiah), commissioned to bring God's kingdom or rule into the world. The kingdom of God represents the wholeness God intends for the entire cosmos. We understand that message best when we interpret Jesus in the light of the Old Testament prophets.[1] Jesus taught his disciples to pray that the kingdom of God might come on earth as it is in heaven (Matt 6:10). The kingdom entails liberation from bondage to powers that are destructive of life.

One vivid story of this transformation is Zacchaeus' encounter with Jesus. His repentance turned his life in a direction that led to the redistribution of his wealth and the liberation to practice justice by a redistribution of his resources to those in need. This brought salvation to his house today, not some distant future.

Jesus stood in solidarity with the marginalized. Those treated as outcasts in the social context of Jesus's time were the very ones for whom Jesus had compassion (the poor, widows, the sick, Samaritans, women, those labeled "sinners"). Jesus's call to "seek first God's kingdom and God's righteousness" (Matt 6:33) "means the restoring of just relations among us personally, in society, and with God. It points to God's gracious initiative in delivering us from sin, guilt, and oppression, and into a new community of justice, peace, and freedom through obedient participation in God's way of deliverance."[2] To respond to the initiative by which God inaugurates the kingdom through Christ thus entails our responsibility to help develop a "gospel order" to sustain the flourishing of life against threats that destroy and threaten life.

Second, a "thick" understanding of Christ keeps us focused on the integral connection between "means" and "ends." Nonviolent peacemaking (the wisdom of the cross) is the way God's Kingdom breaks into the world. Both in his own life and in his teachings, Jesus offered a model of how to confront evil nonviolently. Instead of legitimating the dominant culture's view that violence must finally confront pathological evil, Jesus modeled a creative third way of nonviolent resistance to evil, an alternative to the use of violent force and passive resignation to evil. Followers of Jesus are committed to a pilgrimage seeking concrete initiatives within the culture in which we live, initiatives that can creatively transform conditions of injustice and violence into occasions of justice and peace.[3] The resurrection of Jesus Christ is a sign of God's affirmation for the kind of power that Christ exhibited and that is now also open to us.

D. Security is integral to a biblical vision of shalom.

God has created us to live in community with each other and in right relationship with the larger cosmos. The Old Testament prophets used the word *shalom* to describe the order God intends for creation. This positive definition of peace is a social environmental condition in which righteousness and justice prevail. It is not just the absence of violence or war. The prophet Micah envisioned a future of peace and social justice without fear: "Everyone will sit under their own vine and fig tree and no one will make them afraid" (Mic 4:4). In the words of Zechariah in Luke, the hope of redemption is that "we would be saved from our enemies and from the hand of all who hate us . . . that we being rescued from the hands of our enemies, might serve him without fear" (Luke 1:71, 73).

The Hebrew prophets viewed people's security and safety from the perspective of the poor and marginal. So too did Jesus in his life and ministry. Security is not a "war against terrorism" to protect the interests of the dominant economic military power in the world, then or now. Security is not achieved through wars that attempt to keep the violence in other people's yards (Iraq and Afghanistan) in order to keep us safe at home. Security is not about the privileged, who want law and order, and more police and prisons, in order to protect their gated communities. Resentment and violent reactions cannot help but spread in a world of such gaping inequities.

Militaristic strategies to protect the interest of the privileged will only produce greater insecurity. Genuine security seeks the well being of people who yearn for the basic necessities of life: work that can support families to meet minimal needs for food and clothing, adequate and affordable housing, effective schools, access to health care, stable communities free of drugs and crime, systems of policing that support community rather than tear it down through repression and brutality, and a safe environment with clean air and fresh water. A theology of "order" and "security" is grounded in a "gospel order," an order that is good news for the poor, and liberty to the captives (Luke 4:16).

THE CONTEXT

We live in a world where systems both of order and of disorder destroy human life and dignity. As we consider our calling to be people of shalom in a broken world, we are mindful of the political and economic context of our work: state-sanctioned repression, violence, and war; terrorist violence intentionally directed against civilian non-combatants for the purpose of achieving ideological, political, or personal ends;[4]

ethnic violence within states; criminal behavior that violates recognized societal norms codified in law; the breakdown of infrastructures of economic and political order and the rule of law that sustain community well being;[5] and weak or ineffective systems of law to sustain the common good at local, regional, national, and international levels.

Empire and globalization are the two overarching contexts within which we must find our way as we address these issues. One of the greatest threats to human life and dignity is the "United States empire," the most powerful and dominant military power in world history. President Bush's proposed 2005 military budget of $421 billion exceeds the combined military budgets of the 25 next largest military spenders in the world. When combined with the additional costs of the wars in Iraq and Afghanistan, this budget equals the combined military budgets of all the other countries of the world. In the name of security this empire is engaged in a state of perpetual war, which in turn leads to increased threats of terrorism against its citizens and its friends, thus contributing to a vicious cycle of violence and counter-violence. The war in Iraq exposes the deep contradiction of U.S. foreign policy. The longer the occupation of Iraq, the more counterinsurgent violence, and the less likely that democratic institutions can emerge, which is the declared goal of U.S. policy. The invasion and occupation of Muslim Iraq by a "Christian" Western nation plays into the hands of those who believe they are engaged in a sacred jihad against the evil forces of the West that can only be defeated by violent force.

A second consequence of empire is the loss of democracy and constitutional rights, what Chalmers Johnson has called a "pentagonized presidency."[6] Power in the United States has increasingly shifted to the executive branch of government, which is able to mobilize congress and a docile press in the name of national security.[7] The USA Patriot Act, passed quickly after September 11 by Congress with essentially no debate, undermines basic human rights and basic American values. So too does the presidential designation of hundreds of prisoners at Guantanamo Bay in Cuba as "enemy combatants," imprisoned indefinitely without documented charges based on evidence, and without legal access to U.S. courts.

Third, the needs of empire have shredded principles of truthfulness and straightforwardness. Though the 9/11 commission reported that there was no evidence linking Saddam Hussein and Al Qaeda, many Americans believe there was a connection, since the Bush administration continuously linked the war against terror that September 11 triggered to the war in Iraq.

Fourth, military spending is bankrupting society. Huge problems of poverty, hunger, housing, and basic healthcare are not being addressed. Grandiose military projects like missile defense systems take precedence while the United States is unable to provide basic healthcare for many of its citizens. While the nation spends vast sums on the war in Iraq, citizens in U.S. cities experience the daily insecurity of neighborhood violence triggered by hopelessness at a lack of decent jobs and addiction to drugs. School boards cut funding for education; local governments are forced to cut resources for the infrastructure of towns and cities that provide for the basic welfare and safety of citizens.

Globalization is a public-order issue because it raises the twin ethical issues of threats to the sustainability of life on the planet and the just distribution of economic resources.[8] We cannot sustain the levels and types of consumption that have characterized industrialized nations and at the same time protect the natural environment. One of the greatest long-term security issues is the ticking time-bomb of global warming.

With regard to the issue of distributive justice, "globalization is a two-edged sword, bringing benefits to some and misery to others."[9] While the rich as well as many in the middle class enjoy the benefits of free trade and the increased variety and availability of consumer goods in a competitive global market, the numbers of poor and hungry in the world are increasing. Kofi Annan, UN Secretary General, has stated the issue dramatically:

> Throughout much of the developing world, globaliza-
> tion is seen, not as a term describing objective reality, but
> as an ideology of predatory capitalism. Whatever reality
> there is in this view, the perception of a siege is unmis-
> takable. Millions of people are suffering; savings have
> been decimated; decades of hard-won progress in the
> fight against poverty are imperiled.[10]

The book of Revelation aptly describes the reality of our
world. The "beast from the abyss" tramples the poor, kills the
innocent, and seduces millions of Christians who give this
beast their allegiance, and then put salve on their troubled con-
sciences through charity. While charitable giving is laudable,
the cry of the poor to wealthy and privileged Christians is for
justice and for the beast to get off their backs.

These critical observations about the state of the world,
however, should not cause us to miss other more hopeful signs,
namely those emerging cooperative forces in the international
system that are moving us in more positive directions, despite
opposition from "the beast." The establishment of the
International Criminal Court, the Kyoto Treaty to reduce green-
house emissions, the Nuclear Non-Proliferation Treaty, and the
Treaty to Ban Land Mines are all signs of global cooperation.
Unfortunately, U.S. unilateralism has led the Bush administration to refuse to become a signatory to the International
Criminal Court, Kyoto, and the land mine treaties.

The Universal Declaration of Human Rights is another
positive sign. Though human rights are violated around the
world, nevertheless a commitment to human rights has
increasingly become a plumb line for evaluating the behavior
of nations. Human rights has its roots not only in the
Enlightenment, but also in the Christian tradition. The
Anabaptist heritage played an important role in establishing
the principle of freedom of religion and the right of conscience
to dissent from the authority of the state. Richard Overton, the
seventeenth-century Baptist, grounded human rights in the
Bible and Christian theology.[11] Christopher Marshall has noted
that the Bible "offers the most profound justification for ascrib-

ing dignity and rights to human beings: they have been made in the image of God, occupying a place 'a little lower than God' (Ps 8:5). They have been crowned with glory and honor and are the object of God's love and redemptive activity, with God taking on human nature (John 1:14) so that humans may become participants of the divine nature."[12] Human rights are especially important as an arena in which Christians can find common ground with others searching for a common good that protects the life and dignity of persons.

Mennonites have seldom addressed public order and security directly. Still, these concerns flow directly out of our calling as Mennonite Christians to be messengers of a gospel of peace as it intersects with the desperate needs of the world. Concern for people's safety and security is an extension of the biblical mandate to be a people of shalom. Work by Mennonite Central Committee (MCC) on these issues continues an evolving tradition—a growing enlargement of how Mennonites understand God's call to Christians to be a people of peace in a broken world. The MCC story, which began with relief aid and assistance for fellow Mennonites in Russia in the 1920s, has expanded to concerns for justice and peace building in over fifty countries of the world. As Christians are present on the ground, in the name of Christ, compassion for neighbor impels them to address issues of public order.

We also draw on a body of scholarly work in Anabaptist-Mennonite history and peace theology.[13] The pioneering work of John Howard Yoder in *The Politics of Jesus* established that Jesus's voluntary cross is an alternative to both quietist withdrawal and to violent revolution. With his message of compassion and justice for the marginal and the poor, Jesus passionately engaged the powers and principalities of his day concerning matters of public order.

In North America, Mennonites' work is also shaped by changes in our communities. Mennonites are increasingly serving in public office, working as civil servants, and entering into professions such as criminal justice, law, and social work that regularly engage issues of public order. The research team that produced this volume has heard from many who are asking for guidance from the church to help them discern what it means to be faithful disciples within their professional life.

Fifth, we have many opportunities for cooperation and dialogue with fellow pilgrims in the search for a secure and just peace. All over the world we work with people of many faiths. Especially significant is our relationship and cooperative work with Muslims amid a context of increasing polarization between Islam and the West.

We are collaborating with fellow Christians in local communities, are participating in a growing dialogue with Roman Catholics, and we have contributed to the World Council of Churches, most recently in the Decade to Overcome Violence. Our MCC witness to government in Ottawa, Washington, D.C., and at the United Nations is a collaborative endeavor.

Finally, we benefit from new widely shared emerging paradigms of just peacemaking theory and practice, models of conflict resolution, peace and conflict studies, nonviolence theory and practice, and community restorative justice.

CLARIFICATION OF THEOLOGICAL ISSUES

If safety and security is so important in a biblical vision of peace, why have Christians committed to nonviolence so seldom addressed these issues of order and security? We have opposed violence, emphasized the link between justice and peace, and made important contributions to the theology and practice of peacemaking. But we have not said much about how to address terrorism, or violations of order (like crime), or the abuse of human rights (like ethnic cleansing and genocide).

These questions are challenging because many Christians committed to nonviolence have accepted the assumption that public order is ultimately dependent upon violent force. We assume that in a sinful world, only "the sword" can ultimately maintain order. Christians often cite Romans 13 to support the necessity of violence. Underlying most social and political theory is Christian acceptance of an "ontology of violence," that is, a reading of the world which assumes that the force of evil is "best managed and confined by counter-force."[14]

A. A theological alternative to an ontology of violence

To develop an alternative to the ontology of violence, we must be clear about the narrative that shapes our basic identity as Christians, the narrative of God calling a people to be a blessing among the nations, culminating in the story of Jesus. Christians begin with a different understanding of how the world works and an alternative ontology to "the myth of redemptive violence." According to this powerful myth, when harm threatens human life and well-being, violence is the only saving power that will ultimately overcome these threats. But the Christian vision of life is based on the conviction that in the life, death, and resurrection of Jesus Christ we have a vision of the Kingdom of God, and of how God's reign of justice and peace breaks into a sinful world. In Christ we have a revelation of the way God's sovereign power works in history, a vision of the nonviolent cross as the way in which God's victory over evil is accomplished. This "wisdom of the cross" affirms that safety and security are ultimately grounded not in violence, but in peacemaking practices that build on trust and interdependence to secure a more just social order.

If we begin with this assumption, we imagine a different world and see that violence is not the answer to security. This does not mean that we have "answers" for every threat, or that nonviolence will always be successful in protecting us from harm. But those who support violent force cannot guarantee success either, and there is ample evidence that violence is counter-productive. When we start with a different claim upon the imagination, we are drawn to ways of being and acting through non-lethal methods of nonviolence in the face of threats to people's security and well-being.

Seeing the world from the perspective of the nonviolent wisdom of the cross leads to an ethic of risk, grounded in a different eschatology—that is, a different hope about how the future is secured. The use of violence also involves an eschatology. A conviction that violence can guarantee security is a "utopian dream," a quite astounding claim given the historical record of the escalating cycles of violence. To confess that Jesus Christ really is Lord is to state a conviction about what reality is at its core; we must then risk embodying this view in an alternative political reality.

We cannot concede that "violence" is empirically grounded, therefore, nor that nonviolence is simply a "leap of faith." With a different ontology and eschatology we can point to signs of practices that create a safer and more secure world through nonviolence. But we must not claim too much, and thus fall into our own form of hubris and self-righteousness. We must humbly acknowledge that nonviolence ultimately rests on an eschatological vision, a trust that the future is secured only if we are willing to follow the way of the cross. There is no guarantee of success. Nonviolence requires the same kind of courage as warriors who are willing to die in battle.

B. Response to the dangers of Constantinianism

We must guard against any kind of Christian hubris that would claim we can manage history better. We must address the dangers of Constantinianism by thinking carefully about the relationship between the norms of "faithfulness" and "effectiveness."

Christians must begin with a principled commitment to a reconciling and nonviolent ethic of discipleship. But an equally important dimension of following Christ faithfully is love of our neighbor, which includes work for just systems to protect our neighbors from harm. As Christians we must be willing to put our bodies on the line in defense of our neighbor. Nonviolence cannot be a cover for cowardice and withdrawal from engagement with evil forces that threaten human life. Jesus ended up on the cross because he engaged the principalities and powers. He did not withdraw to the desert. At the same time, we must never separate protection against harm from Jesus's call to love enemies and to live a life of nonviolence. Ultimately, Jesus calls us to follow the way of the cross, to follow his model of engagement, rather than succumb to temptations to take up the sword ourselves in a just cause.

We acknowledge the tension between living nonviolent love and doing justice to protect the life and dignity of our neighbor. In many situations we can do much to further both of these moral norms. We should seek to be effective at contributing to the ordering of a just society, and we can often do that nonviolently. Yet when push comes to shove, we should not weight the two norms of "faithfulness" and "effectiveness" as if we are balancing two equal principles.[15]

Instrumental reasoning for the just ordering of society plays a very important role within the moral life, so long as it operates within a deeper and more profound commitment to an ethic of discipleship that includes love of an enemy we may be tempted to kill. We can often address threats to people's safety effectively through nonviolent strategies. So to reject all instrumental reasoning monolithically is not defensible. A proper blend of instrumental reasoning and nonviolent principle is evident in the practice of both Mohandas K. Gandhi and Martin Luther King Jr. They were both committed to nonviolence and justice and sought to be effective within that framework.

In the long run faithfulness and effectiveness ultimately converge. If we start with an ontology of nonviolent love, which sees the "wisdom of the cross" rather than an ontology of violence at the heart of reality, then faithful following of this wisdom and the pursuit of effectiveness are not contradictory. For if Christ is truly Lord, then the "grain of the universe" is a nonviolent and reconciling ordering that underlies genuine security.[16] This is how God in Christ engages the evil that threatens human life. And if this is true, then we can point to "signs" of "effective" ordering that protect people from harm through nonviolent means.

C. How shall we view systems of public order?

The New Testament engages the question of public order with the language of "principalities and powers." Walter Wink argues that the New Testament views the powers as good because systems of public order (institutions, laws, and practices) are foundational to the flourishing of human life.[17] At the same time these very systems are fallen and in need of redemption. If we assume Wink's basic analysis, what implications do these ideas have for how we think theologically about public order?

1. Order, justice, and peace belong together. A public order that protects the security and the safety of people is inseparable from justice and a commitment to the peaceful resolution of conflict. Order, justice, and peace belong together in creative tension, even though we must acknowledge that it is often difficult to hold all these values together. Sometimes, perhaps often, they do conflict with each other. Nevertheless, we cannot consider "law and order" or "security" apart from either a search for justice or a commitment to resolve conflict nonviolently. Systems of ordering that rely on violent force to achieve security simply perpetuate vicious cycles of violence.

Crime, for example, correlates with our neglect of the infrastructure for adequate education, meaningful jobs that provide an adequate standard of living, and decent and affordable housing. If we do not address the root causes of crime, strengthening police forces and building more prisons will not give us security. A military budget obsessed with buying security through sophisticated weapons systems that rob domestic programs is an illusion. We cannot get cheap security divorced from justice.

2. We need to unmask systems of order that undermine human life and dignity. Though systems that order our corporate life are essential to the flourishing of human life, too often these very systems of order contribute to disorder. For many the police are part of the problem, as police departments militarize, engage in racial profiling, and commit acts of police brutality.

God has created "powers and authorities" to order, sustain, and help life to flourish. But these powers are fallen and in need of redemption. Our task as Christians, then, is to unmask prevailing illusions about order that are often based on repressive, unjust, and violent notions about security.

3. We recognize a creative tension between order and freedom/novelty. The flourishing of life depends upon both order—a determinate structure and lawfulness to reality that is predictable and reliable—and a freedom and openness to the future that is the basis for adaptation and change. This dialectic of order/novelty is foundational in both the natural world and the social and cultural world we humans create. Without either dimension, life in the universe as we know it could not flourish, including human life. Too much lawfulness/order and we would be unable to develop as communities or individuals with unique aspirations and gifts, having lost the capacity to adapt to change.

Conversely, if we could not depend upon a world that is orderly and predictable (from climate to economic and political systems) we could not function. In fact, our freedom is only meaningful when the deliberate actions we choose are likely to bring about reliable outcomes, thanks to the lawful connections between our actions and their consequences. Farmers who work hard, realistically utilizing the best agricultural practices within the givens of their ecosystems, expect a return from their labor that can support their families. Activists advocating minority rights expect to structure just patterns of cultural diversity. Communities who live peacefully in any given society without threatening their neighbors expect a social order that can provide a safe environment.

Elise Boulding has described a number of tensions involved in developing lawful systems. First, balancing the "passion for order" (rational, efficient, just, and peaceful behavioral protocols) with the more "organic" or impulsive side of human life (the spontaneous, irrational, creative); second, balancing centralization against de-centralization; third, weighting complete restructuring of institutions against re-education and evolutionary change; and fourth, balancing relationships between the micro and macro levels.[18]

4. Order does not depend only upon "top-down" imple-

mentation by the state. When we think about order, we need to be mindful that the socialization process to sustain an ordered, just, and peaceful society does not only depend upon a top-down implementation of law by the state. Though the state is important, we tend to focus too much upon the state "to protect the good and punish the evil" (Rom 13). Though political structures are crucial in ordering, creating a culture of peace is integrally linked to what Elise Boulding has called the "underside of history," the daily life of families and communities through whom we learn how to order our lives.

The principle of subsidiarity (from the Latin *subsidium*, meaning "help"), is a notion in Roman Catholic social thought that suggests the limited but positive role of the state while recognizing institutions such as the family and other intermediate associations in ordering society. The principle appears in the writing of Thomas Aquinas, though it was first defined as such by Pope Pius XI in 1931: "Just as it is gravely wrong to take from individuals what they can accomplish by their own initiative and industry and give it to the community, so also it is an injustice and at the same time a grave evil and disturbance of right order to assign to a greater and higher association what lesser and subordinate organizations can do."[19]

5. We must address root causes, not simply symptoms. We must understand security broadly.[20] It is a mistake to view it primarily as an issue of applying force when symptoms of disorder appear. We believe it is important to address the underlying causes of violence and disorder, whether these are the causes of homicide, the factors that lead to the outbreak of ethnic violence as in Rwanda, or the causes of terrorism.

D. Distinguishing between violence and coercion in addressing issues of public order

The word "violence" is rooted in the Latin verb "to violate," which is the same in Latin as the verb "to rape." Violence is harm to the dignity or integrity of a person. We should not restrict its meaning to physical or bodily harm. Violence is an attack upon a person's psychosomatic wholeness. Verbal abuse of a person that harms a person's dignity is no less violent than bodily injury. Killing is the most serious and extreme form of violence because it is irreversible. Violence can be done through direct actions against persons, but also by withholding the necessities, such as love or systems for health and well-being, that human life needs to flourish.

Nor should we equate coercion with violence. Coercion is an element in the process of socialization that "orders" individual human life to serve a broader communal good. "Coercion" is the application of pressure to "order" community life. Even though coercion compels persons to behave in ways that may go against their will, coercion is not inherently violent. Of course sin often taints the use of coercive force in a fallen world, and too often it is used destructively. But whereas violence is not integral to God's intention for humans, coercion is an integral element of the socialization process.

We observe how coercive force functions to shape the common good at a number of levels: within the family, the local community, churches, educational systems, political institutions, and the larger global community. The rule of law (informal for family systems and more formalized within political institutions) "orders" our social behavior in ways that benefit individuals and, at the same time, the larger system. One of the functions of law is to protect the community and individuals from those who are ruled by pathological passions, as well as the unscrupulous who are governed by greed, power, pride, and self-interest and thus led to exploit, steal, defraud, and kill. The challenge for Christians committed to nonviolence and justice is to imagine and develop practices of coercion that do not presuppose violence.

One of the fundamental problems of the global market capitalism, for example, is that it promotes greed and the gratification of individual desire without constraints. To secure a public order that protects the environment and fosters justice, we need to ask what coercive constraints our communities need to place on unlimited individual freedom.

E. Christian witness is multilingual

Christians need to be multilingual, but first we need to learn our own language well. Our primary confessional language is the narrative that shapes our identity as Christians, the story of the people of God from Abraham through Pentecost and beyond. The language of scripture and liturgy, hymn and sacrament, creeds and confessions of faith must nourish any genuinely understanding of security. When the church is an authentic worshipping and discerning community, we learn virtues such as the fruits of the Spirit in Galatians 5:22 and the Beatitudes of the Sermon on the Mount, as well as the ethical practices that mark the Body of Christ. These would include hospitality, forgiveness, and mutual aid to those in need.

At the same time, we need to develop other languages that link us to the worlds beyond the church. In addressing how we engage issues of public order and security, we need to employ wisely at least four additional languages: prophetic witness, Christian vocation, the common good in democratic discourse, and middle axioms. One of the most important functions of the congregation is to help members discern when, where, and how to use these other languages in ways that are consistent with their primary identity as followers of Jesus Christ. As Lydia Harder points out elsewhere in this book, timing is one of the most important elements of wisdom, that is to say, knowing what is appropriate at a particular time in the varied contexts of our lives.

1. *Prophetic witness.* There is an appropriate time and place for language that unmasks the powers and names evil for what it is. We do live in times that call on us to employ the prophetic message of Jesus, whose engagement of the powers led him to the cross. As it compares these powers to a "beast from the abyss," the book of Revelation is all too relevant for our time. Walter Wink insists upon the importance of naming and unmasking the powers. He points out how difficult it is to break through the manufactured idolatry of the powers otherwise. What kind of speech will be required?

Illusion requires incessant repetition in order to mimic the appearance of reality. Propaganda works only through constant reiteration. It is only in quantity that corrupt values, false perceptions, and bogus facts can be sold. Truth, by contrast, though its lot is never easy, makes its way with but a few friends, or even a single utterance. It does not need the apparatus of salesmanship, because reality itself is waiting to confirm it. Hence the power of the beleaguered prophet, or the mothers of the "disappeared" demonstrating daily in Argentina or El Salvador. Normal people with no economic stake never choose to suffer this much just to lie.[21]

2. *Christian vocation.* We need language to engage the professional worlds beyond the church. What does it mean to practice law or medicine well, to be a competent historian, to farm well, or to use entrepreneurial skills in service to the kingdom of God? Our challenge comes when we place our practices and disciplines within a theological context. How do we conceive of our work when we see it as a calling, as a vocation?

Vocation, which comes from the Latin root *vocatio*, suggests that we should live our lives in "response" to God. The danger is that we will simply approve uncritically the "autonomy" of a particular way of thinking or being in the world as defined by the profession that we choose. In other words, we may uncritically accept what it means to be a "good" police officer, lawyer, or public office holder according to the given rules of that profession, without reference to our primary vocation, that of living lives that witness to the way of Christ. Contemporary ecumenical discourse has often used the words "responsibility" or "responsible society" uncritically to bless practices that are in tension with discipleship. The purported necessity of violent force to protect the good and punish evil is only one example. Martin Luther's concept of vocation supports the acceptance of a given order or structure. He believed that faith should be active in love within the various roles persons have within society. Faith, for example, was active in love through the "offices" of magistrate or hangman, even as they employed the sword to protect the good and punish the evil. Luther's two-kingdom theology is problematic because it legitimates the accepted practice of public office holders who bear the sword, rather than challenging them to practice their faith differently because they are called to follow the teaching and example of Jesus.

It would be a mistake for a congregation with police officers as members simply to accept the fact that the rules of that profession must define what it means to faithfully follow Christ within that profession. When we address issues of public order and security, we need to ask how police officers in our congregations serve the public order by following Christ, who calls us to seek justice nonviolently. How do we employ wise language and practice in ways that bring to bear the "wisdom of the cross" in these matters of public order and safety?

3. *The common good within the discourse of democracy.* Christians are called to participate in the public square by contributing their voice to its discourse about the common good. Some assume that in order for Christians to participate in this discourse we must leave behind our convictions as Christians and accept a neutral, secular discourse. The philosopher John Rawls was especially influential in arguing that in a religiously plural society citizens must adopt a public reason or "reason in common" that does not presuppose any particular religious commitment.

Jeffrey Stout has been arguing to the contrary.[22] In a genuine democracy persons of diverse points of view should bring to the table their convictions about what is best for the common good. As Christians, we come to the table as followers of Christ committed to nonviolence and to a view of justice that is biased toward the poor and the marginal. Within this framework we are called to give an account of our convictions by giving reasons and empirical evidence for why we believe policies that flow from our convictions will contribute to the common good. It is surely appropriate to state openly and directly the theological basis for our convictions. However, because our conversation partners represent a plurality of points of view, we appropriately speak differently than we do when we speak to fellow believers, just to be understood. Still, it is not the case that we must leave at the door our convictions and assume that we must water down our point of view in order to find some a neutral secularized common reason. Stout has quoted Nicholas Wolterstorff to support his view: "Given that it is the very essence of liberal democracy that citizens enjoy equal freedom in law to live out their lives as they see fit, how can it be compatible with liberal democracy for its citizens to be morally restrained from deciding and discussing political issues as they see fit?"[23]

Certainly we need wisdom about how to engage in this public discourse. Wisdom is a blend of theological conviction with reason, experience, and an empirical understanding of how the world works.[24] A good example of wisdom language is just peacemaking theory. This theory identifies ten normative practices that are grounded in the moral commitment to Jesus's way of nonviolent peacemaking and at the same time have a track record bringing peaceful social change. They are "wise" practices because experience and empirical data show that these practices actually work and do contribute to the common good.[25]

Democratic discourse also requires virtues that some Christians transgress when they participate in the public square, thus undermining their witness.

> There are people who lack civility, or the ability to listen with an open mind, or the will to pursue justice where it leads, or the temperance to avoid talking and causing offense needlessly, or the practical wisdom to discern the subtleties of a discursive situation. There are also people who lack the courage to speak candidly, or the tact to avoid sanctimonious cant, or the poise to respond to unexpected arguments, or the humility to ask forgiveness from those who have been wronged. Such people are unlikely to express their reasons appropriately, whatever those reasons may be. When it comes to expressing religious reasons, it can take a citizen of considerable virtue to avoid even the most obvious pitfalls. I know of no set of rules for getting such matters right. My advice, therefore, is to cultivate the virtues of democratic speech, to love justice, and then to say what you please.[26]

4. *Middle axioms.* In *The Christian Witness to the State,* John Howard Yoder argued for the importance of still another level of discourse. Here we use language to address institutions or people and call them to live up to their own moral principles or ideals. For example, a government that is not committed to principled nonviolence may nevertheless be held accountable to do everything in its power to seek a just peace without violence. When it does resort to force, pacifists can hold it accountable to principles of just war theory. Likewise, they can hold a police force accountable to serve the community welfare by employing the least amount of force and use force only as a last resort.

Middle axioms discourse arises out of the complex issues of security that involve political actors, many of whom do not share Christian assumptions, and may even be hostile to Christian ethical principles. These complex situations raise age-old questions concerning the relationship of the church to authorities who may advocate and employ the use of violent force to remedy a situation. How do Christians committed to the way of Jesus nevertheless "witness" to authorities who employ violent force?

The use of violent force to solve problems is paradoxical. While in the short run violent force may provide some relative good or accomplish some limited short-range goals, the resort to armed force, even in defense of just causes and for the sake of order, perpetuates the cycle of violence. The U.S. invasion of Iraq may have accomplished some relative good by ending the dictatorial rule of Saddam Hussein. But in the absence of an alternative public order in place of Hussein, and in the presence of a foreign occupying military force, violence has escalated and led to deep misery and suffering for the Iraqi people. A Christian witness to governmental authority, therefore, seeks to communicate a vision of just peacemaking without recourse to violent force. When governmental actors do resort to violent force, a Christian witness will reason by analogy from nonviolent convictions to proposals for how institutions beyond the church (especially government, where the "sword" is operative and assumed) might live up to their own ideals.

At the middle axiom level, just war language is useful as a set of guidelines for governments who do not start with the presuppositions of Christian pacifism, provided that policy-makers have conscientiously pursued just peacemaking practices first. Followers of Christ, then, may appropriately use the language of just war reasoning to critically reflect on public policy, asking: 1. is there a just cause; 2. is the use of violent force a last resort; 3. are the aims in the employment of force clearly stated to one's opponent and does the opponent know what to do to prevent further violence; 4. is the employment of violent force conducted under the auspices of a legitimate authority; 5. does the overall good outweigh the evil that is likely to result; 6. are the principles of noncombatant immunity being protected; 7. and is the employment of force likely to contribute to a just peace?

SHALOM PRACTICES: SECURING HUMAN LIFE AND DIGNITY

The church's witness is multi-faceted: it witnesses simply through being what it is called to be, through its public testimony and witness, through institutions and exemplary programs that model service and help to meet human needs, through work and the professions in which church members engage, and through participation in the common political life as citizens. Abstract principles are not sufficient. We must be able to show that practices are available which secure human life and dignity, constitute alternatives to violence, and thus are not just utopian dreams. We need to do the empirical research to demonstrate that these alternative practices work and that the wisdom of the cross indeed runs with "the grain of the universe."[27]

Especially important is the participation of Christians in non-governmental voluntary organizations and citizens' groups that bring together people from a wide variety of racial, ethnic, religious, and national backgrounds who seek to address the common good. These grassroots groups and voluntary associations, from the local to the international level, stand between the individual and the state. They empower persons imaginatively and courageously to create alternatives to violence in response to issues of safety and security. Grassroots voluntary associations of fellow citizens who seek to achieve security goals through nonviolence often are most effective at carrying out the practices listed below.[28]

These shalom practices appear in two major sections below. Part A describes nonviolent practices that are consistent with Jesus's teaching and life of nonviolence. It provides examples of ways in which the church can help extend the application of nonviolence to secure human life and dignity. Part B describes examples of practices that are more ambiguous. In these situations public witness often requires the language of middle axioms because institutions or political actors presuppose the threat or use of violent force to gain security. As we have seen, these situations challenge us to be multilingual, that is, reasoning about limits and restraints on violence while remaining fully committed to Jesus's way of nonviolence.

The practices that follow are a suggestive sample. It invites people to "see" the world in a new way. Where are nonviolent practices for securing people's lives already being practiced, and what empirical evidence is there for the success of these practices? The sample also invites us to imagine other practices that we might invent if we were no longer to assume that violent force is the primary way in which we secure human life and dignity.

A. Nonviolent Practices

1. Daily life in civil society. Daily life in civil society sustains civil behavior, without which public order would not exist. Security does not depend primarily on the imposition of order through the threat of violent force by the state. Most people, most of the time, learn civil behavior through nurturing institutions like the family, tribal structures and rituals, schools, churches, and other voluntary institutions. Even when states fail, life may go on because of the enduring foundations of order that civil society maintains. We tend to focus too much upon using the state "to protect the good and punish the evil"

(Rom 13). As Elise Boulding has noted, it is precisely the "daili-ness of life" or the "common round from dawn to dawn that sustains human existence."[29]

We learn how to order human life especially through the civil society that mediates between the individual and the state. John Janzen, an anthropologist who did extensive field research in the Congo, noted how long-established local cus-toms and practices assert themselves when larger state systems fail. People find ways to order life by keeping markets func-tioning and roads or paths accessible to traffic. Bruce Bradshaw, with extensive experience in Somalia in the early 1990s as a regional liaison officer for the U.S. Agency for International Development, has described how existing clan structures continued to function to help people meet their basic daily needs, even when states failed.[30]

2. Accompaniment. One of the most important witnesses of the church is to accompany the marginal whose life and dignity are threatened. The church is called to a ministry of incarnation-al presence, to simply be there with people in their struggle, even when we do not see "a way out of no way." The martyred archbishop of El Salvador, Oscar Romero, stated our mandate forcefully and clearly: "A church that does not join the poor in order to speak out from the side of the poor against the injustices committed against them is not the true church of Jesus Christ. The Christian who does not want to live this commitment of sol-idarity with the poor is not worthy to be called Christian."[31]

Intervention teams such as Christian Peacemaker Teams can act as observers and provide public testimony on issues of justice. The development of a corps of interveners called on to be a presence in emergency situations may be one answer to crises like Kosovo or Rwanda. Peacekeeping forces could have a role in cooperation with the United Nations. One of the first recorded uses of the term "white helmets" was in a 1993 speech by Argentina's then-president Carlos Menem, who envisioned an increased role for civilian personnel in UN peace operations. "He dreamed of a national volunteer group, whose objective would be to make men and women of good will available to the United Nations, with the aim of strengthening the reserve capacity of developing countries in support of UN activities in the field of emergency humanitarian assistance and the gradual transition from relief to rehabilitation, reconstruction to development."[32]

Today there is a need for the presence of trained persons to monitor, advise, and otherwise assist the local police in many intrastate conflicts in order to support standards of internationally recognized human rights and fundamental freedoms. Despite many challenges to developing such intervention teams it is clear that military "blue helmets" cannot build peace alone. "Enter the white helmets: a group of civilians with expertise in diverse areas—policing, elections, judiciary, civilian administration, etc.—volunteering to rebuild the foundations upon which a society—and a lasting peace—can flourish."[33]

A good example of third party intervention is the involvement in election monitoring in 2004 in Venezuela. After a significant period of unrest in the country, a recall vote of Hugo Chavez occurred in November 2003, but the results were widely contested. So another recall referendum was held in August 2004, with election assistance and monitoring from the Carter Center and the Organization of American States (OAS). Both organizations worked together to assure that the processes and structures of the election were free and fair. The recall failed, with 59 percent supporting Chavez. Julie Hart, who was one of the volunteers in monitoring the process, commented, "Without this outside confirmation, the government and opposition, both with significant access to resources, could have spiraled the nation into a violent conflict."[34]

3. Community organizing. People's security is grounded in healthy communities that are organized to address the interdependent web of issues that nurture the common good. People's security (and the prevention of crime) is linked to the health of communities. The just peacemaking practice of fostering just and sustainable economic development is an important ingredient of building healthy communities. One example is the Harlem Children's Zone Inc., which integrates a mix of strategies that create safe and healthy communities. Founded in 1970, Harlem Children's Zone Inc., is a pioneering, non-profit, community-based organization that works to enhance the quality of life for children and families in some of New York City's most devastated neighborhoods.[35] The program has evolved into an on-the-ground, resident-driven community-building initiative that serves 3,000 children annually. The work over the past several years has reaffirmed the belief that in order to create positive opportunities and outcomes for all of the children who live in the Harlem Children's Zone Project, there must be an integrated network of services and support for children. Such a network provides family stability, opportunities for employment, decent and affordable housing, a quality education, and youth development activities for adolescents.

4. Human rights advocacy within constitutional democracies. An important factor in the security and safety of people is the role of human rights within constitutional democracies. Charles R. Epp has documented the crucial role of civil society in furthering these rights. In presenting a crucial case study he described how "on October 19, 1958, at five forty-five in the morning, nine Chicago police officers acting without a warrant forced their way into James and Flossie Monroe's home, pulled the Monroes and their six children out of bed, and forced them to stand half-naked in the living room while they ransacked the home." Officers beat family members and humiliated them with racial epithets. "The Monroe family sued the officers under a federal civil rights statute, but the federal district court and the court of appeals rejected their right to sue in federal court. In 1961, to the surprise of many, the United States Supreme Court reversed and granted them this right."[36]

Epp asked how such an expansion of human rights comes about. To answer he did a comparative analysis of the "rights revolution" in four countries: the United States, Canada, Great Britain, and India. Epp meant by the expansion of individual rights the transition from viewing rights as primarily about "the rights of property and contract, to encompass among other rights, freedom of speech and the press; free exercise of religion and prohibitions on official establishment of religion; prohibitions against invidious discrimination on the basis of race, sex, . . . the right to privacy, and the right to due process in law enforcement and administrative procedures."[37] He focused particularly on the rights of women, criminal defendants, and prisoners.

Epp argued against the view of Robert Bork, for example, that the rights revolution has actually circumvented democracy —that liberal activist judges have taken on a strong role in going against the wishes of the majority, and that this is the reason for the revolution. He also argues that it takes more than a strong constitution (e.g. the Bill of Rights) for change to occur. His central thesis is that change occurs because of the activist role of the civil society. In all four countries the expansion of individual rights (or the inhibition of the expansion) is critically dependent upon a vigorous and active civil society—an indicator of a healthy democratic society.

This evidence supports the importance of a nonviolent grassroots view of how order develops to protect humans from harm. The critical factor is "bottom up" grassroots democratic activity, rather than the imposition of order from the top down. Epp's evidence also supports one of the principles of just peacemaking, "to encourage grassroots peacemaking groups and voluntary associations."[38] Epp concluded:

> Neither a written constitution, a rights-supportive culture, nor sympathetic judges is sufficient for sustained judicial attention to and support of rights. Protection of civil liberties and civil rights depend, in addition, on a support structure in civil society. Without a support structure, even the clearest constitutional rights guarantees are likely to become meaningless in the courts; but a vibrant support structure can extend and expand the feeblest of rights. Participants in constitutional democracy would do well to focus their efforts not only in framing or revising constitutional provisions, and not only on selecting the judges who interpret them, but also on shaping the support structure that defends and develops those rights in practice.[39]

5. *Cooperative conflict resolution.* John Paul Lederach has shown how important it is to think of conflict as a dynamic process that has a time frame, for peace building is a long process. Lederach's analysis of top-level, middle-level, and grassroots-level actors in intrastate conflict is especially relevant to issues of safety and security. In his work at peacebuilding, Lederach has learned that it is important to focus on the middle level.[40] Peace practitioners must view the structure of a conflict both in terms of immediate micro-issues and broader, more systemic concerns. His argument draws on a four dimensional "nested paradigm" that Marie Dugan has proposed. For example, an issue (violence in school) points to underlying relational factors (group stereotypes), which occur in a larger sub-system (a school system) within the broader social system (racism in society).

6. *Nonviolent direct action.* Most people assume that violent revolution or war is the only way to respond to brutal dictatorial regimes. Yet nonviolent action ended a dictatorship in the Philippines and rule by the Shah in Iran. Nonviolent revolutions in Poland, East Germany, and Central Europe contributed to the crumbling of the Soviet empire. In historical accounts of the end of the Cold War, a battle over how to see these conflicts is being waged. Most commentators who memorialize President Ronald Reagan credit him with bringing down the Soviet Union through the military might of the United States. Rarely if ever do they speak about the role of nonviolent movements of the people in the countries within the Soviet bloc. Such a reading of history reinforces the myth of redemptive violence and support for militarism. Christians committed to nonviolence can play a critical role in how we write history.[41]

A theology that sees the world differently invites imaginative thinking about alternatives such as Civilian-Based Defense. This is

> a developing defense policy designed to deter and defeat both foreign military occupations and internal takeovers by prepared non-cooperation and political defiance by trained populations. It employs social, economic, political, and psychological "weapons" (or spe-

cific methods of action). This policy would operate by preventing the attackers from ruling the attacked society, denying them their other objectives, subverting their troops and functionaries, and mobilizing international opposition to the attack. All this is to be done in ways that are most difficult for the attackers to counter. The term "civilian-based defense" indicates defense by civilians (as distinguished from military personnel) using civilian means of struggle (as distinct from military or paramilitary means). Weapons of violence are not required and would in fact be counterproductive.[42]

Civilian-Based Defense has in fact been employed in numerous cases. Results have ranged from short-term defeats, to partial successes, to full successes. East German resistance against the Soviets, for example, was unsuccessful in 1953, but very successful in 1989. The Czechs had some short-term success resisting a Soviet Invasion in 1968-69, and successfully achieved their freedom in 1989. The First Intifada in 1989 in the West Bank and Gaza, largely nonviolent, had short-term success by gaining support of world public opinion against the Israeli occupation and forcing the development of a peace process. But since then, with the Second Intifada, which began in 2000 and turned much more violent, the situation of the Palestinians has only worsened.

7. *Other practices.* Woven into this essay at a number of points are the practices of just peacemaking. One of the most important practices is repentance and forgiveness: to "acknowledge responsibility for conflict and injustice and seek repentance and forgiveness." This practice is very important to break the cycle of violence in interpersonal and small group conflicts. More recently, however, it has been applied to the behavior of nations. Examples are Germany since World War II, Japan and Korea, President Clinton apologizing in Africa for slavery, the U.S. apology toward Japanese-Americans in World War II, and the Truth and Reconciliation Commission led by Bishop Tutu in South Africa.[43]

The theory and practice of restorative community justice is

an approach to criminal behavior that seeks to bring healing to both victims and offenders. A restorative concept of justice is an alternative to viewing crime primarily as a violation against the state. Instead of responding to crime primarily with punishment by sending people to prison, only to see them return to society and become repeat offenders, restorative justice seeks to intervene in the lives of offenders by helping them take responsibility for their action, face their victims, repent of their action, and make restitution. This approach also helps victims, otherwise often forgotten, into the criminal justice process. We have evidence that this approach works in preventing a cycle of continuing criminal behavior, thus contributing to safer and more secure communities.[44]

B. Practices that Presuppose the Language of Middle Axioms

1. Just policing. Though just policing is categorized with practices that presuppose the language of middle axioms, that should not lead us to assume that policing necessarily involves the threat of violent force. In fact, our goal should be to develop just policing practices that move in the direction of nonviolence to secure the public order.

It is important clearly to understand the distinction between the use of force in war and police action: 1. Policing is a discriminate use of force, applied only to the offending party; 2. a police officer's use of force is subject to review by higher authorities; 3. the authorized force is within a society where an offender knows the laws apply to both officers and offenders; 4. safeguards exist to contain police force lest it be used on the innocent; 5. police power is a monopoly of force within an existing state and thus is usually sufficient to overwhelm the offender such that resistance is pointless. Most arrests are made without any violence.

Second, it is essential to understand the community function of policing. The aim of community policing is to nurture the common good of the community by establishing relationships between police and families, clergy, social workers, and other community leaders. The community then views police as an extension of itself. In community policing the image and role of police is "de-militarized" from their role as primarily or exclusively enforcers of the law through the use of violent force. Their primary role is to be participants in the community in crime prevention.[45]

Crime is a complex social problem that cannot be solved by any single agency. When we recognize the complexity of crime problems, we also acknowledge that police are not solely responsible for their solution. Crime problems can then be de-constructed into manageable pieces. The police may partici-pate in a community effort to address underlying conditions that breed crime, such as poverty, lack of good jobs, affordable housing, healthcare, and the loss of meaning that leads to drug and alcohol abuse. The police are partners in the community, and their training includes skills in conflict resolution, mediation, negotiation, and personal relationships and communication.

One key success story of community policing came in Boston in the 1990s when the number of homicides plummeted from 152 in 1990 to only 31 in 1999. Much of the drop occurred among individuals under twenty-four years of age. This so-called "Boston Miracle" involved the cooperation of the police department with a group of inner city black ministers, known as the "Ten Point Coalition." This was extraordinary given the city's history of highly antagonistic race relations. The process included gang forums involving youth, ministers, police, and other social service agencies. Both carrots and sticks gave incentives to change. A comprehensive community approach addressed youth violence by helping youth in a variety of ways—school, jobs, family relationships, and drug problems. The youth also faced the sanction of jail if they did not stop their gang banging.[46]

Another important consideration is the use of non-lethal weapons by police forces. An article in the January 8, 2004, issue of the *Denver Post* read: "Denver cops make gains on non-lethal force." The police officer "kept his distance and holstered his pistol. Then he pulled out a taser . . . and zapped the knife-wielding man with the taser's electrified barbs and took him into custody." The *Post* writer praised the police officer for "employing non-lethal techniques in deadly force situations," and placed this police officer's action over against "the ugly history of cops shooting civilians." Only a year earlier a community dispute in a Denver neighborhood had gone from ugly to lethal when a "kid died because he didn't drop a knife when ordered to do so."

A number of police departments around the country are ordering tasers. The category of non-lethal weapons needs serious ethical analysis, however. Reports of serious injury and death from tasers have surfaced. A story by *Christian Science Monitor* staff writer Brad Knickerbocker reflects the fuzzy ethics of other non-lethal weapons.[47] It reports that Donald Rumsfeld wanted to use non-lethal chemicals in Iraq to incapacitate people without causing death or lasting injury, but these weapons violate international law, specifically the 1993 Chemical Weapons Convention.

Some of the most dangerous situations for police are domestic disputes. Police departments sometimes cooperate with unarmed intervention teams of social workers and counselors who are trained to intervene in volatile situations and resolve a potential lethal conflict.[48]

Sometimes civil authorities call in the police or national guard troops during times of national emergency and disaster. One of the most dramatic examples during the Civil Rights Movement was President Lyndon Johnson's federalizing of almost nineteen hundred men of the Alabama guard's Dixie Division. He also authorized the use of two thousand more regular army troops, as well as a hundred FBI agents and a hundred U.S. marshals. Federal troops then protected the civil rights march that Martin Luther King Jr. was leading from Selma to Montgomery in 1965.[49]

2. Practices that transform international conflict. All the practices of just peacemaking theory are compatible with nonviolence. Some of them, however, involve the participation of government actors who have not given up the threat of violent force, even as they seek to resolve conflicts peacefully. We discuss these practices under the rubric of middle axioms because we are addressing institutions or political actors who presuppose the threat or use of violent force.

a. Independent initiatives. Taking independent initiatives in a situation of danger and potential harm is an alternative to being stymied into doing nothing because of the position of one's opponents. It is also an alternative to using threats against one's opponents that only reinforce their intransigence. "The strategy is to take initiatives to decrease the other side's distrust or threat perception, in order to induce them to take similar initiatives or to negotiate seriously to remove threats." This concept of "independent initiatives," proposed by the social psychologist Charles Osgood in 1962, was widely adopted by church statements and peace movements in Europe and the United States. Governments were persuaded to adopt this concept, with striking success.[50]

b. Support cooperative forces in the international system. This is a broad area that encompasses at least three just peace-making practices. The first is to support changes in the international system that move nations to greater cooperation. Four forces are in fact at work that move nations toward greater cooperation: the decline in the utility of war; the priority of trade and the economy over war; the strength of international exchanges, communications, transactions, and networks; and the gradual ascendancy of liberal representative democracy and a mixture of welfare-state and laissez-faire market economies.[51]

A second practice is to "strengthen the United Nations and international efforts for cooperation and human rights." As we pointed out earlier in our discussion of the role of "white helmets" and civilian monitoring of elections, there is significant potential for cooperation between non-governmental organizations and international bodies like the United Nations.[52]

A third practice is "to reduce offensive weapons and weapons trade." This practice fits middle axiom language because it still does not assume full disarmament, but rather shifts arms toward strictly defensive forces. There is much that can be done in controlling arms sales and imports, in moving toward nuclear disarmament of all nations (as required by the Nuclear Non-Proliferation Treaty), and in banning chemical and biological weapons. We also need to urge all nations into compliance with the treaty to ban land mines.[53]

3. *Crisis intervention based on human rights.* These are very complex and difficult questions that require a book-length analysis. We can only summarize a few general principles here. If we use as a case study the genocide in the Darfur region of the Sudan in 2004, we can identify three principles that should guide the international community and apply to other crises as well. An analysis of the conflict suggests some preventive measures that could be taken to prevent other situations like this from occurring:

a. Attention to economic, political, social, and environmental conditions that are at the root of the conflict.

b. Development of the capacity for early warning and early action to respond to conflicts when there is still time for resolution before they turn violent.

c. Disarmament: limit the capacity for organized violence and militarization of political conflict by limiting arms sales.

When these preventative measures fail or are not taken soon enough, then what? What is the ethic that should guide humanitarian intervention? In an appendix to a book entitled *The Ethics and Politics of Humanitarian Intervention,* a list appears of peacekeeping operations with humanitarian components between 1990 and 1996.[54] It is striking that most of these peacekeeping operations were highly successful and involved no casualties or very few. Still, Robert Johansen and Stanley Hoffmann, two contributors to the book, disagreed on the relative merits of military intervention in humanitarian crises. Johansen identified a number of principles, therefore, for a "third path" between no intervention and military intervention:

1. the devotion of far more resources to conflict mitigation and peace-building;

2. the norms that trigger humanitarian intervention need to be much clearer in advance;

3. violations should be clear and well documented;

4. any intervening agency should have widespread

legitimacy and possess real autonomy from separate states in decision making and action;

5. the means employed should be carefully constrained against excessive use of force and the protection of innocent people;

6. the goals should be to stop wrongdoing of those responsible (not an entire nation), protect victims, and strengthen precedents for the future to prevent future misdeeds; and,

7. there must be a broad and comprehensive vision of human rights that builds an ethos or culture of compliance of nonmilitary yet coercive enforcement.[55]

Should Christians support "limited military intervention"?[56] Clearly, military intervention is contrary to a discipleship ethic of nonviolence. But can Christians support as middle axioms police forms of potentially lethal force. Can they, in other words, support discriminate use of armed force that "protects" people from harm, as opposed to massive military force used to protect troops from harm by first softening up targets with bombing? Ernie Regehr has suggested this principle: "Protection operations have as their primary objective the reduction of risk to civilians, not to the intervening forces."[57] How do we deal with the "risk" of forceful intervention, the danger that peril to innocent people will possibly expand rather than shrink? What if interventions do not "work"? Are such uses of force ever the calling of pacifist Christians?

Here we reach the limits of our ability to calculate consequences. To press on for measures that will supposedly guarantee success in every case would be to fall into the age-old Constantinian temptation of managing history to make it come out right. As Christians we should do all we can to seek justice and address the needs of persons in these humanitarian crises, but at the same time remain faithful to our call to be followers of Christ, to live by the "wisdom of the cross." We may use middle axioms in our appeal to other actors to live up to their best ideals. Those who have committed their lives to follow Jesus, however, should renounce all lethal violence.

4. Creative alternatives to responding to terrorism with violence.

What are the alternatives to responding to terrorism with primary reliance on violent force? The psychology of fear that has overwhelmed so many people in the United States since September 11, 2001, does not serve us well. One of the important contributions Christians can make is to counter the underlying psychology of obsession about security with pastoral resources that liberate people from bondage of fear and lead them to a deeper underlying trust and hope in God. Only then can we become free to think and act differently.

The principles of just peacemaking theory provide a hermeneutical key for international cooperation in preventing terrorism.[58] We can illustrate these principles by utilizing Glen Stassen's description of Turkey's successful antiterrorism efforts in response to the Muslim Kurds in southeastern Turkey. Stassen compared it to an unsuccessful antiterrorism campaign by the Russians against the Muslim Chechens in Southern Russian. In the mid-1990s Turkey changed its strategy from attacking with military force, which had been unsuccessful and had resulted in more than 30,000 deaths since early 1984. Turkish officials developed a fourfold approach:

a. They began practicing the just peacemaking principle of "sustainable economic development." They avoided attacking civilians and introduced a major health and education program for the Kurdish area of Turkey. Recognition was also given to Kurdish language and community customs.

b. Turkey also recognized a second principle of advancing human rights, democracy, and religious liberty by allowing Kurds to gain much more representation in the Turkish parliament, and allowing for the development of democratic civic organizations in the Kurdish areas of Turkey.

c. A third just peacemaking principle is to work with emerging cooperative forces in the international system. Turkey responded positively to pressure from the Western European Union to recognize the Kurds and their economic needs. Other countries also cooperated in arresting Ocalan, the leader of the terrorist organization. He was expelled from Syria, and later arrested in Italy.

d. Turkey then arrested Ocalan, and achieved his cooperation in ending the terrorism in exchange for requiring the death penalty (the principle of "cooperative conflict resolution").[59]

The example of Turkey can give us guidance for addressing September 11. We know that the terrorists who attacked on that day represented a young elite that is alienated from their own repressive regimes in the Middle East. Most came from Saudi Arabia, and were reacting to the presence of U.S. forces on the sacred soil of an Islamic country. Saudi Arabia is also an autocratic regime. We can only achieve success against terrorism when we stop supporting policies that repress democracy, whether in Egypt, Saudi Arabia, the Israeli-occupied West Bank, or elsewhere.

Furthermore, even though the 9/11 terrorists themselves were not poor, they were responding to economic conditions in the world that leave vast numbers of people without the benefits of the global economic system. "Sustainable economic development" separates "the terrorists from the people, and does justice for the people so they separate from the terrorists." As Susan Thistlethwaite has written, "Only justice will actually, finally, stop terrorism. Violence only creates more violence."[60] In Iraq at the time of this writing, the perceived injustice of foreigners occupying the country is the single most important factor fueling the violence. The same is true of the unjust occupation of the West Bank by the Israelis.

If we can address these two underlying causes of terrorism, then we can work even more cooperatively with law enforcement agencies around the globe in identifying, arresting, and bringing to trial those responsible for planning and implementing terrorist acts. A paradigm of just policing rather than the paradigm of war, then, could address terrorism more effectively.

A Concluding Reminder

Our ultimate security rests in God, not in our own power and ingenuity. To live faithfully we need qualities of character (virtues and fruits of the Spirit) that liberate us from the bondage of fear. In being reborn to a security grounded upon faith in God's goodness and providential care, Christians will be a blessing to others. Without this foundation, we will have nothing to offer to the world.

We need the guidance of the Spirit to help us discern, that is, to "see" the world from the standpoint of the wisdom of the cross. Can we see the mustard seed and the mysterious power of the yeast in the dough? Can this new way of seeing liberate in us an alternative imagination that can generate creative alternatives to violence?

The resurrection shapes a spirituality of hope, patience, and expectant waiting—the possibility of "miracle" that goes beyond worldly realism about what is possible. Miracles do happen. The Berlin Wall came down against all expectations. Prayer meetings in St. Thomas Church in Leipzig, East Germany, sowed the seeds of that fall.[61] The church became the space in East Germany where a nation was reborn. Faithful Christians in South Africa who put the lie to apartheid helped bring down that system, again against all expectations. Nelson Mandela became the leader of a nation after twenty-seven years in prison.

To follow the wisdom of the cross takes courage. We need the same courage at these times as the martyrs who laid down their lives as witnesses of Christ's kingdom. "Unless a grain of wheat falls into the earth and dies, it remains just a single grain; but if it dies, it bears much fruit" (John 12:24).

NOTES

1. For an account of Jesus's life and message in the context of the prophetic tradition, especially the prophet Isaiah, see Glen Harold Stassen and David P. Gushee, *Kingdom Ethics: Following Jesus in Contemporary Context* (Downers Grove, Ill.: InterVarsity Press, 2003), 19–54, 90–98.

2. Glen H. Stassen, *Just Peacemaking: Transforming Initiatives for Justice and Peace* (Louisville, Ky.: Westminster/John Knox Press, 1992), 41.

3. See Walter Wink, *Engaging the Powers: Discernment and*

Resistance in a World of Domination (Minneapolis: Fortress Press, 1992).

4. Political leaders often use the word "terrorism" to mask their own ideological and political interests. Two words are key to a definition of terrorism: *intentional* violence directed at *non-combatants*. Palestinians who direct their violence against the Israeli occupation military forces are not terrorists, though suicide bombings on a bus carrying civilians do constitute terrorism. Israelis who demolish homes of the families of suspected terrorists are also engaged in terrorist acts.

5. In a meeting of the MCC Peace Committee, Ricardo Esquivia of Colombia identified the lack of "institutionality" (effective structures of order) as one of the root causes of violence in Colombia.

6. Chalmers A. Johnson, *The Sorrows of Empire: Militarism, Secrecy, and the End of the Republic* (New York: Metropolitan Books, 2004), 287.

7. Major newspapers in the United States such as the *New York Times* and *The Washington Post* admitted some months later that they had not vigorously researched and reported the uncertainties about whether Iraq possessed weapons of mass destruction at the time the Bush administration was using these argument to justify the war.

8. See the linkage of these twin ethical issues in Sallie McFague, *Life Abundant: Rethinking Theology and Economy for a Planet in Peril* (Minneapolis, Minn.: Fortress Press, 2001).

9. Rob van Drimmelen, World Council of Churches Development Office, 1998. Quoted by Pamela K. Brubaker in her book *Globalization at What Price? Economic Change and Daily Life* (Cleveland, Ohio: Pilgrim Press, 2001), 15.

10. Speech given at Harvard University in 1998. Quoted by Brubaker, *Globalization at What Price? Economic Change and Daily Life*, 15.

11. Glen H. Stassen, "The Christian Origin of Human Rights," chapter 6 in *Just Peacemaking: Transforming Initiatives for Justice and Peace* (Louisville, Ky.: Westminster/John Knox Press, 1992), 137–63.

12. Christopher D. Marshall, *Crowned with Glory & Honor: Human Rights in the Biblical Tradition*, Studies in Peace and Scripture Series, no. 6 (Telford, Pa.; Scottdale, Pa.; Auckland, N.Z.: Pandora Press U.S.; Herald Press; Lime Grove House, 2001), 116.

13. See especially two books: Leo Driedger and Donald B. Kraybill, *Mennonite Peacemaking: From Quietism to Activism* (Scottdale, Pa.: Herald Press, 1994); Cynthia Sampson and John Paul Lederach, eds., *From the Ground Up: Mennonite Contributions to International Peacebuilding* (Oxford New York: Oxford University Press, 2000).

14. John Milbank, *Theology and Social Theory: Beyond Secular Reason* (Cambridge, Mass.: Blackwell, 1990), 4.

15. See John Howard Yoder's subtle and nuanced understanding of principled and instrumental ethical reasoning in "The

Hermeneutics of Peoplehood: A Protestant Perspective," in *The Priestly Kingdom: Social Ethics as Gospel* (Notre Dame, Ind.: University of Notre Dame Press, 1984), 15–45.

16. The phrase "grain of the universe" comes from John Howard Yoder, "Armaments and Eschatology," *Studies in Christian Ethics* 1, no. 1 (1988): 58; John Howard Yoder, *The Politics of Jesus*, 2d ed., reprint, 1972 (Grand Rapids: William B. Eerdmans, 1994), 246.

17. Wink, *Engaging the Powers*, 65–89.

18. See Elise Boulding, *Cultures of Peace: The Hidden Side of History*, Syracuse Studies on Peace and Conflict Resolution (Syracuse, N.Y.: Syracuse University Press, 2000).

19. See the quotation of Pius XI in the entry on "Subsidiarity" in *The Westminster Dictionary of Christian Ethics* (Philadelphia: Westminster Press, 1986).

20. See Pamela Leach's chapter in the present volume.

21. Wink, *Engaging the Powers*, 94–95.

22. Jeffrey Stout, *Democracy and Tradition*, New Forum Books (Princeton, N.J.: Princeton University Press, 2004).

23. Ibid., 68.

24. See Lydia Harder's chapter elsewhere in this volume, in particular her discussion of how the category of "wisdom" in the Bible works to bridge the narrative/prophetic tradition in the Bible and "worldly" wisdom.

25. Glen Stassen, ed., *Just Peacemaking: Ten Practices for Abolishing War* (Cleveland: Pilgrim Press, 1998).

26. Stout, *Democracy and Tradition*, 85.

27. See note 16.

28. See practice ten of just peacemaking theory: Duane K. Friesen, "Encourage Grassroots Peacemaking Groups and Voluntary Associations," in *Just Peacemaking: Ten Practices for Abolishing War*, ed. Glen Stassen (Cleveland: Pilgrim Press, 1998), 176–88.

29. Boulding, *Cultures of Peace*, 15.

30. Based on notes of a meeting of the Research Team of the Peace Committee of the Mennonite Central Committee. January 22, 2004, at Bethel College, N. Newton, Kan.

31. Oscar A Romero, *The Violence of Love: The Pastoral Wisdom of Archbishop Oscar Romero*, trans. and ed. James R. Brockman (San Francisco: Harper & Row, 1988), 189. Heidi B. Neumark, pastor since 1984 of the Transfiguration Lutheran Church in the South Bronx, describes an example of incarnational presence there: "One of our initial actions was to hold a series of house meetings at which church leaders could invite other members, friends, and neighbors to voice their anger, dreams, hopes, and concerns for the community. . . . We needed to encourage folks to be concrete" about the problems of

drugs, burnt-out buildings, schools without books and inadequate facilities, the terrible conditions of healthcare, lack of jobs, and so on. Heidi Neumark, *Breathing Space: A Spiritual Journey in the South Bronx* (Boston: Beacon Press, 2003), 75–76.

32. See Shannon-Marie Soni, "White Helmets 101," *Ambassador* (2001), Http://www.cowac.org/whitehelmet101.html.

33. Soni, "White Helmets 101."

34. Julie Hart, "Peacebuilding Through Election Assistance in Unstable Democracies: Observations from the Venezuelan Process," unpublished paper (Bethel College, N. Newton, Kan., 2004).

35. See the website of the Harlem Children's Zone Inc. for more information: http://www.hcz.org/.

36. Charles R. Epp, *The Rights Revolution: Lawyers, Activists, and Supreme Courts in Comparative Perspective* (Chicago: University of Chicago Press, 1998), 6.

37. Ibid., 5.

38. Friesen, "Encourage Grassroots Peacemaking."

39. Epp, *The Rights Revolution*, 205.

40. John Paul Lederach, *Building Peace: Sustainable Reconciliation in Divided Societies* (Washington, D.C.: United States Institute of Peace Press, 1997).

41. James C. Juhnke and Carol M. Hunter, *The Missing Peace: The Search for Nonviolent Alternatives in United States History* (Kitchener, Ont.; Scottdale, Pa.: Pandora Press; Herald Press, 2001).

42. See the summary article by Gene Sharp, "Civilian-Based Defense," in Roger S. Powers and William B. Vogele, eds, *Protest, Power, and Change: An Encyclopedia of Nonviolent Action from ACT-UP to Women's Suffrage*, associate editors Christopher Kruegler and Ronald M. McCarthy, Garland Reference Library of the Humanities, vol. 1625 (New York: Garland Pub., 1997), 101–04.

43. See Alan Geyer, "Acknowledge Responsibility for Conflict and Injustice and Seek Repentance and Forgiveness," in *Just Peacemaking: Ten Practices for Abolishing War*, ed. Glen Stassen (Cleveland: Pilgrim Press, 1998), 77–89. For a more extensive analysis see Donald W. Shriver, *An Ethic for Enemies: Forgiveness in Politics* (New York: Oxford University Press, 1995).

44. See the work of Howard Zehr, leading scholar and practitioner: *Changing Lenses: A New Focus for Crime and Justice*, Christian Peace Shelf Selection (Scottdale, Pa.: Herald Press, 1990).

45. On the differences between policing and warfare, see Gerald W. Schlabach, "Just Policing: How War Could Cease to be a Church-Dividing Issue," in *Just Policing: Mennonite-Catholic Theological Colloquium 2002*, ed. Ivan J. Kauffman, Bridgefolk Series, no. 2 (Kitchener, Ontario: Pandora Press, 2004), 23, 28–31, as well as

Schlabach's chapter elsewhere in the present volume.

46. Christopher Winship, "End of a Miracle? Crime, Faith, and Partnership in Boston in the 1990's" (Harvard University, 2002), 7–8, Http://www.wjh.harvard.edu/society/faculty/winship/End_of_a_Miracle.pdf.

47. Brad Knickerbocker, "The Fuzzy Ethics of Nonlethal Weapons," *Christian Science Monitor*, 14 February 2003.

48. In conversations with the research team of the Peace Committee of the Mennonite Central Committee at Bethel College, N. Newton, Kan. (Jan. 24, 2004), Melvin Goering, CEO of Prairie View Mental Health Center, Newton, Kan., reported on the cooperation between police in Memphis, Tenn., and trained unarmed mental health workers who intervene in crisis situations.

49. Charles E. Fager, *Selma, 1965* (New York: Scribner, 1974), 148.

50. For an account of the success of this principle by governments during the Cold War see Glen Stassen, "Take Independent Initiatives to Reduce Threat," in *Just Peacemaking: Ten Practices for Abolishing War*, ed. Glen Stassen (Cleveland: Pilgrim Press, 1998), 46–52.

51. Based on Paul W. Schroeder, "Work with Emerging Cooperative Forces Within the International System," in *Just Peacemaking: Ten Practices for Abolishing War*, ed. Glen Stassen (Pilgrim Press, 1998), 133–46; see especially p. 138.

52. See Michael Joseph Smith, "Strengthen the United Nations and International Efforts for Cooperation and Human Rights," in *Just Peacemaking: Ten Practices for Abolishing War*, ed. Glen Stassen (Pilgrim Press, 1998), 146–55.

53. See Barbara Green and Glen Stassen, "Reduce Offensive Weapons and Weapons Trade," in *Just Peacemaking: Ten Practices for Abolishing War*, ed. Glen Stassen (Pilgrim Press, 1998), 156–75.

54. Stanley Hoffmann, *The Ethics and Politics of Humanitarian Intervention*, with contributions by Robert C. Johansen, James P. Sterba, and Raimo Väyrynen, Notre Dame Studies on International Peace (Notre Dame: University of Notre Dame Press, 1996).

55. This list is a summary of Robert C. Johansen, "Limits and Opportunities in Humanitarian Intervention," in *The Ethics and Politics of Humanitarian Intervention*, Stanley Hoffmann, Notre Dame Studies on International Peace (Notre Dame: University of Notre Dame Press, 1996), 68–82.

56. Mennonites do not agree on these questions. We can identify at least four positions (and there are probably more): 1. Some can support a limited "police" type of military intervention under U.N. auspices; 2. Some counsel "silence," neither giving support and legitimation to the use of military force, yet not overtly condemning government agencies who do use a limited "police" type force; 3. A third

group counsels that the church and governments should intervene in such crises, but only with nonviolent means and methods; 4. A fourth group would maintain that Christian pacifists are called to faithfulness to Christ's way of non-resistance, but should not involve themselves politically, and should instead pray for those in power and give humanitarian assistance through church aid agencies.

57. Ernie Regehr, "Culpable Nonviolence: The Moral Ambiguity of Pacifism," *Voices Across Boundaries*, Summer 2003, 38–41.

58. Glen H. Stassen, "Just Peacemaking as Hermeneutical Key: The Need for International Cooperation in Preventing Terrorism," *Journal of the Society of Christian Ethics* 24, no. 2 (Fall/Winter 2004): 171–91.

59. This list summarizes Glen H. Stassen, "Just Peacemaking as Hermeneutical Key," 177–79.

60. Susan Brooks Thistlethwaite, "New Wars, Old Wineskins," in *Strike Terror No More: Theology, Ethics, and the New War*, ed. Jon L. Berquist (St. Louis, Mo.: Chalice Press, 2002), 264; cited in Glen H. Stassen, "Just Peacemaking as Hermeneutical Key," 179.

61. See Mark Jantzen's personal account in *The Wrong Side of the Wall: An American in East Berlin During the Peaceful Revolution.* (Mark Jantzen, Bethel College, N. Newton, Kan., 1993.)

FOR FURTHER READING

Boulding, Elise. *Cultures of Peace: The Hidden Side of History.* Syracuse Studies on Peace and Conflict Resolution. Syracuse, N.Y.: Syracuse University Press, 2000.

Epp, Charles R. *The Rights Revolution: Lawyers, Activists, and Supreme Courts in Comparative Perspective.* Chicago: University of Chicago Press, 1998.

Friesen, Duane K. *Artists, Citizens, Philosophers: Seeking the Peace of the City: An Anabaptist Theology of Culture.* Scottdale, Pa.; Waterloo, Ont.: Herald Press, 2000.

Hoffmann, Stanley. *The Ethics and Politics of Humanitarian Intervention.* With contributions by Robert C. Johansen, James P. Sterba, and Raimo Väyrynen. Notre Dame Studies on International Peace. Notre Dame: University of Notre Dame Press, 1996.

Juhnke, James C., and Carol M. Hunter. *The Missing Peace: The Search for Nonviolent Alternatives in United States History.*

Kitchener, Ont.; Scottdale, Pa.: Pandora Press; Herald Press, 2001.

Lederach, John Paul. *Building Peace: Sustainable Reconciliation in Divided Societies*. Washington, D.C.: United States Institute of Peace Press, 1997.

Neumark, Heidi. *Breathing Space: A Spiritual Journey in the South Bronx*. Boston: Beacon Press, 2003.

Shriver, Donald W. *An Ethic for Enemies: Forgiveness in Politics*. New York: Oxford University Press, 1995.

Stassen, Glen H., ed. *Just Peacemaking: Ten Practices for Abolishing War*. Cleveland: Pilgrim Press, 2d edition, 2004.

Stassen, Glen H., and David P. Gushee. *Kingdom Ethics: Following Jesus in Contemporary Context*. Downers Grove, Ill.: InterVarsity Press, 2003.

Stout, Jeffrey. *Democracy and Tradition*. New Forum Books. Princeton, N.J.: Princeton University Press, 2004.

Wink, Walter. *Engaging the Powers: Discernment and Resistance in a World of Domination*. Minneapolis: Fortress Press, 1992.

Yoder, John Howard. *The Christian Witness to the State*. Institute of Mennonite Studies Series, no. 3. Newton, Kan.: Faith and Life Press, 1964.

———. *The Politics of Jesus*. 2d ed. 1972. Grand Rapids: William B. Eerdmans, 1994.

Zehr, Howard. *Changing Lenses: A New Focus for Crime and Justice*. Christian Peace Shelf Selection. Scottdale, Pa.: Herald Press, 1990.

—3—

GADFLY CITIZENSHIP: FAITHFUL PUBLIC PRACTICES BEYOND THE NATIONAL SECURITY MODEL

Pamela Leach

> *"Would that even today you knew the things that make for peace! But now they are hid from your eyes."* Luke 19:42 (RSV)

What obligations do pacifist faith communities feel toward questions of security and of intervention in conditions where there is a breakdown of order? The Peace Theology Project that Mennonite Central Committee (MCC) conducted in 2003 and 2004 sought to learn this from its Mennonite and Brethren in Christ constituencies. Yet to engage the dilemmas that arise amid such a breakdown demands some inquiry into who the actors are who ought to bear this concern. Put in the language of the public sphere, we must unpack the meaning of "citizenship" that stands behind any conception of intervention in questions of "order" and "security."

In other words, to ask about the obligation to intervene is to question whether or how Anabaptists feel themselves morally, spiritually, and politically empowered to act in the public sphere for the purpose of enhancing conditions that may be labeled "security" and "order." This chapter explores that question in the context of the global phenomenon of the securitizing of societies. Since I am a Quaker, privileged to walk, work, and sometimes worship with my Mennonite sisters and brothers, I note that this inquiry is not, at least at the point of inception, an Anabaptist one, but merely that of a Mennophile.

TOWARD A MODEL OF MENNONITE CITIZENSHIP

To invoke "citizenship" today is usually to summon a loaded constellation of liberal values, rights, and duties that make certain claims about human nature. The values of classical liberalism arose in the seventeenth century out of a concern to extend the "public" sphere beyond the state, and to limit the state by rendering it accountable. They were premised on a view of human nature as rational, moral, and self-seeking.

Anabaptists have not always been able to reconcile the implications of citizenship with a life of faith. Perhaps for this reason, and out of a model of discipleship that rejects conformity to the world, some Mennonites have set aside the notion of citizenship as unhelpful or deceptive insofar as it denies or perverts obedience to God's will. This witness illustrates that the concept of citizenship is "contestable," that is, a kind of vessel open to different meanings and possibilities. In a context where Christian pacifists are laboring under their roles in the world, and yet finding total disengagement unacceptable as a path of discipleship, re-examination of "faithful public practices" by the MCC project may be timely.

"Citizenship" describes a relationship of belonging in the public sphere. It suggests a rapport based upon mutual obligation to each other and to the larger social order. Since ancient times, citizenship has been acknowledged as a "privileged" place, in the sense that non-citizens, such as refugees and displaced persons, are marginal. Democratic citizens are distinguished by the role they may play in ordering their society, in establishing its priorities and core values, and in shaping the means by which these are instilled and institutionalized.

Such matters have not been incidental, but of central importance to Mennonites since the sixteenth century. Unlike many other communities of the modern era, Mennonites have engaged often and actively in shaping the social contract under which they have lived, and in exercising their right to be faithful. "Institutionality" is a term that Colombian Mennonite Ricardo Esquivia uses for the healthy institutional practices and structures throughout a society that functions according to the rule of law. Historically, wherever a lack of institutionality has hindered a vibrant life of faith—either because it repressed the church, or because it required unacceptable practices such as military service—Mennonites have found sufficient cause for emigration en masse, at astonishing cost. Today such matters have great significance among Mennonites and Brethren in Christ in Africa, Latin America, and Asia. Insufficient "institutionality," demonstrated in places like Colombia and the Democratic Republic of Congo, has resulted in violence bordering on anarchy, and has threatened the survival and peace witness of Anabaptists.

Mennonites have in fact practiced citizenship, and their citizenship has often broken new ground, bringing important yet under-appreciated correctives to an ailing liberal model. One of the most significant criticisms leveled against liberal citizenship has been its individualism. Critics note its limitations both as an account of human origins, in the classic works of theorists such as Hobbes and Locke, and as the contemporary context from which persons engage in their communities and with the state. Mennonites have consistently asserted that community membership fundamentally shapes the identity, values, and actions of citizens. Not least, the group acts as the steward of core values, socializing its members to these in ways that are useful to the state. The community can instill service as a central tenet, or sanction members who fail to respect the discipline or ethos of the collectivity.

Beyond the inward ordering that Mennonites provide, however, Mennonites have modeled outward ways of relating to the state. By acting collectively to negotiate citizenship, land and tenure practices, non-combatant status, language use, and freedom of worship, Anabaptists through their various practices have demonstrated a robust alternative to the atomism of liberal models of citizenship. They have afforded a prototype that now serves aboriginal and other groups seeking to preserve their identity, faith, and integrity. The obvious implication is a rejection of the notion that values and cultural practices are a matter of individual menu selection. Mennonite patterns of citizenship instead suggest that values and practices stem from much deeper and more fundamentally *social and spiritual origins and identities* that provide meaning and belonging. By contrast, the all-too-common modern condition of alienation, a precondition for so much hurt and violence, has been fostered by states' insistence on the individuation of people.

The Mennonite model challenges the notion that good citizens must be soldiers. Ideologically, the modern state has nurtured a strange form of idolatry in order to "command" the highest loyalty from its citizens—the idolatry of nationalism. Anabaptists have espoused the position that service and commitment can take many other forms, and that the state has only limited hold upon lives. Rather, faithfulness to God, the church, and kin typically trumps allegiance to the state, whose role should be to support this fabric of affection, which is ultimately in its interest. A newfound but widespread secular enthusiasm for "civil society" reflects this truth. Adult baptism, too, supports the view that commitment must be intentional, not coerced. When faced with this challenge, states now prefer to negotiate a space where their members can participate in good conscience, rather than to criminalize or lose a valuable population.

The modern state seems to acquiesce and recognize that it never completely commands the loyalties of its citizens. The genius of certain Mennonite arrangements has been to reflect this reality courageously. Yet by submitting to the sanctions of the state, Mennonites also lend legitimacy to its authority. For conscientious objectors to choose prison over emigration suggests respect for the state, but also constitutes a witness to God's ultimate authority. In this manner, Mennonites have demonstrated that citizenship need not compromise faith, but rather affords an opportunity to call the state to ethical account.

Another constellation of systems with which people of strong conscience often clash is economic. The liberalism that undergirds most modern citizenship focuses upon the protection of a dramatically asymmetrical property system. Yet Mennonite collectivist approaches to land tenure, Anabaptist colony communities, their witness to simplicity and emphasis on service, a remarkable generosity in philanthropy, a heavy investment in church institutions, and exhortations to address basic human needs have all modeled alternatives to this mainstream. At their best, these values and practices illustrate the need to live socially and holistically, to uphold community, to sustain the ethical governance of the marketplace, and to call state powers to their life-giving capacity. To be an intentional citizen is to recognize the importance of bearing witness to an oft-forgotten alternative, to be a reminder that what we experience today is not the only possible order, that the Peaceable Kingdom will be at hand if we ready our world for it.

ENHANCING "SECURITY"?

Any discussion of enhancing security may seem to imply taking God's authority into our own hands. Yet Anabaptist communities have quite intentionally provided material, social, and physical security for their members, often with remarkable effectiveness. To reject all discussions of security may be to deny such achievements. Yet "security" and the breakdown of order do raise sensitive questions of accountability. To discuss these requires us to recognize that loaded terms such as "responsibility" have been misused to bully or belittle ethical stances, especially by playing upon nationalism and fear.

To raise the question of citizenship is then to ask not only how individuals but how peoples relate to the state, the greatest proponent of the "security" ideology. The state makes very significant claims on the lives, energies, resources, and loyalties of citizens, but what it provides in return is too often above scrutiny. Appeals to "security" frequently play upon the longing of every community to live in safety and comfort with dignity and integrity, but do not specify who or what is to be secured, and by what means. Yet for pacifist Christians, both the means and the ends must be in right order.

Mostly, state rhetoric about security focuses on articulating, challenging, and eliminating some "national enemy" through the use of militarism or explicit force, placing its citizens in a condition of conflict. This causes us to ponder, as the American Friends Service Committee did in its 1955 statement, *Speak Truth to Power*: "Is there a method for dealing with conflict which does not involve us in the betrayal of our own beliefs? . . . Is there a way to meet that which threatens us, without relying on our ability to cause pain to the human being who embodies the threat?"[1] Any positive answer to these queries calls into question the notion of national security.

This dilemma of how to achieve peace and allay fears draws us to re-examine what we mean by "security," and the extent to which the concept has been hijacked for political ends. As the United Nations Development Programme laments,

> For too long, the concept of security has been shaped by the potential for conflict between states. For too long, security has been equated with threats to a country's borders. For too long, nations have sought arms to protect their security. For most people today, a feeling of insecurity arises more from worries about daily life than from the dread of a cataclysmic world event. Job security, income security, health security, environmental security, security from crime, these are the emerging concerns of human security all over the world.[2]

The events of September 11, 2001, and their aftermath illustrate the limitations of so-called *national* security, in contrast to other more inclusive notions of security. September 11 made apparent that whatever has been secured under the rubric of national security has come at the expense of countless deaths, of a pervasive culture of violence, of gross inequality as a norm, and of privileging the material over social, cultural, and spiritual well-being. National security seems to have cultivated a retributive, zero-sum, us-versus-them logic that builds one security upon the destruction of another, implying a fundamental breakdown of gospel order and the negation of universal safety and dignity.

Thinking outside of the national security bubble reveals continuities between the local and global, matters of policing and matters of warfare, issues of economics and issues of politics. Imagining inclusive security demands a rejection of compartmentalized experience, insisting rather that all of life is sacred, all people have Christ within and all are worthy of security. Such a concept insists that security is relational (not individual, not a commodity to be possessed and consumed). Since all share a basic need to be unafraid, inclusive security is always local yet global in its reach. Inclusive security acknowledges our mutual dependence on the health of God's creation for our own well-being, in contrast to the environmental degradation perpetrated by militarism. Inclusive security demands that we think about security in spiritual terms, since there can be no divide between faith and daily life. As Micah 4:4 suggests, knowing our need for security, God has ordained that each should be able to live at peace and unafraid. All people must be understood not as the obstacles to or objects of security, but as potential servant-leaders and publishers of truth. As noted Quaker physicist and chemist Kathleen Lonsdale suggested, "the task of creating a peaceful world is one in which there is a place for everybody."[3]

National security's preoccupation with borders is merely symptomatic of a far more devastating abstraction, that is, "state sovereignty," or radical independence. Sovereignty carries a veneer of virtue that shields dark deeds, "validating" the bombing of innocents and the building of weaponry. As former U.S. Secretary of State Robert Lansing noted, "the essence of sovereignty [is] the absence of responsibility."[4] Sovereignty is an elaborate negotiation of power, and between powers, that admits of no higher authority. Its "realism," and the warfare that calibrates this state system, seem fundamentally at odds with any order that recognizes God's power.

Since the Treaty of Westphalia in 1648, this modern state

order has gradually subsumed the world. But from the start it has been disorderly and undermining—for protesting churches without national recognition, for persecuted minority groups, for the poor, and for peoples who suffered conscription, conquest, and annexation into the sovereign order. Sovereignty is paradoxically at odds with self-determination and self-governance, but its abstract character inures us to the loss of security and freedom it entails. Scholar Barry Buzan has argued that "for perhaps a majority of the world's people threats from the state are among the major sources of insecurity in their lives."[5] This fact may go some way to explaining why many Anabaptists have rejected "citizenship" as an ethical category while nonetheless submitting to it.

To denounce national security is not immediately to reject all notions of statehood as an ordering mechanism. It is rather to recognize that much violence arises from the coercive attempts of states to keep populations discrete and to sustain unequal conditions. Of course, states are also capable of providing many benefits: protection and advocacy for minorities and underprivileged groups, social services including health care and education, infrastructure that sustains productivity, trade and communication, stewardship of a just rule of law, and global assistance in times of need. These contributions have the potential to nurture inclusive human security as much as they do to erode relations between peoples.

The resistance of pacifist Christians to national security must be manifested by bearing witness to a love that transcends. It might mean recognizing that criminals, rebels, soldiers, and state officials are also engaged in loving relationships with family, friends, comrades, neighbors, and strangers. The most effective intervention of peace churches may be to work creatively and strategically at cultivating the awareness and practice of this universal capacity, transforming violence in the process. This can be pursued through resourceful abundance that starts, not by building barriers that fragment in an economy of scarcity, but by recognizing humanity as a common heir to manifold divine blessings.

GLOBAL SECURITIZING IN THE WAKE OF 9/11

"Far from making us more secure, our policy is increasing the insecurity of the United States and the rest of the world," lamented Quakers in 1955, for "as our strength approaches infinity, our security approaches zero."[6] Today, through the means of national security, even the United States cannot assure its citizens' safety. We can celebrate that only 34,000-36,000 nuclear warheads now exist, down from a Cold War high of 65,000. Yet this may be overshadowed by the acknowledgment that the remaining capability, 96 percent of which is held by the United States and Russia, could destroy the planet many times over. About 600 million small arms are in circulation, produced in the names of security and profit, and almost all manufactured legally in industrialized states. These arms, in the hands of state agents and citizens, kill an estimated 500,000 people a year.[7]

September 11 confirmed that the world is integrated and that citizenship and security are relational even beyond borders. In the face of this terrible lesson, practices that do not recognize the integrated character of life cannot be said to promote security or order. "National security" is no longer credibly placed to reflect the interests, aspirations, and fears of populations. At best, it deploys a reckoning of the "lowest common denominator," often called the "tyranny of the majority," and is insensitive to the vulnerabilities that give threats purchase. At worst, the state simply assumes that the interests of the population are served by its own agenda. The alternative model of citizenship that some Mennonites practice highlights the manner by which citizens can press the state to be accountable and to limit its appetite for total power. But 9/11 also suggests that pacifist Christian communities simply *must* be intentional about their own citizenship and their relationship to the state. As Buzan cautioned, "unless the idea of the state is firmly planted in the minds of the population (and often it is not), the state as a whole has no secure foundation."[8]

In matters of security as elsewhere, we do reap what we sow. A notable unraveling of community has occurred in our post-9/11 relations: about 50 percent of Muslim Canadians have reported increased negative treatment.[9] It took little time for the invisible enemy or "other" to be personified on the streets and for international travel to decline. "Redemptive violence" was widely endorsed. The laws that had "failed" to provide order were amended, suspending many of the civil rights they were drafted to protect. The sweeping USA Patriot Act and the Canadian Anti-Terrorism Act (Bill C-36) were quickly ratified. Minorities have been detained in disproportionate numbers around the world and the presumption of innocence abrogated.

The decline in trust resulting from heightened national security has eroded webs of connections and associations between people, sometimes odiously called "social capital." People are disinclined to engage, through voluntarism or social encounter, with others who differ in ethnicity, social class, religion, or place of origin. This reflects an impoverishment of community, and anticipates the advent of generations who have few relationships with people unlike themselves. Cleavages will be aggravated as social mobility diminishes and classes again become more rigid and racially defined. A disordering condition called "anomie," associated with alienation and characterized by eroded moral and social standards, may be setting in.

Memory informs any sense of security or insecurity. Both tensions between and identities within Iran and Iraq today are traced to a battle between them in the year 637. Their war in the 1980s took a million lives, in part because of that infamous (but much smaller) battle thirteen centuries before.[10] Security has its own temporality, as broken relationships smart and flex through telling and retelling. Where "commemorative," destructive dialogues are sustained over time, the untelling is an elaborate process. For post-apartheid southern Africa "it will take generations to work the violence of states and their discourse out of the everyday assumptions of the region."[11]

Despite the protracted character of preparation required for military intervention, the shock of 9/11 was due in part to the coordinated and compressed timing of the attacks, which contributed to both the scale of the devastation, and its political and psychological impact. So much of the logic of security and warfare is based on such eleventh-hour logic, which denies the preconditions and the broader context in which peacemaking can occur, thus "justifying" an overwhelming use of force. Conscientious objectors (COs) from the World War II era recall how judges tested their witness by inquiring, "What would you do if someone was attacking your family?" As CO David "Doc" Schroeder responds, while all humans have an inclination to self-defense, this does not right the wrong they may do by employing violence. Such questions usually place the respondent inside an adversarial context, rather than providing contextual information that might highlight non-adversarial alternatives.[12]

Invariably there is a precedent to the threat of violence. When Mennonites in Paraguay's Chaco have felt under threat, the history of their relationships with Latino and Aboriginal peoples of the region comes to bear. Similarly, despite the protests of the U.S. administration, we know that there is a "prehistory" to 9/11, in the extensive U.S. intervention in the Middle East, including support for Israel and Saudi Arabia. Civic acquiescence to the cultivation of national amnesia buttresses the elaborate game of strategic security that officials of the state play. Totalitarian regimes have merely perfected this same tactic of historical denial; yet the truth is never entirely forgotten.

ECONOMIES AND TECHNOLOGIES OF NATIONAL SECURITY

One of the most fascinating ambiguities of recent U.S. foreign policy is its unfailing commitment to both national security and globalization. Globalization has undermined the capacity of states around the world to manage their domestic economies. Cutbacks in social services such as education and healthcare, loss of subsidies for agriculture and foodstuffs, and the retrenchment of jobs, have eroded human security. Global economic integration leaves defense as one of the few areas under the control of state authorities. While globalization is often construed in the North as a force without an author, in the South it is laid squarely at the feet of national governments, international financial institutions, and the U.S. government. The loss of political capacity to manage economic crises has led to loss of legitimacy and eventual overthrow of regimes, and to a consequent breakdown of order in many societies. The globalization fallout includes dizzying asymmetries of wealth and poverty, growth in crime, civil wars, authoritarian responses, and human rights abuses—in short, insecurity writ large.

In the United States and Canada, local increases in poverty, homelessness, and crime have remained largely delinked from international economic policy in public opinion, while desperation on the ground has generated a welcome for conservative, hierarchical solutions. These include gated communities, racialized schooling, the suspension of public welfare and healthcare, the incarceration of the poor, and capital punishment. Together such measures contribute to polarized societies, which undermine community and accountability, provoking vigilantism and racist backlashes as well as dissent, resistance, and violent anti-state action (militias, attacks on state infrastructure, violent engagement with police, etc.).

Strong connections are discernible between deprivation and violent conflict. For example, in the period 1990-1995, only 14 percent of all warfare occurred in developed states. Scarcity creates both incentives for and a vulnerability to violence that is unparalleled in more affluent contexts. Reminiscent of Cold War proxy wars, the North is outsourcing violence. Political "great powers" have significant control over the extent and focus of violence imposed upon their populations, and its costs in terms of productivity and trade.[13] The notion that failed states must be salvaged, for example, seems to invite Western-sponsored armed struggle. This is all the more ironic when so often the very frailty of states (such as the Democratic Republic of Congo, or Haiti) is related to the U.S. foreign policy of shoring up weak, corrupt leaders against the popular will. Some states, such as Somalia, have been "made to fail" by superpower intervention and preferences for neighboring states.[14] The costs in terms of ongoing human security are monumental.

Militarism provides a significant impetus for globalization, generating demand for goods, opening markets, and affording access to weaponry for "protection" in destabilized areas. A peace dividend, resulting from reduced defense costs since the end of the Cold War, should have amounted to a trillion dollars already by 1994.[15] Yet rather than being invested in over-stretched social services, these monies are being eaten up by militarism that curiously remains a "growth" industry. The eastward expansion of NATO illustrates how new military "markets" are being provocatively opened.

Economic factors often cause violence to become structural, or intrinsic to the institution, rather than an exceptional moment. Such institutions are no longer redemptive, and per-haps no longer redeemable. Those who perform the many tiny actions that together cause the vast machine to function may fall prey to what Hannah Arendt called "the banality of evil," or like the persecutor-turned-apostle Paul, they may become the most significant witnesses to truth.

Thanks in part to the longsuffering witness of the historic peace churches, many people are now ready to acknowledge that "in a world where God reigns, to be an idealist is to be a realist. The dreamers are those who suppose that they can avoid war by preparing for it on an ever increasing and fantas-tic scale."[16] It is plain that the failure of national security leads to the perverse increase of technology: the official response to 9/11 was predictably "more, bigger, stronger, fiercer." Escalation is thought to enhance might and to offset the appar-ent shortcomings of national security. Charles Krauthammer, a Pulitzer prize winning columnist for the *Washington Post* and defender of U.S. "unilateralism," argued in 1991 that "our greatest hope for safety in such times, as in difficult times past, is in the American strength and will—the strength and will to lead a unipolar world—unashamedly laying down the rules of the world order and being prepared to enforce them."[17] Yet the hindsight of Robert McNamara, an architect of the Vietnam War, offers a compelling counterpoint to this: "We do not have the God-given right to shape every nation in our image or as we choose."[18]

Notable in recent military actions against Afghanistan and Iraq was a performative quality that sought to employ military superiority as a deterrent—against former allies with few friends. The overt logic of all deterrence is a psychological posturing in which threats of pain or violence are used to achieve compliance. Nuclear deterrence promises "mutually assured destruction" unless states offer their populations as hostages, displaying a perplexing disregard for human security. At times, we in powerful states may imagine we inhabit a massive and deceptively painless video game. In Afghanistan, pilotless Canadian spy planes "peer into mountain ravines or terrorist compounds, instantly relaying images back to safely situated ground stations."[19] These instill terror, disturb the peace, and capture images of innocents who may be targeted because of their "risky" behavior, often simply living in remote areas.

The enthusiasm for national security and the escalation of military capability also hinges on a gross tendency to overestimate the potential of technology to resolve conflicts, as several former proponents have come to realize. Regarding Vietnam, McNamara argued: "We failed then—and have since—to recognize the limitations of modern, high-technology military equipment, forces, and doctrine. . . ." The cost of military technology itself is an incentive to magnify perceived threats. McNamara cautioned: "We misjudged then—and we have since—the geopolitical intentions of our enemies . . . and we exaggerated the dangers to the United States of their actions." George Kennan, an architect of the Cold War policy of containment, later repudiated U.S. militarization as a response to Soviet aspirations.

> I think we should have tried to negotiate with the Russians in a realistic way before we went about rearming the Japanese. . . . War among the great industrial developed countries in this age has lost its rationale. . . .

I think the effort to extend NATO to the borders of Russia is really a mistaken policy, a very dangerous policy and unnecessary. . . . We shouldn't overestimate the military aspirations or the powers of other people.[20]

Kennan emphasized the tendency in a high-tech world to mistake information for wisdom. "What we really need is intelligent guidance in what to do with the information we've got." The astounding investment by states in national security demands that the resulting tools and models be "responsive" to problems that arise; in other words, they cause their authors to see and think through a militarized lens. For example, nervousness over Japanese technical superiority led to nationalist security language that construed Japan as a threat.

Many pacifists are being blinded to the limitations of military technology for peacekeeping and for policing. The pursuit of a technological fix for all insecurity detracts from resolving underlying problems in human relations. As an illustration, increased surveillance enabled by technology functions as a deterrent and an alternative to violence, but is costly to social relations, as those who recall totalitarian contexts attest. David Lyons, Queen's University professor and author of *Surveillance Society: Monitoring Everyday Life*, worries about the culture of suspicion that surveillance foments. "If everyone is a potential suspect you don't know who you can trust—it simply increases the level of paranoia, the level of mistrust and distrust of others."[21]

NATIONAL SECURITY VERSUS COMMUNITY WELL-BEING

The priority of community in the Mennonite practice of citizenship stands in sharp contrast to the "securitizing" that erodes fundamental social relations. Yet today a declassification of military culture into the broader community seems to acculturate the public into the military's normative framework. For example, the new South Africa's purchase of military weaponry (U.S. $6.5 billion worth on just one occasion) is justified by appropriating an apartheid-era national security culture. "The direction promised by the slide toward *endless securitization* includes the *reimmersion of the military into everyday life* and national culture through a reintroduction of the draft, because, as South Africa's minister of defense has put it, conscription is 'a powerful tool [in] nation-building.'"[22] Militarism becomes a political instrument, rather than a recourse when politics fails.

It is not uncommon today to see young children wearing fatigues. Almost no one at a public school fair in Winnipeg thought it was inappropriate to have a tank at the celebration. Popular culture has blurred the distinction between military structures and civil society, between peace and wartime. In the course of these conflations "the everyday processes of the social—including negotiation, mediation, and reconciliation—are set aside in pursuit of asserting state control over the social world."[23] Veterans' organizations, R.O.T.C., cadets, reserves, and military commemorations are now regular features of "civilian" life.

One can no longer imagine an arena of domestic security where the "national interest" is not deemed to be at stake. It can be difficult to discern the difference between community neighborhood patrols, community policing, police auxiliaries, private security officers working as police, and police officers of the state. As the reach of state security extends, it is answered by more and more elements of civil society who push to don the mantle of state authority and to address security issues. Fear engages people who might otherwise take a more critical perspective on this securitizing. Such practices demonstrate the suppression of pacifism and nonviolence as alternatives, while a moral economy of violence is promoted.

The popular media, having failed to function as a responsible opposition to the government and *aide-memoire* to society about life beyond militarism, has promoted and embellished official state positions while vilifying dissenters. Only now are there whispers of sober second thought about the one-dimensional coverage of the 2003 Iraq invasion. This narrow political culture has also permeated American universities, where there have been many recent complaints about sanctions against dissenting academics.

SECURITY AND THE "DEMOCRATIC DEFICIT"

> The organizational, cultural, and spiritual framework of a society prepared to wage modern mass warfare is incompatible with the framework of a society that sustains democratic and human values. War preparation now requires organizing society itself as an army, with information and control wholly in the hands of the wielders of power. Obviously, this is incompatible with democracy.[24]

A democratic deficit grows as "security" is defined without community consensus, suggesting a shortfall in accountability. Far from political development, "deficit" suggests a loss or roll-back in terms of delivering on the priorities of communities. This deficit represents a foreclosure of receptivity to the witness of peace churches and others who seek to sustain the hope for a different order. The predictable outcome of that selective deafness is the erosion of public confidence in state officers and institutions. This is in part a result of national security's executism, characterized by presidential or cabinet decisions that render legislatures and democratic practices irrelevant. For example, Britain acquired nuclear capability without legislative approval.[25] During the Vietnam War (which the U.S. Senate never declared), noted McNamara, "we failed to draw Congress and the American people into a full and frank discussion and debate of the pros and cons of a large-scale military involvement. . . . We did not fully explain what was happening."

Securitized thinking disputes the need for accountability or political responsibility. Buzan describes how "an undefined notion of national security offers scope for power-maximizing strategies to political and military elites. . . . The natural ambiguity of foreign threats during peacetime makes it easy to disguise more sinister intentions in the cloak of national security."[26]

Imputed public ignorance about the complexity of security dilemmas serves as an excuse. Democratic politics is giving way to the high-tech secrecy of national intelligence that falsely asserts its own normative neutrality. This is achieved by portraying states as sentient beings, rights-holders, actors in a community of states, rather than the abstract institutions they are. The "need" of states for national security thus trumps the agendas of living communities.

In this context, creeping securitization progresses. Despite social-service cutbacks, policing is generally on the increase, with most of the growth in private policing, while movements to assure greater civilian oversight of the police and military seem moribund. "Developed states" now have a 2:1 ratio of private to public security personnel. In Canada and the United States, armed private police officers have all the authority of public ones but significantly less accountability. Where international aid was once considered an antidote to militarism, it is now often "embedded"—protected by private or state armies. Corporations retain police and military services with little public accountability or transparency, and no comparable social spending to enhance overall local security. Overseas, for-hire military personnel guard mines, pipelines, train lines, and harbors for corporate interests. They do not secure people so much as property, often posing a hazard to the public with their weaponry. They emphasize the detection of risk for insurers by identifying "pre-criminal" behavior, rather than protecting communities. The *de facto* corrective to the failure of public security is not a more inclusive notion of human security, but the deterioration of governance into the "administration of things," as the nineteenth-century social thinker Henri de Saint-Simon anticipated.

CITIZEN SECURITY INITIATIVES

The narrow range of interests that animate a state in protecting its national security hardly touch on the plethora of struggles that impact the security of individuals, communities, and groups within and beyond the state envelope. Contrary to the old myth that the state alone has the legitimate use of force, 9/11 is among many recent events that demonstrate civil society's engagement with security dilemmas. Yet most citizen security initiatives, ranging from block parents and neighborhood watches to direct defense, accept the national security model. Peter Vale argues that these "secondary sites have securitized the social within an analytical frame that views the progress promised by the state as the best form of protection."[27] They accept the high-tech and the bottom line as key indicators of security and well-being, taking the state perception of threat at face value.

Paradoxically, the search by such citizens for security can be destabilizing. Catholic and Protestant militant groups in Northern Ireland, Asian vigilantes challenging racism in British cities, and nationalist or separatist movements in regions such as Spain's Basque, Canada's Quebec, Nigeria's Biafra, the Democratic Republic of Congo's Katanga, and Indonesia's Aceh have all arguably arisen as a result of states failing to adequately share the "commonwealth."[28] September 11 confirmed that, with sufficient motivation, malevolent ingenuity, and ready access to light, affordable military and communications technology, non-state actors can threaten even the strongest states.

Non-state actors of many kinds compromise security: corporate actors and international financial institutions may undermine economic sovereignty and hence market security and livelihood. Corporate actors may erode indigenous industries and agriculture, forcing dependence on expensive imports. They may irretrievably disturb local ecosystems. Rebel movements and civil wars are not only funded by, but may exist for the purpose of, controlling natural resources such as coltan (short for columbite-tantalite, a mineral used in all cell phones) from the Congo, or diamonds from Sierra Leone.

"Predatory" states are too dysfunctional to deliver services, and sap the well-being and security of their populations. Mobutu's Zaire continued to receive U.S. backing and military aid as he plundered state resources and repressed his people, who responded by reducing their exposure to the state and its vicissitudes. Under such threats, populations strengthen their ties to local rather than international markets, practice alternative resourcing through barter, forge black market networks, and make changes in their production patterns. They employ ethnic associations and faith communities to reinforce their collective communal security. They may also seek protection through complex patron-client relations of mutual indebtedness, or may cast their lot with rebel groups, resistance movements or warlords. The retrieval of any public space or ethical witness to the state after such dysfunction and distrust may take generations.

Groups within civil society also construct parallel, largely unaccountable arrangements for surveillance and patrolling by citizens or private security personnel. These often see themselves as the self-appointed "eyes and ears of the police," although the police have mixed responses to their often unsolicited and untrained assistance. Such groups, who frequently work undercover for fear of retribution, may engage in an exclusive reimagining of the community. This will tend to strengthen the propertied against the unpropertied, and increase the tensions felt by at-risk populations such as youth, visible minorities, street people, and sex trade workers. In Manitoba, well over one thousand individuals spend many nights voluntarily on patrol to "secure" their communities. In Arizona, hundreds of citizens are involved in the Minuteman Project, which uses aircraft and all-terrain vehicles, to prevent Mexicans from illegally entering the United States along the Arizona border.[29] In both cases, there are some indications that firearms may be in use.

The incapacity of states to assure security creates power vacuums into which step other non-state agents, whose means and models are sometimes less desirable than those of national state security. In the absence of legitimate state governance, Somalis, Afghanis, and others have placed their trust and resources with warlords who assure security on a neo-feudal basis. In Colombia, drug cartels provide protection to small farmers who cooperate with them against the violent incursions of the state. In U.S. ghettos, gangs provide security to residents and businesses against police harassment and in police "no-go" areas.[30] At least one regional government in Nigeria has retained the services of vigilante gangs as a means to compensate for national police incapacity and corruption. In Russia, communist-style local citizen security initiatives are being restored. In Western Europe, "skinheads" and white supremacists victimize minorities in localized "racial cleansing," itself stemming from a sense of being under threat.

All members of civil society may have a role to play in reflecting upon and assuring security and order. While voluntarism is overall on the decline, security issues draw citizens out to "take back the streets," seeking re-empowerment. Links can be drawn between the sustained rhetoric of the "war on terror," the excessive media attention to crime, the need of the security industry to perpetuate fear, the popularity of the martial arts, and the Mennonite housewife in southern Manitoba who is on patrol in the dead of night against an unseen threat.[31] The postmodern assertion that power is relational, located in many fluid nodes or webs throughout society, here becomes explicit. But common in the examples above is a lack of accountability to the communities that are "secured," reinforcing the democratic deficit. Shared too may be a lack of consciousness or of concern about the corrosion of trust associated with these citizen actions.

Still, communities and groups often demonstrate innovative and integrated understandings of security and, in this respect, offer considerable hope. A citizens' security group in Nairobi, Kenya, sees waste management as organic to mediating conflict and fending off crime. Garbage is a safety and health hazard that erodes community self-perception and collaboration, yet it is not on the radar of national security! In East St. Paul, Manitoba, a skateboard park has been erected to give youth a safe and interesting place to congregate off the streets. Peruvian women have found a way to deal with the gender insensitivity of exclusively male security patrols or *rondas campesinas.* Their alternative security organization targets microfinance projects, linking economic empowerment and security.

Common to these examples is a holistic approach that recognizes security as complex, entailing several layers of problems that converge to constitute a threat. The issues are local, but linked to the global. A lack of capacity in the Kenyan and Peruvian police is a direct effect of the national security model and of integrated global economics. Yet citizens in both cases are demonstrating that they have an alternative vision that will strengthen community well-being.

Toward Practices of Faithful Citizenship

If national security and its by-products are not the answer, then what are the innovative practices of abundant resource-fulness that might support the development of inclusive human security? A family in El Salvador will share its last chicken with strangers; its deep sense of hospitality reflects intentional mutual obligation that provides social security. Such a long-term "loaves and fishes" perspective is strategically wiser than the siege mentality of hoarding.

September 11 caused a momentary rupture of rampant individualism, suspending the loss of what Rousseau called *pitié*, or compassion for fellow humans. Thousands in the United States and Canada engaged in preparing food, answering phones, raising money, providing shelter, and rescuing or hosting strangers. New Yorkers felt knitted together by an unusual closeness, and thrived on the newfound recognition of one another. Without wishing for disaster, one can observe that a different order, more focused on inclusion and well-being, is possible. The "sanctity of life" is common to many faiths and presents a shared basis for interfaith dialogue. Such initiatives can take place between co-workers or neighbors, as well as around the world.

States struggle not only with a reduced policy envelope, but against a global rejection of militarism as a preferred tool of change.[32] They are in a position, as perhaps never before, to welcome dialogue with groups who are prepared to converse about governance and security. The alternative, as we have been seeing, is a more costly authoritarian bullying approach that strikes out almost randomly in the hope that the perpetrator will be confirmed as the chief bully of the playground.

There is a need to articulate a "theology of security" that recognizes both the risks of discipleship and the obligation we have to our global brothers and sisters. An integrated theology of security would embrace all people. The hardened criminal, the rebel guerrilla, the corrupt politician, the prison guard, and the private enforcement officer are not exempt—their lives too are sacred and their fears are heartfelt. A theology of security must acknowledge diversity of belief, practice, and context, but work at shared understandings. It must recognize the centrality of economics, culture, and politics to security. Most often, insecurity derives from a convergence of two or more threats, yet hierarchies of risk undermine some while channeling resources into the validation and resolution of others. The denial of insecurity's complexity has been a contributing factor to sustained fear and violence.

A theology of security cannot be developed in denial of the global division of security labor that is currently in place: security personnel in North America, and peacekeepers around the world, are now in large majority non-white. There is a direct correlation between the risk of the mission and hue of the force sent in. The current global economic hierarchy ensures a supply of desperate people who will bear arms to feed their families. We must avoid "security greed"—individuated thinking that distracts us from gospel order that is hospitable and inclusive. Are we more ready to place other families at risk to respond to breakdowns of order than to place our own families at risk for the practice of nonviolence? Should we change our lifestyles to bring our needs for security into equilibrium with those of our neighbors?

Most seductive about modern progress is the notion that, with technology, humans are omnipotent; too often have we forgotten the humility to which God calls us. Ironically, we deploy our great power as often in destructive ways as in loving ways. Our awesome sense of expanding human capacity has captured the hearts not only of advocates for the national security model, but also of advocates for nonviolence and a more humane world. Yet quick-fixes are much harder to achieve than to imagine.

Pacifist Christians confront the dilemma of a sense of obligation to help and a recognition that those who intervene often do damage. Under such situations, one must ask with humility whether we have honed the skills and understanding required to practice what we preach: "not violence but love is redemptive." In thinking about human needs and security, there is much room to remember the sin of pride. Technology does not always provide the capacity to extinguish human suffering; indeed, technology aggravates some situations. We are least likely to be effective in eleventh-hour salvage operations where the tactics of national security are adopted in kamikaze efforts to mitigate disasters. Here the recognition that it is not we but God who is omnipotent must guide our involvement.

We are surrounded by evidence of this truth. It was neither through world war, nor through the many proxy wars of the Cold War, that the Soviet Union collapsed. Rather, it imploded from a combination of crises that exposed the internal contradictions of a system that preached equality but fostered hierarchy and oppression, precisely as Karl Marx described how systems collapse. The Soviets' militarized, securitized worldview overcame their primary project, as violence became the means to every end. But the West/North is not immune to this prospect.

We have an opportunity, as citizens, to trace the common grain of physical, social, and spiritual security. A faith-based rejection of the compartmentalization of security and life itself is invitational. By cutting across the cleavages that divide us and by breaking the taboos that seal these different modes of engagement, we may come to new understandings.

Many people already draw connections between global and local insecurity. A marked decline in recent Canadian divorce rates has been construed as a post-9/11 reflection of a need for security and stability.[33] Facing threats and confronting their own vulnerability, people commit to one another, and create innovative means of reciprocity and resourcefulness. Insecurity may breed self-serving behavior, but it also fosters stewardship and mutual accountability, as people take greater responsibility in various aspects of their lives. Community is integral to security and well-being.

There are many signs of hope, of people working at a convergence of interests in order to provide for their common needs. In Toronto, urban planning in the last decade has focused on developing dense mixed-income communities where there is a high degree of contact, shared use of facilities, and a sense of a common future. Refugees ride the subway with a former prime minister. In Winnipeg, families are receiving government support to renovate dilapidated old homes in the urban core. Maintaining middle-class confidence in the public school system allows children to have familiarity with peers from a diversity of backgrounds, and sustains the quality of education. In Manitoba, where one in four children is aboriginal, this is an important investment towards future peace. Old patterns of social cohesion in homogeneous communities are no longer possible. In their place must come new ways of relating, of imagining community. Here hospitality can play a significant role. Hospitality does not present risk to our physical safety so much as to our sense of identity and guilt. We should ask ourselves whether interaction will disrupt the peace and "order" in our lives, and if so, why?

Through collaboration and self-help, marginalized people have responded to the insecurities that violent conflict and globalization create. Communal gardens, kitchens, ovens, and mills allow people to buy in bulk, demonstrate solidarity, share childcare and senior care, while providing and receiving the dignity of hospitality. Cooperatives afford economies of scale in purchasing and marketing by opening the potential for credit, sharing of the skills base, mentoring, and enhancing collective self-determination as members acquire their political voice.

Security requires sociability, not seclusion, and implies that individuals will be enabled to contribute to and receive from the larger community.

Resourceful abundance and inclusive security may require modeling in societies that have developed a mistaken assurance that the way of the sword is essential to their survival. What follows are two examples of projects for faithful citizenship, that communities carrying a concern for inclusive security might collectively undertake.

Example Project 1: Full-Cost Accounting

> We can today perform the miracle of the loaves and the fishes; we can make the desert bloom and yield grain for bread. . . . If half the effort being spent on making tanks, guns, aeroplanes, and atomic bombs were diverted to producing the primary necessities of life the last of poverty in the world would be eliminated in the lifetime of our children.[34]

The just use of social and natural resources is a dimension of the stewardship that faithful citizens must exercise. The "moment" of 9/11 that continues even today represents an opportunity for pacifist Christians to educate about the spiritual, social, ecological price tags of armed conflict. As *Speak Truth to Power* cautioned, "it is the spiritual price that man pays for his willingness to resort to violence that is its most tragic aspect."[35] In particular one might focus on the vast and precarious gray area between conventional warfare and tranquility in which most of us reside.

To take one illustration, national security has used *deterrence* as the rationale for building and testing nuclear warheads that are "not intended for use" but that impose order by raising the specter of their deployment. The same strategy of deterrence is used across the security spectrum: social rights are denied unless young people and immigrants register for taxation, military service, etc. Enforcement officers carry weapons to deter offenses. Video cameras raise the possibility that our actions are being recorded. Such deterrence presses the terms of conflict into a framework of violence. The gun and other "symbols of order" may thus undermine the credibility of the order they set out to symbolize. It becomes important to name practices which carry the implicit suggestion that force or pain will be used to achieve compliance. The paramilitarized enforcement systems behind "community policing" may require scrutiny. Would greater civilian oversight of policing and military institutions render such institutions more humane, or merely sweeten structures that are beyond redemption?

We may need to question publicly the strong trend in the United Nations and other peacekeeping providers toward high readiness brigades and militarized "peacemaking" through authorized force. What has been the UN investment in alternative dispute resolution mechanisms and its own demilitarization? Why, beyond monitoring, is military action the primary intervention considered? The United Nations was created to "save succeeding generations from the scourge of war . . . to reaffirm faith in fundamental human rights, in the dignity and worth of the human person . . . to practice tolerance and live together in peace with one another as good neighbors, to unite our strength to maintain international peace and security."[36]

But the UN too easily has been co-opted by the national security paradigm and the notion that power equals the ability to inflict pain. Most matters of peace and conflict reside with the Security Council, a chief advocate for militarism and the national security perspective that has undermined world peace and security. Its current emphasis is on setting aside the principle of consent, deploying heavily armed "complex peacekeeping operations" which mandate "an operation's authority to use force." This implies "bigger forces, better equipped and more costly but able to be a credible deterrent."[37] By contrast, a spirit of servant leadership might foster a radical culture of reconciliation within the United Nations. Are we providing sufficient moral support and peace resourcing to church representatives and others within the UN context?

Example Project 2: Moralizing the State

Effective peaceful resistance to the national security model will demand that the inhumanity of institutions be overcome. In many instances, people working within oppressive systems have simply succumbed to a suffocating culture of segregation. They bear a terrible load, but also present a sublime opportunity for moralizing the state. Maintaining a humane ethic is an important witness. Song Dae Ri, who defected to Canada, was rejected as a refugee on the grounds that as a former trade officer for the Korean government he is complicit in the regime's oppressive rule. Ri's wife and father were executed by North Korea in retaliation for his escape. Following media attention and a popular outcry, Ri was admitted temporarily on compassionate grounds to parent his young son. It is possible to call the state to greater accountability.

People, we believe, are God's children, always redeemable even where institutions are not. Can good people work within damaged institutions? Can those who have difficulty with the notion of Anabaptist police officers nonetheless affirm the person who chooses this path, resourcing and supporting that officer to discern his or her role and attend to the work of the Spirit in a violent institution? Congregations might consider establishing committees of clearness or care for those working in difficult contexts, where living faithfully and offering an alternative pattern is especially demanding. Examples might include those working in policing, in detention centers, in government, in mental health, in emergency work, in law, in welfare, in youth and street work, in frontline social work, or in affordable housing provision. Creative engagement would provide communal support for the project of humanizing and reframing state functions and institutions. Most important is the process of re-imagining and modeling healthy relationships, and how institutions and citizens may facilitate these.

As a result of political pressure, Canadian immigration policy is now harsher than U.S. policy, causing many Canadians to receive their overseas visitors in the United States. The war on terror is also a war on immigrants, who are at the bottom of the social hierarchy. While there is no evidence that non-citizens pose a greater threat, there is significant indication that immigrants are essential to the future health and social welfare of societies in the North. Further, the generous provision of socially supported services—including health, education, and housing to newcomers—enhances their sense of belonging and their capacity to contribute effectively. Advocacy on behalf of immigrants and refugees is an area where Mennonites continue to make an effective and faithful contribution to the moralizing of the state.

The notion that the moral shortcomings of people can be corrected through forceful suasion has no substantive verification. Yet there is a trend toward replacing morality with police and the use of force, further eroding social capacities for conflict resolution. Inclusive approaches to security might civilianize many of the functions now associated with policing. For example, conflict mediation services, anti-bullying, and peer counseling through schools, race relations efforts, parking, and traffic management are questions of order that could well be managed without paramilitary means. In preparation for South Africa's first post-apartheid elections, renown criminologist Clifford Shearing noted that just as soccer fans keep order among themselves, voters had sufficient interest in a peaceful outcome to take an active role in assuring order. Using the soccer template, election organizers kept police at arm's length from the process and achieved a peaceful outcome.[38]

A significant contribution to the just reordering of society would entail a serious engagement with the rule of law and the justice system. This might imply both education and advocacy, in churches and community settings. Structural violence and prejudice have created a system that often discredits the premise of law as a common reference point for protection. Media reports and popular opinion often convict a person before he or she has received due trial. The costs of such wrongful convictions include damaged lives, the spread of a culture of violence from within the penal system, and the loss of credibility for the rule of law itself. Similarly, the disproportionate number of visible minorities in the justice system point to severe systemic dysfunction.

To favor and nurture a restorative justice system is to improve security for all. That Jesus came to "fulfill the law" suggests we must strive to find the rightful place of law in our societies. The struggle for transformation toward a just rule of law is a cause to be embraced by people of every faith. The idea of covenant, which emphasizes the relational quality of justice, should be restored to a place of centrality. Protecting and restoring rights does not signify acquiescence to individualism; the Mennonite experience suggests that rights are also very significant for the protection of groups and communities. For those whose very humanity is being undermined, Mennonites can retrieve respect and well-being by emphasizing the relationality rather than the entitlement that rights language often implies.

Perhaps the most significant erosion of public accountability over security has resulted from increasingly evident "privatization" and democratic deficit. We should work to enhance the public accountability of the state and of private service providers. Since these authorities claim to act on our behalf with our resources, we as citizens can do no less than advocate responsiveness to community ethics.

Toward Inclusive Security and Faithful Citizenship

When we are fearful, citizenship is most likely to entail a lemming-like conformity to unethical and damaging state policies. This path can be rejected through a retrieval of an alternative pattern of engagement that works collectively, actively, and consciously at the remoralizing of society and the state. Above all such a retrieval must recover human lives from the junk heaps where they have too often been left. We recall that God so loves the world, and has planted us in it embodied and empowered to avoid its temptations and failings.

Given that reality, citizenship may be a path of discipleship when followed faithfully. Practiced mindfully, citizenship provides an opening for good works, for witness, and for the occasion to love wherever people fear. Gadfly citizenship calls people and institutions to accountability, reminding them that means do not justify ends. It invites us to take seriously the exhortation to be patterns, to preach truth in the midst of disorder, and to cast light on disorder that passes for order. The practice of a theology of inclusive security retraces the grain of the universe, which does not cleave us from our sisters and brothers, but connects all human experience with the Divine.

NOTES

1. Stephan G. Cary, ed., *Speak Truth to Power: A Quaker Search for an Alternative to Violence; a Study of International Conflict* (Philadelphia: American Friends Service Committee, 1955), v.

2. United Nations Development Programme, *Human Development Report 1994*:3, as cited in Caroline Thomas, "Introduction" in Caroline Thomas and Peter Wilkin, eds., *Globalization, Human Security, and the African Experience* (Boulder: Lynne Rienner, 1999), *op. cit.* 4.

3. Kathleen Lonsdale, *Removing the Causes of War*, Swarthmore Lecture 1953 (London: George Allen and Unwin, 1953), 74.

4. Michael Robert Marrus, *The Nuremberg War Crimes Trial, 1945–46: A Documentary History* (Boston: Bedford Books, 1997), 8–10, as cited in Samantha Power, *A Problem from Hell: America and the Age of Genocide* (New York: Basic Books, 2002), 14.

5. Barry Buzan, *People, States, and Fear: The National Security Problem in International Relations* (Chapel Hill: University of North Carolina Press, 1983), 26.

6. Cary, *Speak Truth to Power*, 8–9.

7. Douglas J. Roche, *The Human Right to Peace* (Toronto: Novalis, 2003), 11, 73.

8. Buzan, *People, States, and Fear*, 49–50.

9. Frank Armstrong, "Does Technology Fuel 'Culture of Suspicion' in Post-Sept. 11 World," *Whig-Standard*, 11 September 2002.

10. David W. Ziegler, *War, Peace, and International Politics* (New York: Longman, 2000), 79.

11. Peter C. J. Vale, *Security and Politics in South Africa: The Regional Dimension*, Critical Security Studies (Boulder, Colo.: Lynne Rienner Publishers, 2003), 177.

12. Mennonite Heritage Centre, "Hard Questions for Conscientious Objectors," http://www.alternativeservice.ca/hard (accessed 19 February 2005).

13. Thomas and Wilkin, *Globalization, Human Security, and the African Experience*, 4.

14. See Mohamed Salih, "The Horn of Africa: Security in the New World Order" in Thomas and Wilkin, *Globalization, Human Security, and the African Experience*, 129.

15. Thomas and Wilkin, *Globalization, Human Security, and the African Experience*, 5.

16. Lonsdale, *Removing the Causes of War*, 56.

17. C. Krauthammer, "The Unipolar Moment," *Foreign Affairs* 70, 1, as cited in Aswini Ray, "Justice and Security" in Thomas and Wilkin, *Globalization, Human Security, and the African Experience*, 87.

18. All quotes from Robert McNamara are excerpted from Doug Saunders, "It's Just Wrong What We're Doing," *Globe and Mail*, 24 January 2004.

19. Stephen Thorne, "Canadian Spy Plane Grounded in Kabul," *Globe and Mail*, 17 May 2004, A8.

20. All quotes from George Kennan are from PBS interview with David Gergen, April 18, 1996, http://www.pbs.org/newshour/gergen/kennan.html (accessed 19 February 2005).

21. Lyons as cited in Armstrong, "Does Technology Fuel 'Culture of Suspicion.'"

22. Vale, *Security and Politics in South Africa*, 184, 167 (emphasis mine).

23. Ibid., 165.

24. Cary, et al., 19.

25. Ray, "Justice and Security, 89-90, in Thomas and Wilkin, *Globalization, Human Security, and the African Experience*.

26. Buzan, *People, States, and Fear*, 9.

27. Vale, *Security and Politics in South Africa*, 165.

28. See Buzan, *People, States, and Fear*, 31. Here I am suggesting common resources but also a shared and inclusive social vision.

29. Alan Freeman, "Border Blitz Targets 'Invaders' from Mexico," *Globe and Mail*, Friday, 28 January 2005, A12.

30. For a fascinating account of this, see Martín Sánchez Jankowski, *Islands in the Street: Gangs and American Urban Society* (Berkeley: University of California Press, 1991).

31. My interview, 2003.

32. See Richard A. Falk, *On Humane Governance: Toward a New Global Politics*, The World Order Models Project report of the Global Civilization Initiative (University Park, Pa.: Pennsylvania State University Press, 1995), 35.

33. Gloria Galloway, "Canadian Divorce Rates Declining," *Globe and Mail*, May 5, 2004, A7.

34. John Boyd Orr, "Food—the Foundation of World Unity," National Peace Council, 1948. As cited in Lonsdale, 38.

35. Cary, *Speak Truth to Power*, 9.

36. *United Nations Charter*, Preamble.

37. "Report of the Panel on United Nations Peace Operations" Executive Summary, http://www.un.org/peace/reports/peace_operations/documents/summary.htm (accessed 19 February 2005).
38. Shearing, personal communication.

FOR FURTHER READING

Buzan, Barry. *People, States, and Fear: The National Security Problem in International Relations*. Chapel Hill: University of North Carolina Press, 1983.

Cary, Stephan G., ed. *Speak Truth to Power: A Quaker Search for an Alternative to Violence; a Study of International Conflict*. Philadelphia: American Friends Service Committee, 1955.

Falk, Richard A. *On Humane Governance: Toward a New Global Politics*. The World Order Models Project report of the Global Civilization Initiative. University Park, Pa.: Pennsylvania State University Press, 1995.

Jankowski, Martín Sánchez. *Islands in the Street: Gangs and American Urban Society*. Berkeley: University of California Press, 1991.

Kymlicka, Will. *Politics in the Vernacular: Nationalism, Multiculturalism, and Citizenship*. Oxford, UK; New York: Oxford University Press, 2001.

Lonsdale, Kathleen. *Removing the Causes of War*. Swarthmore Lecture 1953. London: George Allen and Unwin, 1953.

Marshall, Christopher D. *Crowned with Glory & Honor: Human Rights in the Biblical Tradition*. Studies in Peace and Scripture Series, no. 6. Telford, Pa.; Scottdale, Pa.; Auckland, N.Z.: Pandora Press U.S.; Herald Press; Lime Grove House, 2001.

Power, Samantha. *A Problem from Hell: America and the Age of Genocide*. New York: Basic Books, 2002.

Thomas, Caroline, and Peter Wilkin, eds. *Globalization, Human Security, and the African Experience*. Critical Security Studies. Boulder, Colo.: Lynne Rienner Publishers, 1999.

Ziegler, David W. *War, Peace, and International Politics*. New York: Longman, 2000.

—4—

SEEKING WISDOM IN THE FACE OF FOOLISHNESS: TOWARD A ROBUST PEACE THEOLOGY

Lydia Harder

It may seem surprising that the Peace Committee which advises Mennonite Central Committee's (MCC) international program would consult with police officers, lawyers, city councilors, and social workers in order to develop a peace theology for Anabaptist-Mennonite witness in the public sphere. A second surprise, however, has been the degree to which I as a theologian and MCC Peace Committee member identified with these persons, who are active in institutions that attempt to create safety and order in society. In the questions and issues they raise I have recognized my own fear, insecurity, and guilt in the face of injustice, disorder, and violence. Often we wish for quick solutions. Often we experience a messiness, ambiguity, or loneliness as we take risks to seek security for our neighbor and community. Or else, overwhelmed with the problems of the world, we succumb to passivity, as hope disappears and we retreat into our own comfortable, safe haven.

This identification is not surprising. I grew up in an immigrant family that had left the Ukraine after the Russian Revolution to seek security in a new land. The loss of family members and a secure home in the Ukraine subtly influenced my early years. My family had experienced the temptations that come when institutions are violently disrupted, disorder reigns, and family and friends are in constant danger in communities that once were considered safe and secure. I remember my father telling us stories of the self-defense group that decided nonresistance did not work in those revolutionary times. I remember him telling of Mennonites who joined whichever group had power at the moment, willing even to betray their brothers and sisters in the faith. But more importantly, I remember him telling us the story of his father's murder and his struggle with feelings of revenge and hate. I marveled that he finally came to a place of forgiveness and could express strong convictions, born of that very time, about nonviolence and peacemaking.

One way that my parents expressed these peace convictions was in helping to build a community in the new land, a community in which trust and freedom would reign. I remember being told of the importance of cooperative ventures in which the church took a leading role: our farm co-op, our church schools, our Mennonite burial society. I remember as a child being one of the first people to join the Mennonite Credit Union being established to serve our whole community. I also learned to trust neighbors of various nationalities and religions as I watched my father and mother interact with others in the arduous task of farming and marketing their produce. In addition, I learned to share our resources with others, particularly with the refugee and the homeless. I grew up feeling secure in my family and community, while vaguely aware of the insecurity of others.

In more recent years I have become more directly involved with persons who continue to face insecurity, danger, prejudice, and fear as part of their daily life. Some feel insecure because they have been robbed of their cultural heritage, language, and family structures, as in the case of First Nations people in Canada. Others, including recent refugees from Colombia, were forced to flee from their homes in the face of violence and unrest. Still others have experienced the abuse and violence that can come about in their own homes when the social safety net in our communities is ineffective. I have realized how much security and safety depend on societal institutions that provide structures and communication channels so that basic needs can be met.

During the consultations that our MCC project team conducted on security and safety, I have become aware that we often do not know how to speak theologically about building institutions to seek the common good. This means that we do not know how to call each other to faithfulness, how to counsel each other when we are afraid, how to face the hard questions that have to do with institutional power and integrity or with coercive intervention. We can speak much more comfortably in social, political, psychological, or business language, unsure of the way these relate to our theological convictions. We sit in church hearing about the "upside-down kingdom" of God, or read our MCC brochures describing the prophetic ministry that we are doing in other lands. But we wonder what these have to do with our daily work, which often focuses more directly on bringing stability and order to our communities.

One of the primary challenges we face at the beginning of the twenty-first century, therefore, is to find ways to speak theologically about the "logic" underlying the kingdom of God and the "logic" underlying our human institutions and structures. We need language that will relate the vision of transformation and peace which God's reign promises to the daily decisions we make as we go about our daily work. We need clear language that will aid our discernment as we struggle to live faithfully, seeking the common good of the society in which we live.

God's Reign and Human Institutions

> *Your kingdom come. Your will be done, on earth as it is in heaven* (Matt 6:10).

Theological language contrasting "the kingdom of God" with "the kingdoms of this world" is one way that the Mennonite tradition has of expressing the relationship between

God's kingdom and human institutions. This contrast implies that Christians must think and act according to a logic *different* from the power calculations of our social, economic, and political institutions. Christians must be nonconformed in their thinking, focusing on being in tune with the logic of Jesus Christ who lived the way of righteousness and shalom, rather than on the logic of the communal good as our society defines it. Thus a tension arises between the alternative community, the church that confesses kingdom values, and all other social institutions and their values. This tension creates a prophetic engagement with society calling all persons and institutions to repentance and to a new way of peace and justice. It fuels the missional mandate of our church communities and focuses our attention on alternative strategies and institutions that can more easily exhibit these kingdom characteristics.[1]

Problems have arisen, however, because this description may too quickly equate the kingdom of God with the church, thus creating a sharp divide between the church and other societal institutions. Furthermore, modernity has created a sharp boundary between the sacred and the secular, which has further reinforced the dualism in Mennonite two-kingdom theology and tempted churches to become triumphalistic and exclusive. They forget that churches are themselves human institutions, influenced by the dominant culture, often embodying other-than-kingdom values. When this happens, Christians are tempted to forget their own culpability in the sin of economic, political, and military institutions and may fail to bring their own everyday reality into God's probing light. In addition, they may become insulated in their communities, forgetting that the biblical vision of shalom encompasses all creation and that God is actively working in the whole world so that God's reign may be effectively realized on earth as it is in heaven. The conflict between kingdoms is then understood as a closed and static conclusion rather than an open and dynamic movement of God toward a sure eschatological fulfillment.[2]

The Mennonite tradition does include a second way to speak of this relationship. In an attempt to counter the temptations of the first approach, this way focuses on the biblical conviction that God is Lord of all creation. Therefore some *similarity* exists between the logic that governs the kingdom of God and the logic by which all institutions, including the church, will be judged. From this perspective God does not work in sharp discontinuity in the church and in society more generally. The kingdom of God that is "at hand" rests on a universal hope for a redeemed creation. The church must therefore be actively engaged in society, working for the common good in ways that Jesus Christ taught and embodied. This may include working within institutions and structures whose values overlap with those of the church. As Christians, we should look for signs of God's activity in the world and align ourselves with the direction that we see God moving within our society and the world at large.

Equally subtle temptations may arise when we too quickly assume continuity between the kingdom of God and the logic underlying our political and social institutions. When the whole social order is understood as the sphere of God's activity, Christians may underestimate the need for the critical discernment and empowerment that is necessary to discern and follow God's way. They may not recognize the point when a governing institution becomes oppressive and thus acts in a manner antithetical to the logic of love and compassion that is basic to the kingdom of God. They may become arrogant, so sure of God's will that they succumb to the temptation to use violence to enforce kingdom values. In using this logic Christians may forget that Christ called the church to be a sign of the reign of God in every society and that its logic may sometimes contradict the values underlying institutional structures. Thus a need remains for some tension and duality in our language in order to point to our primary allegiance to Jesus Christ, and to our calling as a church.

In the consultations that we held during this time of discernment on issues related to security and order, I was puzzled by those who felt no tension between their work as police officers, social workers, lawyers, or scholars, and their identity as people of God. However, I was equally disturbed by those for whom the tension was so great that to work in a "secular" vocation somehow seemed to mean working in another kingdom—that is, not under God's reign. The question with which I have wrestled in these months, therefore, has been this: How shall we acknowledge both the continuity and the tension that exist when we act as citizens within our society while pledging our primary allegiance to God's reign coming on earth? What kind of logic determines how we think and act in our daily professions within institutions that may be intimately connected with the use of power and even violence?

In this search I was drawn back to the Bible and its various theological traditions. In particular, I began to reread a strand of the biblical heritage that Mennonite peace theology does not often acknowledge: wisdom.[3] I immersed myself in writings on wisdom in both testaments and soon realized that these extend far beyond the books that biblical scholars know as classic wisdom literature. In this rereading, I began to note how such writings stood beside the prophetic tradition in the larger story of God's dealing with humankind. I began to wonder if including wisdom would help us affirm a logic that connects the best knowledge humans possess, while maintaining a prophetic tension between God's logic and all lesser wisdoms. Perhaps a more robust theology of peace would emerge that would challenge the sacred/secular divide in Mennonite experience while holding all the more firmly to the cruciform shape of Jesus's way of peace. Perhaps we could discover a "way of life" that we can live within a large variety of institutions while prophetically and creatively challenging those same institutions.

THE PROMISE OF THE WISDOM TRADITION

> *Those who listen to me [wisdom] will be secure and will live at ease, without dread of disaster* (Prov 1:33).

> *Keep sound wisdom and prudence . . . then you will walk in your way securely and your foot will not stumble* (Prov 3:21-23).

In the last few centuries the biblical traditions of wisdom have had only minimal impact on theology or ethics as practiced in the West. It is only recently that historical and literary biblical studies have taken a new interest in wisdom, one that theologians and ethicists have begun to notice, and that theological writings on peace and justice have begun to draw on this source.[4] Yet the book of Proverbs, as well as other wisdom literature, draws a direct connection between wisdom, security, and safety. An overview of recent writings by biblical scholars suggests at least three reasons to hope that a study of wisdom traditions might be fruitful for our quest.[5]

First, in its mix of analysis, generalization, accusation, creativity, and freedom, biblical wisdom mirrors our own struggle with God and our communities in our quest for security, safety, and shalom for all people. Because the wisdom traditions generally begin with experience, they attend to empirical evidence and data. They then reflect on that reality by attempting to link it to the "grain of the universe"[6]—that is, the underlying unity and universality of God who is creator, sustainer, and savior of the world. In its rich variety, wisdom explores order by attending to patterns of consistency in reality, while also recognizing conflict and novelty as it opens out to new and disparate experiences. This holds promise for reflecting anew on the ambiguity of our relationships to institutions of order.

Second, Scripture often presents the language of wisdom as a "middle discourse," a language about reality that can exist between the particular language of other religions, and the particular language of Israelite and Christian faith.[7] The intellectual tradition of Israel, though operating within the constraints of its theological commitments, recognized that God had given gifts of wisdom in varying degrees to people outside of Israel. Truth and goodness, wherever they are found, were considered gifts of God—part of God's revelation to all through the testimony of nature, history, and experience. In fact, parallels to various wisdom teachings can be found in Egyptian and Babylonian wisdom. Thus wisdom speaks in a public language and is dialogical at its core. Wisdom may therefore model constructive ways of speaking about security in the public sphere.

Finally, Wisdom is one of the names that early Christians gave to Jesus. Wisdom thus merits particular attention by those of us who stand in a discipleship tradition of following Jesus. Recent study has recognized anew that New Testament writers did not see true wisdom as a rival truth to the prophetic Word or the gospel. After all, Jesus both taught and modeled for us how to live wisely in conformity with the "normative culture of the reign of God" as confessed in our worship of God, and as revealed (though in a hidden way) through creation.[8] New Testament writings recognize that seeking to follow Jesus, the Wisdom of God, into the marketplaces of our world may be risky. As the wisdom of Christ challenges the dominant values of society, it will thus (and paradoxically) require Jesus's disciples to seek safety and security in risky ways. Reflection on Jesus in relationship to larger wisdom traditions, therefore, should help us see how the prophetic and the wise meet as they challenge false understandings and false prophetic words.

To test these possibilities this paper will sample examples of the wisdom idiom embedded in a variety of literary texts in the Bible, spanning a broad range of thought about the cosmos, human nature, and social organization in relationship to peace and security.

WISDOM'S INVITATION, AN IMAGE OF ABUNDANCE

Come, eat of my bread and drink of the wine I have mixed. Lay aside immaturity, and live, and walk in the way of insight (Prov 9:5-6).

Come to me, all you that are weary and are carrying heavy burdens, and I will give you rest. Take my yoke upon you and learn from me, for I am gentle and humble in heart, and you will find rest for your souls (Matt 11:28-29).

One of the central images of wisdom in both the testaments is that of a banquet table symbolizing the abundant riches of life under the reign of God. The image expresses an invitation to all to partake of the nourishment that Woman Wisdom offers and to receive the promise of blessing and shalom that is freely given through God's abundant generosity.[9] This contrasts markedly with the image of the foolish woman who is a flighty creature, a simpleton who cares for nothing but sits on a seat to invite passers-by indoors (Prov 9:13-18). That invitation leads to death instead of life.

The image of a banquet table highlights at least two aspects of the wisdom of God. Most basic is the conviction that God is generous and it is the desire of God to give abundant life to all creatures. In fact, the book of Proverbs sees wisdom as the first of creation, present with God to delight and rejoice in the human race and in the world that God had made (Prov 8:27-33). The New Testament testifies that God through Christ freely offers wisdom for living to everyone, including the ones weary and heavy laden, so that all can know what makes for life and security. Second, this image suggests that although God is generous to all, God also expects humans to make choices as to whose table they will join. Judgments must be made and choices faced in order to partake of God's goodness. These do not depend on human skill nor on human strength alone, but do require our willingness to accept the lessons that wisdom offers. For it is the wise who hear and gain in learning, but the foolish who despise wisdom and instruction (Prov 1:5-7).

Wisdom is thus the reflective side of our life of faithfulness to God, valuing insight and reasoning in the search for a comprehensive vision of the meaning of life. It is this image of wisdom that will guide our study as we explore its expression in a variety of genres, assumptions, expectancies, and perspectives on life. Though the texts chosen will be those that relate most directly to security and safety, the sampling of texts should also point to the scope and richness of the wisdom tradition in its various literary forms. Perhaps these morsels of insight will whet our appetite to partake of the rich nourishment that wisdom offers us.

A Conversation in Many Modes

> *Wisdom cries out in the street; in the square she raises her voice* (Prov 1:20).

The biblical writings that invite us to wisdom's table are not all of the same literary genre nor are they fully integrated with each other. Though there are biblical books that scholars specifically designate as classic wisdom texts (such as Proverbs, Ecclesiastes, Job, and several apocryphal books), the Bible also contains narratives that model wise action, parables that illuminate the wisdom of God, letters that give wise advice, and psalms and hymns that celebrate God's wisdom.[10] Therefore the interfacing of wisdom texts with each other and with other texts in the canon will be most central to our discussion. This will allow us a glimpse of the intertextual dialogue within the Bible. But more to the point, this will allow us to see how wisdom can be a mode of invitation to all people to work out the meaning of peacemaking in our human societies.

1. Stories

Many of the wisdom stories in the Bible arise out of the popular ethos of the tribe and village circle. They were probably told and retold to generations of youth and adults to inspire them to choose the way of life instead of death. Stories invite identification with their characters in the problems and situations that they encounter. For example, stories with characters like Abigail and Daniel begin with conflict situations or personal threats and gradually, through wise responses to the situations, move to a measure of peace and security. Others such as the stories of Joseph and Esther, Stephen and Paul, lead to further risk but serve to highlight how God used human decisions to further God's peace. The wisdom in all of these stories arises out of the reflection on these events by the storytellers.

Throughout the centuries, many different kind of hearers and readers of the stories have identified with the biblical characters even though they lived in quite different social orders of families, tribes, and empires. Still, many stories contain aspects that make them ambiguous models for our own ethical reflection. Waldemar Janzen has given some helpful perspectives on stories of wisdom. He points out that stories that present an exemplary action are not self-contained wholes "yielding an encapsulated and timeless ethical principle."[11] Instead, ethical action emerges from a situation that a preceding story has shaped, and that in turn contributes to the ongoing movement of the larger narrative. Crucial to the interpretation of these stories is the intertwining of theology and ethics, creating a link between God's ordering providence and human action. In many situations it is God's generosity that redeems human actions that only partially fit with God's ways.

Janzen claims that stories operate at an ethical level prior to law.[12] Thus they invite us to reflect on values that successive storytellers have honed into paradigms of wise thoughts and actions. They help us reflect on our own experiences of life, allowing us to differentiate between wise and foolish actions. They therefore invite us to interpret our experiences in the light of the Creator God's provisions for a good life as well as help us understand our human actions in the context of the larger human story.

2. Didactic Traditions of Wisdom

The didactic traditions of wisdom encompass a wide variety of observations about life, ranging from the seeming naïveté of Proverbs, the pessimism of Ecclesiastes, the subversive wisdom of Jesus's teachings to the practical advice within the epistles. Ponderings on daily life by these sages begin with observations but often turn to questions about the larger design and purpose of creation and the role of humans in that creation. These sages believed that the Creator brought into being an orderly world and that divinely ordered rules for living were there for the curious and discerning to discover.

The forms in which the sages gave these teachings were invitational because of their familiarity, not unlike didactic traditions outside of Scripture. For example, a proverb is a form of teaching that is ingrained in our consciousness because of its brevity and its common sense. Poetic presentations such as those of Job inspire meditation and debate about their inter-pretation of life. Parables such as those in the teachings of Jesus create a metaphorical tension that leads to further reflection. The personal address of the Pauline letters creates relationships that allow the readers to receive good advice. Thus the variety of didactic forms itself invites us to reason further about God's design for our security and safety.

It is the assumptions underlying these teachings, of course, that create the ongoing debate and discussion within the wisdom literature. Unlike the prophets who directly claimed to speak God's word for specific circumstances, the sages were more impressed by the limits of their wisdom and by the mys-tery of God that was beyond their reach. Though they assumed that much wisdom could be distilled from everyday experi-ence, they were also impressed by the vastness of God's work and the need for God's self-manifestation through specific rev-elation. Thus proverbial wisdom could concern itself with seemingly mundane instructions on table manners or on tend-ing the flocks, while other wisdom literature such as Job and Ecclesiastes debated more comprehensive themes such as justice, suffering, the nature of God, and creation.

In the New Testament various didactic traditions lie hid-den within the literary genres of gospels and epistles. Too often, therefore, we have failed to recognize them as wisdom teachings. Nonetheless, the strongest consensus of contempo-rary scholarship is that Jesus was a teacher of wisdom.[13] Early in life he was eager to debate with the rabbis in the temple. As Luke testifies, Jesus grew and became strong, "filled with wis-dom" (Luke 2:40). In the gospel narratives he was addressed as Teacher, he gathered disciples, taught in public places, drew on Old Testament wisdom motifs, and appealed to all to follow the narrow way leading to life rather than the broad way end-ing in death. His parables resembled popular stories, but drew readers into deeper reflection on God and God's ways. He was recognized as a teacher greater than Solomon (Matt 12:42) for he often turned the world of conventional assumptions upside down with his radical and wise interpretations of the tradition.[14] In the epistles there is a renewed interest in wisdom expressed in a variety of forms, including creative restatements of the gospel message as well as proverbial and parabolic wisdom containing direct advice on practical matters.

Too often, instead of leading us to discern and reflect further on wisdom in our day, these didactic traditions have been used to cut off discussion and demand immediate obedience. They have been used dogmatically and applied directly to situations that differ vastly from the biblical times. Yet in the dialogue between these various texts, some tensions remain unresolved and some questions do not receive complete answers, thus creating space for our own reflection. We are invited to discern further, to open ourselves to sustained conversation, and deeper thought. These texts, therefore, ask us not only to receive the wisdom that they contain but also to contribute our own insights thoughtfully from our own experience to the conversation.

3. The Merging of Creation Wisdom and Covenantal Wisdom

> See, just as the Lord my God has charged me, I now teach you statutes and ordinances for you to observe in the land that you are about to enter and occupy. You must observe them diligently, for this will show your wisdom and discernment to the peoples, who, when they hear all these statutes, will say, "Surely this great nation is a wise and discerning people" (Deut 4:5-6).

Already in the Old Testament, some biblical writers suggest that Torah, the revelation of God that Israel received from God within its own particular history, was the highest form of wisdom. The covenant that God established with the people of God included the promises to Abraham, the Law, and also the knowledge they gained through their experience of exodus from slavery. Post-exilic writings identified the Torah with wisdom itself (Sir 24:23), as did several of the Psalms (19, 119). However, the wisdom that comes through observation of God's work in creation and the wisdom that the people of God gain through God's liberating action in the exodus meet in rather complex ways in various writings. In response to threats against their national identity in the centuries just before the time of Jesus, scribes and sages intensified their study of the Law. As the identification of Torah with wisdom intensified, creation blessing and covenantal blessing were sometimes held in tension rather than completely identified with each other.[15] For example, as other nations appeared more and more to be enemies, tensions surfaced between openness to the wisdom of those outside the border of Israel and strong needs for identity and protection of the holy nation. But this merging of traditions had a paradoxical result: Priestly concerns for holiness through separation from the nations, and the sages' concern for openness to a wisdom that extended internationally, drew closer and closer to each other. In this context some understood law, which required immediate obedience, as wisdom personified.

Gerald Sheppard has suggested that during the late Old Testament period, wisdom became a theological category that formed a perspective from which to interpret Torah and the prophetic traditions.[16] Wisdom could show in practical terms how Torah related to its own concerns for faithful living. In addition, poetic celebrations of Woman Wisdom as the personified daughter of God emerged during this time, bringing Creation and Torah together in the figure of an attractive woman identified with God's activity from Adam to Moses (Wisd of Sol 10:1-2, 15). It is thus no wonder that early Christians explicitly made the connection between Personified Wisdom and Jesus; the later wisdom tradition was doing exactly this with Torah (Wisd of Sol 7:25-26). In using this identification, Jesus's early followers made the radical claim that Jesus Christ is the key to understanding created reality in all of its manifestations and dimensions.

Within the epistles the teaching of the apostles are understood as the wisdom of God, in contrast to "human" wisdom which strives for prestige and status and leads to ruin (1 Cor 1:18-31). The invitation to discern true wisdom became increasingly central as did the role of the Holy Spirit in giving power for that discernment. The book of Ephesians is a good example of an epistle that brings the concerns of traditional wisdom and the concerns of the gospel of Jesus into conversation with each other. Its view of salvation is repeatedly depicted as new creation, stressing the emergence of creation and salvation from the one God. Tom Yoder Neufeld suggests that Ephesians stands firmly in the wisdom tradition of "revelatory reflection," in which the author consciously reformulates and restates the apostolic deposit, while probing its implications.[17]

The merging of traditions, therefore, not only introduced continuity but also a tension into the overall category of wisdom. Do these traditions overlap completely or can one be given highest priority? Biblical literature does not answer this question by suggesting that only the people of God have wisdom. Neither does it subsume the particular experience of God's people under the general category of wisdom. Instead it recognized that foolishness is never far away from any human knowing and therefore discernment is always necessary. In addition, the biblical witness understood all wisdom to be a gift of God, thus leading to the view that only God's eschatological fulfillment would finally and fully integrate all wisdom. In the meantime, wisdom must be sought with all our minds and hearts and actions.

4. Worship Traditions of Wisdom

The worship tradition of wisdom is highly processed, somewhat removed from immediate experience, and often couched in the language of poetry, or at least placed into a context of the cult, such as the Psalter or New Testament hymns.[18] Its poetic form invites prayer, meditation, and doxology more than debate. For example, Psalm 1 is a classic wisdom psalm in its depiction of the two ways, the way of life and the way of destruction. Placed at the beginning of the Psalter, it points to wisdom as of crucial importance in the worship of God. So too

Psalm 34 celebrates God's deliverance and then actively teaches how the fear of the Lord works itself out practically in the daily choices of life that the righteous make.

The Psalms are therefore a celebration of God and God's way. They encourage all to choose that righteous way because this way leads to life and blessing not only for oneself but also for the larger community. The Psalmist assumes that God and others will overhear these meditations and prayers, which reflect on God's gifts of creation, life, law, and social ordering.[19] For the Psalms rest on the twofold assumption that one can learn by wisdom how to pray and that wisdom itself is a gift of God.

It is the hymns of the New Testament that bring wisdom to its climax in the incarnation of God's Wisdom in Jesus. In these hymns creation and new creation merge in the person of Jesus Christ. Jesus becomes the key to understanding reality in all of its manifestations and dimensions (John 1, Col 1, Phil 2). In worship wisdom merges with prophetic speech proclaiming God's gifts to all creation. Christ is Lord of all since he was present in creation as Wisdom. God's active and ongoing care for creation will continue until creation is completed in the gathering up of all things in the fullness of time.

> He is the image of the invisible God, the firstborn of all creation; for in him all things in heaven and on earth were created, visible and invisible, whether thrones, or dominions, or rulers, or powers—all things have been created through him and for him. He himself is before all things, and in him all things hold together (Col 1:15-17).

It is these convictions of God's generosity in both creation and new creation that give the church confidence to witness to the wisdom of God "in its rich variety," even to "rulers and authorities in the heavenly places" (Eph 3:10). A rhythm or dynamic thus underlies the wisdom traditions. It is a dynamic of receiving from God that which makes for life and then inviting others also to experience life in its fullness. It is this dynamic of receiving and giving that compels the church to enter the conversation in the marketplace and to seek the common good of the community. It is also this dynamic that counters all pride and triumphalism, creating instead a conversation at the table where all can hear an invitation both to share their wisdom and to listen to the wisdom of others.

WISDOM'S TRUTH: VALUES, INSIGHTS, CONVICTIONS, AND PRACTICES

> *Therefore walk in the way of the good, and keep to the paths of the just, for the upright will abide in the land* (Prov 2:20).

> *For the gate is narrow and the road is hard that leads to life, and there are few who find it* (Matt 7:14).

Wisdom's invitation is to the narrow and hard way that leads to abundant life, also named the "way of righteousness," "prosperity," "rest," "blessing," "shalom," or the reign of God coming "on earth as it is in heaven." These terms and images hint at the vast horizon of wisdom writings on this abundant life, and on all that preserves and continues life, and on all that gives meaning and purpose to life. This includes access to necessities for physical life: land, food, and security. But it also includes ongoing family and broader social relationships, which help create the structures that make life possible.

Instead of setting down laws or rules for action for every occasion, wisdom traditions are subtle and more open. They suggest values, insights, practices, and convictions that lead to life. Though they do include some basic substantive knowledge, they realize that this knowledge must continually grow and mature as one learns to live in the way of wisdom.

Questions of security and safety are important for the abundant life toward which wisdom aims. The following convergences in the various modes of wisdom demonstrate a direction for any reflection on safety and security. They do not give final answers, yet they do present learnings from the various traditions of biblical wisdom that can challenge Mennonite peace theology as it struggles with its response to threats of violence and insecurity. In each case, one or two short proverbs or teaching distill these learnings.

1. *Keep your heart with all vigilance, for from it flow the springs of life* (Prov 4:23).

Though few have thought of the story of Cain in the fourth chapter of the Genesis as a wisdom text, it affirms the teaching in Proverbs: jealousy and anger within the individual human heart lead to insecurity for the broader human community. The storyteller is specific about the inner feelings of Cain: "Cain was very angry and his countenance fell." The comment that "sin is lurking at the door" suggests someone whose heart is filled with anger (Gen 4:6-7). Cain's killing of his brother Abel and the ensuing curses upon him affect the whole community and are prominent elements in the stories of the succeeding generations. Classic wisdom texts later highlight these inner feelings and attitudes, placing an emphasis on the personal dimensions that create either insecure situations for individuals and communities or lead to peaceful resolutions.

"Those who are hot-tempered stir up strife, but those who are slow to anger calm contention (Prov 15:18). "The greedy person stirs up strife" (Prov 28:25). "The fear of others lays a snare but one who trusts in the Lord is secure (Prov 29:25). These proverbs arise from common sense observations but point to deeper truth about the role that the inner self plays in communal security and safety. Many of the verses use terms such as the "perverted mind," the "wicked heart," the "jealous," the "self–indulgent," and the "haughty" to indicate those inner attitudes that cause a person to refuse to learn and instead devise wicked plans that lead to violence. Yet there is also sensitivity to the loneliness within one's inner self and to the pain that others cause.

"The heart knows its own bitterness, and no stranger shares its joy" (Prov 14:10). "By sorrow of heart the spirit is broken" (Prov 15:13b). The book of Proverbs is particularly aware of how hasty words can create conflict and turmoil, and it sees the need for self-discipline to avoid the chain of violence that these words can unleash. It thus calls for prudence and thought before acting.

"Fools show their anger at once but the prudent ignore an insult" (Prov 12:16). "A fool's lips bring strife" (Prov 18:6). Jesus in his teachings suggests that the personal aspects of our lives are indeed crucial, for it is there that violence is born. "It is from within, from the human heart, that evil intentions come" (Mark 7:21). Jesus's teachings reiterate the importance of tending to our inner being, even suggesting that uncontrolled anger and insults are just as liable to judgment as is murder (Matt 5:21-26). But Jesus also understands the worry, the valuing of earthly treasures, the envy, and fear that arise within the human heart. His rhetorical questions, such as: "And can any of you by worrying add a single hour to your span of life?" (Matt 6:27) function to bring about deeper reflection on the hidden self that often lies behind violent actions.

In his practical advice James summarizes the need for gentle practices that are born within the heart. But he also recognizes that these can only come from God as a gift when one is open to receive it. Righteousness and peace follow the practice of "keeping ones heart with all diligence."

> Who is wise and understanding among you? Show by your good life that your works are one with gentleness born of wisdom. But if you have bitter envy and selfish ambition in your hearts, do not be boastful and false to the truth. Such wisdom does not come from above, but is earthy, unspiritual, devilish. For where there is envy and selfish ambition, there will also be disorder and wickedness of every kind. But wisdom from above is first pure, then peaceable, gentle, willing to yield, full of mercy and good fruits without a trace of partiality or hypocrisy. And a harvest of righteousness is sown in peace for those who make peace (James 3:13-18).

Perhaps one aspect of security that needs further attention in Mennonite theology is the relationship of the personal and the social/political in responding to issues of violence and insecurity. The scientific approach to knowledge has tended to divide psychology from sociology and political science, as well as the social sciences from theology, thus narrowing our conversation about safety and security. In Mennonite congregations, separation of the domestic sphere from the public has also created barriers to talking more directly about the fear, the worry, the anger, and the trauma that help to create violent responses in our world. Attention to factors that lead to insecurity must include those that arise within the self, thus suggesting that more inclusive conversations are mandatory for those who are wise.

2. *Whoever walks in integrity walks securely* (Prov 10:9). *The righteous find a refuge in their integrity* (Prov 14:32).

In the book of Proverbs righteousness and integrity are almost synonymous with the wisdom that brings security, while unrighteousness and wickedness lead to destruction. There is an assumption that individual righteous and wise persons, especially among the powerful, can uphold a pattern of life that brings security to a community (blessing) while individual foolish actions will bring disaster and conflict (curses).

Solomon is the best-known model of royal wisdom within Israel, thanks to his request to God "to give your servant therefore an understanding mind to govern your people, able to discern between good and evil" (1 Kings 3:9). In the biblical corpus 1 Kings and 2 Chronicles link Solomon to wisdom just as Moses is linked to Torah.[20] The assertion of Solomonic authorship of the book of Proverbs and several of the wisdom psalms fits well with the international fame that the narrative attributes to Solomon and his wisdom. Yet his story illustrates both the blessing and the destruction that come when wisdom does not coincide with integrity.

The story of Solomon begins with the young king having a dream in which he receives the divine gift of wisdom (1 Kings 3ff.). As the narrative progresses, wisdom and right action are associated with varied examples of creative judgment in cases of conflict (such as the famous case of two women claiming the same baby); intelligence and skill in the building of the temple and the royal retinue; overseeing of priests in service at the temple; and the ability to answer riddles and questions from the visiting queen of Sheba, who had heard of Solomon's wisdom.

Repeatedly in the narrative Solomon is also cautioned to exercise his gift of wisdom by obeying the Torah. In the end, the story faults him because "his heart was not true to the Lord his God, as was the heart of his father David. . . . So Solomon did what was evil in the sight of the Lord" (1 Kings 11:4, 6). The story ends with the Lord becoming angry with Solomon and raising up adversaries against him, resulting in conflict, warfare, and disaster.

In the book of Proverbs the individual and institutional interest coincide in the language of building a "house" (24:3). Many proverbs assume contemporary social structures, of course, including the institution of kings and warriors (Prov 24:5, 21-22). Various spheres of order that we moderns often separate in our understanding—including cosmology, societal order, and human nature—are integrated in the notion of a righteous order.[21] In the end, however, reliance for security cannot stay with social or institutional powers because they tend to become unjust. True righteousness is evident in the response of rulers to the poor and vulnerable. Thus it is God's righteousness, with its preferential option for the poor, that judges the righteousness of any institution: "Those who oppress the poor insult the Maker, but those who are kind to the needy honor him" (Prov 14:31). "The Lord tears down the house of the proud, but maintains the widow's boundaries" (Prov 15:25).

The book of Ecclesiastes is rather cynical in its portrayal of the present social order. The writer knows that this order can easily become tyrannical in its hierarchy and its rigidity. He also recognizes the presence of war but knows that wise reflection can find better ways to solve conflict: "If you see in a province the oppression of the poor and the violation of justice and right, do not be amazed at the matter; for the high official is watched over by a higher, and there are yet higher ones over them" (Eccles 5:8). "Wisdom is better than weapons of war, but one bungler destroys much good" (Eccles 9:18).

These learnings already suggest that there is a tension between the wisdom of God and conventional wisdom, between the righteousness of God and commonly held definitions of justice. Thus wisdom's quest for discernment often takes the shape of a struggle characterized by ambiguity and even contradiction in the expected patterns of life. In this struggle divine forces of creation and chaos contend for the domination of the cosmos, resulting in threats to the processes of life. Social life mirrors this struggle. It is in times of crises that significant tensions develop, raising new questions as to which patterns of living and which institutions are in tune with God's way.

In the face of this uncertainty the people of God turned to the particular revelation of God in history, to Torah and to gospel, in order to gain more light into the mystery and purpose of God. Jesus entered this struggle and affirmed the way of justice, nonviolence, peacemaking, and reconciliation toward which earlier sages had already pointed. At the heart of his teachings was the coming of the kingdom of God and its righteousness. In many ways this righteousness challenged the conventional way of power, especially in its way of seeking security. In Jesus's teachings, power and authority did not give the right to insist on higher status or to act as a tyrant but rather gave the opportunity for service and might even lead to death for the sake of the other (Mark 10:42-45).

Thus the way of wisdom with its concern for the vulnerable and poor merged with the righteousness that Jesus defined and embodied. It is not surprising that the epistles associate "learning Christ" with "true righteousness" (Eph 4:24). The letter to the Ephesians admonishes Christians to learn to live as "wise" people, living righteously in a way that exposes the "unfruitful works of darkness" (5:3-20). For righteousness can be defined by its fruits, that which is "good and right and true" (5:9).

Mennonite peace theology has often talked about the struggle between righteousness and unrighteousness as a struggle between the church and the world. This suggests little continuity between integrity and justice as society generally understands such virtues and the righteousness that Christians understand to be God's gift through Jesus. But if wisdom and righteousness connect more directly, we may understand both to be gifts of God, available to all who are open to learning wisdom.

Any prophetic engagement will certainly require the church to name the sharp opposition between unrighteousness and righteousness. But the church must acknowledge that it too, like Solomon, has often contributed to warfare and insecurity. The church too has sought prestige and power and contributed to injustice and oppression.

If we understand wisdom as the righteousness Jesus embodied in his wise and compassionate response to the poor and vulnerable, we realize that this wisdom is a gift of God given also to reflective persons who learn through their experience. Thus Mennonite theology must continue to accept and testify to the incompatibility between justice and injustice, righteousness and unrighteousness, which is basic to true wisdom. At the same time, however, Mennonites dare not use their status as church to assert power in the marketplace, but rather must act wisely, choosing to act justly and compassionately for those who are most vulnerable.

3. If your enemies are hungry, give them bread to eat; and if they are thirsty, give them water to drink (Prov 25:21; Rom 12:20).

The story of Abigail in 1 Samuel 25, which some scholars identify as a model wisdom tale, invites us to consider this practice as a way to gain security. The story begins with the foolishness of Nabal who refuses traditional tribal hospitality to David the fugitive. Abigail, a woman who is "clever and beautiful," averts the tragedy that David's revenge would have created. Going out to meet David, she takes with her rich gifts of food and drink and appeals to him to forgive. David summarizes the story in this way: "Blessed be the Lord who has judged the case of Nabal's insult to me, and has kept back his servant from evil" (25:39).

Abigail, in wisdom born of life experience and ordinary good sense, thus takes her place in the larger story of David, a story in turn linked to God's gracious purposes of blessing the whole world through God's people. Abigail chooses to pre-serve life by pursuing hospitality and intervening in a timely way when her family is under threat. As a result of this action she not only protects her family but builds community security and good will. Abigail moves outward from kinship hospitality to embrace the stranger, even while protecting the tribal inter-ests to which she is committed.

In a story in 2 Kings 6:15-23, Elisha the prophet suggests that this kind of hospitality can also be extended to national enemies. He instructs the king to provide a generous feast for his enemies, thus averting further raids upon his own land. In these stories hospitality overlaps with traditional values, but moves to a deeper level when that hospitality extends not only to strangers but also enemies. Interestingly enough, Egyptian and Akkadian proverbs also assert this direction in some of their proverbs.[22]

Biblical wisdom teachings give a number of reasons for not seeking revenge. One of them is simply that the wise will not answer another's folly by being foolish themselves (Prov 26:5). But other reasons focus on what one's actions do to the enemy. Heaping "coals of fire" on your enemy suggests shaming them but also suggests overcoming evil with good. It points to the space that one ought to leave for God's actions, since we should not "claim to be wiser than [we] are" (Rom 12:14-21).

Jesus recommends the practice of hospitality for a yet-deeper reason—the generosity of God who makes rain to fall on both the just and unjust (Matt 5:43-45). Jesus in his earthly life rejected the way of revenge and extended hospitality. He ate with sinners, had compassion on the outsider, and forgave those who injured him. Likewise, the epistles confirm this prac-tical alternative to revenge (Rom 12:14-21).

Mennonites have understood hospitality as a key practice

of peacemaking, but have not always recognized the inclusive nature of this hospitality. In addition, they have not always understood that others beyond the church may long for exactly this kind of wisdom to overcome vengeance. Thus Mennonites must more readily seize the opportunity to witness to practices of hospitality in the marketplace beyond the church and enter into discussions of what it means in our present global context.

4. For everything there is a season, and a time for every matter under heaven (Eccles 3:1).

The book of Esther does not explicitly mention God's action, yet the presence of God's people with their wisdom surrounds this story, in which a woman chooses wisely in moments of great insecurity and fear. Esther's great beauty allows her into the harem of the Persian king. She then uses the power structure of the Persian court skillfully in order to attain her goal, the security of her people. This goal takes precedence over any personal fear she may have had for her own life. What is striking is the advice of Mordecai, Esther's mentor. "For if you keep silence at such a time as this, relief and deliverance will rise for the Jews from another quarter, but you and your father's family will perish. Who knows? Perhaps you have come to royal dignity for such a time as this" (Esther 4:14). Beneath these words lie subtle assumptions about God's providence and the place of human action in God's plans.

The book of Proverbs assumes that people are capable of choosing their attitudes and course of action in situations that are often ambiguous and confusing. Few of the behaviors are universally applicable. Instead the proverbs call for the flexibility of mind to determine which are appropriate for a particular situation. Statements that seem contradictory or at best confusing when we attempt to follow them dogmatically are helpful if understood as needing further discernment as to when they are most appropriate. Thus "do not speak harshly" and "do not refrain from rebuking" seem opposite but may each be appropriate for a particular time. What is crucial is not just doing right but doing right at the right time.

Though wisdom has a particular understanding of time, focusing on the present, in writers such as the authors of Ecclesiastes and Job there is also a growing discontent about limiting the results of righteous actions to this life. After all, experience clearly shows that often the wicked prosper and the righteous fail in their endeavors (Eccles 7:15). Tom Yoder Neufeld suggests that wisdom introduces an eschatological hope that "loads the present to overflowing while also seeing it as movement toward culminating the process of reconciling the cosmos in Christ, a process that began already before the beginning, so to speak."[23] Thus the heart of Jesus's message had to do with the fulfillment of time, for the reign of God is at hand. This suggests that Jesus understood wisdom's concern with God's timing and the place of human action within God's overall design. His willingness to trust God and risk even death in order to fit into God's plan is in line with the wisdom of the sages of old who also took risks in order to live in allegiance to God's reign. This becomes particularly clear in Ephesians, with its focus on reconciliation.

> With all wisdom and insight he has made known to us the mystery of his will, according to his good pleasure that he set forth in Christ, as a plan for the fullness of time, to gather up all things in him, things in heaven and things on earth (Eph 1:8-10).

To discern the times in a spirit of hope thus becomes a crucial practice for the people of God as they seek to witness to God's wisdom in the marketplace. Wisdom cautions us that doing the right thing at the right time is crucial and requires discernment, but also requires hope in God's action of full reconciliation. In any Mennonite concern for security, deliberate attention to time in light of eternity will be necessary in order to know when to wait for God's action and when to act in God's name.

5. In the fear of the Lord one has strong confidence and one's children will have a refuge (Prov 14:26).

To recognize the limitations of human life and the human inability to control its direction is part of the wisdom tradition, as is trust in God as our refuge and strength. It is the book of Ecclesiastes that reminds us most clearly of human limitations, the ambiguity of all human achievement, and the impossibility of securing anything permanent as human beings. The writer laments these limitations particularly in the area of intellectual capabilities and wisdom. "All is vanity," he cries. Ecclesiastes' unique niche among wisdom teachings seems to be to bring out exceptions to the rule, to keep wisdom honest in its reflections, and to encourage a deeper pondering of the seeming contradictions that belie God's intention and purpose in creation.[24]

Similar to the book of Job, the writer contests a world that operates according to principles of fairness and justice as defined by human rules of behavior. It delves beneath these assumptions to ask questions at the limits of human understanding. Thus the book of Ecclesiastes suggests the futility of conventional wisdom and points to the search for a deeper wisdom that does not come from mere observation of life.

The story of Joseph in Genesis 37-50 is actually a wisdom tale. It prompts similar reflections because Joseph's actions do not directly fit the outcomes in the story. It begins as a story of family strife and violence yet struggles with the broader social political question of brothers ruling over brothers. Joseph, though misunderstood, falsely accused, and even threatened with death makes decisions that preserve his own life in face of great insecurity. But these decisions also lead him to become the chief adviser to Pharaoh, because there was no one "as discerning and wise" as he. His eventual reconciliation with his brothers, who had betrayed him, was possible because he recognized God's leading beyond his own actions and could set aside revenge in favor of reconciliation. His acknowledgment of God suggests the fear of God that is the beginning of wisdom: "God sent me before you to preserve for you a remnant on earth, and to keep alive for you many survivors" (Gen 45:7).

Though the book of Proverbs seems to suggest that human

logic and keen observation can discern the way of blessing that God has revealed through God's creation, it also acknowledges that the way of the foolish is the more popular course. Many do not understand the limits that God has written into creation in order to allow life to flourish for all.

The most decisive shift in focus toward God, however, occurs in the worship tradition of wisdom. It is this shift that brings a sense of security, patience, and purposeful action to those who are wise, despite the apparent flourishing of the wicked. Thus meditation and prayer in the context of the community of God's people become a crucial practice of the righteous witnessing to God and to the life that God intends (Ps 34).

A major temptation of the modern world is the dualism that would divorce secular from sacred; such a dualism in turn tends to separate intellectual activity from worship. Mennonites have not been immune from this temptation. At times, in fact, Mennonites have narrowed their operative theology to a humanistic ethic, which does not adequately acknowledge God as prior to that ethic. Biblical wisdom suggests that the practice of worship is necessary in order to keep our wisdom honest by acknowledging the limits of its knowledge.

6. For the message of the cross is foolishness to those who are perishing, but to us who are being saved it is the power of God (1 Cor 1:18).

Already in the stories of the Old Testament, faithful interpretation of God's way in the marketplace includes risk, suffering, and death. Daniel models wisdom in situations where the overwhelming reality is the exercise of power by foreign rulers. In Daniel's specific role as courtier, he exhibits his fidelity to the true God in his observance of Jewish food laws and in his faithfulness in prayer, despite threats to his life. The story suggests that it was God who gave Daniel wisdom and skill in every aspect of life as well as insight into dreams and visions (Dan 1:17, 5:14.). It also suggests that any power a ruler enjoys comes as a gift from God (2:36), who could also take it away. Threats to Daniel's own security, however, find their answer through trust in the "Most High God," the King over all creation, whom he served.

Daniel's story reminds us that to choose wisdom over foolishness involves risk. Temptations abound as persons struggle to choose the way of life amidst opposition and persecution. Idolatry, misuse of power, and a seeking of prestige or status are temptations of the wise as they gain in power. Being wise, therefore, may require us to go to the halls of power, but it also requires us to claim an alternative power based on faith in God the creator and sustainer of the universe. The New Testament confirms this in the story of Jesus, who in his willingness to risk death on the cross fully embodied trust in the loving God. The resurrection assures us that the power of God can bring life from death. Thus the presence of God through the Holy Spirit encourages the wise to make risky choices in the face of threats and violence, secure in the knowledge that God's power will ultimately intervene.

In the book of Acts, Stephen and Paul as well as other followers of the Way demonstrate a security based on a trust in God in their public witness. Paul knew from his own experience the "wisdom of the cross" and the "power of the resurrection," which allowed him to be confident even when there were risks of death. First Corinthians 1-2 suggests that a willingness to suffer will help discern between the wise and foolish. For the wise are those who depend fully on God's creative and redemptive power instead of conventional learning, status, or eloquent speech. The cross represents for Paul God's loving will to stand with the suffering world against the "rulers of this age," even to death (1 Cor 2:8). True power is thus born not of oppressive control or violence, but of solidarity in divine love. This power of the cross is revealed through the Spirit (2:10). The cross, therefore, is also the wisdom that will reconcile enemies and bring together those who are alienated. Paul reiterates this theme in Ephesians when he calls Christ Jesus "our peace," the one who has broken down the dividing wall between Jews and Gentiles, creating one humanity in place of the two, thus making peace.

What is clear in all of these discussions is that wisdom's willingness to risk life for the other is not based on a depreciation of biological life but rather on trust that mere physical death does not present a limit to life. Rather, it is an opening to full eternal life. Eternal life, by definition, overflows for the other. Jesus Christ most directly embodies it, for the totality of his life and death took on a cruciform shape in order to bring abundant life to others. Wisdom recognizes the need to suffer on behalf of others, but it also strongly asserts that fear of death, insecurity, and violence are not God's will for humans. Thus the "wisdom of the cross" makes sense only within the larger rhythm of receiving and giving, a rhythm in which life and power are received from God, and voluntary vulnerability and suffering are given for the sake of the life of the other. It is this wisdom that is crucial so that teaching self denial does not just become another way to assert power over another—another temptation from which Mennonites have not always been immune.

Conclusion: The Promise of Wisdom for Discernment of the Common Good

This sampling of various biblical texts confirms that the Bible does use the language of wisdom to describe the relationship of the logic of the kingdom of God and the logic underlying the good in our human institutions and structures. It suggests the value of human reasoning in seeking the good but also seeks to define aspects of righteousness and goodness that only those who are ready to follow wisdom's invitation can learn. It helps us understand the many persons in our pews, who like my parents, participate actively in their communities by building institutions of ordering even as they maintain a prophetic witness against all violence.

The term "wisdom" has the advantage of a broad range of meanings—from folk wisdom to royal wisdom, from personal insight to the common sense of a community, from compassionate practice to skillful calculation, from careful orderly reasoning to unpredictable revelatory knowledge. It encompasses a way of doing things as well as a way of reasoning, an attitude of the heart as well as some substantive assertions of truth. It is not limited to one area of life but plays itself out in the family circle as easily as in the royal palace. Thus wisdom is not a static, closed characteristic of the sort that a strict formula can capture, but is rather defined by particular values, attitudes, insights, and practices at particular moments in time. Foolishness is never far away; discernment is always necessary for the kind of wisdom that gains in breadth and depth as it receives new insights.

The image that most directly points to this dynamic definition of wisdom is God inviting all to a banquet of life-giving food. This invitation is open to all and no person or community can hoard it. For it is God who creates and sustains life, and who knows therefore what is needed for the ongoing sustenance of all throughout God's creation. Yet anyone at any time can refuse God's invitation to partake of this nourishment. Only the indiscriminate pattern of God's gracious gift of insight allows life to continue despite human foolishness and pride.

Yet to partake of this nourishment is to take one's place at a larger table of participants, each offering the gift of wisdom to the other. The invitation can come in many forms, but the process of becoming wise is always one of receiving and giving —of receiving life, land, justice, and blessing from God, and of giving life, land, justice, and blessing to others. It is about choosing life for oneself and then acting in life-giving, generous ways toward others. It is about receiving power and then empowering others. By implication, it is also about not being violated and killed oneself while in turn refusing to inflict violence and death on others. It is about not being controlled by others, while in turn not abusing and controlling others. It is this rhythm of righteousness that creates the dynamic of life in the kingdom of God.

It is also this rhythm that sustains life in human community, thus creating an interconnection and solidarity with all people in their quest for security and safety.[25] Wisdom rejects a dualistic view of reality that would draw a strict boundary between sacred and secular wisdom, between faith and reason, or between church and the marketplace. It insists that God has traced a grain of wisdom through the universe, which humans are to discover and respect. Yet wisdom is keenly aware of the limits to human understanding, knowing that truth is frequently hidden from human eyes, and that only God understands fully the direction of the universe.

A tension arises when we accept this limit to wisdom and when we look more closely at the description of the security of life that we find in wisdom literature. Biblical wisdom would understand biological life as a mere starting point as it reflects on what makes for the "way of life" that we are urged to choose. For wisdom, life is that abundance which terms such as land, family, rest, and security indicate, but it also includes justice and righteousness, blessing and shalom. To receive life, therefore, is to receive the kind of life that God intends, not merely existence as it so frequently presents itself in human experience. Biblical wisdom strongly challenges lesser definitions of life, no matter who presents them.

Wise persons who understand this rhythm recognize "kairos" moments when the wise must take action and challenge lesser wisdoms. They become prophetic in their willingness to witness to life in its fullness and are empowered to suffer through the power of the Holy Spirit. In this sense, wisdom and prophetic speech intersect in their dependence on the indwelling of God's Spirit of Wisdom that we need to discern wisely as to when and where to speak and act.[26]

One can name a number of key practices as wise in the way they seek the common good or life of our world. These include interpreting situations truthfully, probing all experiences for their life-giving qualities, extending hospitality to others, forgoing revenge and forgiving the other, conscientious objection to injustice and greed, generosity and care for the needy, seeking reconciliation with the enemy, and patient waiting for God's action. How does wisdom answer the question of whether we should be involved in institutions and structures that order human life? It asks us to demonstrate practically how our engagement is determined by the rhythm of life that we have discovered in our own experience of God's grace. After all, wisdom takes seriously the importance of personal virtues and individual initiatives that witness to truth and justice within institutional structures.

This rhythm of life is also important for the way we enter into public discourse. Wisdom as understood in the Bible counters discourse that would seek a control or monopoly of the truth. This includes the power that one can exert by using the idiosyncratic language of the faith community or the selective language of a particular political institution in order to dominate the other. It counters all triumphalism, tribalism, and forceful insistence on one's own way. But it does not hide its own insights, nor shy away from sharing its distinctive interpretation of reality while inviting others to share their unique perspectives. This means that the church must learn to be dialogical and "multilingual," that is, willing to speak and listen in many languages.[27]

First, the church must be fluent in its own particular tongue, arising out of its own historical experience, where identity is forged, virtues are learned and taught, and God is worshipped. This language of worship and caring community becomes the institutional witness that points to the source of all wisdom while recognizing the limits of human wisdom.

But second, the church must also speak the language of a middle discourse "on the wall" between communities of discourse, where witness for the gospel logic and the struggle for the good intersect.[28] In that conversation Christians must participate wisely and prophetically for the sake of the abundant life of the whole community.

In the final analysis, all wisdom is accountable to God, who is both the source and sustainer of life. As Christians we can turn to Jesus Christ, who embodied wisdom in his very being, and to the Holy Spirit, who continues to enliven the whole universe, in order to learn the rhythm of wisdom. Our calling as people of God is to become wise, to speak and act according to the limits of our understanding and to trust in the promise of God, "I will bless you and make you a blessing." With that hope we can wait with eagerness for God's promise to be fulfilled, when all things will be "gathered in him, things in heaven and things on earth." In the meantime, we participate in God's rhythm of life, in tune with Jesus and the sages of old, willing to transcend lesser wisdoms for the sake of the "wisdom of the cross." This way of life is aptly characterized as "walking in the resurrection"[29] while seeking the common good of our communities and nations.

NOTES

1. For an overview of this trend toward the prophetic see Leo Driedger and Donald B. Kraybill, *Mennonite Peacemaking: From Quietism to Activism* (Scottdale, Pa.: Herald Press, 1994), 150–52.

2. My reflections in this and following paragraphs owes a debt to Gerald W. Schlabach, "Beyond Two- Versus One-Kingdom Theology: Abrahamic Community as a Mennonite Paradigm for Engagement in Society," *Conrad Grebel Review* 11, no. 3 (Fall 1993): 187–210.

3. However, note two contributions on wisdom and peace theology by Douglas Miller and Tom Yoder Neufeld in Ted Grimsrud and Loren J. Johns, eds., *Peace and Justice Shall Embrace: Power and Theopolitics in the Bible; Essays in Honor of Milard Lind* (Telford, Pa.; Scottdale, Pa.: Pandora Press U.S.; Herald Press, 1999).

4. Note for example the almost complete neglect of the classical wisdom texts in the biblical index of Perry B. Yoder and Willard M. Swartley, eds., *The Meaning of Peace: Biblical Studies*, Studies in Peace and Scripture (Louisville, Ky.: Westminster/John Knox Press, 1992), 279–87.

5. I recognize that there is a great deal of debate among scholars as to what constitutes wisdom writing and how wisdom should be defined. However, for our purposes I will deliberately use a very broad definition. For an extensive survey of the highly varied wisdom tradition and the extensive secondary literature see Roland E. Murphy, "Wisdom in the Old Testament," *Anchor Bible Dictionary*, ed. David Noel Freedman (New York, N.Y.: Doubleday, 1992), 6:920–31.

6. This term comes from John Howard Yoder, "Armaments and Eschatology," *Studies in Christian Ethics* 1, no. 1 (1988): 58.

7. Gerald T. Sheppard, "Biblical Wisdom Literature at the End of the Modern Age," in *Congress Volume*, Papers read at the 16th Congress of the International Organization for the Study of the Old Testament, held in Oslo from 2 to 7 August 1998, eds. André Lemaire and Magne Sæbø (Leiden; Boston: Brill, 2000), 396–97. Middle dis-

course may take the place of middle axioms as understood by John H. Yoder because it can include the practice of speaking as well as to the substance of what is spoken. See Duane Friesen's essay in this book.

8. Daniel S. Schipani, *The Way of Wisdom in Pastoral Counseling* (Elkhart, Ind.: Institute of Mennonite Studies, 2003), 39.

9. This fits well with Pamela Leach's emphasis on the "abundant resourcefulness" of God's creation, challenging ideologies that promote scarcity and competition. See page 104.

10. Though a chronological study of the development of the wisdom traditions would be helpful, in this preliminary overview we will take a more canonical approach to our quest. See Waldemar Janzen, "A Canonical Rethinking of the Anabaptist-Mennonite New Testament Orientation," in *The Church as Theological Community: Essays in Honour of David Schroeder*, ed. Harry John Huebner (Winnipeg, Man.: CMBC Publications, 1990), 107.

11. Janzen, "A Canonical Rethinking of the Anabaptist-Mennonite New Testament Orientation," 11.

12. Ibid., 64f.

13. Marcus J. Borg, "Teaching of Jesus," in *Anchor Bible Dictionary*, 3:806.

14. Marcus J. Borg, *Meeting Jesus Again for the First Time: The Historical Jesus & the Heart of Contemporary Faith* (San Francisco: HarperSanFrancisco, 1994), 27–32.

15. Waldemar Janzen, *Old Testament Ethics: A Paradigmatic Approach* (Louisville, Ky.: Westminster/John Knox Press, 1994), 195.

16. Gerald T. Sheppard, *Wisdom as a Hermeneutical Construct: A Study in the Sapientializing of the Old Testament*, Beiheft Zur Zeitschrift Für die Alttestamentliche Wissenschaft, no. 151 (Berlin; New York: W. de Gruyter, 1980), 13.

17. Thomas R. Neufeld, *Ephesians*, Believers Church Bible Commentary (Waterloo, Ont.; Scottdale, Pa.: Herald Press, 2002), 364.

18. Robert Davidson, *Wisdom and Worship*, The Edward Cadbury Lectures (London; Philadelphia: SCM Press; Trinity Press International, 1990).

19. Erhard S. Gerstenberger, "Practicing the Presence of God: The Wisdom Psalms as Prayer," in *To Hear and Obey: Essays in Honor of Fredrick Carlson Holmgren*, eds. Bradley J. Bergfalk and Paul Edward Koptak (Chicago, Ill.: Covenant Publications, 1997), 20–41.

20. Gerald T. Sheppard, "The Relation of Solomon's Wisdom and Biblical Prayer," *Toronto Journal of Theology* 8, no. 1 (1992): 11.

21. Leo G. Perdue, "Cosmology and the Social Order in the Wisdom Tradition," in John G. Gammie and Leo G. Perdue, eds., *The Sage in Israel and the Ancient Near East* (Winona Lake, Ind.: Eisenbrauns, 1990), 271.

22. William Klassen, *Love of Enemies: The Way to Peace*, Overtures to Biblical Theology (Philadelphia: Fortress Press, 1984), 34–35.

23. Neufeld, *Ephesians*, 51.

24. Roland Murphy, "The Sage in Ecclesiastes and Qoheleth the Sage" in Gammie and Perdue, *The Sage in Israel and the Ancient Near East*, 271.

25. "Holy interconnectedness" is Walter Brueggeman's term; see *The Creative Word: Canon as a Model for Biblical Education* (Philadelphia: Fortress Press, 1982), 81. "Inclusivity" and "indivisibility" are terms Pamela Leach uses for the coming together of all people, since all wisdom has its source in one Creator God.

26. Wisdom of Solomon 7:27 already suggests that Wisdom is but one; she passes into holy souls and makes them friends of God and prophets.

27. Note Duane Friesen's work on this multilingual practice in his essay in this book.

28. Walter Brueggemann, *Interpretation and Obedience: From Faithful Reading to Faithful Living* (Minneapolis: Fortress Press, 1991), 41–69.

29. This phrase was used in the Schleitheim Confession of 1527, though it was interpreted in a rather dualistic manner. See Howard Loewen, *One Lord, One Church, One Hope, and One God: Mennonite Confessions of Faith in North America: An Introduction*, Text Reader Series (Elkhart, Ind.: Institute of Mennonite Studies, 1985), 79.

FOR FURTHER READING

Brueggemann, Walter. *The Creative Word: Canon as a Model for Biblical Education*. Philadelphia: Fortress Press, 1982.

Ceresko, Anthony R. *Introduction to Old Testament Wisdom: A Spirituality for Liberation*. Maryknoll, N.Y.: Orbis Books, 1999.

Davidson, Robert. *Wisdom and Worship*. The Edward Cadbury Lectures. London; Philadelphia: SCM Press; Trinity Press International, 1990.

Janzen, Waldemar. *Old Testament Ethics: A Paradigmatic Approach*. Louisville, Ky.: Westminster/John Knox Press, 1994.

Murphy, Roland Edmund. *The Tree of Life: An Exploration of Biblical Wisdom Literature*. Grand Rapids, Mich.: William B. Eerdmans Pub., 1996.

O'Connor, Kathleen M. *The Wisdom Literature*. Message of Biblical Spirituality, vol. 5. Collegeville, Minn.: Liturgical Press, 1993.

APPENDIX TO PART I

PEACE THEOLOGY: A VISUAL MODEL WITH NARRATIVE EXPLANATION

by the MCC Peace Theology Project Team

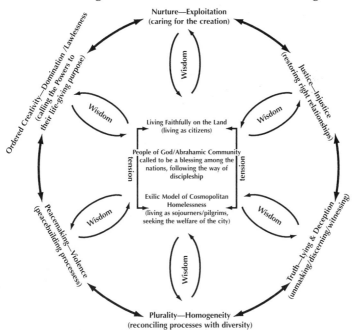

KINGDOM OF GOD
God's gracious deliverance/shalom-making

Nurture—Exploitation
(caring for the creation)

Ordered Creativity—Domination /Lawlessness
(calling the Powers to their life-giving purpose)

Justice—Injustice
(restoring right relationships)

Wisdom

Living Faithfully on the Land
(living as citizens)

People of God/Abrahamic Community
called to be a blessing among the
nations, following the way of
discipleship

Exilic Model of Cosmopolitan
Homelessness
(living as sojourners/pilgrims,
seeking the welfare of the city)

tension

Peacemaking—Violence
(peacebuilding processes)

Truth—Lying & Deception
(unmasking/discerning witnessing)

Plurality—Homogeneity
(reconciling processes with diversity)

KINGDOM OF GOD
God's gracious deliverance/shalom-making

I. The All-Encompassing Reality of the Kingdom of God

The controlling image or concept that frames the model is the *kingdom of God*. The kingdom is central to Jesus's teaching in the Synoptic Gospels. It is a political metaphor. It signifies the power of God that is breaking into human life and culture to liberate people from the bondage of destructive powers and systems, thus restoring all of life to the wholeness God intends for the creation.

The Synoptic Gospels interpret Jesus's teaching of the kingdom of God within the Old Testament prophetic tradition. Glen Stassen and David Gushee show seven significant connections between Jesus's teachings of the characteristics of God's reign in the prophet Isaiah: deliverance or salvation, righteousness/justice, peace, joy, God's presence as Spirit or light, healing, and return from exile.[1] One of these seven themes, return to the land (Isa 61:7), correlates with the Matthew's beatitude, "blessed are the meek, for they shall inherit the earth" (Matt 5:5). The liberating power of God restores people to a healed relationship to land, a connection to "place" that sustains healthy communities and human well-being.

The kingdom symbolizes the creative and liberating healing of God in every dimension of human life and culture. It is physical/personal, as is evident in the story of the exorcism of Luke 11. In the words of Jesus: "If it is by the finger of God that I cast out the demons, then the kingdom of God has come to you" (Luke 11:20). The kingdom is social/political: "Blessed are you who are poor, for yours in the kingdom of God" (Luke 6:20). After his encounter with Jesus, Zacchaeus is liberated from his complicity with the Roman domination system and thus freed to redistribute his wealth. "Look, half of my possessions, Lord, I will give to the poor; and if I have defrauded anyone of anything, I will pay back four times as much" (Luke 19:8).

The kingdom is not strictly a place; it is a process that is happening in the world, though it must always be embodied in particular people and communities at particular moments.

Suggesting this process are the gospel metaphors of leaven and the mustard seed that grows into a bush where birds can nest (Luke 13:18-21). The kingdom is both present and future. It is already breaking into history. The good news of its coming is "near" or "at hand." (Mark 1:15). It is "among you" (Luke 17:21). At the same time, it is still not fully present, so in the words of the Lord's Prayer we are instructed to pray that the "kingdom come . . . on earth as it is in heaven" (Matt 6:10). The kingdom of God breaks into this world, into history. It does not refer only to a place like "heaven," which in popular North American culture is viewed as "beyond" or "off the map" of the created world and human history. God's liberating power is a process that transforms the creation, human history, and human culture.

The kingdom of God is not something we humans bring about through our own power. It is a reality *in process* that God is ever initiating. We are invited to participate in God's transformative process to deliver the world from bondage and inaugurate shalom. Participating in this process requires commitment and loyalty to what God is doing in the world.

It is both liberating and demanding, as Jesus suggests in Luke: "No one who puts his hand to the plow and looks back is fit for the kingdom of God" (Luke 9:62).

Thus, our visual model of peace theology emphasizes that the kingdom surrounds everything that is in the inner circle. The kingdom is in fact broader than the church. The kingdom of God also surrounds the outer circle in the diagram, which identifies key dynamics in all human life. It includes God's work in the world: nurturing a caring creation, sustaining the powers to order life so it flourishes, and building truthful, just, and peaceful relationships. The kingdom of God represents God's work in the world to bring wholeness to the entire cosmos.

As Perry Yoder has shown, "shalom" (wholeness, well-being, *and* peace, in Hebrew understandings) is integrally connected with words in the Bible for salvation and justice (the restoration of right relationships).[2] Walter Wink refers to the reign of God as "God's domination free order." Under this rubric Wink incorporates a broad spectrum of arenas of life: what God's rule means for gender, for human relationships in general, for the distribution and ordering of power, for the ordering of political institutions, for the nature of economic structures and transactions, and for human relationships with the natural order.[3]

In short, the term "kingdom of God" is a comprehensive and integrative rubric for all of God's work in creation. By it we designate the processes through which we participate in God's work: 1) ordering of the world; 2) caring for the creation; 3) serving justice; 4) contributing to the nonviolent resolution of conflict; 5) respecting the plurality of human cultures; and 6) witnessing to truth while unmasking the lies we tell each other and the world.

II. THE CENTER OF THE MODEL: THE CHURCH

While the kingdom of God is the most comprehensive and integrative theological framework for our work, God calls out particular communities of people in history to embody and carry out God's mission in the world. Therefore *at the center of the model is the church.* Beginning with Abraham, God has been calling a people to be a blessing among the nations. "You are a chosen race, a royal priesthood, a holy nation, God's own people, in order that you may proclaim the mighty acts of him who called you out of darkness into his marvelous light" (1 Peter 2:9).

The center of the church's loyalty is Jesus Christ, Lord of history and the model of discipleship. The people of God live in the dynamic tension between being "sojourners/pilgrims" and "living as citizens in the land." On the one hand, as witnesses of Christ's alternative way of being in the world, the church is in tension with the dominant culture wherever it exists. Jeremiah's letter to the exiles reflects this side of the tension. They were living as a faith community in exile in pagan Babylon. Later the early Christians saw Rome as "Babylon" (Rev 14 and 18), and some Christians today see the "American Empire" as "Babylon." Nevertheless, in this pagan context,

Jeremiah urges the exiles to seek the peace of the city where they live.

Mennonites have historically tended to emphasize being pilgrims and witnesses to God's kingdom, a kingdom which is "not of this world" (John 18:36). Some have interpreted this to mean "otherworldly," a stance of withdrawal from the world or culture. Often in the Gospel of John, "world" does not mean the good creation, or all human culture. Rather it means the world as estranged or separated from God. Jesus is saying that we are to be witnesses of another way *in* the world, a witness that does not conform to the destructive practices of the world. We can see this illustrated when Jesus identifies the distinguishing mark of his kingdom with nonviolence. He says that if his kingdom were of this world, "my followers would be fighting to keep me from being handed over."

John Howard Yoder coined the phrase, "cosmopolitan homelessness" to emphasize this pilgrim side of the tension. The church is a transnational group of people (cosmopolitan) who live among the nations by following another Lord, one who calls all Christians to nonviolent peacemaking. This is homelessness from the point of view of traditional dominant cultures, which assume the true test of social loyalty is a willingness to kill to "save" the nation. The second century Epistle of Diognetus puts it this way: Christians "live in countries of their own, but simply as sojourners." Yoder's emphasis upon this side of the tension is a warning about the dangers of "Constantinianism," the adoption of a pretentious theological and ethical stance in which the church seeks to "manage history to make it come out right," and in the process waters down discipleship. One of the first practices that they compromise when they do so is nonviolence.

At the same time Christians live in particular places, within particular nations. While Mennonites have often migrated to find a safe haven to practice their faith, Mennonites historically also have lived as citizens in many lands (and not simply as "exiles"). This side of the tension—living as citizens in the land—has required Mennonites to think through what it means to live faithfully in the land once we have become a settled people, no longer on the move. This is a special challenge for Mennonites now settled in North America. Gerald Schlabach has argued that "to define Constantinianism as the basic problem for Christian social ethics is to concentrate our ethical reflection on the effort to avoid evil and unfaithfulness —rather than the challenge of embracing the good in a faithful manner."[4]

In the North American context, we need to ask what it means to be "good" citizens. At the same time, we need to ask how we do that in ways that are faithful to the gospel. What does it mean to live as Christian citizens who participate in the political process, engage in professional work such as law, social work, and public administration? In Mennonite Central Committee's (MCC) work in the Middle East, how do Mennonites work with Palestinians who have lived in exile too long and are struggling to live well in the land without the violence of occupation? How do Mennonites in Colombia live faithfully in a land where the disorder of armed violence is destroying the basic fabric of society? How do we Mennonites live as settled people, without becoming defenders of our own self-interest, legitimating a status-quo fallen order, or who allow the rules of our professions to dictate practice?

III. THE INTEGRATIVE FUNCTION OF WISDOM

Wisdom is a bridge-building concept in our model. It links the narrative theological orientation of the people of God with knowledge of the world (reality) in the broad sense (empirical data, social theory, reasoned discourse, experience, human desire). The pattern of twin arrows suggest that to gain and apply wisdom is an ongoing process, not something we settle once and for all. The arrows move in two directions to suggest how our theological orientation shapes the way we see the world, and at the same time that our knowledge of the world is the context for our theological thinking. Wisdom helps us to be multilingual as we speak to each other in the church in the light of God's call, and at the same time in the context of our work as citizens, social workers, lawyers, accountants, and administrators. Wisdom is the link we make between our theological commitments and orientation with everything else we know about the world.

Wisdom literature in the Bible provides a model for understanding divine revelation in a mode that links the historical (salvation history) to the underlying unity and universality of all truth implicit in a Trinitarian view of reality. God is not only the ground of the created order who is revealed supremely in Jesus Christ, but also the living Spirit present in all of life.

Wisdom is properly a way to bring together theory and practice (as the book of James illustrates), as well as theology and applied ethics (as evident in the letters of Paul). Wisdom is the bridge by which we live faithfully in our particular context in the light of what we know about the world. Wisdom focuses on the "how"—doing the right thing at the right time. Wisdom (in the light of God's reign, as God calls us to be a people) is a way for lay persons in their professions to think about responsibility in society (how to live faithfully in the land).

Wisdom is, furthermore, a way to incorporate arenas of discourse, like the "created order" and "natural law." We insist, however, that such wisdom be integrally connected with Christology and the wisdom of the cross, so as not to become an independent, autonomous sphere (e.g. a separate "orders of creation," as in Luther's theology). Wisdom is a way to incorporate secular knowledge, while at the same time subjecting such knowledge to our theological and ethical plumb line of the wisdom of the cross.

In our Mennonite peace theology, we have tended to focus our attention on prophetic modes of discourse in the Bible, modes that emphasize our critique and stand over against the fallen social order. While not ignoring these modes of discourse, in this project we focus on how we faithfully live as citizens *within* the social order, not only on how we live *over against* it. We think this concept of wisdom helps us move beyond the impasse of one- or two-kingdom theology. We do live in the tension between God's call to be faithful and the fallen orders of the world, (hence our use of two-kingdom language). Nevertheless, God's kingdom is one, a liberating power within the world. Our task is to discern how God is working in the world, so that the narrative of God's calling us as a people is integrated with wise living in the land. It is this kind of wise living that will transform social orders in the direction of God's will. Thus we attempt to follow Jesus, who as a prophet also embodied wisdom in his words and actions.

IV. ORDERING WITHIN A PEACE THEOLOGY

Around the outer circle we have identified six areas of concern that need consideration if we are to live faithfully in the land. The arrows suggest dynamic movement, that these six areas connect integrally with each other and overlap. The reader should not assume that this list of six areas is comprehensive or complete. Our model focuses primarily on social systems and how one orders societal institutions such as a legal systems, political organizations, and economic structures so that they serve the common good. We recognize that we could address other important issues such as gender, education, the family, the arts, or other aspects of culture. At the same time the six areas do cover a wide spectrum of concerns: creation care, justice, truth-telling, peacemaking, order, and diversity. These are some of the most important elements to be factored into any consideration of what it means to live faithfully in the land.

Our primary focus in this project is on what we have tentatively labeled "ordered creativity—domination/lawlessness." In the earlier stages of our research project we used the language of "order/disorder." However, we soon realized the problems with this language. These two terms are not simply opposites, the one "bad" and the other "good." Sometimes the most ordered systems are violent and repressive. At the same time, disorder is not completely negative. Some chaos or disorder can lead to creativity and change. However, we also recognized the destructive consequences of lawlessness. So we have searched to find language to recognize the positive polar tension between proper order and dysfunctional disorder. Thus we juxtapose the positive concept "ordered creativity" with both extremes of "domination" and "lawlessness." To flourish, people do depend upon ordered systems upon which they can rely for life. At the same time, within this order there must be the opportunity for novelty, for creative freedom to initiate processes that acknowledge greater complexity and create new opportunities. Regardless of the language we use to describe this relationship between order and novelty, the important focus of this project is the positive task suggested by the words in the parentheses under these categories: "calling the powers to their life-giving purpose," for example.

How do we call the powers to their life-giving purpose? We recognize that one cannot consider ordering apart from doing justice, peacemaking, truth-telling, living with diversity, and caring for creation. We intentionally state our engagement with these issues as verbs, as an active process. We want to avoid the presumption of a kind of utopian thinking, a recipe for the good society that could paralyze us from acting because it is "impossible" to achieve. Though the concept of the kingdom of God does suggest a vision of a gospel order, nevertheless, as we have already pointed out, the kingdom of God calls us to participate in a transforming process. Our focus on process suggests that we identify doable, practical, empirically verifiable processes of faithful living in the land that serve the common good.

Mennonites have usually viewed the ordering function of government as an institution of the fall. However, this is too limited a view. Even if we could imagine a world free of sin, we humans would still need to order our lives together. We would need rules/laws, structures of decision making, and assignments of differentiated roles. Ordering is integral to a doctrine of creation that recognizes human beings as social animals. Ordering takes place in the actual world, not in a perfect world without sin, but in a world in which human pride and egoistic self-interest taint all human behavior. We live in an imperfect world, and sometimes human beings behave in ways that threaten the peace and well-being of others. These factors of human sinfulness and imperfection complicate immensely the question of how to rightly order our lives together. There is much work that Mennonites need to do on these questions in order to develop a more adequate and comprehensive peace theology.

Some Mennonites have resolved these questions by handing over the ordering functions (policing, responsibility for the legal order) to others (non-Christians who are "outside the perfection of Christ," as the 1527 Anabaptist Schleitheim Confession of Faith puts it). We do not think that this way of understanding a two-kingdom position is adequate in a comprehensive peace theology that calls Christians "to seek the peace of the city where we live." We believe that Christians need to participate in helping build a well-ordered society that is just and reliable. We do not see a reason to exclude this arena from Christian responsibility. Neither did other Anabaptist leaders like Pilgram Marpeck or Menno Simons.

Many of us living in Canada and the United States tend to take for granted the stable institutional structures of law, the courts, electoral processes for the transfer of power, legislative processes for decision making, and a stable economic system. But these systems often do not serve well the marginal and poor within North America. And when we listen to our brothers and sisters in areas of the world like Palestine or Colombia,[5] an ordered system that is reliable and just is often the need. Can these responsibilities simply be passed off to others? We believe our responsibility is to imagine creative ways in which Christians can contribute to this ordering dimension of the peace of the city. North American Mennonites benefit from these structures of order (and some are at the same time harmful to others in the larger global community). Furthermore, many of us are direct participants in these structures through professions like law, teaching, social work, and public administration. We need to think theologically about what these involvements mean, and how we can live faithfully to avoid simply being acculturated to the "standards" of our profession.

These then are some of the questions that have shaped this project:

1. How do we view the institutions of law and order, whether at local, provincial and state, or international levels? At what level (international to local) should different types of issues be addressed? How should law be theologically grounded? Is there a common basis of law in a pluralistic world? What is our view of the United Nations Universal Declaration of Human Rights? What are the ethical norms for good law? How do we view the processes for the administration of law? . . . litigation? . . . criminal law? . . . the role of coercive functions of the police in upholding law? What are the causes of disorder and security, and how do we address these underlying causes?

2. What is the place of policing in a peace theology? How do we view the intervention of the police function to arrest, bring to trial, and punish behavior that is a threat to the well-being and safety of people? Are there nonviolent practices that could be brought to bear in order to protect the good and prevent harm? Does this "sword" function ultimately rest on the threat of violent force? Or is a nonviolent approach to force possible? Can we identity non-lethal forms of coercive force that we as pacifists could use and support? How do we distinguish between policing and war?

3. Do we have a special contribution to make to the above questions from the standpoint of a peace theology and ethic? Can we make a contribution that provides a creative leaven in wider thinking about these issue, similar to the contributions Mennonites have made in restorative justice (Howard Zehr) and in peacebuilding (John Paul Lederach)? What knowledge can we as Mennonites draw upon that goes beyond mere theoretical knowledge? Do we have wisdom—grounded in empirical research and experiences of living with the struggle of what it means to be faithful—to practice the right ordering of society?

NOTES

1. Glen Harold Stassen and David P. Gushee, *Kingdom Ethics: Following Jesus in Contemporary Context* (Downers Grove, Ill.: InterVarsity Press, 2003).

2. Perry B. Yoder, *Shalom: The Bible's Word for Salvation, Justice, and Peace* (Newton, Kan.: Faith and Life Press, 1987).

3. Walter Wink, *Engaging the Powers: Discernment and Resistance in a World of Domination* (Minneapolis: Fortress Press, 1992).

4. Gerald W. Schlabach, "Deuteronomic or Constantinian: What is the Most Basic Problem for Christian Social Ethics?" in *The Wisdom of the Cross: Essays in Honor of John Howard Yoder*, eds. Stanley Hauerwas, et al. (Grand Rapids: Eerdmans, 1999), 450.

5. In the MCC Peace Committee meeting in Akron in March 2003, Ricardo Esquivia, Director of Justapaz in Colombia, used the word "institutionality" to describe the structures which are necessary in any society. In Colombia there is a need to strengthen the rule of law or institutionality, and the civil structures that offer the possibility of life.

PART II

SEEKING THE WELFARE OF THE CITY: ESSAYS ON PUBLIC PEACE, JUSTICE, AND ORDER

Conference Papers

_____

SECTION A

A Church Perspective on Security, Safety, and the Common Good

—5—

PARTNERS IN GOD'S PASSION

Mary H. Schertz

Concern for public security and debates over how to work toward the common good have been polarizing. Recent U.S. elections make this abundantly clear, but it is not just true for countries. Mennonite denominations in North America have also found these issues polarizing.

Many Mennonites take national security very seriously and compromise their traditional commitments to pacifism and nonviolence as they seek the welfare of their neighbors and communities. Our civil obedience to God-ordained public orders, and concern for the safety and well-being of our neighbors, they believe, demand that we support national efforts to protect the state even if we do not personally take up arms. Other Mennonites take the commitments to pacifism and nonviolence very seriously and dismiss national security as a concern unworthy of a truly trusting Christian. We are citizens of the world, not of a particular nation, they insist, and our concern is for the welfare of the entire inhabitants of that world, not just those around us.

Both trains of thought can lead to a callous disregard for the concerns of real human beings. Well-intentioned support for national values can neither face squarely the numbers of Iraqi casualties nor the innocence of many of these dead people. But neither can well-intentioned dismissal of national values face squarely the fears of our neighbors across the street.

Some of our theological and ecclesiological understandings have fed this polarization. Our concern to know and practice the will of God, our concepts of the world or the state,[1] and our assumptions about how we relate to it have been especially divisive. My argument in this essay is that if we discern and practice the will of God within the larger framework of God's passion—both God's love and God's fury—we may find a view of the relationship between church and world that bridges our polarization. Doing so should help us move into more positive and helpful interactions with our neighbors, our countries, and our world as we face issues of real and lasting security for all God's creatures.

Attempts to define the state in terms of the will of God have actually contributed to our impasse. If we understand the ordination of the state as God's will, then we too quickly understand the will of the state as the will of God. Ordination confers blessing and approval on the actions of the state. If we understand the state to be fallen—a vanquished foe of God's victory over the principalities and powers—then we too quickly dismiss its role as an agent ordained by God for the common good. However, if we understand the state, both ordained and fallen, as the object of God's passion, God's love, and fury, we are freed to participate in the public arena fully as God's partner in loving the world and telling the truth.

God's ordination of the state does not necessarily confer approval of all its decisions; God regards with divine passion what God does not approve. Nor does fallenness or recognition that the state is a "power" limit God's ability to work in, with, and through a political or civic situation in all its sinful reality. The divine passion fully encompasses the world, with all its peoples and its structures. Recognizing our world as the object of God's passion and recognizing that we discern and obey God's will as partners with that passion frees us to act creatively for the security of God's creatures at home and abroad.

GOD'S WORLD

Just how we think about the question of the relationship of believers to the world is not immediately apparent. One of our fundamental issues is where to enter into the biblical material. Typically we have begun inquiries into how believers should relate to the world in which we find ourselves by thinking about nature or politics. We think cosmologically or sociologically. Both series of questions, as points of entry into the construction of a biblical theology, are complex and large. The canonical material on cosmology (that is, how to think about nature and the universe) is vast, almost as big as the world itself. We could profitably talk about creation, concepts of multiple heavens (2 Cor 12:2), as well as nature in all its glorious beauty and consummate indifference. In the pursuit of these questions, we would discover that some of the biblical assumptions about the cosmos are obscure and barely understandable to people with modern and postmodern mindsets. How do we deal with an earth inhabited by giants who copulate with human women, as in Genesis 6? Or how do we think about spirits imprisoned since the time of Noah to whom Jesus goes to preach after his death, as in 1 Peter 4? Then, of course, we could look at Ezekiel or Revelation!

The scholarship regarding the biblical canon from a sociological perspective is equally vast and complex. Many of the biblical references to entities such as the state and its governance reflect politics and social realities that are not much more available to us than ancient cosmologies. How then do we understand ancient Israel to be God's nation? What about the other nations to which Israel is to be a light? How do we understand Cyrus, as God's messiah, God's anointed one, in Isaiah 45:1? In the New Testament does the church assume the role of Israel as God's state? What about the governments ordained by God? If they are ordained by God what is our civil obedience? What do we do about conflicting strands of thought and vastly differing attitudes toward these principalities and powers within the Bible itself?

The cosmological and sociological tasks are both challenging and vital. What I want to propose, however, is that there is a consideration that stands prior to issues of world and state. That prior consideration is rooted in theology rather than cosmology, sociology, or even Christology. I am proposing that an appropriate understanding of God's passion as lover and judge of the world might empower us to be more fully engaged in the world as citizens and peacemakers.

To recognize God's passion for the world, a passion that expresses itself in both love and wrath, should empower us as citizens of God's kingdom and peacemakers in God's world. It should empower us to participate in the life of the nation and to wrestle with it for the common security, the common good. In so doing, we will discern and practice God's will but we will do so as bodies that inhabit spaces and nations in solidarity with all God's creatures. To use more familiar terminology, my proposal is that the exercise of imagining God's passion for the world frees us to seek the peace of the city, the city that is also us. The moral agenda of seeking that peace is by no means diminished if we understand it within the rubric of grace. There is no more vigorous morality than that which compassion and truth demand.

LOVE

For many of us, the most familiar (and no doubt over-used) passage of the entire Bible is John 3:16. I am certain that most of us can recite it in flawless King James English. A good, traditional understanding of this text assumes that what the evangelist is talking about when he says that God loves the world is that God loves the individual people in the world. The giving of God's Son has to do with God sending Jesus to die on the cross for our sins. Believing and not perishing has to do with individual sinners who become convinced of a particular confession about Jesus and, as a result, will go to heaven instead of hell when they die.

I say "good, traditional" understanding because Jesus is talking to one man—Nicodemus—and the text uses singular verbs and participles through out. Clearly, the salvation envisioned in this text demands that individuals choose whether they will indeed love the light or love the darkness. Like Nicodemus, and like every Israelite from the time God gave

Moses the law at Sinai, each individual at the end of the day must determine his or her own allegiance. What will we ultimately choose? Will we work the deeds of evil or the deeds worked out in God (3:19-21)?

Individual salvation is not, however, the only thing this text has in view. The text does not, in fact, say that God loves and saves us as individuals. This text says that God loves the world. It is the world as created, as collective, that God loves. It is also, in 3:17, the created world, the world as collective that is not condemned but saved through this giving of the Son. Yes, the text goes on to say that this salvation of the world involves individual choice, but that is the second thing the text says, not the first thing.

The text also does not say anything about the death of Jesus. We have read God's love for the world so long in light of the cross that we have a hard time thinking about it any other way. Again, it is appropriate to include the cross in references to "giving" and "sending" the Son. But it is not appropriate to limit the giving and sending to the cross. The more immediate context here is the incarnation, not the death and resurrection. At this point, we are in John's third chapter, not the end of the gospel. Jesus is still very much alive and the cross is a cloud on the horizon. The miracle of the incarnation is what the introduction of the gospel insists upon communicating. Birth, new birth, is the image that Nicodemus struggles to comprehend in this immediate story. The images of birth, Jesus's incarnation, and the new birth that he wants to impart are the first references for the giving and sending. It is important to consider the narrative framework for this understanding even if it transcends that narrative framework.

God's love for the world is embodied in the incarnation as well as the cross. Incarnation, as John Howard Yoder once said so powerfully in a meditation on John 1, means that "God acted in a totally human way; he unhesitatingly entrusted his own cause to the hands of ordinary people."[2] In that same meditation, Yoder follows Raymond Brown's translation of the grace and truth of the incarnation (1:14) as "enduring love."[3]

God as Jesus, tenting among us, is described as God's enduring love—God's grace and truth. This incarnation of God in Jesus holds together creation and redemption. The reality that Jesus preexisted, that he was part of the creation (1:3), establishes that there is one set of principles underlying the natural order (as we have sometimes termed it) and the redemptive order.[4] That conviction, of course, became one of the primary tenets of Yoder's work as it developed and grew through the years. He concludes that mediation with an affirmation that

> [John] is not trying to say anything about whether it is possible that the impossible has happened. He is rather testifying that what God always was, and what the Word of God was always trying to do, in creation and in the Garden of Eden, and in Abraham and in Moses and in the prophets, shining on faithfully even though the darkness did not receive it, continues. That same revelatory thrust within the very nature of God has now reached its culmination. One grace has succeeded another. Enduring love, which was always there, could now be beheld in its fulfillment. That this has happened is not a puzzle at all; it is the way it had to be if God is the God he always was, the God of enduring love.[5]

The central resounding note of the incarnation is that God loves the world, as a whole, as it can become certainly, but also as it is. What is more, God loves the world passionately, wildly, nonsensically, unconditionally as, in fact, only God can love. When we render John 3:16 with only individual salvation in mind, or even salvation of the whole world one-by-one (another version of individualism), we miss a central link between creation and redemption. The same passion that conceived and birthed the world is also the passion that is quite intent upon saving the world.

FURY

As God's love is an expression of the divine passion, so is God's wrath. I suspect that as humans we are always courting dualism. We have trouble wrapping our minds around the divine paradox that God's love and God's wrath are concomitant components of God's passion. Our proclivity is to emphasize one and downplay the other. We have indeed all had our fill of a traditional emphasis on judgment over love. So now, in our contemporary culture and in our contemporary peace church culture, God's wrath is a hugely unpopular notion. But I would contend that a peace theology can no more ignore the one than the other.

We ought to know, simply from our own experience with human relationships, that love and fury are not oppositions. We can know these passions intimately in the same relationship, sometimes in the same moment. Long ago, Beverly Harrison from Union Seminary in New York wrote an article she called "The Work of Anger in the Power of Love."[6] She argued there that the opposite of love is apathy, not anger. Anger, she continued, is an essential indication that something is not right. It is an essential element of truth, upon which love—true love, that is—is built.

It follows, therefore, that the divine wrath springs from the same well as the divine love. The wrath of God is the truth-telling face of God's love. As John W. de Gruchy notes in his case study of the Truth in Reconciliation Commission in South Africa, "If we are truly going to understand the relationship between justice and forgiveness in the process of reconciliation from a biblical perspective, we must keep in mind that 'God's wrath' against evil is presupposed."[7]

Again, an analogy from human relationship seems useful. In human terms, we are "saved"—that is, we grow, we become more than we were, we learn forgiveness, we learn to laugh and cry, we become fully human—through the love and anger of those with whom we are intimate. Love and anger, unconditional acceptance and rigorous expectations, paradoxical as they may seem, are by no means oppositions. Together they become the very life blood of our most important human interactions. Why would that not also be true of both our own relationship with God and God's relationship to the world?

As Miroslav Volf put it so eloquently when he was at the Associated Mennonite Biblical Seminary in early 2004,

> God is not only the creator of all reality. God is also its redeemer. The aim of God's redemptive activity is to overcome oppositional dualities so as to leave room in the whole of reality only for reconciled differences. By becoming flesh, the Word united itself intimately precisely to that which has alienated itself from God (1:14). Moreover, God loved the world which was opposed to him (3:16) so by becoming flesh the Word may also be the "Lamb of God who takes away the sin of the world."[8]

HUMAN RESPONSIBILITY

What does God as lover and judge of the world have to do with us as citizens and peacemakers? What does it have to do with the polarization in our denomination on questions of support and participation in national agenda?

I know, from many conversations with students, that troubling questions arise from biblical notions of God's fury. Is God violent? If we grant God's prerogative to judge, sometimes violently, at least as the biblical canon reports God's actions at some points, do we relinquish the ethical basis for nonviolence? Can God be a God of peace and a God of war at the same time? Does that tilt the discussion of our participation in the national forum toward support for just wars? Important, and intriguing, as those questions are, I would contend that they are not really the most important ones.

Our task, I believe is to define our human responsibility as partners in God's passion rather than as mirrors or extensions of God's passion. The parameters of human responsibility look different under the rubric of divine passion than they do under the rubric of divine will. Again, I am certainly not suggesting that the discernment and practice of God's will is not part of Christian faithfulness. Those acts of Christian faithfulness are vital. But our practice of faith must reflect the reality that we are not God and we are not responsible to implement God's will in the world. We are to obey God's will for us.

Simply put, we are God's creatures, God's bodies. We are located in both nature and politics, but as God's servants rather than as God's agents. We are part of the world that God loves. In creaturely solidarity with that loved and judged world we are to love each other and our enemies. We are to practice the discernment of church discipline. The God who created the world, the God who is in love with the creation, is the lover and judge of the world. That God is the one who acts in the world in both love and judgment.

Understanding and responding to God's passion—becoming partners in God's passion—requires profound relinquishment and profound activism. We need to give up the effort to transform the world and join our God, who is already at work transforming the world.

We must relinquish notions of the world as a soulless wasteland. The world, including our communities and our nations, is exactly what God is in love with. When we cannot love this world, we simply need to recognize that God does. We must also relinquish notions that the salvation of the world happens through us and that it happens as the world becomes more like us, or joins us. Salvation demands each of our allegiances but salvation is not about us. Humanity, ancient and contemporary, overwhelmed with evil, overwhelmed with indifference, and overwhelmed with the size of the redemptive task, is prone to settle with "us," whether that is Israel or the church or any other social group. But the message of the incarnation is that God is not about to settle for a fragment of the world. As we have known from the beginning of Israel's history, the biblical God is a jealous God, a greedy God, a creative and endlessly resourceful God with a passionate and imaginative love for the entire world. In light of that love, our careful boundaries between the world and us seem not only pretentious but also irrelevant.

Finally, we must relinquish both violence and powerlessness. As Ray Gingerich argues, nonviolence is power and violence is a failure of power. An example he cites, one that I find moving and compelling, is the amount of power to work toward freedom and democracy in the world that the United States relinquished by invading Iraq.[9] As partners with God in God's passion for the world, we have the power to be faithful stewards of, and witnesses to, the peace and justice we cherish. As partners of God's passion, we have the power to participate in healing acts of compassion and in healing acts of telling the truth. Those acts of compassion and truth-telling require generous-but-critical participation in the public arena.

In our relinquishment and in our taking up of responsibility to be active partners with God in the world, our example is none other than Jesus Christ. If our understanding of the world is primarily theological, our understanding of ethics is primarily Christological. For the communities to whom the epistle of 1 Peter was written, the most important meaning of the cross was not that Jesus died for sinners. The most important meaning of the cross, the way Jesus's suffering was "for us," was his example of radical trust.

For this early interpretation of the cross, its crucial meaning was two actions that Jesus took in dying. First Peter 2:21-24 is a chiastic hymn, a common literary form in the biblical material in which the main emphasis gets pulled into the center. In this case, verse 23 makes the point.

> For to this you have been called, because Christ suffered also for you, leaving you an example,
> So that you should follow in his steps—
>> WHO did not sin, and there was no deceit found in his mouth [*stomatos*].
>>> WHO, being abused, did not reply with a curse, *Suffering* did not threaten,
>>> But entrusted himself to the one who judges justly.
>> WHO himself bore our sins in his body [*somatos*] on the tree),
> So that free from sins, we might live for justice.
> For by his wounds you have been healed.

As those middle three lines state so clearly, Jesus's first action was a decision not to retaliate, not to revile in return for reviling. But his second action was even more important because it grounded his first action. His second action was to entrust himself to the Just Judge. The life and ministry of Jesus, and the purpose toward which he had been moving since his temptations in the wilderness, culminated in this testimony that reconciliation—between God and the world, and among the peoples of the world—is not a matter of containing evil but of transforming evil. It is a freely chosen, decisive action. It is a simple but powerful decision to break the cycle of violence. At the heart of the cross is a relinquishment of revenge. At the heart of the cross is a handing over of revenge to the just judge.

In the end, creation cannot be separated from redemption, the incarnation cannot be separated from the cross, love cannot be separated from fury. Nor can the ordination of the state be separated from God's victory over the principalities and powers. But for our moment in the river of life and faith, we are called to be partners with God's passion for the world. We are called to join God in the hard work of transformation, and, in that work, to fully enjoy the loving and holy God.

Notes

1. The issues of the world and state cannot be collapsed, of course. Yet in this discussion they are more or less interchangeable. When it becomes important to distinguish I will do so.

2. John Howard Yoder, "Glory in a Tent," unpublished paper from *Festival of the Word*, Goshen, Indiana, April 19, 1974, p. 4. Associated Mennonite Biblical Seminary library, general papers.

3. Ibid., 6.

4. Ibid., 10.

5. Ibid., 3-4.

6. Beverly Wildung Harrison, "The Power of Anger in the Work of Love," in *Making the Connections: Essays in Feminist Social Ethics*, ed. Carol S. Robb (Boston: Beacon Press, 1985), 3–21.

7. John W. De Gruchy, *Reconciliation: Restoring Justice* (Minneapolis: Fortress Press, 2002), 168.

8. Miroslav Volf, "Johannine Dualism and Contemporary

Pluralism," Paper from Lecture Series, Associated Mennonite Biblical Seminary, February 2004, 25.

9. Ray Gingerich, "The Resurrection: The Nonviolent Politics of God," *Vision* 5, no. 1 (Fall 2004): 79–87. This is a ground breaking analysis of power in relation to violence and nonviolence.

FOR FURTHER READING

De Gruchy, John W. *Reconciliation: Restoring Justice.* Minneapolis: Fortress Press, 2002.

Gingerich, Ray. "The Resurrection: The Nonviolent Politics of God." *Vision* 5, no. 1 (Fall 2004): 79–87.

Harrison, Beverly Wildung. "The Power of Anger in the Work of Love." In *Making the Connections: Essays in Feminist Social Ethics*, edited by Carol S. Robb, 3–21. Boston: Beacon Press, 1985.

6

Becoming Strategic Doves in a Land of Hawks: Alternative Security Through an Anabaptist Lens

J. Daryl Byler and Lisa Schirch

Where do Anabaptists in the United States look for security, order, and justice? Do we fall in line alongside millions of Republicans and Democrats to support policies that urge a strong military response to terrorism? Or does the call of Jesus to "be wise as serpents and innocent as doves" (Matt 10:16) offer a distinctive, less militaristic, alternative? Do we base our support on a traditional two-kingdom understanding, where Christians live out a pacifist lifestyle, while refusing to criticize governments who use unbridled lethal force in attempts to create order and security? Or do we believe that the ethic of Jesus has application for both the church and the state? Are we tempted by quick military solutions to the complex problems associated with an age of terror, or do we in fact trust God's promise to care for us?

These questions make us think about our unique position in Christian history. Post-9/11 American Christians are in a different situation than when Jesus talked of the Roman Empire and its effect on the Jewish people it was oppressing. We also face something different from early Anabaptists whose own repressive governments were persecuting them. Today, Anabaptists in the United States are no longer oppressed or martyred for their beliefs or lifestyles. We benefit from, and are complicit with, our fellow citizens in consuming a disproportionate share of the world's resources, gained in part from unfair U.S. trade and military policies. We come from a long tradition of Anabaptists who did not support the state. But this time, the state is fighting "on our behalf" rather than against us. How will we respond?

Can we be "strategic doves" who are innocent of harming others, yet, in the words of Matthew, "wise as serpents" in thinking about global security issues? Can we blend peace theology and practical strategies for building a secure world for ourselves and people in other countries?

In this chapter we are attempting to use images of hawks and doves without simply associating them with right-leaning or left-leaning politics. Indeed, in the post-9/11 world, both Republicans and Democrats have overwhelmingly supported militaristic or "hawkish" responses in an attempt to make Americans feel more secure.

The biblical image of doves, which long predates its current political usage, is associated with both the presence of God's Spirit and peace. This symbol is familiar to Anabaptists today, being incorporated into the logos or both Mennonite Church USA and Mennonite Central Committee. In now-standard political terms, "doves" often connote naïveté and an underestimation of the power of evil in the world. The goal of this chapter, however, is to encourage Christians, specifically Anabaptist Christians living in the United States, to become "strategic doves" who are able to articulate the complexity of current security challenges, and to offer realistic options for addressing these challenges.

The War on Terror

Many U.S. citizens answer the question, "What will make us safe?" with the simple answer "a war on terror." Following on the heels of a "war on poverty" and a "war on drugs," the war on terror takes a "get tough" approach to security issues. Several broad themes guide this new war.

First, the war on terror defines terror as the primary form of evil in the world. There has been little introspection or nuance about any United States or Western contributions to evil. The war on terror has focused on direct violence, specifically acts of terror, but has ignored structural violence, like unjust economic policies, war, or occupation.

Second, the war on terror emphasizes military responses over the rule of law. Rather than emphasizing accountable policing techniques and judicial processes to apprehend then try those who have planned or perpetrated acts of terror, the war on terror has depended on overwhelming force and has badly undermined notions of due process.

Third, the war on terror has relied on unilateral over multilateral approaches. For example, when the United States could not get United Nations authorization for a war against Iraq, it simply bypassed this legitimate international body and created a weak "coalition of the willing." While there are instances of increased U.S. cooperation with other countries (e.g. intelligence sharing, freezing assets of suspected terror cells, and security training), by in large the war on terror has isolated the United States from the rest of the world and contributed to widespread anti-American sentiment.

The U.S. war on terror, which may go on for decades, already has many faces:

• The United States has fought wars in Afghanistan and Iraq. The human cost includes: 28,000-31,500 Afghan and Iraqi civilian deaths (one study says more than 100,000 Iraqi civilians); along with more than 2,300 U.S. and allied troops; and unnumbered thousands of Taliban, al Qaeda, and Iraqi fighters. Additionally, tens of thousands of civilians and troops have been injured. As of April 2005, the U.S. Congress has appropriated some $300 billion to fund these wars.

• The war with Iraq introduced the concept of "preventive war"—that is, going to war, not in response to actual or imminent attack, but out of fear that the nation *might* be attacked in the unknown future. This policy is especially problematic when those fears are based on faulty intelligence, as in the case of Iraq. And it sets a frightening precedent for the rest of the world.

• The United States has increased military spending from $300 billion to nearly $500 billion a year, including the cost of the current wars. For the first time ever, the U.S. military budget roughly equals the rest of the world's military budgets combined. To put this amount in perspective, for $500 billion, the United States could instead:

-fully fund global anti-hunger efforts for 20 years; or

-fully fund worldwide AIDS programs for 50 years; or

-insure that every child in the world is given basic immunizations for the next 166 years; or

-provide 24.2 million students with full four-year scholarships at public universities in the United States; or

-hire 8.6 million new public school teachers in the United States for a year.

• The war on terror has been used to justify fast-track deployment of a U.S. missile defense shield—which violates long-term international treaty commitments—and to promote research for new types of "usable" nuclear weapons. This latter effort places the United States in the awkward and duplicitous position of trying to convince other countries to get rid of their nuclear weapons programs, while planning new nuclear weapons for itself.

• The United States has dramatically abridged the civil liberties of some U.S. citizens and legal residents. It has selectively applied the Geneva Conventions to detainees held in U.S. custody in Afghanistan, Guantanamo Bay, and Iraq. According to Christian Peacemaker Teams, the International Red Cross, and Amnesty International, the graphic pictures of abuse at Abu Ghraib prison made public in the spring of 2004 are only part of a much broader pattern of abuse.

In spite of all these efforts, most Americans feel less secure today, several years after embarking on the war on terror, according to an Associate Press poll in April 2004. In both Afghanistan and Iraq, politicians and military strategists argued the war would be quick and decisive, as they assumed the military forces within these two countries would quickly surrender once they recognized America's superior fighting capacity.

While war produced some dramatic changes, today both Afghanistan and Iraq face uncertain futures. Both countries have held elections, but neither yet has a well-functioning government. Insurgents in both countries continue to resist U.S. forces and those who are seen as U.S. collaborators. According to recent research by reputable security think tanks in Washington, D.C., and London the number of Al Qaeda members has *increased* since 2001. Every war waged on Afghanistan or Iraq becomes, in the words of a British Minister of Parliament, a self-defeating "recruiting drive for terrorists."

Military solutions to current security issues fail because they prompt rather than quell the desire for people to fight the United States. Some military strategists now acknowledge that America's superior military power cannot keep it safe. The United States cannot win a war against militant religious extremists with old military strategies based on overwhelming the enemy with coercive military power.

The war on terror makes us less safe because it is based on the faulty assumption that U.S. military power can crush the will of others to fight. Reactions in the United States to September 11 are exactly those predicted by Al Qaeda, which portrays the United States as greedy, domineering, and aggressive. For example, as noted earlier, U.S. military spending continues to increase every year, taking money away from government spending on social services, education, healthcare or infrastructure programs that could save lives in the face of natural disasters such as Hurricane Katrina. Despite its wealth, the United States is at the bottom of the list of per capita economic aid to other countries. Other developed nations give ten-to-twenty times more per capita in development aid than does the United States.

The Nature of the Global Security Challenge

Eastern Mennonite University's Center for Justice and Peacebuilding and Mennonite Central Committee's Washington Office are seeking to understand and analyze the changing and complex nature of global security by listening closely to our partners in North America and abroad in order to understand how people from different parts of the world view security challenges. We must in fact recognize that Al Qaeda-brand terrorism is a new and different security challenge.

First, today's security challenge is outside of the state system; it is global rather than national or regional. Internal conflicts and civil wars in other countries are increasingly framed as part of the global war on terror, giving governments everywhere the excuse to use violence rather than dialogue and negotiation to address issues of injustice that spawned these internal conflicts. While many of these conflicts have had nothing to do with Al Qaeda or any global terrorist network in the past, government repression is in fact making the connections a self-fulfilling prophecy. Now there are links, for example, between militants in Iraq fighting U.S. occupation and Al Qaeda. Intelligence research shows these links did not exist before the U.S. war against Iraq.

Military strategies have worked best when there is an identifiable center to attack. And traditional diplomacy is based on negotiations between top level national leaders. Al Qaeda does not fit into the traditional state structure. Al Qaeda is dispersed and decentralized around the world. It is more like a group of hornets stirred up from their nest than a large beast that can be captured or killed. It is virtually impossible to disarm or kill everyone who supports Al Qaeda or groups with similar visions.

Second, because Al Qaeda is not part of the state system, communication with them is limited. While strategists typically think of war as a continuation of diplomacy by other means, today's war on terror has no diplomatic channels such as embassies or hotlines to communicate and negotiate with those who threaten us. Osama bin Laden asserts that the United

States does not understand anything but the language of violence. A psychology of fear and insecurity contributes to the same feelings here in the United States. Many Americans see violence as the only language to communicate to Al Qaeda that they must stop their terror. Both sides use a "hawkish" strategy based on lethal force.

Third, Al Qaeda-brand terrorism will only get more terrifying as laboratories around the world produce new, more compact, and more deadly weapons. Weapons of mass destruction have gone from a complexity, price, and size that only a few wealthy countries could produce to inexpensive suitcase-sized bombs that could allow a few individuals to kill millions. In addition, travel has become much easier over the last few decades despite new security checks at airports and borders. The ability of people to use weapons of mass destruction and terror is increasing faster than the U.S. military's capacity to attempt to deter or stop them.

Fourth, Al Qaeda-brand terrorism calls for a change in global structures, not territorial lines or state power. Al Qaeda fights for ideas, not territory. Militaries, on the other hand, protect territories and economic interests, not ideas. According to bin Laden's "Letter to America," which was published by the British press but not in the United States, Al Qaeda engages in terrorism both to live out its understanding of Islam and to resist what it perceives to be Western political, economic, cultural, and military imperialism. Al Qaeda wants the United States to stop supporting Israel, to stop supporting dictatorships in Middle Eastern countries who promise continued U.S. access to oil at the expense of real democracy, and to withdraw U.S. troops from the "holy soil of Islam."

Today's anti-Western sentiment is a mutation of an older anti-colonial message that resonates with many people in the world, even though they may despise the methods of terrorism. The popularity of the anti-Western message is unlikely to fade over time or to disappear in the face of overwhelming coercive force. People everywhere have a basic need for self-determination and feel angry and frustrated when they see outsiders from the West intervening in their countries. These anti-colonial ideas also hold wide appeal for many people in the world in an era when economic policies backed by Western countries have led to increased global poverty.

Poverty increases the insults brought by U.S. and Western cultural, political, and military presence in the Middle East and other places around the globe. Poverty is a breeding ground of terrorism in two ways. First, some desperately poor people look for ways of fighting the system that provide no opportunities for them to improve their lives. Western economic policies and support for unjust governments in the developing world are often seen as the biggest obstacle to development. Second, the relatively well-educated and middle class planners within Al Qaeda who orchestrated September 11 and other large acts of terror use the poverty and humiliation of their people as a mobilizing force to increase anger against the West.

The Church's Response

Where do people of faith enter into this increasingly complex and insecure world? What has God taught us about strategy, in particular strategy for global security? How do people of faith understand the causes of conflict and insecurity? And if continuing to increase U.S. military power is not the solution to these challenges, what is?

While Anabaptists seek to be pacifists, we too frequently ignore the fact that we live within violent structures that make it impossible for us to be complete pacifists. We often fail to acknowledge our own complicity in violent systems and are too quick to judge others for their violence. We sometimes succumb to the temptation of believing that we are pure and pacifist. We allow the state's military to do the dirty work of fighting wars on our behalf, while we reap the benefits.

God's strategy calls us to move away from violence, to seek nonviolence in a violent world, and to be doves bringing peace rather than hawks calling for war. It focuses on long-term approaches that seek to prevent, reduce, transform, and help people recover from violence in all forms, even structural violence that has not yet led to massive civil unrest. At the same time it empowers people to foster relationships at all levels that sustain people and their environment. (For specific recommendations about how to engage in these tasks, see chapter 20.)

The Bible gives us wisdom and stories about human nature. It illustrates the role of human choice and responsibility. Jesus tells his followers that those who live by the sword will die by the sword. Those who seek their security through military power will become entangled and strangled in its web. Jesus provided examples for us and inspires us to make different choices—to love our neighbors and our enemies, and to share what we have with others. Jesus calls us away from greed and aggression toward compassion and love. He commissioned us to receive, enter into, and bear witness to the reign of God.

The rich biblical understanding of shalom recognizes that no one can be truly secure until all are secure. U.S. security is inherently tied to global and human security. God's strategy is to create a world where everyone is able to satisfy their basic needs for food, shelter, clothing, education, jobs, healthcare, respect, participation, self-determination, meaning, and bonding with others in "right relationships" (e.g. Isa 58; Mic 4:4; Matt 25:31-46; Luke 4:18-19). Many now refer to this notion of security as "human security," in contrast to traditional notions of "national security" or "military security."

In order for Anabaptist Christians to engage society and government in discussions of global security, we must begin by remembering three things: our baptism, our mission, and our context. The first is a matter of identity. The second is a matter of calling. And the third is a matter of citizenship.

1. Remembering our baptism

In the midst of the mighty Babylonian empire, Shadrach, Meshach, and Abednego remained true to their faith by remembering their identity. They were Hebrews and, therefore, would not bow before Nebuchadnezzar's golden statue (Dan 3:19-30). For Christians, baptism defines our own core identity.

It defines how we understand ourselves and our relationships. To the church at Galatia, Paul wrote: "As many of you as were baptized into Christ have clothed yourselves with Christ" (Gal 3:27). That is to say, in our baptism we are joined or yoked with Christ, or as the New Testament writers frequently describe it, we are "in Christ." That means that we fully identify ourselves with the life, teachings, death, and resurrection of Jesus. Like Jesus, we begin with the simple affirmation that God is our security.

But there is still more to our baptism. Paul wrote: "There is no longer Jew or Greek, there is no longer slave or free, there is no longer male and female . . ."—today Paul might add: there is no longer Canadian and American and Iraqi—"for all of you are one in Christ Jesus" (Gal 3:28). This is not to say that there are no longer distinctions. But these distinctions are no longer the core basis of our identity in the new order created in Christ. As Christians around the world, we have been baptized into one body. Every time we take communion we reaffirm that we are part of this global body. This body is the new creation (2 Cor 5:17), the new political reality that God is creating as a global witness to God's mighty power to reconcile.

Those who are bound together by faith are better able to traverse national boundaries and imagine approaches that focus on concerns for human and global security, not simply on national security interests. For Christians, citizenship in a particular nation must always be secondary to our Christian identity or citizenship as members of the body of Christ that transcends national borders and interests.

However there is also a danger in denying the power that these national identities still carry in the fallen world in which we live. As U.S. or Canadian citizens, we have enormous power and privileges that our sisters and brothers in the global South do not have. Even in the body of Christ, we cannot divorce ourselves of this reality of national citizenship.

2. Remembering our mission

Our mission seeks to answer the question of why we exist.

The New Testament has described our Christian mission in various ways: loving God completely and neighbor as self (Matt 22:37b-39); making disciples of all nations, teaching the way of Jesus (Matt 28:19-20); being "ambassadors for Christ," charged with the ministry of reconciliation (2 Cor 5:18-20); and making known the manifold wisdom of God to the principalities and powers (Eph 3:10). There is no space or time in this mission for dominating, hating, or seeking to destroy our enemies. Showing concern for and seeking the well-being of neighbor and enemy alike keeps us busy, full-time.

Menno Simons inspired early Anabaptists to practice an evangelical faith by clothing the naked, feeding the hungry, and sheltering the destitute. As development expert Jeffrey Sachs suggests, what the world needs to effectively stop terrorism are weapons of mass salvation. To restructure global trade and reorient the forces of globalization may reduce Western profits in the short run, but should lead to vast improvements in the quality of life in the developing world. Spending money on effective development programs is far more cost-effective compared to money spent to wage the ongoing military operations the U.S. government says are necessary to continue the war on terror. With better distribution, there are enough resources in the world to educate, feed, clothe, house, and provide healthcare for everyone.

3. Remembering our context

For citizens of the United States, it is also imperative to remember our context: We are Christians living in the world's sole superpower, the empire that is leading the global war on terror. *Theologically*, we do well to view ourselves as exiles living in this midst of the empire. We should never feel at home with policies of dominance, militarism, and unilateralism. We are people of the cross, not people of cruise missiles. But *politically*, we are very much citizens of this empire. Our global sisters and brothers remind us of this constantly. As citizens of the empire, we bear some responsibility for engaging the empire.

Temptation for exiles. If we see ourselves primarily as exiles living in the midst of the empire, our temptation may be to withdraw and isolate ourselves in an attempt to be distinct or pure. Indeed, many Anabaptists have taken comfort over the years in texts like Romans 13, which speak of government's role in bearing the sword. When our government engages in violence around the world, we may not be happy about it, but we have sometimes said that this is the way governments are and it is not our place to challenge them.

But we should not read Romans 13 as a carte blanche authorization of military force. Indeed, a *plain* reading of Romans 13 must recognize tight parameters for government's role in restraining evil. Romans 13 only permits the state to punish "the wrongdoer" (13:4). This suggests very limited, focused actions, more akin to police powers and judicial processes, which are used to restrain the wrongdoer without putting innocent civilians at risk. A plain reading of Romans 13 would seem to exclude modern warfare altogether, given its high rate of innocent civilian casualties. Declaring war to punish Saddam Hussein is like amputating your arm in order to get rid of a splinter in your finger.

Non-engagement also seems at odds with our stated mission as a church to love our neighbors as ourselves. For years, Anabaptists in the United States have engaged government about concerns that affect us, like the draft. So why would we not also engage government when our global sisters and brothers ask us to do so on their behalf?

Temptation for citizens. The primary temptation we face as citizens is one of assimilation. This has been the church's challenge since the time of Constantine. It has led many in the church to forge strong alliances with the state and embrace an uncritical patriotism. Even in our Anabaptist churches, we have seen a strong resurgence of this uncritical patriotism since September 11. But assimilation is certainly counter to the biblical teaching that the church not be "conformed to this world" (Rom 12:2).

Temptation for both exiles and citizens. Both exiles and citizens can face a third temptation: to undermine or overthrow the empire. Today, most Anabaptist peace and justice proponents would not advocate violent overthrow of the empire. But we do find it easy to lash out in anger, criticizing the empire's many faults, often without offering constructive alternatives. This approach lacks a posture of humility. The church has too often failed to live up to its own mission. So there is little room to be hypercritical of the government's failures. Indeed, both Peter and Paul remind us to show respect for governing authorities (1 Pet 2:13-17; Titus 3:1).

AN ANABAPTIST APPEAL TO GOVERNMENT

If neither isolation, nor assimilation, nor overthrow are appropriate, what does a healthy engagement look like? The prophet Jeremiah told the Jewish exiles in the heart of the Babylonian empire to "seek the welfare of the city where I have sent you into exile" (Jer 29:7a). What might it look like for Christians today to seek the welfare of the empire to which we "have been sent"?

An Anabaptist understanding of engaging or witnessing to the state always begins with a demonstration—not a march on Washington, but a demonstration of what God's reign looks like. The *Confession of Faith in a Mennonite Perspective* states: "We witness to the nations by being that 'city on a hill' which demonstrates the way of Christ" (Article 23). Can the North American church model something radically different by sharing global resources and power more equitably? Our relationships in the Mennonite World Conference offer us a demonstration plot to offer an alternative to the practices of empire.

But our confession of faith also says we are to call the nations "to move toward justice, peace, and compassion for all people" (Article 23). We must base any appeal to government on our best practices in the church. But such an appeal also requires us to extrapolate from those practices and articulate principles that are more broadly useful for governing authorities and society at large.

GOOD AND EVIL

Specifically, with regards to the war on terror, Anabaptists can make a significant contribution based on our theological understanding of good and evil. President Bush has declared that the war on terror is a battle between good and evil. Romans 12, a widely cited text among Anabaptist Christians, makes these basic points about good and evil:

a. We are to hate what is evil (Rom 12:9a). Christians are not neutral about evil. The Bible admonishes us to *turn from* (Ps 34:14, 37:27); *hate* (Ps 97:10, Rom 12:9); *have nothing to do with* (Ps 101:4); *shun* (Prov 14:16); *and avoid* (1 Thess 5:22) *evil.* So the church will do well to name and confront evil in its many forms. All of us have a tendency to see the worst evil as something that others do, however. Aleksandr Solzhenitsyn has wisely written: "If only there were evil people somewhere insidiously committing evil deeds, and it were necessary only to separate them from the rest of us and destroy them. But the line dividing good and evil cuts through the heart of every human being. And who is willing to destroy a piece of his own heart?" (*The Gulag Archipelago*, 2002, Harper Perennial).

The church should hold up a mirror to evil in all its multi-faceted forms. One of the problems since September 11 has been that some "progressive" Christians seemed ready almost immediately to "justify" the acts of terror by focusing on the sins of the United States. What happened on September 11 was clearly evil. All acts of terrorism represent a cruel disregard for human life. On the other hand, some "conservative" Christians focused only on the evil that the September 11 terrorists perpetrated, while refusing to consider the U.S. actions and policies that led to the anger behind the attacks.

The church will do well to name and confront evil in its many forms and to call governing authorities to do the same. We must ask that governments oppose the violence of militarism and imperialism and racism just as much as they oppose the violence of terror. A broader understanding of evil, and our own complicity in that evil, will lead to more humble and consistent international policies.

b. Only good is strong enough to overcome evil (Rom 12:17, 21). Our theology also teaches us something about how God overcomes evil in the world. Paul wrote to the Romans that "While we still were sinners, Christ died for us" (Rom 5:8). The cross is God's antidote for evil. Later, in Romans, Paul said: "Do not repay anyone evil for evil, but take thought for what is noble in the sight of all" (12:17). Paul concluded chapter 12 with these words: "Do not be overcome by evil, but overcome evil with good" (12:21). In an age of terror, the church needs to redouble its efforts to do good, "to take thought for what is noble in the sight of all." How might the church do a better job of listening to our global partners, entering ministries of accompaniment and solidarity, and actively seeking justice? In chapter 20 we offer specific suggestions.

While governments will likely not embrace the message of the cross fully, the church still does well to remind governing authorities of the basic principle that evil can only be overcome with good. By its example and analysis, the church must appeal to governing authorities to develop policies and practices that consistently show respect for human rights and the rule of law, and which promote just and mutual relationships and fair distribution of global resources.

Ultimately, it is strategies that seek the common good, and that aim to increase the security of all nations, which hold the greatest promise of increasing security for Americans who now live in fear of the next act of terror.

FOR FURTHER READING

Juhnke, James C., and Carol M. Hunter. *The Missing Peace: The Search for Nonviolent Alternatives in United States History*. Kitchener, Ont.; Scottdale, Pa.: Pandora Press; Herald Press, 2001.

Miller, Keith Graber. *Wise as Serpents, Harmless as Doves: American Mennonites Engage Washington*. Knoxville: The University of Tennessee Press, 1996.

Sampson, Cynthia, and John Paul Lederach, eds. *From the Ground Up: Mennonite Contributions to International Peacebuilding*. Oxford New York: Oxford University Press, 2000.

[Scheuer, Michael]. *Imperial Hubris: Why the West Is Losing the War on Terror*. Washington, D.C.: Brassey's, 2004.

Wallis, Jim. *God's Politics: Why the Right Gets It Wrong and the Left Doesn't Get It*. [San Francisco]: HarperSanFrancisco, 2005.

Yoder, John Howard. *The Politics of Jesus*. 2d ed. 1972. Grand Rapids: William B. Eerdmans, 1994.

7

How Inclusive Is the Inclusive Church?

Carol Penner

I grew up learning stories about a Jesus who loved tax collectors, harlots, and thieves on crosses. I learned that Jesus loves everyone, even though we are all sinners. The church's job is to be like Jesus, welcoming sinners and inviting them to new life. This early Sunday-school theology is not something I have outgrown; rather, it has deepened as I have matured in the Mennonite church. It is commitment to this very theology that has prompted me to struggle deeply with how we work out these simple statements amid the hurly-burly of congregational life.

I have just finished a pastoral assignment in an urban church that has a history of welcoming people who have sexually offended against children. This context stretched me to examine the practicalities of inclusiveness. Pain, conflict, ambivalence, humility, and awe have filled this stretching. I have had to examine the heart of what I believe about the church of Christ and its witness to the world.

What happens when churches attempt to include people who have committed sexual offenses against children? Wondering whether my church's experience was unique, I decided to interview five pastors whose churches have worked at inclusiveness. I was able to find these pastors through my contacts with "Circles of Support and Accountability," a non-profit organization sponsored by Mennonite Central Committee, which provides both support and accountability to people who have sexually offended and are coming out of prison. The quotations in this paper come from these five pastors, as well as from my own experience. We all serve in Protestant denominations, and our churches range in membership from 60 to 1500 people. All of the people in our congregations whom we know to have offended are men.

I will begin by talking about how inclusiveness seems to threaten public peace and safe space. I will briefly outline theological reasons for inclusiveness and then discuss its nitty-gritty practicalities. I will conclude by commenting on the contribution that inclusive churches make to society at large.

Public Peace and Safe Space

The plain fact is that our society directs anger and hatred toward people who have sexually offended against children. People who hurt children in a sexual way are viewed as a threat to public safety. Their actions provoke a visceral sort of disgust in people's minds. They are treated as unclean, often hounded from community to community. No one wants someone who has offended in their neighborhood. Popular opinion suggests that public peace is best served by getting rid of people who have sexually offended against children. Popular opinion would wish them locked away for life—if not killed outright.

Canada does not have capital punishment, and Canadians rarely incarcerate for life. So people who have committed horrible sexual offenses against children often do re-enter society. In order not to re-offend, these people need an accountability structure and a supportive community. The stigma of their crime means that it is often very difficult for them to find a place to live, to work, or to socialize. When we direct hatred against these people and make it difficult for them to reintegrate into normal life, we are tragically creating conditions that make it likely that they will re-offend.

Given this social reality of anger and hatred against people who have committed sexual offenses against children, it is not surprising that church members rarely react positively to inclusive approaches. Congregants want their church to be safe. Including a "dangerous person" is seen to compromise that feeling of security. All of the pastors I interviewed said there was some resistance to being inclusive from within their congregations. Pastors heard these comments:

> If he comes, we're out of here.

> People like that don't belong in church.

> They should burn in hell, where they belong.

> I guess they belong in church, but I don't want them coming to my congregation.

> You don't care about the children if you let him come.

> I know in my mind that he should be welcome in the church, but every time I see him in church I get upset.

> If people in the community find out, no one will want to come to our church.

> If he comes, that means our youth program is never going to get off the ground. Who will let their children come to our church?

> If he is in the church you will never see my family here. [This final comment was from a junior member of the pastoral team to the senior member.]

The pastors I interviewed sometimes faced anger from congregants over inclusiveness, whatever their congregation decided:

> We had three people leave the church after we made the community decision to be welcoming. They were angry and bitter.

There was a lot of emotion in our discussions, but in the end, not a single person left the church over it. We were stronger after facing this issue.

Pastors also faced anger from people in the community who did not want anyone to help the person who had offended.

People who have committed offenses against children are not a homogenous group who pose similar risks. When pastors told their stories of inclusiveness, the variety of the offenses and circumstances was striking. Here is a partial list of the people who pastors were working to include (names and details have been changed):

Blake is a man who was convicted of abusing over twenty children, and has just been released from ten years in prison. He has no friends, no job, no support system, and is under twenty-four-hour police surveillance. His picture has appeared in the local paper. He had made a connection with the pastor of a local church when he was in prison. The pastor asks his church whether he can invite Blake to attend services.

Roberto is a retired teacher active in the church. Three former students recently filed charges, and Roberto's sexual abuse conviction shocked the church community. The pastor maintained contact with Roberto throughout his incarceration. Roberto, who maintains his innocence, wants to re-integrate into his church community upon his release from prison.

Jeff is a developmentally delayed young man who is in his early thirties. He grew up in the church. A neighbor calls and tells the pastor that Jeff is about to be arrested because he abused a young boy.

Ted has recently joined the church. He confides to the pastor that he abused his step-daughter and has just come out of jail. He has no court-ordered restrictions except to stay away from his family.

Larry is a forty-year-old married man with two small children. He served time twenty-one years ago for having sexual intercourse with a girl who was fourteen. No one in his church knows about his history except for his wife and the pastor.

Casey abused two girls twenty years ago when he was abusing alcohol and drugs. Filled with guilt, he turned himself in, served time and went for addiction counseling and straightened out his life. He is active in the church as well as Narcotics Anonymous, but very few people know of his history of abuse.

Simply to name these people and their offenses is fraught with theological and pastoral challenges. When people think about including those who have committed offenses against children, their minds turn immediately to someone like Blake with a long history of assaulting numerous children. The stories I heard reveal the complexity of sexual offenses, and the challenge to be inclusive. One pastor talked about church members using words like "pedophile" and "child molester" for those who had committed a relatively minor offense. Yet one uses the term "minor offense" reluctantly and only in relation to other offenses, since any type of sexual abuse is devastating in the life of the survivor.

In my own writing, I prefer the term "people who have sexually offended" rather than the more common term, "sexual offenders." As a church community we do not habitually refer to our church members as liars, adulterers, embezzlers, or tax evaders, even when they may have committed these sins. By referring to individuals as people, and refusing the temptation to label, the church signals that we are holding out the possibility of change.

GOD'S JUSTICE, GOD'S LOVE

What motivates a church to be inclusive? How does God call us to relate to Blake, Roberto, Jeff, Ted, Larry, and Casey? I asked the pastors about the theology behind their actions and their comments speak for themselves. Three theological themes do emerge from their comments, however—grace, following God's call, and the Body of Christ.

Grace

What is Christ calling us to do in the church? We are supposed to call people to repentance, and expect that God can change them.

The grace of God is there for all of us. These men have sins of a certain kind. My sins are bad too. Although society sees their sins as worse than mine, God might not look at it the same way. The grace of God has to be big enough to include all kinds of sins.

God has called us to this charism, to be a place of hope for these people in our city. Could we really tell this man, "We have no hope to give you"? We had to include him if we believed that God loves everyone.

Following God's Call

I can't deny that including these men involves risk, but aren't we called as Christians to accept risks? Think about Ananias in Acts 9. It was very risky to that whole congregation to include Paul. What would have happened to the early church if they had refused to accept him because of the risk? We are called to step out in faith.

As a church we're called to break down barriers between people. Our congregation breaks down barriers and makes community with people from different cultures, different generations, different social backgrounds. God will call his people from every tribe and nation. I see the barrier between offenders/non-offenders as just one more barrier that needs to be bridged.

These men are the least in our society, the most looked-down-on. They are like the Gerasene demoniac, a naked, screaming person who was pushed away as sub-human. Jesus says, "What's your name?" We're called to treat these people with respect.

As a church, we're called to take care of children, because Jesus cared about the children so much. How does rejecting these guys protect children? It just isolates them, and makes them more likely to re-offend. It's a lot of work to walk with a sexual offender, but if it means one child is not victimized, it's worth it.

The Body of Christ
First Corinthians 12 talks about the body of Christ. People who have offended are part of the body of Christ. If we reject them, we are losing gifts that they bring to the church. The church will be poorer.

When he first started coming to church, someone prayed for him, "Let his life be a gift." And that was what I saw happen. He was able to bring something to our community that no one else could have brought.

I was so scared to include him. I thought we might be run out of town, that the press would hound us like they'd hounded him. I didn't see him as a safe bet not to re-offend. I felt it would ruin our community if he re-offended. Yet I knew it was God's thing to have him in our church.

I have seen our compassion in the church grow because of the presence of this man. He isn't some faceless monster, but a real person who has had a terrible life. He has good qualities too.

Our foundation must be embrace and not exclusion. Society wants to exclude these guys from any type of community. The church includes them. That's a strong message about the value of human life, the strength of God's love. It's a model of the kingdom.

Including a sexual offender wasn't a new thing. Our community was all about including misfits, people whom society rejected. This was just one more step along that path. It's a sign of God's power that he can build a church that brings life with these types of dangerous people.

According to pastors I interviewed, Christian community was a gift that churches could give to people who had committed sexual offenses against children. The men were almost invariably isolated and cut off from any human contact. Most of them could not return to the community where they had offended, and so had to integrate into a community where people did not know them. Some of them had police surveillance and the media followed their movements. Others were afraid to talk about their offenses, because they feared ostracism if people knew the truth. The church could be a home for these men who were profoundly homeless.

∾

Providing a community to people who have offended was also a gift that churches could give to the larger society. Social isolation increases the risk of re-offense. Every pastor I interviewed said that protecting children was in fact a motivation for their work. The pastors hoped that the church could help prevent another offense.

It is important at this point to state plainly that not one pastor suggested that these men were safe to be with children. I emphasize this because churches have historically minimized the pain of abuse that women and children have suffered. Many feminist writers have pointed out that the church has a terrible pattern of forgiving men who have been abusive without holding them accountable. The church has a history of being suspicious of women's shelters and other organizations designed to help survivors of abuse. In the past, churches naïvely trusted the repentance of people who have offended, and were over-confident about their ability to counsel people with complex problems. This has resulted in the re-victimization of many women and children.

In the interviews I did, however, no one minimized the crimes these men had committed. On the contrary, all demonstrated a sober understanding of the depth and breadth of the men's crimes. The pastors all admitted that Christian faith was not enough to stop people from re-offending. None of the pastors interviewed said, "This person will not re-offend because he is a Christian now." Likewise, none of the pastors claimed to be qualified to counsel a person who had sexually offended. They relied on professionals involved in the men's lives to provide that type of care. Pastors wanted to provide the support of a social community that was positive and hopeful for the person. "We want to help them so they don't re-offend," said one. "We want to do everything in our power to protect them from re-offending."

All of the pastors I interviewed saw the church working as part of a team with community agencies set up to protect society. None of the pastors felt that they were working in isolation. Most of the pastors had contact with parole officers, and all of them interacted with "Circles of Support and Accountability." Several of the pastors spoke about medical treatment, and the importance of medication in controlling behaviors. The pastors believed that Christian faith and a welcoming community were part of the net that might keep this person from re-offending.

A number of the pastors talked about the stress of pastoring people who have sexually offended against children.

> There is no doubt that including him was a huge drain on me personally. I was never relaxed when I knew he was in the building; I was always vigilant. I'm not saying we shouldn't have done it, it's just that we have to be aware that there is a high pastoral cost to this work.

Another pastor commented:

> I felt a huge responsibility, and always felt that I could be doing more. I did not have limitless time to devote to these men as I had a congregation of hurting people that also demanded my time. I had to remind myself that there were many people working with them. I had to trust God, and admit that I could ultimately not stop them from re-offending. . . . It was important to have people to talk to; talking to the parole officer, the social service worker, and the circle coordinator were important supports for me in this work.

Talking with other pastors who were doing this kind of ministry was also a significant support.

ORDERING FOR SAFETY

How does a church protect its members from danger as it is being inclusive? All of the pastors tried to minimize the risk of re-offense by helping to put into place structures to order the church's life and the life of the person who had offended.

All of the churches in this study have safety policies regarding children. Abuse prevention strategies include volunteer screening and police checks for people working with children. Policies dictate that children are never alone with one adult, and children use a buddy system when they walk in the church to go to the washroom. One pastor remarked, "Think about what reasonable standards you could expect a church to take in terms of safety. We've raised the bar on this by 100 percent."

None of the pastors interviewed kept knowledge about sexual offenses to themselves. Depending on the offense, various numbers of people received information. For a high profile case that was in the media, "We had two congregational meetings where we talked about this fellow, and whether we would welcome him. Everyone knew what he had done." In another case, when someone within the congregation committed an offense, the church made an announcement to the whole congregation that charges were being filed and held a series of meetings with an outside facilitator. Information about sentencing was also shared publicly on Sunday morning. In another situation, when a former church member wanted to re-integrate into the community, the pastor spoke to every family with children in the church. In one case, when information arose about an offense in the past, people on the pastoral team were alerted as well as other key people in the church.

Sharing information was an easy decision for some pastors, but others found it more difficult to decide who needed to know. Pastors experienced conflict with church members over information: "One woman was adamant that everyone should know this information, but I had decided to tell only key leadership people. She was very unhappy with my decision and let me know it every time she saw me." On the other hand, the same pastor spoke of other people being angry when they shared information: "Some people were furious with me that I had shared this man's secret. They wondered whether their own secrets were safe with me or whether I would be broadcasting them too."

There is a delicate balance between the need for public awareness and the reality of stigmatization. One pastor of a very large congregation said, "Not everyone needs to know. It would just spook people. We are taking very strong precautions with this person, and there has to be a degree of trust that people in leadership will make decisions with the community's safety in mind." Another pastor commented, "It's a case-by-case thing. In one situation we might tell the church, in another case, only key people will be told. Different people pose different levels of risk. We don't want to paint everyone with the same brush."

Churches sometimes processed information as a group, but one pastor talked about the difficulty of new members joining the congregation after the process was completed: "How do I share information about people who have offended with newcomers to the church? How long do they have to attend before I share this information with them?" There was a fear of scaring potential congregants away by sharing information too soon: "It's difficult to distinguish between people who are just visiting and may not need to know, and people who are church shopping, and need this information to make an informed decision."

Church leaders set parameters for how people who had offended could be involved in the church. It was a given that they simply could have nothing to do with children. Screening of volunteers already precluded them from this. One person was only allowed to attend mid-week services where children were rarely present because for him simply to be in the same room with children was considered a risk. Some people had to agree to be buddied (shadowed) by someone when they were at church. Some restrictions addressed life outside the church building. The person who had offended was asked not to accept any social invitations to homes where there would be children present. Several people had written agreements about what hours they would be present in the church building and which washrooms they would use. Some could not participate in church retreats or other events where monitoring might be difficult.

A number of pastors spoke of resistance to these measures by the person with the history of offending. One man showed up in church even though the pastor had told him that the church needed time to process his involvement. He was asked not to return for a period of time; he never came back. In another case the pastor felt that the whole congregation needed to know the nature of a person's offense. The person did not want the information shared and so he decided not to attend the church.

One pastor talked about the conflict that arose when church members tried to be more inclusive than the agreements allowed. For example, after attending for some time, a person with a history of offending received an invitation to sing in the worship band. The pastor had to speak to the people involved and say that it was not appropriate because this person could not have a public role in the church. In another situation when a person was facing charges, some people in the congregation believed in the person's innocence, and resented that the church placed restrictions on the accused:

> I was told that as a pastor, I had a duty to believe my congregant when he said he was innocent. But most people who are accused say they are innocent, at least at first, so we have to put restrictions on them. They can clear their name in court.

Ordering the church so it can be a safe place for both survivors of abuse and people who have committed offenses against children can be a challenge for pastors. One commented:

We have welcomed this person who has offended, but we would not have been able to do that if his victim was in the congregation. In that case, we would clearly have had to provide a home for the victim, and ask the person who had offended to find another church. It wouldn't be fair to ask the survivor to face their abuser every Sunday morning.

A number of pastors commented on the fact that once a church has successfully supported someone with a history of sexual offending, they are likely to attract other people who have offended and who know they will not be turned away. For a small congregation this can have a dramatic effect. One small congregation had four or five people with a history of offending against children. The pastor commented:

The reality is that because of our success in supporting people who have offended, we have a number of them here. A survivor of abuse would probably not choose to attend this church. It would just be too difficult for them. I have tried to be sensitive to the needs of survivors, and have run a program for female survivors of abuse with the help of our local sexual assault center. But perhaps different churches are good at different things. We can't be everything to everyone. Our church does a good job of providing a home for people who have offended. Not many churches do that. . . . A number of survivors of abuse left the church when he came, in spite of the meetings we held to process everything. But a number of survivors did stay.

CONCLUSION

Society seeks to make itself safe by rejecting and stigmatizing people who have sexually offended against children. Tragically, this isolation often leads to further offenses and more victimization. The church, following the lead of Jesus, is trying to include these people who are cast out. It is empowered in this work by a God who loves beyond our love and hopes beyond our hope. By taking the path of inclusiveness, the church is able to see the humanity of the person who has offended. Calling on that humanity, the church extends an invitation to new life. Providing support, accountability, and community to people who have sexually offended—in conjunction with the courts, parole officers, social service workers, and medical professionals—does help to minimize the risk of reoffense, and makes our society safer. The church contributes an important piece of this work that social service professionals cannot manufacture, a loving community.

Inclusiveness brings with it conflict, strong emotions, and risk. In my congregation, inclusiveness was a turbulent experience that challenged me both personally and as a pastor. In our case, the man had assaulted a boy in the neighborhood who was the same age as my own son. I went to court with him and heard the charges read, and listened to the testimony of the young boy at the preliminary hearing. I was disgusted and repelled by my church member's actions. That Sunday when it came time to serve communion, I really did not want to give him the bread and the juice. I did serve him, praying that God would help me grow into the pastoral shoes I was wearing. Over the course of eighteen months, I spent a lot of time with this man, and I came to see his humanity, and his beauty, in spite of myself.

The journey toward inclusiveness has profoundly shaped our church. We have experienced strong and passionate conflict, division, and hurt feelings. Including this one man turned out to be a process that tested our strength as a community. Could we simultaneously be inclusive of people who took strong stands against inclusiveness?

The struggle tested our patience and willingness to walk the long journey. We would have liked to see quick and complete repentance, which certainly would have made my job as an advocate for inclusiveness easier. People who commit serious crimes, however, are rarely able to recognize immediately the harm they have done. We decided to walk with our church member as he faced criminal charges. We tried to be inclusive. We did not do this perfectly, or happily, or easily.

Eighteen months later in court he entered a plea of guilty, and received a suspended sentence. One month later he suddenly died of a heart attack. At his funeral a church member reflected that we had tried to be a home for him. We did not always succeed, and at times he felt alone and isolated, but we tried our best. He always knew that we were trying to be inclusive.

The church goes against popular opinion, and it even goes against the common-sense feelings of its members, as it works at inclusiveness. By refusing to exclude, and trying to include people in loving communities, churches hope to minimize the risk of re-offending. The irony is that people who have served time and are publicly identified as sexual offenders are not the only threat. Given the abuse statistics in our society, one can assume that every church has someone in it that has committed a sexual offense against a child. By fostering openness, refusing to stigmatize people, and being inclusive, we are encouraging people who have committed offenses to come forward and get help for their problems. Carefully including people who are dangerous and risky may paradoxically be the best way to create communities that are safer for our children.

FOR FURTHER READING

Cooper-White, Pamela. "Ministry with Violent Men." In *The Cry of Tamar: Violence Against Women and the Church's Response*, 206–28. Minneapolis, Minn.: Fortress Press, 1995.

Fortune, Marie, and James Poling. "Calling to Accountability: The Church's Responses to Abusers." In *Violence Against Women and Children: A Christian Theological Sourcebook*, eds. Carol J. Adams and Marie M. Fortune, 451–63. New York: Continuum, 1995.

Miles, Al. "Once an Abuser, Always an Abuser?" In *Domestic Violence: What Every Pastor Needs to Know*, 101–28. Minneapolis, Minn.: Fortress Press, 2000.

Poling, James N. "Preaching to Perpetrators of Violence." In *Telling the Truth: Preaching About Sexual and Domestic*

Violence, eds. John S. McClure and Nancy J. Ramsay, 71–82. Cleveland, Ohio: United Church Press, 1998.

——. "Stories of Recovering Perpetrators." In *The Abuse of Power: A Theological Problem*, 49–73. Nashville, Tenn.: Abingdon Press, 1991.

Yantzi, Mark. *Sexual Offending and Restoration*. Waterloo, Ont.; Scottdale, Pa.: Herald Press, 1998.

8

CONSIDER THE LILIES:
EMBRACING THE VALUE OF VULNERABILITY

Pamela S. Nath

While preparing a sermon for a nearby church in the weeks following the September 11 attacks, I found the following quote
posted on an Internet discussion group:

> My best friend was in the South tower [of the World Trade
> Center] when this terrible tragedy took place and she is still
> unaccounted for. She left behind a five-year-old daughter,
> a loving husband and family, and many friends. . . . Last
> night I spoke to her daughter, who is the same age as my
> little girl. . . . She asked me, whether, if she prayed really
> hard, her Mommy would come back to her. . . . I feel so
> helpless. Why does a five-year-old girl have to ask such a
> terrible question? Why did this senseless thing have to take
> place? I am crying and grieving for my friend that I grew
> up with, for all the victims and their families. I am praying
> for all their souls and the souls of those who did this. May
> God have mercy on them! There is so much hatred now,
> but this will not change what happened and it will not help
> how we feel. I cannot find forgiveness in my heart for the
> people responsible, but I am praying for the strength to do
> just that. Hate and revenge will only take this further and
> it will lead to a war that will leave the world in ruins. . . .
> How many more children have to pray for their parents to
> come home before this nightmare will end?

This poignant quote illustrates many of the raw emotions that U.S. citizens and others experienced around the globe following the tragic attacks on the World Trade Center and the Pentagon on September 11, 2001. The woman who posted the message expresses sadness, grief, and anger about the ending of so many lives and in particular the life of her best friend. She shares her confusion about how to respond to the difficult questions that violence and suffering raise, not only for five-year-olds, but also for all of us. Finally, she voices an uncertainty about the future—a fear about what the future will hold in terms of further suffering and violence. Her emotions and questions are not just her own, but are shared by many others. If Anabaptist peace theology is to be compelling in a post-9/11 world, it must be responsive to the emotional, cognitive, and spiritual needs that result from the lack of peace, justice, and security in our world. In this paper, I seek to highlight these needs in the hope of stimulating further conversation about ways that our theology might respond to them.

THE TRAUMA OF SHATTERED ASSUMPTIONS OF SAFETY

As we move through our lives, we all make assumptions about ourselves, about others, and about our world. Psychological research has demonstrated that white middle-class inhabitants of the Western world tend to assume that the world is a predictable and fair place in which outcomes are contingent upon merit. Good things happen to good people and to people who work hard; bad things happen to bad people, or at least those who make bad choices. Those living in Western cultures also overestimate the extent of control that we have over events. A high percentage of Americans possess an internal locus of control, that is, a tendency to see themselves as in control of outcomes in their lives. These assumptions are more pervasive and subtle than beliefs, operating not only on a cognitive but also an emotional and a behavioral level. They provide a sense of security and invulnerability in an otherwise frightening world.

Traumatic events experienced personally or vicariously

have the potential to "shatter" these assumptions of justice and control, and leave both victims and bystanders with a heightened sense of vulnerability in a world that is, in reality, not always a safe, predictable, or just place. For many in the world, of course, including the oppressed and poor in the United States, these illusions of invulnerability, security, and the inherent justice of the world have never been sustainable. Still, the intense reactions of many to the events of September 11 indicate the extent to which many residents of the United States and other countries in the Western world had successfully avoided the terrible reality of the extent of suffering in the world, at least emotionally.

Strikingly, both in the media and in my everyday life many people suggested that September 11 had "changed everything." Though September 11 was without doubt a tragedy, it was not the first horrendous event experienced in the history of humankind. Yet somehow in the United States many had managed to distance themselves from the reality of suffering in the world, and September 11 did change that for them. Polls and surveys in the days and weeks following September 11 revealed that the effects were not limited to those whom the attacks had directly affected; as many as two-thirds of Americans reported that they had experienced a loss of safety and security connected to the attacks. Even six months after the attacks, 37.5 percent of respondents to one survey reported that they experienced a fear of future terrorism at least some of the time.

In addition to coping with the shattering of everyday illusions of a safe and just world, those who experience trauma or loss confront what trauma researcher Ronnie Janoff-Bulman has called the "terror of meaninglessness." In its wake, trauma often leaves many pressing existential questions about the "meaning" of the event and of life in general, along with the significance of one's own individual life. Philosopher Thomas Attig articulates the mysteries of "finiteness, change, imperfection, uncertainty, and vulnerability" that confront victims of loss and trauma:

> Is it OK that we are small and insignificant when compared with the vast expanses of space, time, and history that surround us? Is it OK that change and impermanence pervade our lives, and that we have little to no control over many of the things that happen in them? Is it OK that we are imperfect; that we fall far short of our highest aspirations? Is it OK that our knowledge is limited, our judgment is fallible, and certainty eludes us? Is it OK that we are vulnerable to suffering and death?[1]

In the aftermath of trauma, religion has the potential to help people struggling with these sorts of existential questions. Religion can assist those who struggle to cope with a sense of insecurity and uncertainty in a world that suddenly seems dangerous, unpredictable, and potentially meaningless. But religion is only one potential source of answers to the questions that trauma raises. National ideologies offer a competing source of meaning in the chaos immediately following a violent trauma. Research by Thomas Pyszczynski of the University of Colorado and his colleagues has provided evidence that national culture functions in this manner.[2]

These researchers have found that when people are reminded of their own mortality, even in subtle ways, they have a tendency to defend their worldviews by reacting more punitively toward others who demonstrate differences in identity, belief, or behavior. In one of their studies, for example, college students rated anti-American essays more harshly and pro-American essays more generously if they had previously answered questions about their own death.

In another study, researchers told municipal court judges that they were examining the relationship between personality traits, attitudes, and bond decisions. The judges completed a series of questionnaires assessing personality, and then received a brief from a hypothetical legal case in which they were to set bond. Embedded in the packet for half the subjects was an additional questionnaire that required the subject to write short responses to questions about their own death. The judges who took the questionnaire that reminded them of their own mortality set an average bond of $455, in comparison to an average bond of $50 for the judges who completed all the same procedures except for this particular questionnaire.

In yet another study, German citizens were interviewed about their attitudes toward German immigration policies either in front of, or a short distance (100 meters) away from, a funeral parlor. Researchers then asked them to estimate the percentage of the German public who agreed with their opinion. Groups interviewed in front of the mortuary gave higher estimates of the percentage that agreed with their opinions.

In study after study, researchers have found evidence that people become particularly defensive about their worldview in situations that make them aware of their own vulnerability and mortality. Thus, individuals who have seen the United States as both good and invulnerable may become even more resistant to challenges to those beliefs in the aftermath of September 11, a particularly vivid reminder of human mortality.

In the immediate aftermath of September 11, social science researchers found an increase in anger and aggressive attitudes; hate crimes toward Arab Americans were on the increase and support for military action was high. In their desire to recover a sense of security and control, and to defend the national worldview, people may be particularly susceptible to arguments for a violent response in the aftermath of a traumatic experience. Echoing the earlier writings of psychologist William James, Veteran war correspondent Chris Hedges describes how violent action may help to restore a sense of meaning that can be disrupted in trauma:

> War makes the world understandable, a black-and-white tableau of them and us. It suspends thought, especially self-critical thought. All bow before the supreme effort. We are one. Most of us willingly accept war as long as we can fold it into a belief system that paints the ensuing suffering as necessary for a higher good, for human beings seek not only happiness but also meaning. And tragically war is sometimes the most powerful way in human society to achieve meaning.[3]

In an address to Congress in the days following the September 2001 terrorist attacks, President Bush tried to reassure the public with these words: "Freedom and fear..., [j]ustice and cruelty..., have always been at war. And we know that God is not neutral between them." Intentionally or not, the president was helping people to "make sense" of the tragedy in a way that maintained a belief in American right and merit, as well as a sense that the United States was carrying out God's larger purpose in the world. Certainly, the patriotic fervor and the high levels of support for military action in the United States following 9/11 suggested that Bush's argument was consistent with the worldview of many Americans and helped them "make sense" of the events. American national ideology envisions security as the result of strength and control. The assumption appears to be that with the right choices, the United States will be able to avoid another attack like 9/11, and the right choices are assumed to be actions like strengthening the nation's borders, enhancing its intelligence capabilities, and building or perhaps demonstrating U.S. military might.

Trauma and the Possibility of Transformation

Although a belief in military might as critical to security is deeply embedded in American national consciousness, traumatic experiences also hold the potential for a transformation of one's traditional ways of viewing the world. Trauma and loss may expose limitations in cultural understandings and make current worldviews impossible to maintain. Although the tendency may be to defend one's worldview in response to vulnerability, survivors must find some way to revise their worldviews or replace them with alternative perspectives when those worldviews can no longer accommodate the realities that trauma and loss have revealed. This task, difficult and painful though it may be, also provides the potential of positive, as well as negative change.

Studies of trauma victims have demonstrated that many if not most trauma victims experience positive growth in the aftermath of traumatic victimization and loss. In response to the existential questions that trauma raises, trauma victims can work to reestablish a sense of value and meaning to life through multiple pro-social channels. Such channels include enhanced interpersonal relationships, participation in altruistic social causes, and engagement in spirituality. Survivors often report a newfound sense of their own competence. Although they recognize that their future is not secure, they increasingly trust their ability to handle what challenges may come.

Many trauma victims never recover their earlier sense of safety and invulnerability, but rather than being something negative, this enduring sense of their own vulnerability provides them with a newfound appreciation for life, a stronger sense of the priorities in life, a sense of compassion for others who suffer, and a deeper ability to be intimate with others. Ronnie Janoff-Bulman, a leading trauma researcher, describes the growing acceptance of vulnerability that is evident in the healing process:

> Schooled in anxiety and disillusionment, victims are "educated by dread." Once you know that catastrophe dwells next door and can strike at any time, you interpret reality differently. Trauma survivors no longer move through life unmindful of existence; they can more readily relish the good, for they all too well know the bad. They have made their peace with the inevitable shortcomings of our existence and have a new appreciation of life and a realization of what is really important. The wisdom of maturity, which acknowledges the possibility that catastrophe will disrupt ordinary routine, replaces the ignorance of naïveté. And the trauma survivor emerges somewhat sadder, but considerably wiser.[4]

Whereas American ideology attempts to base its security on strength and control, survivors' experiences of living and healing in the midst of vulnerability suggest an alternative vision of security, a security that is rooted in relationships and a sense of ultimate purpose in life. Just as developmental psychologists have demonstrated the ways in which our earliest attachment relationships provide us with a base of security from which we explore the world, our security may ultimately rest in our relationships with others. For example, the desire for justice in the wake of the terrorist attacks on September 11 is an understandable and legitimate human response to these violent acts. That said, a distinction is necessary between acts of war and a stance that looks to the international community as a partner in our attempt to find, disarm, and even punish the perpetrators.

Military actions do not just punish the guilty parties, but also result in the "collateral damage" of civilian casualties. To recognize the ultimate futility of attempting to reestablish a permanent sense of security through military action, one need only remind oneself that to increase the sense of vulnerability, victimization, and insecurity in civilians of other nations through a violent retaliatory response leaves them with a similar sense that they are susceptible to aggressive actions by the United States. This sense of powerlessness and vulnerability is likely to enhance the ability of terrorist groups to find new recruits. A cycle of violence can easily develop, therefore, fed by the emotions of victimization on all sides. In fact, recent research in Iraq and Afghanistan, supervised by Mike Wessells of the Christian Children's Fund, has documented that many youth have recently joined radical Islamicist organizations because of anger and frustration about U.S. involvement and continuing problems with security and rebuilding in their country.

A security based on invulnerability is an elusive goal for mortal human beings who do not have ultimate control over events and cannot protect themselves against all catastrophes. In contrast, embracing our common human vulnerability may paradoxically serve to increase rather than weaken our security. In a paper calling for a "complete reconsideration of the relationship between vulnerability and security,"[5] a Church of Norway commission argues that mutual vulnerability and dependence promotes cooperative solutions rather than conflict or the use of force and creates a climate of mutual trust and confidence.

Ultimately, it will be unfortunate if the strengthening of U.S. national security post-9/11 allows U.S. citizens to maintain their illusions of invulnerability, safety, and control—particularly if these illusions prevent us from turning to others in the world community in relationships of mutual dependence. One might ask what impact it has on U.S. international relationships for so many in the country to have felt such safety before 9/11, when this is not the experience of so many others in the world. A security that acknowledges that we are not entirely in control and that relies upon relationship would recommend and allow a different sort of involvement in the world community. Such an involvement would seek to strengthen international ties through humanitarian and cultural connections. It would be willing to listen to the counsel of the international community. And it would not be based on wielding our strength but on fulfilling our responsibilities as a partner to others.

A sense of security *is* necessary for human development and health. The promise of a strong military response and the potential to protect America from future violence offers a compelling response to the psychological needs of a traumatized nation. If the church is to compete with this worldview, then we need to offer an equally compelling alternative perspective that helps people make sense of their experiences of trauma and vulnerability. Theologians and psychologists alike have identified that to acknowledge our own vulnerability and dependence upon realities beyond ourselves is a critical step in spiritual development. At its best, religion calls us to recognize the limits of our control and to recognize that our security ultimately depends upon God.

Conclusion

Military actions promise to reestablish security and control, but ultimately fail to fulfill that promise. Information from the social sciences regarding creative ways that trauma victims cope with their experiences may provide a resource to the church as it sorts out how to offer alternative ways of coping with the newfound vulnerability in the nation following terrorist attacks. Like the trauma survivors who learn to live with a newfound sense of vulnerability, we can develop our compassion for others who are also suffering, strengthen our relationships with others, and ultimately recognize a Power greater than us upon which we must rely. We can seek a sense of security rooted in relationship, like that which forms in our earliest years of life in our attachment relationship with our caregivers.

In doing so, we are likely to foster a deeper sense of meaning and purpose for our lives. This is a different type of power and security than the type of power that is too often exerted in global politics. If this message seems "unrealistic," I would argue that this is because it runs counter to the cultural worldview of the United States, which views peace as the result of superior military strength. It is thus essential that our theology articulate a well-developed alternative view of security, of vulnerability, of suffering, of control, and of power.

NOTES

1. Thomas Attig, "Relearning the World: Making and Finding Meanings," in *Meaning Reconstruction and the Experience of Loss*, ed. Robert A. Neimeyer (Washington, DC: American Psychological Association, 2000), 45.

2. Thomas A. Pyszczynski, Jeff Greenberg, and Sheldon Solomon, *In the Wake of 9/11: The Psychology of Terror* (Washington, DC: American Psychological Association, 2003), 27.

3. Chris Hedges, *War Is a Force That Gives Us Meaning* (New York: PublicAffairs, 2002), 10.

4. Ronnie Janoff-Bulman, *Shattered Assumptions: Towards a New Psychology of Trauma* (New York: Free Press, 1992), 175. Janoff-Bulman takes the phrase "educated by dread" from Kierkegaard.

5. Commission on International Affairs in Church of Norway Council on Ecumenical and International Relations, *Vulnerability and Security: Current Challenges in Security Policy from an Ethical and Theological Perspective* (2002), 4, Http://www.kirken.no/engelsk /VULNERABIL.doc.

FOR FURTHER READING

Commission on International Affairs in Church of Norway Council on Ecumenical and International Relations. *Vulnerability and Security: Current Challenges in Security Policy from an Ethical and Theological Perspective*, 2002. Http://www.kirken.no/engelsk/VULNERABIL.doc.

Hedges, Chris. *War Is a Force That Gives Us Meaning*. New York: PublicAffairs, 2002.

Janoff-Bulman, Ronnie. *Shattered Assumptions: Towards a New Psychology of Trauma*. New York: Free Press, 1992.

Janoff-Bulman, Ronnie, and Andrea R. Berger. "The Other Side of Trauma: Toward a Psychology of Appreciation." In *Loss and Trauma: General and Close Relationship Perspectives*, eds. John H. Harvey and Eric D. Miller, 29–44. Philadelphia: Brunner-Routledge, 2000.

Neimeyer, Robert A., ed. *Meaning Reconstruction and the Experience of Loss*. Washington, DC: American Psychological Association, 2000.

Pyszczynski, Thomas A., Jeff Greenberg, and Sheldon Solomon. *In the Wake of 9/11: The Psychology of Terror*. Washington, DC: American Psychological Association, 2003.

Stout, Chris E., ed. *A Public Understanding*. Vol. 1 of *The Psychology of Terrorism*. With a foreword by Klaus Schwab. Psychological Dimensions to War and Peace. Westport, Conn.: Praeger, 2002.

Tedeschi, Richard G., Crystal L. Park, and Lawrence G. Calhoun, eds. *Posttraumatic Growth: Positive Changes in the Aftermath of Crisis*. The LEA Series in Personality and Clinical Psychology. Mahwah, N.J.: Lawrence Erlbaum Associates, 1998.

Wagner, Richard V., and Katherine R. Long. "Terrorism from a Peace Psychology Perspective." In *Understanding Terrorism: Psychosocial Roots, Consequences, and Interventions*, eds. Fathali M. Moghaddam and Anthony J. Marsella, 207–20. Washington, DC: American Psychological Association, 2004.

9

ANABAPTIST THEOLOGY AND ISSUES OF HUMAN SECURITY IN PARAGUAY TODAY

Alfred Neufeld

According to Transparency International, Paraguay has led the list of most corrupt Latin American countries for the last fifteen years. In the company of Haiti and Cameroon, Paraguay also ranks high on the international list. Yet the high index of corruption is only a thermometer indicating many different social and economic evils that afflict the country. This makes human well-being highly insecure and distances it greatly from the biblical ideal of *shalom*.

René Padilla has recently shown that corruption and insecurity are closely interwoven with "the way in which the global capitalist system often affects whole countries."[1] As Padilla rightly states for Argentina, there are at least four reasons for corruption and poverty, which also apply to Paraguay:

- the corruption of the governing classes
- the corruption of the global economic system
- the foreign debt, which becomes some kind of "imperial tribute" and makes the national budget inadequate to provide social benefits such as education, healthcare, and retirement funds

- and the "fluctuations of a market controlled by global economic structures," which leads to growing gap between the rich and the poor on a global scale.[2]

Paraguay holds a large number of different immigrant Mennonite communities. Mennonite Central Committee (MCC), Mennonite Economic Development Association (MEDA), and local initiatives like *Christliche Dienste* and the ASCIM program (a cooperation between First Nations and Mennonite communities) have worked hard to bridge the gap between rich and poor, and to foster the idea of biblical *shalom*. In the last decades Mennonite educational institutions as well as media initiatives and political participation have had a visible impact on Paraguayan social and cultural life.

In May 2003, however, Mennonite participation in Paraguayan national life entered a new phase. In order to give his anti-corruption campaign nonpartisan credibility, a new president invited four Mennonite professionals into his cabinet. After careful congregational discernment, they agreed. In their first two years of office they have made considerable efforts to improve government performance, though progress and improvement in social economic well-being have been very slow.

SETTING THE STAGE

Paraguayan history and national debates have vacillated between greatness and humiliation. Long military rules under Francia (1811-1840), the Lopez father and son (1840-1870), and later Alfredo Stroessner (1954-1989) have sapped the country, both morally and economically. Two terrible wars (1864-1870; 1932-1935), triggered mostly by foreign interests, brought further devastation. Further still, the Cold War was very "hot" in Paraguay, as was usually the case in the global South.

Mennonites came to Paraguay as refugees. In 1927, the first group of South Manitoba immigrants came as what we might call "cultural refugees," escaping the pressure of the Canadian government to have their schools integrated into the national education system. A second large segment came in 1930 and 1948 as religious-political refugees, escaping from Soviet Russia. Later immigrations of Amish, Mexican Old Colony, and other groups looked to Paraguay the way some sixteenth-century Anabaptists looked to Bohemia and Moravia, as a place where government would not interfere with Mennonite churches or community ideals. All immigrated under Law 514, which guaranteed freedom from military service and, to a large extent, autonomy so that Mennonite communities might manage their social, economic, religious, educational, and health needs on their own. Most so-called colonies developed in an almost complete absence of national government.

All this is now changing very rapidly, precisely because the communities have been opening up to missions and social services. Many young Mennonite churches have emerged out of the national Paraguayan community, as well as various Indian tribes. Mennonites have had no coherent political theology, however, to guide them in their new roles.

The Anabaptist heritage has oscillated between the Schleitheim Confession and the pastoral practice of Menno Simons. Where Schleitheim viewed the state as an order of God "outside the perfection of Christ," Menno implied an openness to the possibility of Christian rulers. In national politics, Mennonites have tended to apply the Schleitheim formula of no political participation strictly. Menno Simons and his idea of a Christian society have been applied more to politics within Mennonites' own communities and colonies.

The Paraguayan experience is again somewhat *sui generis*, however. With good reason, Calvin Redekop has described Mennonite colonies as "a state within the church."[3] Mennonite community life in Paraguay has combined old Russian colony traditions, which go back to the immigration policies of Catherine II, with the early Soviet introduction of a system of economic cooperatives (Raiffeisen-Genossenschaften). At an early meeting of Mennonite World Conference in Danzig 1938 that prepared for Mennonite migration out of war-torn areas of Europe, Harold S. Bender and B. H. Unruh envisioned something like a "Mennonite republic" in Paraguay, which MCC and other international Mennonite institutions would help shape.[4]

Actually the colonies have come close to the vision that the early Anabaptist thinker Balthasar Hubmaier had for the village of Waldshut, along the Austrian Rhine. Hubmaier imagined a whole town that might be more or less identified with Anabaptism and have its parallel form of "law and order," looked after in a normally nonviolent way. Mennonite *Ordnungsdienst* in the colonies of Paraguay might be considered an attempt to put into practice Menno Simons' idea of "a sword without blood."[5] Mennonite communities have usually appointed *Ordnungsmaenner* in order to enforce community rules, intervene, and resolve conflicts instead of calling the police. In that sense they are an amazing case study in mediation and conflict resolution without arms. Of course there have also been darker sides to the system. At this moment the *Mennonitische Ordnungsdienst* is undergoing some kind of revision, in order to redefine its relationship to the national police. One option is to transform it into more of a peace and mediation service.

The national state and government have rarely interfered with the dynamics of life in these parallel Mennonite communities. Nonetheless, the system suffered a major crisis during World War II, when Mennonites hotly debated whether to return to the nation of Germany and reintegrate with German peoplehood. During that time a more Lutheran approach to two-kingdom theology, with its double set of ethics for private and political affairs, emerged in some quarters. It was especially prominent among those who favored a return to Europe and an integration into the wider German nation, the so called *Deutsch-Voelkische Bewegung*.[6]

A second impulse to rethink historic political attitudes came after the end of the Cold War, with the overthrow of the Stroessner military regime in November 1989. Until then democracy, free elections, and the participation of all citizens in political life was a mere facade, which Mennonites mainly avoided. Now, however, strong motives emerged to become part of the nation's future, to run democratically for public offices, and to make the social Mennonite heritage understandable and accessible to Paraguayan society. Eventually a deeper process of Anabaptist theological reflection began to accompany this political optimism. Mennonite integration and political participation became topics for several study conferences.

To be sure, Mennonite communities have keenly felt issues of human need and human security before and sought to address them. They have also made considerable efforts to reach out to their non-Mennonite neighborhood, especially those whom society has marginalized—First Nations, victims of leprosy, the mentally challenged, the aged, and street children. A broader theological and political reflection about issues of human security, however, is only in its beginning stages.

Mennonite churches and organizations have elaborated only a few documents concerning political participation. The Faith and Life Commission of the Mennonite Brethren Conference (2004) and the Mennonite Peace Committee (2003) provided a basic position and study material. Generally they redefine political engagement and responsibility as a search for the well-being of all, as a way to model servant leadership, and as an effort to make the social practices of the church accessible and applicable to wider society. They define political engagement as service more than an exercise of power. They try to uphold the priority of the church in social transformation. They insist on faithfulness to the way of Jesus in all areas of Christian social responsibility.

Starting with the first free elections of the early 1990s, Mennonite church members have been campaigning and winning elections. Heinz Ratzlaff, Kornelius Sawatzky, Orlando Penner, and Werner Thielmann have held office as either senators or deputies in the nation's two chambers of the Parliament. Kornelius Sawatzky, Orlando Penner, and David Sawatzky have also held the position of governor in the Chaco department of Boqueron. There are mixed feelings within the churches about the usefulness and adequacy of this kind of political participation.

Matters took a new turn in May 2003. Nicanor Duarte Frutos ran as presidential candidate for the old ruling party

(Partido Colorado) and, surprisingly, won the election. Through his contacts as former Minister of Education, through his wife Gloria Penayo—a baptized member of a local Mennonite church—and through developing friendships, Duarte Frutos had become increasingly interested in the Anabaptist heritage of social justice and nonviolence. Once elected, he invited professionals and entrepreneurs he knew from local Asunción Mennonite church into his government and cabinet to help in the areas of economics, industry, health, education, and state finances. None of these were party members nor had they shown previous political ambitions. They all went through a rather intense discernment process together with a pastoral team before stepping into political offices.

Ernst Ferdinand Bergen is a younger businessman and owner of several important firms in Asunción. His sensitivity for social concerns grew through long involvement as chairman of the Mennonite prison ministry and the need for former prisoners to get a second chance in the labor market. His wife Lucy, daughter of a former Mennonite *Oberschulze*, developed a close friendship with the now First Lady while both were leading women's societies in their respective Mennonite churches. They now work closely together in the First Ladies' Foundation for Human Development (Red Paraguaya de Desarrollo Humanitario, or REPADEH) to assist single mothers. Ernst Ferdinand has become Minister of Industry and Commerce, and has been co-decorated by the U.S. Congress for his fight against piracy and corruption.

Carlos Walde was president of a large family firm, Chacomer. He hosted several home Bible studies for businessmen and politicians. The present government called him to be a main economic adviser and negotiator with foreign economic institutions.

Andreas Neufeld was CEO at the Menno Colony cooperative branch in Asunción. He was offered the post of vice-minister for tax recollection and has been recognized as quite successful at improving state finances in a historic context of massive tax evasion.

Carlos Wiens was for a decade the chief surgeon and medical director of the Mennonite Leprosy Mission at Km. 81, the long-standing Mennonite mission for victims of leprosy. He accepted an invitation to become medical director of the national social security system.

Victor Wall has been a pastor and school administrator. He has become part of the national advisory board on educational questions.

After eighteen months of work, however, the Duarte Frutos administration can hardly claim dramatic and visible improvements. Yes, it has received recognition for its fight against corruption and piracy, as well as an important improvement in state finances and macro economics. But it has found it hard to reconcile the needs of the poor, marginalized, and peasants with the interests of large national and international capital, industrialized agriculture, and legal reforms required by the International Monetary Fund. Crime and violence are on the rise. Two years in, the present administration, with a considerable Mennonite presence, is under attack from left and right, from rich and poor.

BIBLICAL SHALOM AND SOURCES OF INSECURITY IN PRESENT PARAGUAYAN SOCIETY

Human insecurity in Paraguay is increasing. Walls and fences to protect property are growing higher. Electronic security companies do big business. Private armed security service has become one of the main new sources of employment. On the other hand, common criminality, robbery, and kidnapping create almost a paranoia in the population. In the countryside road blockings and private property invasions by landless farmers cause disturbance, discouraging investments in general and the very much needed foreign investments in particular.

Establishing a political consensus that looks toward the future is difficult, therefore. As Monsignor Ortiz, Catholic bishop of the impoverished province of Concepción, said in his Sunday sermon at the national cathedral of Caacupe on October 24, 2004: "We are full of drugs, alcohol, and violence."

One commonly hears clergy and sociologists say that church and society are sick. But this sickness, this lack of biblical *shalom*, has sources: historic sources, cultural sources, sociological sources, economic sources, spiritual sources.

1. Poverty and the dangers of the social gap

Historically the wealth of Paraguay was in cotton. Cotton was a family business and the main source of income for a large population of *campesinos*, or small farmers. A sadly famous class of *acopiadores*, who bought up the harvest and financed campesinos families and production for the next year at high interest rates, exploited the cotton business above all.

A collapse in the cotton market is the main reason why the campesino culture is in crisis. Big business has now turned to soy beans and beef, so the campesinos sell their small properties and immigrate to urban slums or find jobs in the informal economy, mostly related to piracy, smuggling, and marijuana production. During election periods they often sell their vote willingly, in order to gain a bit of cash. The number of street children and the amount of informal street commerce are rising. So is criminality and robbery. The main problem is agro-economic, since the vast majority of campesinos has no way to make a living in the new technological conditions of big agriculture.

2. Culture of resignation and rebellion

Throughout its history the Paraguayan population has often felt overpowered. The experience of powerlessness tends to produce two opposite reactions: resignation or rebellion. Both are common. Prominent intellectuals such as the philosopher Adriano Burgos, the agro-sociologist Milda Rivarola, and the former director of the social program of the Paraguayan Catholic church, Dionisio Gauto, all have argued that fatalism has become a serious cultural problem. As Gauto has said, "El sentimiento fatalista es lo que mas predomina"—fatalistic beliefs are the predominant characteristic of our society.

Cecilo Baez, who wrote *La Tirania en el Paraguay* a century ago, as well as prominent 20th-century novelist Augusto Roa

Bastos, both blamed the abuse of power for alternating tendencies toward resignation or rebellion. Roa Bastos talked of the "monotheism of power," which has been the basic historic belief in Paraguay. In his novel *El Trueno entre las Hojas* [*Thunder in the Leaves*] Roa Bastos portrayed violence as an endemic evil. Much of the insecurity and criminality that the country is suffering at this moment seems to derive from a basic resignation as well as a basic enchantment with power.

3. Structural sin

Wise lawmaking has not been a characteristic of Paraguayan social structure. And many of the nation's better laws are not being reinforced. This has favored a pronounced inequality in society. Paraguayan social structures support the gap between rich and poor, between powerful and powerless. Fiscal resources to protect the old, the poor, the sick, and those without access to education are very limited. They are especially limited, however, so many who are capable of paying taxes practice tax evasion.

The international and globalized economy has not shown real interest in giving weaker countries a chance either. Apostles of the free market usually preach from countries where the markets are very well protected. So for Paraguayan beef it is almost impossible to find an open market in Europe or North America. Prices for soy and cotton only improve for our country if there has been bad luck with climate and harvests in North America or in China.

On the other hand, companies making and promoting foreign products—not just acceptable ones like McDonalds and Coca Cola, but European and North American sellers of tobacco, beer, and liquor—are carrying out far more aggressive propaganda in the local media than their home countries would allow. So resignation, violence, and alcohol go hand-in-hand.

Even our major national problems of corruption and piracy have a global component. All of our pirated products find willing buyers outside of our country. As Ernst Bergen notes, "You can only dance the tango of corruption if you have a willing partner."

4. Violent criminality, violent police

After the downfall of the military government in 1989, civil society and police both struggled to adapt. Civil society was not accustomed to a wide range of liberties nor to the responsibility of democratic citizenship. Police were not in the habit of respecting human rights or using nonviolent methods of investigation. Furthermore, Paraguayans have a long tradition of arming themselves in public and protecting private property through private security forces, body guards, and personal firearms. So once people lost fear of the government, some forms of criminality rose dramatically. People expected the police to react in a more violent way, despite too many proven cases of criminal-police collusion. The "itchy finger" became very common and the press did not object. But this was no solution, as the police themselves now realize, after many police officers have lost their lives.

To fight criminality mainly through intelligence and non-violent methods is a new and unknown approach in Paraguay. And to establish a penitentiary system that aims at restoration and rehabilitation is still a far-off dream.

5. Loss of social fabric, culture of solidarity, and nationhood

The big changes in the campesino culture that industrialized agriculture and global competitiveness have caused are weakening the social fabric. Migration toward cities and a lifestyle based almost exclusively on cash has disrupted historic social solidarity. Old traditions surrounding cotton and campesino community life were strongly based on helping one another out. This was not unlike the historic solidarity of Mennonite community and colony life.

But the historic national culture of Paraguay has one other root. Spanish culture came through the *conquistadores*, who worshipped the ideal of feudalism—that is, a social elite holding most of the property, basically being served by the larger population. The dream of the ideal life as one of not laboring, but instead making others work for you, is still very strong. And capitalistic economy makes it stronger. Historically, after all, a good boss or *patron* at least had to assume major social responsibility and solidarity with his employees. It usually was considered to be an honor and good luck to find a good *patron*, be loyal to him, and depend on his solidarity.

A newer social trend among the poor has tended to spoil what remains of these traditions. As they seek to be close to the rich and powerful in order to gain some benefit or another, solidarity among the poor themselves has declined. One campesino saying puts it this way: "Society of the poor and society of the dogs always end in fight." Or another: "What good does it do to be in solidarity with another poor bastard like you?" The disruption of solidarity among the poor and opportunistic relationships of the poor to the rich have had critical moral consequences. It puts democracy in danger, since political parties tend to manipulate or buy the votes of the poor. It also fosters the informal and illegal economy, since the poor are often loyal to their *patrones*, whether or not their business is legal or corrupt.

ANABAPTIST ECCLESIOLOGY AND "POLITICAL EVANGELIZATION"

Various political parties in Paraguay have begun to identify the Mennonite immigrant communities as a model for social solidarity. As a matter of fact, average per capita income within the Mennonite communities is several times higher than the national average. The social system of cooperativism in agriculture, welfare, health, education, and other areas of life has had impressive economic benefits. In the last election campaign, therefore, most of the presidential candidates made reference to "the Mennonite social model" as a new paradigm for restoring the fabric and economy of the country.

Until recently immigrant Mennonite communities themselves were basically worried about their own security. They tended to see the outside society as something completely incompatible with the Mennonite social tradition. That is why membership in the cooperatives still continues to follow a mostly "ethno-religious" line. Only in recent years have Mennonites begun to think in encouraging ways about their social experience as something that might also apply to the wider Paraguayan society. Previously they approached outside society mainly along the lines of charity.

More and more, however, Mennonite traditions of serving their own community translate into political responsibility based upon a "search and service for the well-being of all." The Mennonite experience in Paraguay has been rich in models of community development, basic healthcare, schooling rooted in community, economic solidarity, and so on. Cooperatives have provided a very effective way of relating directly to the national and international market without the interference of those *intermediarios* who buy low from the producers and sell high to the market. Furthermore, Mennonites have a significant tradition of preventing crime and dealing with crime in nonviolent ways through community-based solidarity, with almost no intervention from the national police.

My own personal search for a coherent Anabaptist political theology has led me to the concept of "political evangelization." With this concept I wish to stress two dimensions: On the one hand, Anabaptist-Mennonite political involvement will most often continue to limit itself to the "prophetic-proclamation" presence of the church and its witness to the world. On the other hand, we must not limit evangelization to "saving souls"; rather it must be a way to permeate the whole of social and cultural life with the way of Jesus and the good news of the gospel.

Christian nonviolence and public policies for human security must relate to one another. In his paradigmatic approach to Christian discipleship, John Howard Yoder insisted that for a follower of Jesus, church ethics is always public ethics. Here he linked Karl Barth's political ethics closely to a believers church orientation. In doing so, Yoder may well have produced a political theology with a dynamic synthesis of Schleitheim's insistence on living within the perfection of Christ, Menno Simons' hints that public order might be possible through "a sword without blood," and Pilgram Marpeck's active citizen with a strong believers church orientation. In that same spirit and hope, I would like to suggest some very preliminary thoughts on Anabaptism and policies for human security, in the form of ten theses:

1. Christian policies of human security must be grounded broadly in overall biblical theology, bringing salvation history, the Trinitarian character of God, and the Christological identity of the church into synthesis.

2. At least seven perspectives of a "Christian worldview" must sustain the church in its work for human security: the sovereignty of God as chief protagonist in creation and redemption; basic aspects of Torah as *summum bonum* (or highest good) of human living; the covenant character of the people of God; the teleological character of history as it moves purposefully toward *shalom*; the cultural and ethical implications of conversion; the human dignity of cooperation with God's design; and the kingdom tension between the present age and the age to come.[7]

3. Criminal violence is always rebellion against God, a violation of human dignity and a disruption of the social fabric. Usually it also violates existing law. But every human being and all societies are capable of becoming violent and criminal.

4. Violence and criminality are usually directed against private property. Although the protection of private property is legitimate, there is also a danger of materialism. Sins against property must not be overemphasized in comparison to other sins.

5. The gospel and the local church nurture many resources and practices that are key to overcoming violence and fostering security: reconciliation, the gift of the Spirit, unconditional acceptance of sinners, new peoplehood and family belonging, restitution, Torah-shalom ethics, and responsible lifestyle in light of the last judgment. In the area of practical theology, local churches are able to offer competence in conflict management, mediation, and peace services.

6. For followers of the way of Jesus and his church, the search for security and the fight against criminality have limits: All pastoral care aims at restitution and can never accept

killing in any form. In seeking security, whether private or public, Christians who follow the model of Jesus (or for that matter Michael Sattler) will prefer to give up their lives instead of taking other life. Further still, they will do this in light of the eternal destiny of unrepentant criminals, conscious of how Jesus shared the last moments of his life with two criminals. When Menno Simons suggested that "the sword of Christian authority shall be without blood"[8] he seemed to have hoped that there might be a way of reinforcing law without shedding blood through lethal coercive force. Whether or not this is applicable in all situations, it is worth exploring further within the believers church tradition. A country like Costa Rica has managed to live without military force. Traditionally, much of the British police force has helped maintain public order without the use of arms.

7. Security and the fight against criminal violence cannot be divorced from the search for social justice. That is why the church will pursue specific concerns for adequate lawmaking, by which society strives to bring together peace and social justice. Both are biblical values. But in pursuing them, the Christian and the church often will often suffer a lack of peace and justice.

8. The church will pursue a special interest in understanding the social and cultural roots of criminality, violence, and insecurity. It will critically review the construction of national history, family and role model traditions, the school system, economic structures, the overall cultural value system, as well as the repercussions of global society.

9. A synthesis of church, society, and state must never become so intense that no one can separate them neatly from each other. Church and state need enough independence from each other that they may speak to one other in a responsible manner. Furthermore, the church cannot assume responsibility for the whole of society, and even less for those not willing to follow the way of Christ. It is the task of the church to witness toward the way of the cross by repaying evil with good, and by embracing the world in its ungodliness. The foolishness of the

cross is wisdom also in the search for human security.

10. Therefore an Anabaptist political theology of human security might best be called "political evangelization." There is only one ethic for the church and for human society outside of the church. This is the ethics of life in the New Jerusalem, toward which humanity is called to walk. The political responsibility of the church consists in proclaiming and living out the one kingdom of God. By witnessing faithfully and prophetically, the church is engaged in the "evangelization of culture," whether consciously or not.

NOTES

1. C. René Padilla, *Transforming Church and Mission*, 2004 Forum for World Evangelization, Thailand (San Clemente, Calif.: Lausanne Committee for World Evangelization, 2004), 53.

2. Ibid., 54.

3. Calvin Redekop, "A State Within a Church," *Mennonite Quarterly Review* 48, no. 4 (October 1973): 339–57; quoted in Gerhard Ratzlaff, *Ein Leib, viele Glieder: die mennonitischen Gemeinden in Paraguay* (Asunción, Paraguay: Gemeindekomitee [Asociación Evangélica Mennonita del Paraguay], 2001), 233.

4. Ratzlaff, *Ein Leib, Viele Glieder*, 233.

5. Cornelius Krahn, *Menno Simons (1496–1561): ein beitrag zur geschichte und theologie der taufgesinnten* (Karlsruhe: H. Schneider, 1936), 166–69.

6. See John D. Thiesen, *Mennonite and Nazi?: Attitudes Among Mennonite Colonists in Latin America, 1933–1945*, Studies in Anabaptist and Mennonite History, no. 37 (Kitchener, Ont.: Pandora Press, 1999).

7. Alfred Neufeld, *Fatalismus als missionstheologisches Problem: die Kontextualisation des Evangeliums in einer Kultur fatalistischen Denkens das Beispiel Paraguay*, Missiologica Evangelica, vol. 6 (Bonn: Verlag für Kultur und Wissenschaft, 1994), 473.

8. Krahn, *Menno Simons*, 166–69.

FOR FURTHER READING

Barrett, Rafael. *El dolor paraguayo.* Edited by Miguel A. Fernández. Caracas, Venezuela: Biblioteca Ayacucho, 1987.

————. *Mirando vivir.* Edited by Carlos Meneses. Barcelona: Tusquets, 1976.

Godoy Ziogas, Marylin, Olga Caballero Aquino, and Manuelita Escobar de Peña. *Pintadas por sí mismas: historia de diez vidas.* Asunción, Paraguay, 1986.

Neufeld, Alfred. *Fatalismus als missionstheologisches Problem: die Kontextualisation des Evangeliums in einer Kultur fatalistischen Denkens das Beispiel Paraguay.* Missiologica Evangelica, vol. 6. Bonn: Verlag für Kultur und Wissenschaft, 1994.

————. "Menno und die Obrigkeiten: Ein früher Fall von politischer Evangelisation?" In *Mission im Zeichen des Friedens: Beiträge zur Geschichte täuferisch-mennonitischer Mission,* eds. Heinrich Klassen and Johannes Reimer. Edition AFEM, vol. 14. Lage [Nürnberg]: Logos VTR, 2003.

Padilla, C. René. *Transforming Church and Mission.* 2004 Forum for World Evangelization, Thailand. San Clemente, Calif.: Lausanne Committee for World Evangelization, 2004.

Paraguayan Conference of Catholic Bishops. *El hombre paraguayo en su cultura.* Cuadernos de Pastoral Social, no. 7. Asunción: Conferencia Episcopal Paraguaya, Equipo Nacional de Pastoral Social, 1986.

Ratzlaff, Gerhard. *Ein Leib, viele Glieder: die mennonitischen Gemeinden in Paraguay.* Asunción, Paraguay: Gemeindekomitee [Asociación Evangélica Mennonita del Paraguay], 2001.

Redekop, Calvin. "A State Within a Church." *Mennonite Quarterly Review* 48, no. 4 (October 1973): 339–57.

Thiesen, John D. *Mennonite and Nazi?: Attitudes Among Mennonite Colonists in Latin America, 1933–1945.* Studies in Anabaptist and Mennonite History, no. 37. Kitchener, Ont.: Pandora Press, 1999.

Yoder, John Howard. *Body Politics: Five Practices of the Christian Community Before the Watching World.* Nashville, Tenn.: Discipleship Resources, 1992.

PART II

SEEKING THE WELFARE OF THE CITY: ESSAYS ON PUBLIC PEACE, JUSTICE, AND ORDER

Conference Papers

_____

SECTION B

The Global Context of the Church's Witness

10

Public Peace, Justice, and Order in Ecumenical Conversation

Fernando Enns

> The pacifist witness of the Historic Peace Churches—
> such as Mennonites—has all our respect. It is an impres-
> sive expression of a Christian lifestyle but it contains no
> further productive contribution to the ongoing debate
> on international conflict resolution and it can therefore
> be neglected in the further reflection.[1]

This statement appears in a recently published German book on the ethics of peace by Michael Haspel. The author, a gifted young theologian, strongly criticizes his own Protestant state church in Germany for being too optimistic about military interventions, for being too wedded to traditional just-war thinking, and for failing to develop new strategies for nonviolent peacebuilding. Haspel does not seem to find a real alternative in the position of the historic peace churches. But neither does he identify their position as one that requires serious consider-ation as Christians struggle to defend those who cannot defend themselves against the threat of violence.

Haspel's statement is symptomatic of how other Christians respond to the peace church position. One finds much respect for a traditional, firm, and consistent nonviolent witness by committed Christians. But thinkers from mainstream churches do not consider it a serious option for the "real problems" of the "real world." They continue to see it as a possibility only for small groups at the edge of society who are not in power, who are not taking responsibility for what is going on outside their own church circles—a nice icon in the ecumenical museum of interesting exotic species.

In this paper I will illustrate the ecumenical conversation on the "real problem" of protection of civilian populations, looking both at history and at continuing debates within the World Council of Churches (WCC). My hope is to gain insights on challenges that face the ecumenical family in general, as well as Mennonites in particular. I will present this debate within the framework of the international Decade to Overcome Violence 2001-2010 (DOV), which offers a new common ecumenical space for reflection on peace, justice, and order. The DOV is a great step, perhaps even a paradigm shift within the ecumenical movement. It provides an opportunity to reflect together on ethically justified reactions to the threat of violence.

History of the Ecumenical Movement

One of the strongest motivations behind the early twentieth-century movement that led to the WCC was the experience of World War I. Christians were perplexed at the inability of the churches to prevent this terrible war. In 1937, a decade before the WCC was finally founded, one of the conferences that prepared the way met at Oxford around the theme of "Church, Community, and State." Facing the danger of yet another world war, the conference declared:

> If war breaks out, then pre-eminently the church must manifestly be the church, still united as the one Body of Christ, though the nations wherein it is planted fight each other, consciously offering the same prayers that God´s name be hallowed, his kingdom come, and his will be done, in both, or all, the warring nations.

The Second World War in fact delayed the founding of the WCC. Once again churches in the afflicted nations proved unable to stop the violence and to present to the world another reality—that of world communion, a body of sisters and brothers whose interrelatedness would be stronger than their respective loyalties to their nations.

Finally in 1948 the WCC was founded. Meeting in Amsterdam, the first assembly made what would become a well-known pronouncement:

> War as a method of settling disputes is incompatible with the teaching and example of our Lord Jesus Christ. The part which war plays in our present international life is a sign against God and a degradation of man.

Although the whole council adopted this powerful statement, it needed clarification. The perspectives of Christians on matters of war and the use of armed force differed at the time, and still differ radically, continuing to threaten the unity of the church. The Amsterdam assembly identified the differences frankly:

1. "In the absence of impartial supranational institutions, there are those who hold that military action is the ultimate sanction of the rule of law, and that citizens must be distinctly taught that it is their duty to defend the law by force if necessary." This position remains the official one in a large number of churches. It reflects the well-known two-kingdom theory: that God rules in the world through worldly order, and that it is God´s will to maintain this order, to act against oppressors, to protect the weak, and to punish the evil-doers.

2. "There are those who hold that, even though entering a war may be a Christian's duty in particular circumstances, modern warfare, with its mass destruction, can never be an act of justice." This position is grounded in the same theological argument. Nonetheless, it seriously applies one criterion in the just war theory—those requiring that a war be waged by just and appropriate means. Thus it speaks against the legitimacy of war in times of weapons of mass destruction.

3. "Others, again, refuse military service of all kinds, convinced that an absolute witness against war and for peace is for

them the will of God, and they desire that the Church should speak of the same effect." Pacifist traditions, including Mennonites, represented this position, along with individuals from other traditions.

Following Amsterdam, Willem A. Visser 't Hooft, the first WCC General Secretary, invited the historic peace churches (HPCs) to share their convictions with the wider ecumenical family. The result was a well-known series of Puidoux Conferences. All major theological arguments on war, peace, and the relation of church and state had a voice in these conferences. The opportunity and challenge for Mennonites to spell out their ethical position helped them enormously. In ecumenical circles, John Howard Yoder became the most persuasive spokesperson for a nonviolent position grounded in the ethics of Jesus. It was a serious and timely witness, for which we should be immensely grateful. But in the end it did not convince other traditions to adopt the Mennonite position as an ecumenical family, although it did attract many individuals who became strong protagonists for a consistently nonviolent position in their own churches.

During the past decades, WCC meetings have continued to debate the appropriate Christian response to violent conflicts and repeatedly taken a stand. In some situations they have condemned the use of disproportionate armed force. In others, they have criticized the failure of the international community to protect populations in the face of predictable massive violence. But the question remains: Is the use of armed coercion an acceptable tool to protect human rights and enforce the international rule of law in violent or potentially violent situations, and if so, under what conditions?

Basically, the same positions that the WCC outlined in 1948 continue to dominate the member churches and denominations of the WCC and within the denominations, even today. Still, the debate is progressing.

THE "REAL CHALLENGE": PROTECTING CIVILIAN POPULATIONS IN TIMES OF VIOLENT HUMANITARIAN CRISIS

In 1999 the Central Committee (CC) of the WCC adopted a "Memorandum and Recommendations on International Security and Response to Armed Conflict" that called for new approaches to international peace and security in the post-Cold War world. The document highlights dilemmas surrounding "humanitarian intervention," particularly as they became evident in Kosovo and in the failure of the international community to prevent genocide in Rwanda. Mennonites supported this memorandum, first and foremost because of the emphasis it places on the need for "new approaches." The memo led to a study process, with initial findings going to the CC in Potsdam 2001, the same meeting that launched the international DOV at the Brandenburg gate in Berlin, just eight months before 9/11.

1. Potsdam 2001

The Commission of the Churches on International Affairs presented those initial findings in a document entitled "The Protection of Endangered Populations in Situations of Armed Violence." Its promising subtitle reads: "An Ecumenical Ethical Approach," but basically it offered nothing but a new formulation of the just war theory in modern terms without even reflecting its complexity. It included a list of criteria to guide UN reforms and to serve "in the interim whenever armed intervention for humanitarian purposes is undertaken."

The original goal had been to clarify issues and develop guidelines to assist the churches. What is the central issue? The document formulates it correctly: "The moral obligation of the international community to protect lives of civilian populations that are at risk in situations where their government is unable or unwilling to act is widely accepted." The WCC Eighth Assembly in Harare had affirmed

> the emphasis of the Gospel on the value of all human beings in the sight of God, on the atoning and redeeming work of Christ that has given every person true dignity,

> on love as the motive for action, and on love for one's neighbors as the practical expression of active faith in Christ. We are members of one another, and when one suffers all are hurt. This is the responsibility Christians bear to ensure the human rights of every person.

The Potsdam document does include some valuable phrases, such as these:

> Fundamental to conflict-prevention efforts is the task of building cultures of peace, reconciliation, and metanoia which make conflict transformation a preferred option to violence. Peace education, election monitoring, civic education, inter-faith dialogue, and awareness raising on human rights are all activities which can successfully prevent escalation of conflicts in some areas. These are long-term measures in which the churches can and must play a particularly active role.

The document also speaks about the responsibility of the churches in post-conflict situations and pastoral responsibility for processes of reconciliation and forgiveness. Finally, it ends with a realistic analysis: "In practice the international community has seldom been capable of such [ethical] consistency." Therefore: "Many now believe that the international community has a right—or even a duty—to use armed force to help protect and assist people at risk in such situations."

In the end, however, the document does not propose "new approaches" but instead returns to the just war theory, and does no more than apply its traditional catalogue of criteria to the situation of the twenty-first century. At most, it correctly analyzes the failures of the international community in so many instances but in the end sounds like an effort to put new wine in old wineskins.

The long and heated debate that ensued was revealing in many ways. From a Mennonite perspective it was at first shocking that so many delegates from other traditions did not seem to realize what was at stake here. For the first time in history the WCC was going to adopt a document listing criteria for the use of military intervention; by doing so it would implicitly confirm the just war theory as a consensus within the ecumenical family. Once the discussion started, however, it was satisfying to discover how much time the committee was willing to dedicate to hearing the peace church perspective, and how much it was valued. It became obvious that the WCC could not adopt a document that so clearly conflicted with the ecclesiological identity of one of its member churches.

As debates proceeded confessional borderlines that initially seemed clear-cut turned out to be more diverse. It became increasingly obvious that personal and contextual experiences were also shaping the ethical convictions of delegates. A Lutheran theologian from Norway was convinced that it had been the Christian duty of his father to fight and kill German Nazis in order to defend his own people. Therefore he would not even accept an argument like Bonhoeffer's that one becomes guilty by killing another person, even if one acts with the best of motivations. Some Lutherans from Germany said the opposite. Some representatives from the southern hemisphere, mainly women from Africa, made clear that they could not understand why the men present were so eager to legitimize the use of military intervention. From their experience military intervention has never proven helpful but only given birth to new hatred, killing, and suffering. A pacifist voice turned out to represent many more than just the small Mennonite family.

Still others spoke against the proposal of the adoption for different motivations. Delegates from the Russian Orthodox Church, for example, were skeptical of what they saw as a Western-dominated United Nations. This drove them to oppose any implementation of a redefined just war theory.

Debates like these are highlights in the life of the WCC. It is through just such interaction that the different confessional, cultural, and contextual perspectives emerge and churches call each other to account. Delegates must present their best arguments. Even if we do not agree in the end, we stay committed to each other, growing together in this communion of churches through honest struggles. It is a peace witness in itself. This itself suggests a thesis: A peace church is always ecumenically oriented.

In the end, the document changed greatly. The committee replaced the euphemistic term "humanitarian intervention" with another: "The protection of endangered populations in situations of armed violence." The revised document lists fundamentally different opinions. The proposed set of criteria for military intervention was separated from the document. Above all, the Central Committee did not adopt the document but merely *received* it as a study paper for further reflection, and invited member churches to react.[2] One can criticize this as a compromise, but the decision realistically reflects the diversity within Christian churches on this very matter.

What is most disappointing is the failure of the study process to identify any truly "new approaches," as it had promised. The question thus remains: How is the world communion of churches reacting in times of armed conflict when it becomes necessary to protect the very lives of our brothers and sisters?

2. The Historic Peace Churches' Response

Several months after the meeting of the WCC's Central Committee in Potsdam—but still prior to 9/11—representatives from all three historic peace churches gathered in Bienenberg, Switzerland. This was the first such meeting in the context of the Decade to Overcome Violence. HPC theologians came together to share and reflect critically on our respective peace theologies. (A second meeting took place in Nairobi, Kenya, in 2004.[3]) Representatives did not simply reformulate their diverse peace theologies but also sent a reaction to the WCC, entitled "Just Peacemaking: Toward an Ecumenical Ethical Approach from the Perspective of the Historic Peace Churches." It starts with a confession of their own complicity in violence:

We have often failed to live up to our commitment to the Spirit of Jesus Christ. We have often been silent and failed to act on behalf of those who are suffering the scourge of injustice and violence. We do not always know exactly what constitutes justice—or peace—in a given situation; we lack wisdom in addressing the complex issues of our time. In particular we share with the wider church and the larger world the perplexities of addressing the complex issues raised by conflicts such as those in Rwanda, Iraq, the Middles East, Somalia, Southern Sudan, Kosovo, Colombia, South Africa, and many other places.[4]

In five paragraphs the paper goes on to accept the challenge of finding ways to protect endangered populations in situations of armed violence, but also to explain why the approach of the WCC-study paper cannot be helpful. It calls for deeper theological and ethical reflection, and correlates peace with justice:

1. "A biblically and theologically grounded pacifism regards seeking God´s justice as central and integral to a nonviolent philosophy of life. To state the issue as if we have to choose between nonviolence and justice is a false dichotomy."

2. The HPC theologians then identified a number of normative practices for seeking justice within "principled pacifism," and which those who accept "just war" reasoning can also affirm.

3. "The use of violent force as a 'last resort' to secure justice creates conditions that inhibit the achievement of justice. Too often we work under the false assumption that, if we cannot find a nonviolent solution to a conflict, the use of violent force will take care of the problem."

4. "We call on the churches to emphasize the distinctive witness to the world that flows from our commitment to the spirit of Jesus Christ and our identity as the body of Christ in the world."

5. "Though both pacifists and those who reason with 'just war' principles seek justice, neither tradition can guarantee that justice will be accomplished. The pacifist commitment to nonviolence is ultimately grounded in an eschatology of trust

in the victory over evil of God revealed in Jesus's life, teachings, death, and resurrection."

Clearly this response does not offer a sufficient answer to all aspects of the question at stake. The Bienenberg group formulated its statement in a humble and honest way, trying to avoid the impression that peace churches think they know all the answers. Still, it also exposes the shortfalls and the weaknesses of the WCC paper by questioning traditional arguments and by inviting the WCC to broaden its discussion rather than attempt to close it. New wine, after all, requires new wineskins.

3. Central Committee Geneva 2003

At its 2003 meeting the WCC's Central Committee received an update on the study process. By now the events of September 11, 2001, had taken place, as well as wars in Afghanistan and Iraq. These events have added new dimensions to the debate: On the one hand, globalized terrorism has sharpened awareness of human security in the northern hemisphere; on the other hand the United States has waged a unilateral "preemptive" war against another sovereign state in defiance of international law and the will of the UN Security Council. These developments show that the power of the nation-state, which seemed to be fading in the post-modern era and times of economic globalization, is back. The WCC spoke unanimously against the war in Iraq and also condemned terrorist attacks.

In the 2003 report to the CC, responses to its 2001 study document include one from the Lutheran Church of Norway, called "Vulnerability and Security."[5] The Norwegian response stresses the deep interrelationship between vulnerability and security. It also focuses on the question of humanitarian intervention, defining it as "the international use of force on the territory of other states and without their consent with the aim of (re-)establishing elementary human security when it has been grossly and persistently violated." It then revisits criteria for a "just war," insisting that while discussions continue on the validity of the criteria, they nonetheless represent an important ethical framework.[6] Listing criteria in itself does not endorse a general ethical legitimization of military intervention, it insists. Meanwhile, a more fundamental consideration of the relationship between human vulnerability and security, combined with a broad approach to the security problem, opens the way for a wider perspective.

The Norwegian statement points to two specific contributions that churches can make in the context of security policy—highlighting the perspective of victims and offering the service of reconciliation. The victim's perspective (Matt 25:35) reinforces the concept of human security the document advocates. And since reconciliation is at the very core of the Christian message (2 Cor 5:18), the churches must be the first to insist on peaceful solutions to confrontation and conflict. Reconciliation processes require respect for truth and justice, remorse, forgiveness, and a new beginning.

The Protestant Church in Germany (EKD) also responded officially in a letter that echoes reflections it had previously made in a document entitled, "Steps on the Way to Peace: Points of Reference on Ethics and Peace Policy."[7] Strikingly, the EKD response also insists on relating the issue of how to protect innocent populations to a broader perspective on security. According to this perspective a reliable structure of peace and security will require the rule of international law, ensure the protection of freedom and economic justice, strengthen international organizations, and establish a culture of social behavior, as well as respect for minorities. Hence it includes conflict prevention, conflict resolution, and post-conflict reconciliation. The concept of "just peace" (instead of just war) conveys the basic idea of Christian peace ethics. It calls for the strengthening of the international peace system as intended and drawn up in the Charter of the United Nations. The universal acceptance and implementation of human rights is an important factor for strengthening international peace as a legal system.

The EKD document continues to allow for the use of military force but insists that it remains a borderline case. The use of military force as "last resort" has been vehemently criticized within the church's internal discussion; thus the document calls for further careful analysis. The document ends by recognizing that the fundamental ethical debate over whether to use violence or maintain a radically pacifist position will not and probably cannot be resolved. The EKD does not believe it can ever entirely exclude a defensive war. But the prime task is of peace promotion, which requires strategies and policies that promote democracy and economic justice.

The third response that WCC study process had received between 2001 and 2003 was the statement of historic peace church theologians at Bienenberg. The report to the Central Committee summarized the HPC position adequately, quoting the five arguments listed above, and making the following points:[8]

> a. The HPC position sets forth a vision of justice that is holistic and social, distinguishing it from a view that emphasizes individual autonomy and freedom, protection of private property, or a narrow perspective on human rights such as freedom of speech and association. The biblical tradition of covenant justice includes social solidarity, religious liberty, and a comprehensive vision of human rights.

> b. The HPCs list five available practices as possible nonviolent alternatives to explore: nonviolent forms of defense and social transformation; citizens' corps of observers / interveners / advocates; acknowledging responsibility for violence and injustice, and seeking repentance and forgiveness (e.g. truth and reconciliation commissions); training persons in cooperative conflict methods and strategies; the church's witness and advocacy on behalf of the marginalized and those whose lives are threatened by injustice.

> c. A presumed "humanitarian intervention" may mask egoistic self-interests and the partisan political agendas of the parties who intervene. Implicitly, the church has accepted the assumption that violent force is inevitable,

and therefore we must support the preparation for that possibility. Last resort thinking cuts short imaginative thinking and creative action to find alternative ways to make peace.

d. The HPCs express disappointment that the language and content of the WCC study document is dominated largely by political analysis and prudential calculation about when resort to armed intervention might be justified and what restraints should be placed on it. It questions whether this can really help to develop an "ecumenical ethical approach" as the subtitle suggests.

In addition the 2003 report lists other contributions from governmental and non-governmental organizations.

How the Debate Has Been Reshaped

The question that arises from a survey of recent WCC conversations is this: Is the process of discernment actually developing in any fresh direction? The debate is clearly in transition. The contributions of the churches have reshaped that debate. Together with responses by other traditions, historic peace church participation cannot be underestimated. Despite diverse assessments of just war argumentation over the use of war as a "last resort," statements by all traditions demonstrate a clear tendency to approach the challenge of protecting innocent populations in a much more holistic framework. This became visible as the 2003 meeting of the WCC's Central Committee reached an agreement:

1. The next step of the study will have the title "The Responsibility to Protect: Ethical and Theological Reflections." Protection includes prevention, reaction, and rebuilding. Different aspects of conflict management and peace-building can be unfolded. All reactions called for effective non-military means for the treatment and solution of conflicts, in the conflict prevention, mediation, and the post-conflict reconciliation moments.

The ethical demand to protect those who are in danger cannot be isolated from the broader framework of conflict resolution. The responsibility to protect includes a long-term involvement, working for sustainable reconciliation. The shift in emphasis here prevents the ecumenical family from limiting debates on the single question, that of whether and when the "last resort" of military intervention is legitimate. This will require churches to discern together and emphasize how to prevent conflicts, mediate, and rebuild communities instead of ending every discussion by simply restating our differences. This is an opportunity for peace churches to feed in their insights and experience at nonviolent peacebuilding.

> 2. The ethical and theological perspective of the churches will be clearly highlighted. This means to make explicit the criteria for discernment in these particular cases in which the action to be taken cannot clearly be foreseen. Only an ethical and theological analysis could show the unique role of the churches in this area.

This agreement helps to shift the whole debate to the role of the churches in society. At Potsdam, Mennonites demanded that the ecumenical family must argue first of all as churches— that is, explore their own theological and ethical wisdom in order to not repeat what any non-governmental or governmental organization could say as well, simply building on humanistic arguments. This is how the churches best serve the societies within which they live; this is the service a world communion of churches owes to the world. From the peace churches it demands that they share more than a simple pacifist witness. It also requires them to offer theological and ethical reasoning through engagement in ecumenical debates.

> 3. [We agreed on a shift] from security understood as something related only to states, to human security. This includes physical safety, economic and social well-being, respect for the dignity and worth as human beings, and the protection of human rights and fundamental freedoms.

> In the present world circumstances, the question of what is the determining authority to decide intervention remains crucial.

Again the debate is opening into a more inclusive approach. It is not the states or the nations that are at the center of the ecumenical debate. It is the human being in relation to others, created in the image of God, loved by God as revealed in Jesus Christ, sustained by the work of the Holy Spirit. On the grounds of a Christian anthropology we will be able to approach the issue of security in a much more coherent way. Hopefully we will not fall into the trap of an individualistic approach but will start with a relational anthropology. We will have to recognize ways that human beings are interrelated to their respective communities and cultures. We will have to emphasize how much social well-being plays a role in conflict resolution.

The question of authority will also require discernment. Should the church allow the United Nations Security Council, in all its problematic format, to be the institution that decides whether and how to intervene? Clearly we have no better political instrument yet. Political institutions will have to make these kinds of decisions. What then is the role of religious institutions in the process of decision making? What is their relation to political institutions? A theology that takes seriously the fallenness of creation in general will also have to include human political institutions in this perspective.

> 4. The conflict, between on one part the respect to the state sovereignty and on the other the protection of human rights violated in a state, is at the core of the discussion on intervention and human security. The international system is built on the principle of national sovereignty. The principle of non-intervention, on the other hand, has been broken several times, justifying intervention based on the argument of serious human rights violations committed by a state against its own citizens as a threat to peace.

Former state-churches have often used arguments on the basis of international law, concerning respect of the sovereignty of a nation-state, for example. But this is not a theological argument. Mennonites have not considered this way of reasoning appropriate for the churches, mostly because they have not identified themselves with the nation-state as other churches have done. The "untouchable" sovereignty of a state as an absolute law needs, in fact, to be questioned. Mennonites share an understanding that the body of Christ—the church worldwide, the ecumenical communion of churches—transcends all other loyalties. This will become a controversial issue with those traditions that have seen their linkage to a nation or ethnic group as an identity-marker of the church.

> 5. Issues of protection cannot be separated from the respect and promotion of human rights and the strengthening of democracy. As many documents stated, measures to reinforce civil and political, economic, social and cultural rights, as well as a strong democracy, are strategies perceived as central in prevention, mediation, and reconciliation processes.

Mennonites know from history that the violation of human rights, such as freedom of religion or conscientious objection to military service, is basic to their identity. They have developed theological arguments to affirm such rights. This implies responsibility for the human rights of all others as well, including people of other faiths. Some would conclude, however, that to fight for democracy is an obligation for Christians because fundamental human rights such as free will, education, free press, free expression of opinions, and freedom from discrimination of race or gender are preserved only in a democratic system. Interchurch debates should not assume that democracy as practiced in the West is the one ideal model for the rest of the world. The best way to ensure human rights, and the religious grounds for doing so, needs discussion among people from all cultures, which might result in various social expressions.

6. [We have agreed that] international law is not static, but in a constant process of evolution; the new configuration of the world requires continuous reflection. The recent war against Iraq brought some issues into consideration: multilateralism and unilateralism, the role of the UN Security Council, the relationships between military intervention and humanitarian assistance. Besides ethical criteria, legal and political criteria should be considered to go beyond the present situation. The specific roles of the International Court of Justice and the recently established International Criminal Court in the pursuing of justice should also be included in the reflection.

We recognize that law is not something given, divine, but is something that humans shape. It is our responsibility. The churches need to pay attention to the development of international law, using the power of law in order to bring peace and reconciliation. We have to share our insights concerning restorative or transformative justice and inform ongoing political debates wherever we can. Justice—empowered by law—is one of the most effective tools in situations where all other means for nonviolent conflict resolution have failed. This implies law enforcement. And yet we know that law is a limited tool. It is not a synonym for reconciliation. The theological distinction between God´s justice and human justice is crucial.

7. All the related ecumenical documents emphatically underlined the priority of non-military instruments in safeguarding peace and related the prior option of freedom from violence to the roots of the Decade to Overcome Violence. In the responses coming from the churches, divergence in opinion is again clearly perceived. While some try to specify criteria for the use of military force as last resort, the document from the Historic Peace Churches directly criticizes this option. Recent discussions on just war and preemptive war will be included in a future study.

I am sensing a serious willingness in all churches to take up the crucial questions. It will be necessary to share our respective wisdom with one another. Every tradition needs to be challenged. Mennonites will have to prove that their beliefs have something to contribute to the "real challenges" of the "real world," without subscribing to a revised just war theory, without necessarily giving in to the temptation of theological legitimization for the use of violence, but with a firm commitment to engage in theological and ethical debate.

DECADE TO OVERCOME VIOLENCE: CHURCHES SEEKING RECONCILIATION AND PEACE, 2001-2010

The DOV offers an ecumenical space for these debates in a new dimension. The decade is considered a journey of common discernment. It is an opportunity to reshape the whole debate, moving it from the question just war theory versus radical pacifism to a common search for prevention, mediation, and reconciliation. DOV is a challenge to all churches—including HPCs—to become more creative in nonviolent ways of conflict resolution, thus becoming more faithful. And it is a commitment of all churches to take up this responsibility seriously, not limiting debates to the one ethical issue of whether to use violence as a last resort. Rather, we are called to explore together how overcoming violence and building sustainable peace is at the heart of the Christian confession, belief, and mission—a way of living, a "regulative principle" in Christian theological ethics.

NOTES

1. Michael Haspel, *Friedensethik und Humanitäre Intervention: der Kosovo-Krieg als Herausforderung evangelischer Friedensethik* (Neukirchen-Vluyn: Neukirchener, 2002), 82.

2. To read the document as received, see http://www.wcc-coe.org/wcc/who/cc2001/pi2rev-e.html.

3. Cf. the DVD documentation *Watu Wa Amani. People of Peace. The Decade to Overcome Violence*, April 24, 2005. Written documentation is in preparation.

4. Enns, Fernando, Scott Holland, and Ann Riggs, eds. *Seeking Cultures of Peace: A Peace Church Conversation* (Telford, Pa., Scottdale, Pa.: Cascadia Pub. House, Herald Press, 2004) 232-42.

5. Available at http://www.kirken.no/engelsk/VULNERABIL.doc.

6. "Vulnerability and Security" presents the following just war criteria as most important: a. just cause, b. just intention, c. rightful authority, d. compliance with current rules for the waging of warfare (*jus in bello*), e. last resort, f. proportionality.

7. Third edition, 2001, available at http://www.ekd.de/english/2230_peace_ethics_on_probation.html.

8. These are my summary paraphrases.

FOR FURTHER READING

Durnbaugh, Donald, ed. *On Earth Peace: Discussions on War/Peace Issues Between Friends, Mennonites, Brethren, and European Churches, 1935–75.* Elgin, Ill.: The Brethren Press, 1978.

Enns, Fernando. *Friedenskirche in der Ökumene: Mennonitische Wurzeln einer Ethik der Gewaltfreiheit.* Kirche - Konfession - Religion, no. 46. Göttingen: Vandenhoeck & Ruprecht, 2003. [An English translation is in preparation, to be published by Pandora Press as *The Peace Church in the Ecumenical Context: Mennonite Roots of an Ethic of Nonviolence.*]

Enns, Fernando, Scott Holland, and Ann Riggs, eds. *Seeking Cultures of Peace: A Peace Church Conversation.* Telford, Pa., Scottdale, Pa.: Cascadia Pub. House, Herald Press, 2004.

Gros, Jeffrey, and John D. Rempel, eds. *The Fragmentation of the Church and Its Unity in Peacemaking.* Grand Rapids, Mich.: Wm. B. Eerdmans Pub. Co., 2001.

Haspel, Michael. *Friedensethik und Humanitäre Intervention: der Kosovo-Krieg als Herausforderung evangelischer Friedensethik.* Neukirchen-Vluyn: Neukirchener, 2002.

Van der Bent, Ans. *Commitment to God's World: A Concise Critical Survey of Ecumenical Social Thought.* Geneva: WCC Publications, 1995.

—11—

RECOGNIZING THE OTHER'S INSECURITY: EXPERIENCES OF CHRISTIAN-MUSLIM RELATIONS IN INDONESIA

Paulus S. Widjaja

September 11, 2001, shook the entire world, not just the United States. In a single incident in the land of the world's super-power, thousands of people had been killed. Evidence soon showed that a group of Muslim hardliners had carried out the 9/11 attack. Then, thirteen months later, came the 10/12 attack in Bali, Indonesia. Hundreds of Westerners, mostly Australians, died in a bomb blast also carried out by Muslim hardliners. As a result of these incidents, along with U.S. attacks on Afghanistan and Iraq, many people in the world are eager to know more about Islam and the Muslims. Academic, religious, and civic institutions have held seminars to explore Christian-Muslim relations. Many universities around the globe have established centers in Islamic studies to research Islam and the character of the Muslims.

Westerners have learned that they can no longer ignore the existence of Muslims. Many Westerners have recognized that Muslims are fellow human beings and that they can become outraged when they feel threatened and oppressed by the world hegemony that U.S. and British governments presumably lead. At the same time, Westerners now realize that

Muslims have real power to strike back when they feel threatened. They may not have smart bombs, but they obviously have such strong feelings about their dignity and honor that they will not let others oppress them.

In all this, certain questions press upon our minds and hearts: What is actually going on behind all these attacks and counter attacks? How can we make sense of incidents that do not seem to make any sense at all, such as suicide bombing? What are the dynamics and complexities that underlie Christian-Muslim relationships? Are these two communities destined to destroy each other, as sometimes seems? And how, finally, should we respond?

THE ABC TRIANGLE

I am not pretending that I know the best answers to these questions, nor am I pretending to be an expert in Islam. The purpose of my paper is not to give an academic lecture about Islam or Muslims. My intention is simply to share the experience of Christian-Muslim relations in Indonesia, and talk about some of the flash points in those relations.

Too often we jump to conclusions about the behavior of a group of people and forget that behind one's behavior, there are always certain attitudes. We also tend to forget that both attitudes and behaviors are shaped by one's context. There is, in other words, a correlation between *attitude*, *behavior*, and *context*, what Johan Galtung has called the "ABC triangle."

Thus if we want to understand the attitude and behavior of Muslims, it is important for us to understand the context that has shaped their struggle. By trying to understand, I am not suggesting that we excuse Muslims for the evil that some have done, nor am I suggesting that we have to agree with everything they are doing. Glen Stassen, my professor at Fuller Theological Seminary, has said correctly in his book *Just Peacemaking* that an important criteria for just peacemaking is "validating the other's interest." By validating the others' needs, hopes, fear, and desires, we can better understand empathize with them, and we are enabled to make peace.

Ultimately, only Muslims themselves are fully competent to articulate their own interests. But we who seek to listen carefully are also responsible to speak what we believe we are hearing, always with humility and awareness of our limitations or biases.

One dimension of the context requires clarification before all else. Many Westerners have asked my opinion on what they perceive as religious conflict between Christians and Muslims in Indonesia. This is indeed a difficult question. On the one hand, there have been bloody conflicts between Christians and Muslims in Indonesia, such as those in Central Sulawesi and the Mollucas. Tens of thousands of people from both sides have been killed, and residential and religious buildings have been looted, burned, and demolished.

On the other hand, it is not quite accurate to call the conflict religious. This would imply that the two communities are fighting because of different religious belief and practices. The conflict has *become* religious because the two communities heavily use religious texts, symbols, and rituals in the conflict. Churches and mosques alike have blessed the warriors and their weaponry before they have gone to war. They also wear religious clothes in the war. But a closer look at the conflict reveals that its basic thrust is not religion itself, but starts from somewhere else and ends up in religion. So the real task for us is to locate the root of the conflict.

THE IDENTITY CONFLICT

Some people have criticized books such as Benjamin Barber's *Jihad vs. McWorld* or Samuel Huntington's *The Clash of Civilizations and the Remaking of World Order* for potentially contributing to the clash of which they warn.[1] Their merit, however, has been to demonstrate that the clash is not simply between military or economic forces. Rather it is a clash of identities. And one of the root causes underneath this clash of identity, in my opinion, is globalization.

Globalization is not simply about the promotion of free trade. Mostly and ultimately, it is about the worldwide promotion of the culture and way of life of the West. As such, globalization has threatened local people in many places in the world and forced them to withdraw to their primordial communities, where they can feel safe and keep their identity intact. When the force of globalization persuades everybody in the world to eat McDonald's, drink Coke, smoke Marlboro, and enjoy a "free" and individualistic lifestyle, some people, especially those from proud and ancient cultures, are naturally forced to defend and maintain their identity by all means. The stronger the force of globalization is, the stronger the drive to withdraw to the primordial enclave and to defend the primordial culture.

This dynamic becomes all the more inevitable when local people perceive their national governments as having failed to safeguard their identity. Michael Walzer describes the dynamics of membership within a nation well. When a nation, he says, loosens its grip and becomes more open to infiltration of culture and values, the people within that nation will naturally tighten their own grip so that the infiltration does not reach them in the local community. Conversely, when a nation tightens its grip, the people will loosen theirs.[2]

This may explain why when the Indonesian government becomes more open to globalization and eagerly joins with the other nations in organizations such as the World Bank, International Monetary Fund, or World Trade Organization, Indonesian Muslims increasingly show their Islamic identity publicly. More and more Muslim women wear *jilbab*; more and more Muslim men wear white robes, *sorban*, and keep long beards. All this was rare when I was a kid. Everywhere in the cities we can also find stickers, posters, and banners with phrases like "We are a Muslim family," "I am proud to be Muslim," "Born to be Muslim," "Islam is the best," etc. Such a phenomenon, in my opinion, reflects the natural way for Muslims to demonstrate their identity in the face of the sweeping force of globalization. It is not simply a matter of demonstrating their faithfulness to religious command. It functions as a message to the global community that Indonesian Muslims can still hold their ground and keep their identity intact vis-à-vis the sweeping force of globalization.

While the Indonesian Christians are also experiencing the force of globalization, it affects Christian cultural identity far less than that of Muslims. This may be because Christianity, from its inception in Indonesia centuries ago, has already been Westernized. Therefore Christians do not feel strange to many aspects of Western culture that come along with globalization. It does not mean that more Christians than Muslims can accept McDonald's, Coke, Marlboro, or a free and individualistic lifestyle. Many Christians cannot accept those Western commodities. But it does mean that the Indonesian Christians have less resistance to the Western culture that globalization brings than do Muslims.

Such a difference of attitude toward globalization has brought another dynamic to the relationship between Christians and Muslims in Indonesia. Globalization is not perceived simply as a cultural threat to Muslim identity; it is also perceived as a political threat from the powerful West toward less powerful Indonesians. Hence globalization appears to many a Western strategy to conquer the world, including Indonesia. And because the Indonesian Christians are identified as Westernized people, these two sentiments—the defense of Indonesian/Muslim identity against the force of globalization, and the perception that Western-Christians are conquerors—create conditions for conflict between Christians and Muslims.

Further encouraging these sentiments are certain events, articles, brochures, and even songs that take place or circulate among some groups of Christian hardliners, indicating the intention to defeat the Muslims and conquer the whole world. Conservative Christian leaders in the United States like Franklin Graham and Pat Robertson have blamed Muslims for problems in the United States and the world. Their words have indeed offended Indonesian Muslims, who often cite them in national magazines as evidence of the hostile attitude of Christians toward Muslims.

An Indonesian Muslim cleric has also lamented that

Muslims do not like Christians because they often sing songs that contain quite triumphalistic phrases, such as, "Our Lord shall tread down our adversaries" (the lyric is actually inspired by Psalms 60:12; 108:13). The Muslim cleric pointed out that if that is the attitude of Christians toward Muslims, who are perceived as enemies of Christians, then Muslims have the right to stamp down Christians first before the Christians do it to them. Another very famous Christian song declares the desire of Christians "to win Indonesia for Jesus." Such formulas place Christian-Muslim relations into the framework of winning and losing. These and many other examples show the insensitivity of Christians to the interests of Muslims.

A mission strategy to reach "unreached" peoples called "The 10/40 Window" has also become popular evidence among the Muslims about the intention of the Christians to conquer the world and make the Muslims the top priority target to be conquered.[3] We may wonder why it is that Hollywood and the Pentagon, which are also located within the "10/40 Window," have brought such devastating impacts throughout the world, yet are never spoken of as mission targets? Simply to speak of Muslims with the label of "unreached" people is itself offensive. The Muslims may rightly ask why Western Christians should use such a negative adjective with reference to them. Outside the church, these people are called the "uncivilized" people. Inside the church, they are called the "unreached" people. Can we not find a better and more positive way to speak of Muslims without using such triumphalistic-imperialistic terms?

One recent case that demonstrates Christian triumphalism is the building of the Jakarta Tower, known among Christians as the Jakarta Revival Center. This is a project of some Christian evangelicals. The building will become the highest building in the world. When asked why they are doing such a mega-project, the leaders of the development group say that it is necessary to show a visible, concrete, and identifiable presence of the Christians in Indonesia. In other words, it is meant to be a show of force by some Christians rather than a reflection of a humble desire to serve society.

These and other similar cases send a message of Christian triumphalism to Muslims and create enmity between the two communities. If we want to make peace with Muslims, we have to validate their fear and concerns. The fear of losing one's identity and being conquered reflects a very basic need for survival. Of course, we can also make a list of similar cases of triumphalism by which some groups of Muslim hardliners have threatened Christians. But it is not my intention to make such a list. It is better for us to examine ourselves rather than to blame others for the bad things we do. Another important practice of just peacemaking, according to Glen Stassen, is "taking the transforming initiative." That is to say, we make peace better by first taking steps to correct ourselves, to repent, and to approach the other, rather than to wait for the other to take the first step.

THE POWER GAME

The desire of the Muslims to defend their identity in the face of globalization determines their attitude not only toward nations in the international community but also their fellow citizens, who they perceive as comrades of the dominating power of the West. Their anxiety then manifests itself outwardly in the form of enmity toward the West, and also inwardly in the form of struggles to gain political power within the nation. This partly explains why some Muslim hardliners are demanding the national implementation of Islamic *shari'ah* (law). When a group of people feels threatened by a powerful foreign force to the extent that they might lose their identity, dignity, and right to self-determination, they will naturally fight back by trying to gain the power to control the course of the nation. This is not simply a matter of determining who is really in charge in the nation; it is a matter of survival, a matter of life and death.

Unfortunately, Christians have responded unwisely. A minority complex has made many Christians paranoid. Seeing some Muslims move for political power, some Christians are tempted to do the same thing because they are afraid if they do not, then they will have no political power at all, resulting in a resurgent persecution of Christians. This paranoia was already obvious in the waning years of the last dictatorial regime of Suharto. Suharto tried to win the support of Muslims by placing a significant number of Muslim leaders in his cabinet while removing the Christian ones, which prompted anxieties among many Christians.

The logic behind this anxiety is quite naïve. If Christians are no longer holding key positions in the cabinet and military leadership, then the assumption is that Christians might have no control over the national politics whatsoever. I was once involved in the nominating committee for the leadership of the Communion of Churches in Indonesia (CCI). Within the committee there was a hot debate about who was the most appropriate Christian military general for the CCI advisory board. Some churches thought this was necessary, not only to safeguard Christians and Christian interests, but also to open the door for Christians to take part in controlling national politics.

Such an attitude reflects a theology of prosperity, in which God's blessing coincides with achievement and success, in this case political success. It also reflects a sort of pragmatism in which effectiveness is the measure of a church's success. Whether or not churches can effect society and direct its course is the test of faithfulness. Within this mindset, churches feel a strong drive to take control of the nation. Christian leaders holding key positions in the cabinet and military leadership had once been signs of such success. But since this is no longer the case, some Christians are trying to repeat their earlier "effectiveness" by establishing a Christian political party.

The only Christian political party eligible for the legislative election of April 2004 was Partai Damai Sejahtera (PDS), which means Peace Party. What a name! Establishing and supporting this party have been so-called evangelical churches. Party leaders said their purpose in establishing the PDS was to voice Christian aspiration and interests, a very sound mission. A closer look, however, reveals that this party was intended as a way for some Christians to gain political power.

The name of the most recent PDS campaign was "Joseph Enters The Palace 2004." The theme suggests the desire of the Christians in PDS is not simply to voice Christian aspiration and interests, but to gain political power, just like Joseph did. Perhaps such political power is necessary if the Christians want to direct the course of the nation for its betterment. But this represents a very naïve pragmatism. Moreover, choosing the figure of Joseph is itself quite telling. Behind such a choice there is the spirit of triumphalism and self-righteousness. The theme portrays the Christians as Josephs, the good guys, and the rest of the nation as Pharaohs, the bad guys, living in unbelief. The theme also reflects Christian self-righteousness insofar as it portrays Christians as messiahs who can save the nation.

One may wonder why it should be Joseph who serves as the model for Christian political engagement. Why not Isaiah with his vision of "new heavens and a new earth" where "no longer will there be in it an infant who lives but a few days, or an old man who does not live out his days"? Why not a new heaven and new earth where people "will build houses and inhabit them; they will also plant vineyards and eat their fruit" (Isa 65:17, 20-21)? Or why not Jeremiah with his call to seek "the welfare of the city . . . and pray to the LORD on its behalf" (Jer 29:7)? These prophets also went to the palace just like Joseph. But they did not enter as triumphant heroes who resumed political control over the entire nation, though they did strive for justice and repentance of the whole nation.

Motivating Christian political engagement in Indonesia is an interest in gaining political power, rather than a brokenheartedness due to the spread of injustice. As such, Christian political engagement appears to be merely a countermovement against Muslims within the very same power game. The first round of recent presidential elections in July 2004 revealed this clearly. The strongest presidential candidate, Susilo Bambang Yudhoyono (SBY), made a political coalition with the Star Moon Party, a very small unpopular Islamic party that strives for the implementation of the Islamic *shari'ah* in Indonesia. This prompted PDS leaders to urge Christians not to give their votes to the retired general. As a counter-measure, PDS soon declared that they had decided to join a political coalition with the current regime against SBY, even though this regime has been proven ineffective due to its heavy internal conflicts. It is no wonder that Muslims become outraged and perceive Christians not as friends, but as enemies who pose a clear and present danger to their lives. The most prominent Christian political movement in the country does not reflect a genuine act motivated by the desire to do justice, to love kindness, and to walk humbly (Mic 6:8).

So What?

In contrast to all this, I would propose that the key for a peaceful pro-existence between the Christians and the Muslims is the capacity for empathy toward each other. In a peaceful pro-existence, the two communities should not simply meet each other halfway through a balance of assertions and concessions. Each community must go all the way through to the other side and learn to see reality from the other's point of view. Each must seek to understand and validate the other's interests—their needs, hopes, fears, and desires—in order to empathize with them. Only then will we find capacity not only to support each other's existence, but also to transcend the conflict and tension that exist between the two communities.

A simple way to do this empathy-building is to create opportunities in which people from each community may comfortably cross to the other side and live out the other's experience. One way to do this is by providing a chance to role play. In the training on peacebuilding and conflict transformation that the Center for the Study and Promotion of Peace gives to the two communities in conflict areas, we often ask the communities to exchange experiences with each other.[4] We do this by asking each group to write out a conflict scenario based on real-life experiences in which they feel that the other group has treated them unjustly or misunderstood them. Then the groups exchange the scenarios and play them out in front of the whole group. During the preparation for the play, each group is allowed to ask for clarifications from the group that wrote the scenario.

From such a simple exercise, people often gain new aware-ness, new sensitivity, and even new respect for the other. For now they can see reality from the other's point of view and empathize with the other. Thus the Christians learn that the alcoholic drink that many Christians in the middle and eastern part of Indonesia like to make, sell, and consume really poses not only a moral problem to the Muslims, but also a religious one. So too, Muslims learn that the sweeping of ID cards in public buses that many Muslims like to do in some big cities is hurtful, humiliating, and unjust to the Christians. In one of the trainings, Muslims even learn that there is a big difference between Catholic and Pentecostal worship; this is quite differ-ent from the situation among the Muslims, where all different groups have the very same rituals. Of course such role play alone is not sufficient to build mutual empathy between Christians and Muslims. But something has to be done to bridge the gap between the two communities. A Chinese proverb says, "Every walk in a long journey always starts with a first small step."

Another similar method to build empathy is to provide opportunities for people from each community to live in each other's contexts, even if only for a short time. In my seminary, we have a program in which students live in an Islamic board-ing school for a time, and *santris* from the Islamic boarding school, in exchange, also live in our dormitory. In 1995, a Youth Discovery Team that Mennonite Central Committee sponsored brought together youth from North America, India, and Indonesia, and gave them the opportunity to live in various non-Christian contexts. Such opportunities are great for pro-viding space and time to people from the two communities to build mutual empathy toward each other. They allow people from both communities to see others as subjects who have dignity, not as objects to be conquered.

Another effective way the Center for the Study and Promotion of Peace uses is to co-facilitate training on peacebuilding and conflict transformation, especially in places that conflict between Christians and Muslims has torn apart. The presence of Christian and Muslim facilitators who are working together as co-facilitators carries a powerful message about the possibility of peaceful pro-existence between the two communities. Of course, there are many suspicions toward such arrangements. In our experience, some Muslim participants quite often see our Muslim co-facilitators as traitors who have been co-opted and Christianized. But as the training goes on and they can see that the relationship between Christian and Muslim facilitators is a genuine relationship based on equality, mutual trust, and respect, they come to honor us and are convinced that cooperation between Christians and Muslims in peacebuilding is a real possibility.

Before I close my paper, there is more important matter to mention. Based on my experience in reconciliation projects between Christians and Muslims, a challenging task we need to address carefully is the different emphases regarding the concept of reconciliation. Muslims usually put more emphasis on justice, while Christians put more emphasis on love and forgiveness. Thus, for Muslims, the establishment of justice should precede any kind of reconciliation work, by first identifying who is right and who is wrong in the conflict and what will be a just punishment for the wrongdoers. For Christians, in contrast, the effort to put away and forget the pain of the past must precede any reconciliation work.

In this matter, Muslims might learn from Christians that reconciliation is not achievable without the offer of love and forgiveness. While justice is surely very important, love and forgiveness should become the prerequisite for reconciliation, not the result of reconciliation. Furthermore, the concept of justice that Muslims hold dear should expand so that justice is understood not merely in term of punishment, that is, punitive or retributive justice, but also as the restoration of the broken relationships, that is, what we call restorative justice.

On the other hand, Christians might learn from Muslims that true and genuine reconciliation must also involve the painstaking work of addressing injustice. While it is true that love and forgiveness are important for reconciliation, without justice love and forgiveness can easily become a cover-up for past injustices and can downgrade the hurt and pain of victims. The concept of love and forgiveness that Christians hold dear should therefore expand so that love and forgiveness are not understood merely in terms of forgetting, but also in terms of remembering the wrongdoing that prompted the need for forgiveness.

Once again, my intention in writing this paper has not been to defend Muslims nor to justify the evil some of them have done. My point is simply to state that if we want to make sense and understand the attitude and behavior of the Muslims, we have to understand their context first and validate their interests—their needs, hopes, fear, and desires. The way to survive this tense relationship between Christians and Muslims is not by erecting a barrier between us to shield the Muslims off, nor by gaining power over them, but by making friends with them. Just as not all Christians are good, so are not all Muslims bad. An old adage says, "What we see is what we get." This is very true in regard to our relations with Muslims as well. If what we want to see in Islam are Muslims who are violent and full of enmity, then that is what we will get. If what we want to see in Islam is the friendly and peaceful Muslim, then that is also what we will surely find.

Rebecca Seiling and Tim Corlis, members of the Youth Discovery Team 1995, give us a simple but profound suggestion: Take off your shoes!

> Shoes speak loudly. They represent a person's identity and symbolize wealth, power, and privilege. They protect us from blisters, bruises, scratches, and pain. They serve to blind us from the realities and hardships of life. By taking off our shoes, we are vulnerable. By taking off

our shoes, we humble ourselves in respect for the other person. In taking off our shoes, we are able to see more clearly.

NOTES

1. Benjamin R. Barber, *Jihad Vs. McWorld* (New York: Random House, 1995); Samuel P. Huntington, *The Clash of Civilizations and the Remaking of World Order* (New York: Simon & Schuster, 1996). *The Clash of Civilizations* has been translated into Middle Eastern languages and read widely by many people in the Middle East. This has been taken as evidence that it has provoked the clash between the Muslims and the West.

2. Michael Walzer, *Spheres of Justice: A Defense of Pluralism and Equality* (New York: Basic Books, 1983), 38–39.

3. The web site 1040window.org explains: "The 10/40 Window is an area of the world that contains the largest population of non-Christians in the world. The area extends from 10 degrees to 40 degrees North of the equator, and stretches from North Africa across to China."

4. The Center for the Study and Promotion of Peace is a center for community service of Duta Wacana Christian University in Jogjakarta, Indonesia. This university is owned by twelve different churches in Indonesia. Two of them are Mennonite.

FOR FURTHER READING

Appleby, R. Scott. *The Ambivalence of the Sacred: Religion, Violence, and Reconciliation*. With a foreword by Theodore M. Hesburgh. Rowman and Littlefield Publishers, 1998.

Avruch, Kevin. *Culture and Conflict Resolution*. United States Institute of Peace Press, 1998.

Gopin, Marc. *Between Eden and Armageddon: The Future of World Religions, Violence, and Peacemaking*. Oxford University Press, 2000.

Volf, Miroslav. *Exclusion and Embrace: A Theological Exploration of Identity, Otherness, and Reconciliation*. Abingdon Press, 1996.

12

THE POWER OF DIASPORA: SEEKING THE PEACE OF PALESTINE-ISRAEL

Alain Epp Weaver

In their recent book *Powers of Diaspora*, Daniel and Jonathan Boyarin raise an impassioned plea for "taking diaspora provisionally as a 'normal' situation rather than a negative symptom of disorder." Daniel Boyarin is professor of Talmudic Culture at the University of California, Berkeley. He and his brother, the cultural critic Jonathan Boyarin, celebrate what they call "the diasporic genius of Jewishness, that genius that consists in the exercise and preservation of cultural power separate from the coercive power of the state."

The Boyarins point out that while living as minority communities in Europe, North Africa, the Middle East, and North America—that is, in the *galut*—Jews have presented a cultural-political witness that should not be dismissed or ignored simply because it was rarely connected to state or governmental power. Diaspora, for the Boyarins, represents a political model, a way for a community to preserve its identity in the world without needing to be in charge of the state's mechanisms of violence, and without seeking to exclude other communities from particular territories. Diaspora as a political form counters nationalism, since diaspora involves the "dissociation of ethnicities and political hegemonies." But diaspora also poses an alternative to any type of political liberalism that seeks to homogenize or erase ethnic and cultural differences.

Not surprisingly, the Boyarins' appropriation and celebration of diaspora as a critical and political model has implications for thinking about Zionism and the Palestinian-Israeli conflict. Their diasporic politics also bears on the question of what it means to seek the peace of the city, because to raise this question—at least for Christians and, as the Boyarins suggest, for some Jews—is also to ask what it means to be God's people in exile.

The dispersion of God's people opens up new vistas for understanding what it means to receive God's gift of land, and what it means to live securely in the land. The prophet Jeremiah's counsel to the exiles in Babylon who yearned for the streets of Jerusalem was unexpected and perhaps even harsh. Plant trees and build homes in the diaspora to seek the peace of this pagan city, he told them, for in Babylon's welfare they would find their own welfare.

The witness of Scripture consistently returns to the theme that land is finally God's possession, as are the people Israel. When the people enjoy landed security, this can only be attributed to the radical, undeserved graciousness of God. The people Israel are not ultimately in charge of their own destiny, but must rely completely on God, both when they enter into the land of Canaan and as they are taken into exile. At times, the biblical account of God's gifting of land is profoundly disturbing: "I gave you a land on which you had not labored, and towns that you had not built, and you live in them," God tells the people. "You eat the fruit of vineyards and oliveyards that you did not plant" (Josh 24:13; see also Deut 6:10-11). Setting aside the question of their historicity, the Deuteronomic accounts of the conquest of the land present the people Israel as called to be utterly dependent on a God who will dispossess their enemies, even exterminate them; these accounts appear to presuppose that landed security depends on exclusive control of fixed territory by a single ethnic group.

Life in exile, in contrast, means life as a minority, a life where God's people are "not in charge." As the late John Howard Yoder insisted, Jeremiah's call to the exiles to seek the peace of city marked a new chapter in the story of God's people learning what it means to depend radically upon God. If at other points in the biblical account God's people have appropriated God's gift of land by setting up kings for themselves and pursuing exclusive ethnic control over territory, the experience of exile forces a new form of dependence on God, a dependence on God to preserve his people when they live as a minority among other peoples and do not have access to military might to secure and defend borders.

An exilic politics, it should be stressed, does not need to relinquish attachment to particular territories or reject concern for landed security. Jeremiah's appeal to the exiles in Babylon to plant trees and build houses instead presents the people Israel with a new model of landed security, one in which Israel's well-being is intimately bound to the flourishing of those communities in whose midst it lives. Jeremiah's call to the exiles is not the celebration of a rootless cosmopolitanism that keeps its distance from any particular attachments. Rather it is a call to identify with the particular societies in which God's people find themselves, even while understanding that in the end our homeland is found in God. Putting down roots in Babylon, furthermore, does not mean that hopes for return to a yearned-for physical Zion are to be dismissed out of hand. The lessons of exile, however, should be remembered even if the community returns physically to the land: authentic return will not involve the dispossession of other peoples in order to establish demographic control and territorial domination but will instead mean searching for the welfare of all in the land. An exilic consciousness should persist even after any return to the land, teaching us to maintain a constant, creative tension with landedness, reminding us that land is not an exclusive gift.

The prophet Micah offers a vision of the future in which each person will sit under vine and fig tree, with no one to make them afraid (4:4). The Palestinian reality for the past fifty-six years, however, has been one of being progressively driven out from under their vines and fig trees, dispossessed of land and rights on the land. Military, legal, architectural, and planning mechanisms have all been deployed to dispossess Palestinians from land and other natural resources. The walls and fences of the separation barrier that Israel is constructing in the Occupied Territories is only the most recent and blatant example. Neither Palestinians nor Israeli Jews, meanwhile, enjoy personal bodily security. This is obvious in the unspeakable horror of Palestinian bombings that tear through buses and cafes in Tel Aviv, Jerusalem, and Haifa; the death of a seventy-year-old man in Khan Younis, killed as he sat in his wheelchair with his house demolished on top of him; a Palestinian man shackled at the Hawara checkpoint near Nablus and beaten by Israeli soldiers in front of his wife and children. Thousands of Palestinians and Israeli Jews have been killed during the past four years alone, and tens of thousands have been injured. Each death demands mourning, every injury calls for grief. What will bring bodily security for Palestinians and Israelis? What will make them secure under vine and fig tree?

In what follows I argue that Christians can rightly engage in two basic forms of political witness: first, the critique of and action against particular abuses of power through legal argument and appeals, and through nonviolent direct action; and second, by offering positive visions of a more just future for the wider body politic. In the case of Palestine/Israel, I argue that Christians can, and even should, on both pragmatic and theological grounds, work for a one-state future for Palestinians and Israelis, a future in which the two nations live in equality in one political body. The theological basis for a Christian endorsement of a one-state solution to the Palestinian-Israeli conflict resides, I suggest, in the Ephesian vision of two peoples made one, two peoples whose differences are not erased but who are nevertheless reconciled into one body, the dividing wall of hostility between them torn down.

APPEALS TO INTERNATIONAL LAW

Palestinians rightly understand the separation barrier that Israel is constructing in the Occupied Territories, as well as of the plan by Israeli Prime Minister Ariel Sharon to "disengage" from Gaza and parts of the West Bank, as devastating to any hopes to establish a Palestinian state along the 1949 Armistice Line. A state established along this so-called "Green Line" would itself comprise only 22 percent of Mandate Palestine, the territorial unit west of the Jordan River that Britain administered prior to 1948. The barrier, many increasingly argue, is a second Nakba, or Catastrophe, for the Palestinian nation, the first one being the expulsion of hundreds of thousands of refugees in 1948. The U.S. seal of approval for the disengagement plan, its declaration that some settlements beyond the Green Line will inevitably be incorporated into Israel in any final status agreement, and its negation of the right of Palestinian refugees to return to their homes and properties, have been characterized as a second Balfour Declaration.

How to respond to a military regime that seeks to consolidate the territorial gains of conquest and colonization through the imposition of de facto borders? One approach is legal. A recent International Court of Justice (ICJ) ruling against Israel's wall in the Occupied Territories found Israel to be in violation of international law and called for a halt to its construction, the dismantling of those sections already built, and compensation for land and properties destroyed during its erection. But can the United Nations be moved, in face of the ever-present U.S. veto on matters related to Israel, to give the ICJ ruling teeth? Diana Buttu, a legal adviser to the Palestinian Liberation Organization, poignantly observes that, in the wake of the ICJ ruling, the question is now "what the international community will do: Will it apply the power of law or the law of power?"

For nearly six decades, Palestinians have found time and again that they might have law and international resolutions on their side, but find no will in the international community to press for the application of laws and resolutions. UN General Assembly Resolution 194 may affirm the right of Palestinian refugees to return home, but no international political will is mobilized to counter Israel's blunt refusal to allow refugees to return. Israeli colonization of the Occupied Territories in the form of constructing Jewish-only settlements on confiscated

Palestinian land, Israeli policies and practice of house demolitions, and various other forms of collective punishment carried out by Israel against the Palestinian civilian population, are, according to jurists, human rights groups, and almost all governments of the world, violations of the Fourth Geneva Convention. But the High Contracting Parties to that Convention refuse to convene to address Israel's repeated and ongoing violations.

Not surprisingly, Palestinian experience with the Israeli legal system has been even less satisfying. While some glimmers of hope might be visible in a June 2004 ruling by Israel's High Court that thirty kilometers of the wall should be re-routed to minimize the humanitarian impact on Palestinian communities, in the end the court avoided, as it has consistently since 1967, granting the applicability of international law to the West Bank and the Gaza Strip (what Israel calls the "administered" territories, or Judea, Samaria, and Gaza). As David Kretzmer outlines in his study of Israeli court rulings regarding the Occupied Territories, political and military considerations have, in the end, always won out over legal considerations in the court's rulings.

Torture, land confiscation, construction of settlements (that is, colonies), house demolitions—the Israeli courts have provided legal justifications for all of these actions. When Israeli court rulings have placed limitations on the actions of the military government in the Occupied Territories, other government entities have routinely circumvented them. For Palestinians, in short, the power of law is strikingly weak: UN resolutions regarding Palestinians and their rights fill up over five large volumes; Palestinian, Israeli, and international human rights groups painstakingly document Israeli violations of international law, but the law of Israeli power–backed by U.S. military, financial, and political support–holds sway.

"A Few Meters": Quantifying the Efficacy of Nonviolent Action

Fishi haq bidun warahi mtalib, says an Arabic proverb: No right disappears as long as someone puts a claim to it. Palestinians put claim to their rights through *sumud,* an obdurate steadfastness, a blunt refusal to disappear. They hold on to the keys of homes destroyed in 1948, stand in lines at checkpoints, and negotiate paths through hills and fields in order to get to work, school, and family. In the face of dispersion and dispossession, Palestinians have maintained a hope for a future of landed security.

As the walls and fences have gone up over the past two years, this hope has been more difficult to maintain. *Maa fii 'amal*, there is no hope, many Palestinians increasingly say. Israeli Prime Minister Ariel Sharon has boasted that "The Palestinians understand that [the disengagement] plan is, to a great extent, the end of their dreams, a very heavy blow to them." For those Palestinians who refuse to quit dreaming, the question is how best to counter the ideology and practice of the physical and spiritual walls of separation erected by Israel.

An increasing number of Palestinians are answering, "Nonviolence."

Ayid Murar from the village of Budrus near Ramallah, a village that has been at the forefront of nonviolent protest against the separation wall, perceptively observes that nonviolent action can empower a broader segment of the population than can violence. "We have to bring the entire Palestinian people into the struggle against the occupation," says Murar, "women, children, the aged—and they cannot take part in a violent struggle. But they can take part in this kind of struggle, which also contributes to the unity of our nation. We also know that a nonviolent struggle puts more pressure on the Israelis," he continues, noting that while soldiers know how to respond to armed attacks, nonviolent protest catches them off guard.

While revenge attacks might provide emotional catharsis for some, such catharsis soon dissipates, leaving no lasting basis for hope. That is all the more true because the effectiveness of Palestinian armed struggle against massive Israeli military might is limited at best. In contrast, daily protests in Biddu, Budrus, Beit Surik, and many other villages have been inspiring and galvanizing, even as a predictable Israeli stigmatizing of nonviolent protest as "terrorism" has been depressing.

The fact that after years of roadblocks, curfews, economic siege, and daily violence Palestinian communities are finding the resources to organize to try to stop bulldozers from uprooting trees and clearing the path for the wall is truly a testament to God's Spirit at work to bring blessing and hope in the midst of destruction, apathy, and hopelessness.

One should not minimize the challenges before those communities who gather to face the bulldozers, of course. In the summer of 2002, residents of villages such as Jayyous and Falamiyeh in the Qalqilyah district were organizing to try to stop the uprooting of their trees and the construction of the separation barrier on their lands. Now the wall has been in place for over two years. In October 2003, the Israeli civil administration of the military government announced that non-Israelis would require a permit, issued by the civil administration, in order to enter the "seam area" between the wall and the 1949 Armistice Line, or the Green Line. This meant, for example, that villagers in Jayyous would have to obtain a permit if they wanted to work land on the other side of the wall. Should people try to negotiate the hostile, Kafkaesque bureaucracy of the civil administration in order to try to get a permit to pass through the gates in the wall? Or should they refuse on principle? As it is, only a minority of farmers in Jayyous and other affected communities have managed to obtain the required permits, and most fear that it is only a matter of time before Israel begins confiscating land behind the wall on the pretext that it is not cultivated.

Were the nonviolent protests in Jayyous three years ago then for naught? Will the protests in villages around Ramallah, Salfit, and Jerusalem be for naught? Aziz Armani from Khirbata, one village near Ramallah where the wall is going up now, suggests not: "The main thing," he says, "is that we feel we are doing something, if not for ourselves then for the coming generations. Even if we are able to get the fence moved two meters and save a few meters of our land, that will be something."

The Bi-National State: A Vision of Reconciliation

Armani's words might seem to provide little comfort and hope, measuring success in the nonviolent struggle by getting walls and fences moved a couple of meters and saving a little bit of one's land from the bulldozer's teeth. In addition to the construction delays and the adjustments in the wall's path that nonviolent action has managed to affect, however, there is a longer-term reason for hope, even if this hope might at times appear faint. Over the past few months, Israelis, at the invitation of Palestinian communities, have been joining with Palestinians in nonviolent attempts to stop the uprooting of trees, to halt the wall's seemingly inexorable path of destruction. In addition to whatever short-term successes these Israelis and Palestinians chalk up, in their shared work for justice, I would suggest, they offer signs of hope for the future.

Perhaps Israel's separation wall will be quickly dismantled, and a two-state solution based on an Israeli withdrawal to the Green Line might be possible; the United States' blessing of Sharon's disengagement plan, however, makes this exceedingly unlikely. Determined not to resolve the conflict, Israel looks to manage it through walls and fences, and one fears that, with its military might and American backing, it will succeed in the medium term—five years? ten years? longer? The walls and fences and the apartheid-style reservations they create will not, however, succeed in the long term. They will fall, just like other physical and legal barriers in Johannesburg and Berlin. The question is what will replace them. Will the future remain captive to the logic of separation, with the violent dispossession that separation has brought with it? Or might a future of integration emerge?

In a much-discussed article in the *New York Review of Books* in 2003, historian Tony Judt surveyed the bleak reality of Palestine/Israel and concluded that a one-state solution to the conflict, routinely dismissed by policymakers as utopian, has become the most realistic way forward. Israel's ethnic nationalism, he suggested, was an anachronism that could only be maintained by new waves of violence and dispossession. A bi-national state would be more realistic than indefinite apartheid or massive ethnic cleansing.

While most Israeli Jews would strongly reject Judt's appeal for a democratic state in all of Mandate Palestine and equate it with national suicide, dissenting voices can be heard. Eyal Weizman, an architectural theorist, for example, suggests that the alternative to wall-and-fence-building is not "more planning 'creativity' of the Ariel Sharon type, but . . . a non-territorial approach based on principles other than partition." Israeli peace campaigner Haim Hanegbi concurs with Weizman, noting that "The purpose of the wall is to separate, to isolate, to imprison the Palestinians in pens. But the wall imprisons the Israelis too. It turns Israel into a ghetto . . . the last desperate act of those who cannot confront the Palestinian issue [or are] compelled to push [that issue] out of their lives and out of their consciousness." The path of separation leads to a dead end. "Our past forces us to believe in the project of a Jewish nation-state that is a hopeless cause," Hanegbi writes. "Our past prevents us from seeing that the whole story of Jewish sovereignty in the Land of Israel is over. Because if you want Jewish sovereignty you must have a border, but . . . this country cannot tolerate a border in its midst. If you want Jewish sovereignty you need a fortified, separatist uni-national structure, but that is contrary to the spirit of the age. Even if Israel surrounds itself with a fence and a moat and a wall, it won't help." In the end, Hanegbi concludes, "we [Israeli Jews] will have to come to terms with the fact that we will live here as a minority." The challenge will be to embrace this fact with hope rather than turn away from it as a tragic horror.

Just as support for a bi-national one-state solution to the conflict remains a minority position among Israelis, so too does it attract at present only a minority of Palestinians. Secular Palestinian political parties have distanced themselves from previous support for the single democratic state in favor of a two-state model; Islamist political parties offer theocratic visions unattractive (at best) to Jews, Christians, and, arguably, the majority of Palestinian Muslims. The late Edward Said, of course, was, in his later writings, a notable exception to the discourse of separation. As Israeli colonization of the Occupied Territories continues with tacit American blessing, however, and as the walls and fences of separation are put in place, more and more Palestinians are starting to doubt the viability of a two-state solution to the conflict. Omar al-Qattan argues that "we have become cornered by Israel's separatist logic, as embodied in the ludicrously unrealizable two-state solution." Faced with an Israeli determination to establish de facto borders with quiet support from the United States, Palestinians must be proactive in offering an alternative vision for the future. "What kind of home would we want to share with our Jewish neighbors?" Al-Qattan asks. He concludes, "We must begin to translate our dream of return to a noble and just project, one that threatens no one and yet is just and fair, one that persuades, indeed seduces, Israelis to accept rather than brutally reject our existence."

Two organizations associated with Mennonite Central Committee, one Palestinian and one Israeli, are working for such a persuasive, seductive future of justice and reconciliation. They are the Badil Resource Center for Residency and Refugee Rights, and the Zochrot Association. For the past five years, Badil (whose name means "alternative" in Arabic) has led the campaign for a rights-based solution to the Palestinian refugee crisis, a solution that does not negate rights of return and compensation. At a consultation in Haifa this past July, Badil brought together Palestinians, Israeli Jews, and experts in international law and refugee return to discuss how the return of Palestinian refugees to homes and properties inside Israel might be a key component of a durable peace agreement rather than a stumbling block, as it is often portrayed by opponents of return. The Zochrot Association, meanwhile, has for the past two years brought busloads of Israeli Jews to the sites of destroyed Palestinian villages, where they hear from Palestinian refugees from the villages about the villages' histories and their destruction. They then erect signs, in Hebrew and in Arabic, bearing the original names of streets and the names of the remains of churches, mosques, and homes. Eytan Bronstein, director of Zochrot, describes the sign-posting project as a re-visioning of the landscape in the service of a just future:

> As long as razed Palestinian villages remain uncommemorated on the Israeli landscape, their existence in the past and their destruction is repressed. Each new sign will change the experience of driving down Israel's roads and walking on its paths. Signs erected over the ruins of Palestinian villages will represent a challenge to written history inscribed on the landscape. Posting signs at villages integrates the past, present, and future and between the ethical, aesthetic, and political. This is taking action upon the landscape in the hope of rediscovering and remodeling it, creating a renewed landscape that will reveal the traces of what has refused to be wiped out, in spite of so many efforts.

Israeli Jews joining with Palestinians to commemorate destroyed Palestinian villages; Palestinians and Israeli Jews examining how a rights-based solution to the Palestinian refugee crisis might be the foundation of a durable peace, a peace that would guarantee legitimate individual and collective rights for both Jew and Palestinian; Israeli Jews and Palestinians holding hunger strikes and nonviolent protests in front of bulldozers coming to uproot trees and pave the way for the wall. These joint actions, I would suggest, have sacramental value. They are, in other words, embodied signs of the good news of reconciliation.

The writer of the epistle to the church at Ephesus celebrates the fact that in Jesus two different peoples, Jew and Gentile, have been reconciled into one body. Today there is one political body, incorporating Jews and Palestinians, between the Jordan River and the Mediterranean Sea, but it is not a body of reconciliation. There is one sovereign state, Israel, controlling territory in which 3.5 million Palestinians live under military occupation without citizenship. There is one sovereign state, Israel, but it is not a state of its citizens, and state power is marshaled to exclude and restrict Palestinian access (both in Israel and in the Occupied Territories) to land and water. There is one sovereign state, Israel, erecting dividing walls that will generate hostility for years to come. The Ephesian vision of two peoples reconciled, the dividing wall of hostility between them broken down, stands in sharp contrast to a reality in which legal, planning, and military walls are built to guarantee demographic superiority and control over resources.

As one of the great peacemaking texts of Scripture, the second chapter of Ephesians presents a practice and vision of reconciliation between two peoples, Jews and Gentiles. Such a practice and vision reconciles into one body the stories and histories of those once divided by hostility. Reconciliation does not erase the difference between the two; peace is not about homogenizing or obliterating difference, but rather about breaking down dividing walls of hostility and about the formation of bridges and bonds between those who remain different. The Ephesian vision is incarnated whenever the dividing walls of injustice, oppression, and violence that fuel hostility are brought down, and opportunities for a shared existence are made possible. It is a vision, I would argue, that is fundamentally more in concert with a one, bi-national state future for Palestinians and Israeli Jews than are projects of separation.

The reshaping and renaming of the landscape involved in Zochrot's signposting project embodies a politics of identity in which Israeli Jews do not gain their identity only in opposition to or differentiation from Palestinians. Rather, the Palestinian story of dispossession is allowed to shape what it means to be Israeli as well.

The Palestinian Muslim theologian, Mustafa Abu Sway, articulates a line of thought parallel to Zochrot's when he suggests the concept of *dar al-hiwar*. The concept echoes traditional categories of *dar al-islam* (the house of submission) and *dar al-harb* (the house of war) but is clearly distinct from them. *Dar al-hiwar*, or the house of conversation, presents a political vision in which distinct identities are maintained but in which one's identity is shaped through conversation with the other.

Zochrot's practice and Abu Sway's notion of *dar al-hiwar* intersect, furthermore, with the Pauline understanding of the body. Paul, in his letter to the Corinthians, articulates a political theology in which the distinct members of Christ's body participate in each other. "If one member suffers, all suffer together with it; if one member is honored, all rejoice together with it," Paul writes (1 Cor 12:26). The bi-national state as a vision of reconciliation will thus not mean the erasure of difference between Palestinian and Jew, but will instead mean that Palestinian and Jew, remaining different, now participate with each other, suffering when the other suffers, rejoicing when the other prospers.

∾

Those who embrace the challenge of diaspora, who seek the peace of the cities to which God has led them, will not be able to embrace ethnic nationalisms, nor endorse legal, architectural, and military tactics deployed to ensure demographic and territorial superiority. In the case of Palestine/Israel, those who seek the peace of its cities, of Haifa and Tel Aviv, Gaza and Nablus, Dimona and Jerusalem, will thus be attracted to a bi-national one-state state solution to the conflict, a solution that undermines exclusive correlations between nation and territory, a solution that could open the door to Palestinian and Israeli Jewish identity being shaped through *hiwar*, or conversation, with the other. True security, secure identity, will be found not behind concrete walls, barbed wire fences, and legalized apartheid, but in participation with the other, in seeking the well-being, the *shalom*, of all the people in the land.

FOR FURTHER READING

Judt, Tony. "Israel: The Alternative." *New York Review of Books* 50, no. 16 (October 23, 2003).

Kimmerling, Baruch. *Politicide: Ariel Sharon's Wars Against the Palestinians.* London New York: VERSO, 2003.

Kretzmer, David. *The Occupation of Justice: The Supreme Court of Israel and the Occupied Territories.* SUNY Series in Israeli Studies. Albany: State University of New York Press, 2002.

Pappé, Ilan. *A History of Modern Palestine: One Land, Two Peoples.* Cambridge, UK, New York: Cambridge University Press, 2004.

Smith-Christopher, Daniel L. *A Biblical Theology of Exile.* Overtures to Biblical Theology. Minneapolis: Fortress Press, 2002.

Weaver, Alain Epp. "On Exile: Yoder, Said, and a Theology of Land and Return." In *A Mind Patient and Untamed: Assessing John Howard Yoder's Contributions to Theology, Ethics, and Peacemaking,* edited by Ben C. Ollenburger and Gayle Gerber Koontz, 161–84. Telford, Pa.: Cascadia Pub. House, 2004.

Yoder, John Howard. *For the Nations: Essays Public and Evangelical.* Grand Rapids, Mich.: Wm. B. Eerdmans Publishing Co., 1997.

Yoder, John Howard. *The Jewish-Christian Schism Revisited.* Eds. Michael G. Cartwright and Peter Ochs. Radical Traditions. Grand Rapids, Mich.: Wm. B. Eerdmans, 2003.

13

A "Weak Church" Seeks Security in a Violent Land: Experiences of the Colombian Mennonite Church

Alix Lozano
Translated by Molly Brandt

The world designates $2.2 billion each day for the production of death. That is, the world devotes this astronomical fortune to promote hunting expeditions in which the hunter and the hunted are of the same species, and in which the most successful hunter is the one who kills more of his own neighbors. Nine days of military expenditures would be enough to provide food, schooling, and medicine to the many children who lack them. At first glance, this goes against common sense. And a second glance? The official story justifies this squandering for the war against terrorism. But common sense tells us that terrorist forces are actually more grateful for this than anyone else. Anyone can see that military expenditures have given the wars in Afghanistan and in Iraq their most powerful vitamins. Wars are acts of state terrorism, and state terrorism and private terrorism feed each other.[1]

In his essay "In Praise of Common Sense," Eduardo Galeano, Uruguayan author and expert in Latin American affairs, invites us to reflect on the kinds of logic that reign in our world—that of death over life, and war over peace. If only we had a bit of "common sense" and would invert that order, perhaps we could escape from this crazy and absurd dead end, war with all of its consequences and with its new face: terrorism.

For Colombians, life is more hazardous and insecure each day. The poor have nowhere to sleep, the rich cannot sleep peacefully, and the middle class is least secure of all, drowning as it is in debt. Each person takes refuge in his or her own space; each person seeks his or her own security and welfare. But the welfare of the city and country depend on the welfare of every person, without distinction of race, creed, or gender.

The security and welfare of a country depend above all on creative strategies in which the best human energies are clearly committed to achieving transformation. A church that is engaged in society must be especially creative and committed if it is to complete its mission as salt and light, thus fulfilling its role in the construction of God's kingdom on earth.

In the face of present realities, in which the current Colombian government proposes the military route as the only way out, the future looks more uncertain and threatening each day. An increasingly desperate search is on for some exit from the situation of crisis. Emigration is on the rise, along with prostitution, the "do whatever you can to survive" resale economy, illicit and high-risk business such as narcotics and arms trafficking. These have brought us to a state of widespread war, with the new face of terrorism. This is where state terrorism and private terrorism feed off each other, as Eduardo Galeano writes.

In order to take up this subject, we will look at the panorama of present sociopolitical and economic realities in Colombia in the light of biblical texts, from the perspective of a theology of peace. In this way I hope to share practical experiences of the Mennonite Church of Colombia as a contribution toward seeking the welfare of a country.

COLOMBIA: THE PRESENT SITUATION[2]

The government of Colombian President Alvaro Uribe has proposed to build a "communitarian state." This is a new euphemism to disguise the usurping character of our carica- ture of a state. It follows the primer of authoritarian neoliberal states that have been imposed all over Latin America.

The objectives of the government plan, it explains, are this: "Our communitarian state will dedicate its resources to eradi- cating poverty, to building social equality, and to providing security. There will be more citizen participation in defining public works, and in their execution and upkeep. Citizen par- ticipation guarantees that resources will reach the people and will not get tangled up in politicking."[3]

Claims to be fair-minded and proposals to eradicate poverty have little credence when the annual investment in "democratic security"—that is, in militarism and repression—rises during a government's first year to twelve billion pesos, close to fifteen percent of the total annual budget of 67.1 billion pesos. This is a figure that equals 4.3 percent of the gross domestic product (GDP). The disproportionate growth of military expenditures explains the rationale behind new taxes on liquid assets to finance the war in areas of "internal upheaval." It also explains the eminently fiscal motivation for so-called reforms in labor, pension, and tax law. Through cuts in social spending and ris- ing burdens on citizens, the government is trying to control the deficit and pay the interest on national debt even while main- taining a policy of war. Since tax revenues will not cover the 2004 budget, however, the government must once again fall back on foreign debt and drastic cuts in social spending.

From another perspective, this state of internal upheaval resuscitates elements from recent history, which went by sinis- ter names such as the "security statute," the "state of siege," and the "law of national security." Implementing a new "anti- terrorist statute," and linking up the program with *campesino* soldiers" and a network of informants, cooperators, or collabo- rators, current programs foreshadow the consolidation of an authoritarian state. This sort of state is based on a highly exclusive model of development that legalizes state terrorism and the rule of paramilitary forces.

As its ideological root, the authoritarian state uses the lamentably famous National Security Doctrine. This doctrine suppresses democracy in every aspect, even in the smallest ways, and gives to the military corporation (the army) the exclusive right to establish national objectives. An "internal enemy" serves as an excuse for the militarization of society, of the people, and of the state. Its consequence is murder and the disappearance of social activists and social organizations.

Meanwhile, in Colombia, we suffer the result of all these programs. That result is not really a governing state but only the imitation of government. It is the hybrid of an old oligarchic state, an authoritarian state, and a dependent neoliberal state.

What is curious is that the current government, even as it implements political, social, and economic counter-reforms, has begun laying out a strong aid program aimed at the poor and desolate. This includes 50,000 new housing subsidies, 50,000 educational placements, and free lunches and dinners. But we should not forget that the regime has a pragmatic need to recruit from the lower echelons of society. These programs are efficient ways to take advantage of the poverty and ideological ignorance of the masses.

Integral to the Colombian context is the political-military intervention of the United States. "The United States trained more military personnel and police in Colombia than in any other country in 2003."[4] A complete complacency toward this policy among many sectors of Colombian society results from a corresponding political-military surge by the guerrillas. Colombia ends up facing the following alternative scenarios: 1) total war, with defeat of the guerrillas; 2) total war, with victory by the guerrillas; 3) prolonged total war without victory by anyone, creating a total social, economic, and political collapse of the current state; or 4) a negotiated political exit solution to conflict, and the implementation of a process of national reconciliation and reconstruction that allows for profound social, economic, and political transformations. This last option would require a development model of redistributive wealth, agricultural programs, self-determination, sovereignty, and peace with social justice.

FEAR AND AUTHORITY[5]

All of these conditions create in the national panorama a state of anxiety, fear, and uncertainty. Because of this, it is urgent to find a speedy solution to Colombia's fratricidal war and culture of violence, which results from a state of violence lasting more than fifty years.

In cities and towns, the average citizen experiences fear in the presence of "agents of order" who abuse their authority. When the arms that they carry, which the state has given them as a dissuasive instrument, turn into threatening objects, the rule that would link citizens with legitimate authority in a relationship of trust is broken. Once social relations pass from a basis in respect to a basis in fear, something grave has happened to a society. What sticks in the consciousness of the victim who is forced to keep quiet about injustice is a resentful feeling of humiliation. Fearing reprisals, the witness never dares to denounce the abuser. One can only exercise the right to complain when one does not fear for one's own physical safety, when the rule of law prevails over the arbitrary whims of the state. Situations such as these create a climate of intimidation and silence, fostering a severe distrust of authorities and of actual laws. Even though people wish to maintain respect for legal institutions, they will always recall the humiliating situation of those who have had to silence themselves and not demand their rights.

Of course, there do exist agents of order inclined to listen to the good sense of citizens and who find the arbitrary use of authority repulsive. But because of a psychological mechanism that perhaps flows from a personal desire to dominate, there are many more for whom carrying arms becomes a form of coercion. The relationship between citizens and the state's armed forces are not entirely cordial. We live at a time in which most Colombians are full of fear toward the people who represent them. When rights and liberties are violated in the name of an order that itself violates order, society does not move toward reestablishing the harmony we desire between citizen and authority. Rather, it moves toward a precipice in which authority imposes itself with repressive power.

This situation has little to do with confronting subversion or terrorism but concerns the use of authority in order to intimidate opposition. Society grants special powers to the authorities, who then convert every suspicion of "rebellion" into guilt, and any resentment of its "network of informants" into definitive proof. Mass detentions are not just a method of subversives, after all, but rather an "investigative" technique that the state delegates to its armed personnel.

PUBLIC POWER VS. PRIVATE POWER

We also see the other side of the coin in cities such as Medellín. The city is very pleasant and dynamic, but it has another face, that of a very violent and savage place. It is, as we say, very complicated. There are whole areas where the authorities are not in control and do not even enter. Instead, private and illegal security forces control the population, often fighting among themselves for domination. It is possible that this is the future that awaits many large cities, that they will become ungovernable for legal authorities, who turn over government functions and policing to private armies financed by extortion, drug money, and other illegal economic activities. Still, these cities are also the object of God's mercy, just as Nineveh was. It is God's desire to liberate our cities and societies, which seem to be so full of problems and out of control.

COLOMBIA AND ITS PERCEPTIONS OF PEACE

The armed conflict that Colombia is suffering has generated a deep sense of worry that holds sway over all sectors of the population. As a consequence, in the last few years people have put forward diverse concepts of peace, each of which requires a different sort of solution.

We observe, with concern, that the present armed conflict

is the result of concurrent factors that have profoundly hurt civil society. We can identify the following among these damaging factors: injustice, the powerlessness of the state, the loss of values, legal immunity for those who commit crimes in the name of the state, corruption, and the indifference of the wealthy class in the face of the suffering of the poor. These factors translate into extremely high levels of poverty, a lack of efficient healthcare, deficient education, the disintegration of the family, unemployment, and severe impoverishment of the population.

The constricted notion of peace that has resulted in much of Colombian society is quite worrisome. Peace has come to mean no more than the absence of guerrillas, narcotics trafficking, paramilitarism, and common crime. This conception leads many to think that if these points of agitation disappear, there will be peace in Colombia. We forget that peace cannot be reduced to confronting the public order, nor to political anarchy. Yet too often, in the speeches of various actors in the armed conflict, and even among representatives of civil society, too many confuse peace with the resolution of armed conflict. In Latin America, we frequently forget that peace is architectural and a construction that generation after generation must make. We forget that peace has spiritual, religious, moral, ethical, political, economic, familial, social, educational, psychological, and anthropological aspects.

It is fundamental, of course, that the armed conflict in Colombia be solved, so that social, economic, and political life can reorganize itself in coherent and convenient ways. The resolution of the armed conflict is essential in order to lead a true peace process. But peace is more than this alone. It is the result of an eclectic, harmonious, and coherent combination of justice, truth, and freedom. Justice, in turn, is a rightness of being and personal self-conduct; it is that integrity in life that makes possible virtuous behavior and the practice of God's will. It is on this basis that we will see social justice, the equitable distribution of resources and opportunities.[6]

MENNONITE CHURCH EXPERIENCES SEEKING THE WELFARE OF COLOMBIA

We live then in a country where tragedies are a daily event. Blows against justice and unfair immunity for crimes are constant. The use and abuse of authority have no boundaries and catastrophes leave huge scars of pain.

How are we to respond when militarism, official violence, and many forms of violence barely allow breathing room? A "weak" church becomes "strong" when it assumes an attitude of service and solidarity alongside the victims, and when it struggles to condemn and change corrupted structures into structures that are more honest, more humane, and more compassionate.[7]

Enlightenment from the Biblical Text

In Jeremiah 29 we find a letter that the prophet wrote to the Jews exiled in Babylon. It was a pastoral letter, meant to correct an error. Someone was creating false hopes by suggesting to the Jews that the time of exile would end soon and that the return to their homeland was imminent. Jeremiah refuted this rumor and affirmed that the time of exile would be long. He then brought them down to earth and established their real situation:

> But seek the welfare of the city where I have sent you into exile, and pray to the Lord on its behalf, for in its welfare you will find your welfare (Jer 29:7).

The book of Esther offers us a dramatic picture of life for those who stayed and established themselves in the Persian empire. At the center of this picture is the Jewish woman Esther. The action takes place in King Ahasuerus's palace in Susa, the capital of his empire. Esther had become queen and discovered the plans of Haman, a high-ranking royal official, to destroy the Jews. Mordecai, her relative, recommended to Esther that she speak personally with the king and beg him to intercede on behalf of the Jewish people. But to make the request, Esther faced a dilemma: she would run the risk of death if she appeared before the king when he had not invited her to see him. In the middle of all this, Mordecai confronted Esther with her true choice:

> For if you keep silence at such a time as this, relief and deliverance will rise for the Jews from another quarter, but you and your father's family will perish. Who knows? Perhaps you have come to royal dignity for just such a time as this. (Esther 4:14)

In chapter four of Micah, we find God's dream for the world. This vision is what God wants—a people who demonstrate hope in the midst of despair. But notice who the protagonists are:

> In that day, says the Lord, I will assemble the lame and gather those who have been driven away, and those whom I have afflicted. The lame I will make the remnant, and those who were cast off, a strong nation; and the Lord will reign over them in Mount Zion now and forevermore. (Mic 4:6-7)

In this passage, God's hallmark is that God will construct a nation with the weak, with the small, with those who can expect nothing from society.

So how can a weak church work in favor of the city? How can a weak church understand that this is a historic moment to be salt and light? It cannot turn away from this historical moment, for to do so would mean the church's own destruction. In Colombia we have had to understand that we are all in the same boat; if the boat sinks, we too will sink.

Working in Favor of the City

In Colombia, we Mennonites are a weak church. Yet we have found ways to work "in favor of the city," above all in matters that are concerned with public peace, justice, and order.

1. Conscientious objection in Colombia.[8] In 1986, the four Anabaptist conferences won approval for a resolution they had presented before CEDECOL (Evangelical Federation Council of Colombia),[9] advocating the legal recognition of conscientious objection to military service and the possibility of doing alternative civil service.

In 1987, Mennonite Central Committee (MCC) financed the visit of a Spanish lawyer to evaluate and advise the Colombian church on this topic. The church managed to get the word out about interest in this new issue for the country. After this initial effort, however, little energy and few resources remained to pursue the matter.

In 1989, a Jesuit contacted us. He was working with a group of young people who had come together after a massacre of ex-guerrillas at the Palace of Justice. Thanks to the prompting of our 1987 news releases, he had become well-informed concerning the issue of conscientious objection and sent other interested people to work on a proposal on the rights of youth. This included the right not to carry arms. "Go talk to the Mennonites," the Jesuit told them. "They've worked on the subject and they have information."

Thus began a new round of collaboration. As the groups began to learn to know each other, they started to put together program plans. MCC funded a small project, and at the end of 1989 they held two open meetings, where people were invited to converse about the subject. A coordinator was named to carry out proposed tasks.

In November 1990 a national forum on military service was organized, and a wide range of speakers were invited. They included a retired general, a bishop of the Catholic Archdiocese, a representative of the Communist Youth, the Executive Secretary of CEDECOL, and a representative from the Mennonite Church, who presented the conscientious objection position from an Anabaptist theological perspective.

Previously the issue of conscientious objection had seemed taboo. Now the forum placed it onto the national agenda. The form also inspired analysis and reflection in newspapers with national circulation about the Colombian armed forces.

In that same year, a National Constituent Assembly was preparing to write a new constitution for the country. Several Mennonites were working on preparatory commissions that the government had named, and they naturally worked on areas related to freedom of conscience. This work resulted in article eighteen of the new constitution, which states that "no one will be forced to act against his or her conscience." It is a human right that must be applied immediately, in spite of all of the government's efforts to keep it sidelined. So conscientious objection to military service slipped itself into the new national constitution.

And just how many people were part of the core movement for conscientious objection in Colombia? A mere eleven. Need I say more?

2. Conciliation and mediation. The subject of conciliation and mediation in Colombia has grown in the measure at which it has been taught. The Christian Center for Justice, Peace, and Nonviolent Action (Justapaz), a ministry of the Mennonite Church of Colombia, has offered classes, together with our seminary. But universities have also taught it, often inviting Mennonites to present the subject. John Paul Lederach, among others, has taken part in developing our curricula. Today conciliation and mediation is a topic that has taken hold in many educational and national debates.

3. Alternative justice. Justapaz has been participating in different restorative justice groups, and the government has expressed great interest in these. Eastern Mennonite University has facilitated everything we have needed in terms of academic theory. The goal has been to look for alternative forms of punishment in which it becomes possible for both victim and offender to be restored. The traditional model of justice includes the state and the offender, but the victim is not restored. To respond to this, Justapaz and the Confraternidad Carcelaria (Prison Brotherhood) of Colombia work in several of the country's prisons so that people deprived of their freedom can meet and reestablish their own dignity. On one occasion the Senate Commission on Human Rights told a young man: "Go to the Mennonite church. They can help you with this situation." Although this testifies to the respect our work has won, it is also a cause of concern for the church, since it means that the church is very exposed.

4. *Pan y Paz Project.* "Give food to the hungry" is a prophetic statement, but society's values have it backward. Resources invested in arms are a bad investment. Because of this, Pan y Paz (Bread and Peace) declares that without food, there is no peace, and no justice. A "Forty Meals a Week" program takes up this cause. In this program a given community group prepares the meals, wrapped in plantain leaves, and gives them to poor people in poverty-stricken areas. These too are ways to take up the challenge of well-being with justice.

5. *Moments for peace.* "Moments for peace" creates spaces where people confess their faith that peace and the well-being of the country can come about through prayer. When we permeate our work for peace and social well-being with prayer, people are more likely to become conscious of their reality and take up a commitment to responding. We must pray, in addition to working. Once I heard the testimony of a man who stood every day in front of the capitol and prayed about the war in Vietnam. Someone asked him what he could do by praying, and he responded, "If I can't change the war, at least I don't want the war to change me." In the same way we might now say that through prayer *and* work, we will find dual reasons to combat evil. "One is to change it. The other is so that it doesn't change us. . . . If we can't change the world, we should try to love it. If we can't love it, we shouldn't try to change it."[10]

6. *Ecumenical peace projects.* In the northern Colombia city of Córdoba, specifically in an area with a strong paramilitary, guerrilla, and army presence called "Montes de María," a

foundation called "Red Desarrollo y Paz" (Network for Development and Peace) has begun. Three Catholic dioceses participate, together with the Mennonite Church. The objective is to accompany processes of holistic, autonomous human development that will allow the construction of sustainable peace in the communities of the region. Evangelical churches receive resources through the ASVIDAS foundation on behalf of associations for the improvement of life in this zone that has been so crushed by war. They accompany communities in education and conflict transformation, through mediation that helps the community seek peaceful routes to resolve conflicts, searching for peace through restorative justice.

7. *Processes of reinsertion.* These projects offer pastoral support for the process of demobilizing those who have taken up arms, so that they can find a new life. This means striving for their reinsertion into society by filling gaps in a program that the government has established. Through training, formation, and accompaniment during this process, our hope is that people will grasp the gospel of peace.

8. *A meeting of "peoples."* Our communities of faith have experience with displaced people who are arriving from different parts of the country. These people come fleeing their land because either the FARC guerrillas or the paramilitaries have threatened them with death. Either of these groups regard them as "enemies," or they were living are in "enemy" territory, or they have helped one group or the other. These people arrive at a church, they meet, they participate in the same space, they are baptized together, and they become part of one body. It is the text of Ephesians 2:14-16 in practice:

> For he is our peace; in his flesh he has made both groups into one and has broken down the dividing wall, that is, the hostility between us . . . in one body, through the cross, thus putting to death that hostility through it.

9. "Sanctuary of Peace" churches. We encourage local churches to declare themselves publicly as sanctuaries of peace (Josh 20; Deut 19:8-13). This means being a people of peace, giving a message and a testimony of peace, and being a space for peace. We show this by proclaiming the good news of forgiveness, salvation, and liberation; offering restoration and reconciliation for all Colombians with God and their neighbors through our Lord Jesus Christ; and by spreading the word of God in all corners of our country. To do this is to rescue many fellow citizens from wasted and mutilated lives, and, by the power of the Holy Spirit and the power of transformative love, to restore them into the image of God and the invaluable potential that each person has.

10. Educational processes. Educational action is also necessary in the transformation of society. Transformative education must be united, committed, and participatory. It must create awareness and assume the values of a culture of peace.

a. *SBMC:* The Mennonite Biblical Seminary (SBMC) offers Anabaptist biblical and theological training. It supports society by reading and discerning the times from a contextual theology, responding assertively in the historical situation that we are living as a country. Its work on behalf of Anabaptist identity never ends.

b. *School for peace:* This is a new ecumenical program planned jointly with the seminary, Justapaz, and MENCOLDES, the Colombian Mennonite Foundation for Development. It is a program dedicated to strengthening leadership as well as the social, political, and ethical development of churches and communities from a biblical perspective of peace. We represent this with the Hebrew concept of *shalom*, understood as more than the simple term "peace," which for many means only the absence of conflict. We look to create a culture of justice and peace through "education for peace," by training new generations so that they can be agents of new ways of living. Through this program, we are forming networks with other ecumenical groups, such as Misión de Belén (Bethlehem Mission), who have shown interest in a type of education based on *shalom* during this critical moment in Colombia.

c. *The Mennonite school in La Mesa:* This school in Cudinamarca has trained some of its students as conciliators, and they have led processes of conciliation within the student body itself.

d. *Peace education, opposing the "culture of violence":* We achieve this through workshops that help communities become aware of their situation, as well as subjects like the biblical basis for peace and nonviolence, peaceful resolution and conflict transformation, citizen participation, human dignity, and the construction of a stable infrastructure for peace.

e. *Andean Seminary:* Conversations have begun among Anabaptist conferences in our region with the goal of creating an Andean Anabaptist Seminary for Colombia, Venezuela, Ecuador, and Peru. Its goal will be to offer theological training that is pertinent and contextual in the face of the violence in this region.

11. Other spaces.

a. The church has a presence and works in many spaces, and it hopes to continue to contribute with greater zeal in peace councils on municipal, departmental, and national levels; in citizen roundtables; in the Permanent Assembly of Civil Society for Peace on municipal, departmental, and national levels; in municipal spaces that give services to displaced people; and through positions in the Citizens' Mandate for Peace. It must contribute in all these venues through faith, wisdom, and discernment.

b. We carry out work for justice and peace such as aid to orphaned children and widows, to displaced families, to women who are heads of their households, and in general with all people who are affected by violence. We do this through support activities, halfway houses, spiritual and psychological help, education, medicine, training and support to income-generating projects, support for returning and reconstruction of the social fabric, and so on. In each case, our work must be holistic and reflect God's concern for each person in his or her totality.

c. We participate in public witness, such as vigils for peace, moments of prayer for peace, and other local actions that give a nonviolent testimony.

d. We provide a service of protection for persecuted persons whose lives are in danger. Such efforts open space for a territory of peace, free from any action or intrusion of any armed person, and protected by international human rights protocols.[11]

e. We cooperate with other people of good will who are working in the same areas, beginning with other Christian groups whose confessions are different from our own.

f. We seek prophetic clarity to denounce situations that offend God's project of justice and peace, and to proclaim God's project of abundant life for all of God's creation.

12. International networks of support.

a. *Christian Peacemaker Teams:* CPT has its roots in the historical peace churches of North America. In Colombia, CPT works at the invitation of the Colombian Mennonite Church (IMCOL), which offers legal and spiritual support.

CPT volunteers have been present in Barrancabermeja for the last three years, a zone with a strong paramilitary presence. They actively accompany a community of *campesinos* who decided to return to their homes after living as displaced people because of violence caused by illegal armed groups. Volunteers hold vigils for peace and organize delegations and prayer. They offer spiritual and social accompaniment to each of the residents and are on the lookout for risks from armed groups in the area. Many Colombian Mennonites have joined the team of foreign volunteers.

b. *Witness for Peace:* This is a group that visits and accompanies processes of peace with an attitude of solidarity.

CONCLUSION

Clearly the security and welfare of a country or a city cannot leave the concerns of the people abandoned and off to one side. In our understanding, safety and welfare must be apparent in a child who does not die of hunger, in a disease that does not spread, in a job that is not eliminated, in an ethnic conflict that does not explode into violence, in a dissident who is not silenced, in a natural environment that is free of contamination and exploitation, in a woman who does not die at the hands of her husband and who can freely express who she is.

The security for which we struggle in Colombia is a security that is not preoccupied by weapons. Rather, it defends life and human dignity. We have to address our proposals and orient our political will toward a concept and practices of security that are more humane and less militaristic, less warlike, in which the life of each human being comes first.

Let me close with another excerpt from Eduardo Galeano's essay, "In Praise of Common Sense."

> To save ourselves, we must come together. Like the fingers of a hand. Like ducks in flight. The technology of shared flight: The first duck who lifts off opens the way for the second, who clears the path for the third, and the energy of the third lifts the fourth into flight, who helps the fifth, and the impulse of the fifth pushes the sixth, who lends his strength to the seventh. . . . When the duck who is in front grows tired, he drops to the tail of the flock and leaves his spot to another, who rises to the tip of the inverted V that ducks draw in the air. They all take turns, in front and behind. According to my friend Juan Díaz Bordenave, who isn't a duckologist but who knows about ducks, no duck believes himself to be super-duck because he's flying in front, nor sub-duck because he goes behind. Ducks have not lost their common sense.

NOTES

1. Eduardo Galeano, "Elogio del sentido común," Forum Barcelona 2004 (Barcelona, Spain, 2004), Http://www.barcelona2004.org/esp/banco_del_conocimiento/docs/PO_1_ES_GALEANO.pdf.

2. Most of the ideas in this section come from a presentation made at the Encuentro Continental de Organizaciones del Campo (Continental Encounter of Rural Organizations) and the Encuentro Continental de Lucha contra el ALCA (Continental Encounter of the

Struggle Against the Free Trade Agreement of the Americas), held in Quito, Ecuador, from October 27 through November 1, 2002; sponsored by the Asociación Campesina ACA-FENSUAGRO (Rural Workers' Association).

3. "Manifiesto Democrático: Los 100 puntos de Uribe" [Democratic Declaration: The 100 points of Uribe].

4. "Foreign Military Training: Joint Report to Congress," July 2004, cited in Sergio Gómez Maseri, "Report: The United States Trains More Armed Forces in Colombia," *El Tiempo* (Bogotá, July 15, 2004) 1-11.

5. Information in this section is based on an article of denunciation written by columnist Oscar Collazos in the *El Tiempo* newspaper of Bogotá in June 2004, p. 7a.

6. CEDECOL, unpublished document of proposals to the General Assembly, Cali, 31 May 2003.

7. Pedro Stucky, *Esperanza en el exilio: la iglesia latinoamericana en camino hacia el siglo XXI*, [Hope in Exile: the Latin American Church on the road to the twenty-first century], Colección Horizontes (Guatemala City; Santafé de Bogotá, Colombia: Ediciones Semilla-Clara, 1992), 45.

8. Ibid., 50–54.

9. CEDECOL draws together the majority of the Evangelical Churches of Colombia, and in the last decade has begun to accept socio-political reflection. The Mennonite Christian Church (Iglesia Cristiana Menonita) is a member of the organization.

10. Stucky, *Esperanza en el Exilio*, 60.

11. Guillermo Triana and R. Esquivia, *Declaration of CEDECOL to the Nation*, unpublished document (Bógota) 3.

FOR FURTHER READING

Esquivia, Ricardo. "Building Peace from Below and Inside: The Mennonite Experience in Colombia." With Paul Stucky. In *From the Ground Up: Mennonite Contributions to International Peacebuilding*, eds. Cynthia Sampson and John Paul Lederach, 122–40. New York: Oxford University Press, 2000.

Galeano, Eduardo. "Elogio del sentido común." Forum Barcelona 2004. Barcelona, Spain, 2004. Http://www.barcelona2004.org/especially/banco_del_conocimiento/documents/PO_1_ES_GALEANO.pdf.

Stucky, Pedro. *Esperanza en el exilio: la iglesia latinoamericana en camino hacia el siglo XXI*. [Hope in Exile: the Latin American Church on the road to the twenty-first century]. Colección Horizontes. Guatemala City; Santafé de Bogotá, Colombia: Ediciones Semilla-Clara, 1992.

—14—

ANABAPTIST FAITH AND
"NATIONAL SECURITY"*

Ted Grimsrud

In a world in which "national security" concerns generally are framed in militaristic terms, pacifist heirs of the Radical Reformation seem to face two choices—either step outside of our pacifist assumptions and speak the language of power politics, trying to make some kind of contribution that will make sense within the military-oriented assumptions broadly characteristic of policy makers, or remain within our pacifist world and be content with "irrelevance" concerning public policy formulations, with nothing to say concerning reasonable fears about security that motivate many people in North America.

Of all people, however, spiritual descendants of the sixteenth-century Anabaptists have good reasons to question this either/or. As we confess Jesus Christ as Lord of the entire universe, as we understand security most fundamentally to be found by cohering with the will of God for human life, and as we confess that the evangel (the good news of healing and

* A longer version of this chapter appeared previously as "Anabaptist Faith and American Democracy," *Mennonite Quarterly Review* 78, no. 3 (July 2004): 341–62. Used with permission.

salvation) is for *all* peoples, we make a statement about the relevance of our central faith convictions for all human social structures and patterns of governance.

Of course, the question of how to respond to national security issues poses a complex challenge to Anabaptists living in North America, especially the United States. How are we to think of our citizenship in this nation?

We find ourselves, on the one hand, in a land of freedom. We may look with gratitude for our spiritual forebears' opportunity to find a safe home in North America. We have opportunities, totally unimaginable for the sixteenth-century Anabaptists, to participate in the political life of North America's democracies. Not only are Mennonites tolerated, we may vote, run for office, speak out, serve on school boards and in other ways be fully participating members in North American democratic processes.

Yet, the United States is now the world's only superpower, spending more on its military than nearly all the rest of the world's countries combined. Does this militarism add to or subtract from the genuine security of North Americans? Do pacifist Christians have any insights that might help us better think about national security?

From its beginnings the Anabaptist tradition has expressed a strong suspicion of empires, power politics, and trust in the sword. Present-day Mennonites surely are being faithful to that tradition when we refuse to support the wars of America.

However, what about the "good America" of religious freedom and participatory democracy? Is a traditional Mennonite "two-kingdom" stance—in which Christian convictions are understood primarily to be directly relevant for the faith community's inner existence and not the broader society's existence—adequate for determining our understanding of citizenship today? In our time, people throughout the world plead for participants in American civil society to seek to influence American foreign policy in a more peaceable direction. Do American Anabaptist Christians have a responsibility aggressively to seek to take their pacifist convictions into the public square in a way that might influence our government?

In this essay I suggest we take three distinct stories into account as we reflect on these questions. The first I will call the "Anabaptist Story." The second story speaks of an America that has served as a beacon of hope for self-determination and freedom for the world. We may call this the "Democracy Story." And the third is a story of conquest, domination, and widespread violence, called the "Empire Story." As pacifist followers of Jesus, those adhering to the Anabaptist Story appropriately seek to distance themselves from the Empire Story. Does such distancing also require of present-day Anabaptists a deep suspicion of the Democracy Story?

ANABAPTIST FAITH

Amidst great diversity among sixteenth-century Anabaptists, we may identify one commonality—nearly every movement and leader was looked upon with suspicion, and usually hostility, by the governments and churches of Western Europe.

What was it about the Anabaptists that led so many to identify them as enemies of the state? The answer to this question may provide us with a core set of convictions that their spiritual descendants should carry on and apply to various times and places.

The four points I summarize here are elements of such a core. Anabaptists understood themselves as committed, above all else, to following Jesus's way in all areas of life. As a consequence of that central commitment, they found themselves in conflict with the states and state churches of Western Europe.

1. By establishing themselves as a free church, Anabaptists asserted an unprecedented (and "unacceptable") level of independence from the state, thus challenging the top-down social uniformity that political and religious leaders understood to be foundational for social order. Anabaptists refused to accept the prince as ultimate authority; that is, they gave their ultimate loyalty to God's call for how to live, not to that of the government.

2. By asserting that it is never God's will for Christians to fight, Anabaptists challenged governmental appeals to God as the basis for war. Such governmental appeals play a crucial

role whenever Western nations garner citizens' support for warfare.

3. By rejecting the domination of political and religious hierarchies, Anabaptists pointed toward an upside-down notion of social power. In their view, the gathered community of believers provided the best context for hearing Jesus. So genuine power does not flow from the top of the social pyramid down, nor does it flow through the use of the sword. Discernment of God's will for human beings is not filtered through mediators such as a prince or bishop. Rather, it comes directly to the community that then determines its own approach to faithfulness.

4. By insisting on an alternative approach to economics—separating themselves from worldly materialism by advocating simplicity, economic sharing, mutual aid and, in a few famous cases, common ownership of all property—Anabaptists challenged the emerging economic basis for the Empire Story.

These core Anabaptist convictions provide a basis for pitting Anabaptist faith in clear tension with the core convictions of the Empire Story. The opposition to warfare and exploitative economics clearly apply to our present context. So too do the value of upside-down social power and the commitment to forming a counterculture that remains clearly committed to an identity as followers of Jesus, even though such commitment might be costly.

What, though, about the relationship of Anabaptist convictions to the Democracy Story? Do we gain direction from these core convictions that would also support deep suspicion toward active participation in political life? Are the Anabaptist Story and the Democracy Story by necessity totally separate, even incompatible, stories?

The first Anabaptists, while suspicious of governmental power and willing to separate themselves from activities such as bearing the sword that they saw directly contradicting the way of Jesus, seem nonetheless to have operated with assumptions that they could speak directly to prince, bishop, and all others in their society. They understood that they spoke a common language with others. Hence, they could proclaim their convictions and the religious basis for those convictions without apology, and they expected their interlocutors to be able to understand their proclamations. Anabaptists' voices were met with hostility. Severe persecution is what silenced them, *not* their own beliefs about the social irrelevance of their convictions.

Much later, in North America, Mennonites found a welcome place of toleration. They became a part of the multifaceted religious mosaic of the United States and Canada. From its beginning, the United States had no established state church and made allowance of some sort for conscientious objection during times of war.

Mennonites have experienced (and helped to foster) tolerance, freedom of religion, economic opportunity, protection of rights, free speech—the stuff of the Democracy Story. In their steadfast quest for legal recognition for their conscientious objection to war, Mennonites have made an especially significant contribution to the practice of democracy in North America. Conscientious objection has not so much been a gift from a respectful government as a demand stemming from implacable convictions that meant Mennonite pacifists would suffer a great deal rather than take up arms. Mennonites' perseverance in their peace convictions, even at the cost of great hardship (including, in a few cases, death), eventually played a major role in widening the compass of legal recognition for conscientious objectors.

Do we Mennonites today, in turn, have the responsibility to speak out openly and assertively, thus contributing to democracy by playing a role in the public conversation by which our society arrives at governmental policies?

THE TWO AMERICAS: THE DEMOCRACY STORY AND THE EMPIRE STORY

Emphasizing a distinction between the Democracy Story and the Empire Story might help clarify the question of our responsibilities in public policy conversations. For such a distinction helps us think about democratic participation as an issue separate from our potential complicity in militaristic state violence.

Walter Karp, in an essay entitled "The Two Americas," drew the distinction between "the American republic" (which has sought to embody the ideals expressed, for example, in the Declaration of Independence and the Bill of Rights) and "the American nation" (which has sought dominance, wealth, and power throughout the world). Karp believed that these two are "deadly rivals for the love and loyalty of the American people."

Noam Chomsky, perhaps the foremost critic of the Empire Story writing in the United States today, certainly condemns that story with extraordinary analytical prowess, but he also affirms that the United States is the freest society in the world. The main hope Chomsky offers his readers, in the face of the extremely destructive power of the Empire Story, lies in an expansion of the Democracy Story. He asserts that a reinvigorated American civil society, the planet's "second superpower," has considerable promise for overcoming empire.

Jonathan Schell, in his book *The Unconquerable World*, also argues that for Americans, the choice is at once between two Americas, an "imperial America" and a "republican America." Schell shares Chomsky's use of the image of the world's "second superpower." Schell links these two "superpowers" with two kinds of power, drawing on a distinction that Mohandas Gandhi made: "'One is obtained by the fear of punishment,' [Gandhi] said, 'and the other by acts of love.'" Schell calls these "cooperative power" and "coercive power." His book demonstrates the viability of this second kind of power and presents the case for harnessing cooperative power for the sake of overcoming the destructiveness of coercive power.

Writers loyal to the Democracy Story insist on a distinction between their loyalty to America as a democracy and their critique of America as an empire. The first loyalty provides the basis for denying the second loyalty. Though most of these thinkers have not been pacifists, their vision of democracy understands imperialistic violence to be antithetical to genuine democracy. And, as a rule, they would affirm that pacifists within a genuine democracy have the right—even the responsibility—to seek to influence society to move in more pacifist directions. The role of Quakers in American history testifies to this openness.

Given the extent to which the current American empire impacts the entire world, what we could call the "death struggle" between our Empire Story and our Democracy Story has tremendous significance far beyond our country's borders.

Arundati Roy of India speaks for many around the world who resist U.S. imperialism. In the July 7, 2003, issue of *In These Times*, she argues that those with the most potential are the citizens of the Empire itself:

> The only institution more powerful than the U.S. government is American civil society. The rest of us are subjects of slave nations. We are by no means powerless, but you [Americans] have the power of proximity. You have access to the imperial palace and the emperor's chambers. Empire's conquests are being carried out in your name, and you have the right to refuse. You could refuse to fight. Refuse to move those missiles from the warehouse to the dock. Refuse to wave that flag. Refuse the victory parade.

Anabaptist Americans face a direct challenge. As members of our "powerful" civil society and as pacifists who reject the Empire Story, do we have a special responsibility to become politically active as an expression of our Anabaptist faith?

FAITH AND CITIZENSHIP IN A DEMOCRACY

How does a call such as Roy's toward active participation in public affairs fit with Anabaptist convictions that we must not compromise in our commitment to follow the way of Jesus? May we do both—participate in American public affairs *and* remain consistent in our adherence to Jesus's way?

Religious ethicist Jeffrey Stout, in his recent book *Democracy and Tradition*, indirectly challenges Anabaptist Christians to participate in American democracy even while maintaining our abhorrence of war and empire. Overtly he engages the thought of Stanley Hauerwas. But since Hauerwas affirms Mennonite John Howard Yoder as profoundly influencing his ethics, and famously categorizes himself as a "high-church Mennonite," Stout's challenge to Hauerwas challenges American Anabaptists as well.

Stout uses the term "democracy" for the "civic nation" of the United States that he is passionately seeking to help thrive. Central to democracy for Stout lies the practice of public conversation, wherein citizens take an active role in reasoning together to shape their society. "Citizens" are characterized as those who accept some measure of responsibility for the condition of society—and in a genuine democracy, this possibility is available to all.

Stout argues that authentic democratic conversation *welcomes* all citizens to express whatever premises ground their claims and to do so openly. Democracy seeks to bring as many groups as possible into the conversation, to encourage each group to be straightforward in making their case for their particular perspective, to allow voice to each perspective and then to seek to arrive at the best possible public policies. Thus, pacifist Christians should not bracket their faith-based convictions insofar as these convictions lead to certain social perspectives.

Such conversation is difficult, even under the best circumstances, because participants do not share a common agreement on how to rank their most important values. Still, Stout believes that in practice this difficulty has never been an insurmountable problem in the United States. Analogous to how informal groups of athletes play sandlot baseball or street soccer without umpires or referees, our democratic society—without a monolithic authority recognized by all—still makes sense of commitment and adjudicates right and wrong.

Stout senses that U.S. democratic practices are at risk. The impact of the growth of the power of corporations and the national security state has directly challenged the sustainability of hard-earned democratic traditions in the United States. Stout believes that all people of good will must join together in efforts to protect and reinvigorate these democratic traditions.

Hence, what he perceives to be an antipathy toward the practices of democracy on the part of influential thinkers such as Stanley Hauerwas troubles him greatly. Stout believes that Hauerwas's stated antipathy toward "liberalism" often translates into implicit hostility toward the civic nation and, hence, toward conversational or reasoning democratic practices. As Stout represents him, Hauerwas sees liberalism as a "secularist ideology" that discriminates against religion, forcing Christians to enter into public discourse only if they leave their Christian convictions behind. Hauerwas, in Stout's view, pushes Christians who identify most centrally with their faith community away from engagement with participatory democracy in the broader society at precisely the moment when such engagement has become particularly important, in our age of anti-democratic responses to "terrorism" and corporate domination of civic life.

Stout accuses Hauerwas of emphasizing the difference between Christians and non-Christians in a way that fosters suspicion toward the latter. In seeing his particular religious tradition as seeking to be a community of virtue over against the sinfulness of the surrounding world, Hauerwas undercuts Christian identification with the Democracy Story.

Two Distinct Languages?

Since my concern is primarily with Mennonite understandings of citizenship, I turn to a Mennonite writer who has recently addressed these issues. In a recent essay, "Thinking Theologically About War Against Iraq," Ted Koontz echoes Hauerwas's concern lest Christians proceed too far into public policy discussions.

While expressing support for Mennonites who publicly opposed the U.S. war on Iraq "largely in terms of pragmatic or secular considerations" (such as just war reasoning, national self-interest, and general humanitarian concerns), Koontz argues that Christian pacifists must continue to think and speak in explicitly Christian terms, above all. He distinguishes between pacifist Christians' "first language" (the language of faith, most centrally based on fundamental convictions about God and Jesus Christ) and our "second language" (the language of pragmatic or secular considerations).

Koontz gives four reasons why using the first language is so important. First, because "Christians should always reject all wars," even when there are not strong second language reasons for doing so, we may at times have to rely on our first language reasons as the only reasons for remaining committed to pacifism. Secondly, if we spend too much time speaking and thinking in our second language, we may actually lose our first language. Third, we do best to speak from our strength; few Christian pacifists are experts in the second language. Fourth, we have allies who speak what is our second language as their first language, and thus have much more expertise than we do to speak against war on pragmatic grounds.

Koontz's distinction between first and second languages helps us be clear about our convictions and articulate in how we communicate them. However, Koontz's first language/ second language distinction is ultimately not very coherent. On the one hand, he states that the first language includes "all those who name themselves Christian." But then, when he tries to flesh out core Christian doctrinal convictions, he sounds specifically Anabaptist. This first language Koontz that articulates seems to be only the first language of *pacifist* Christians. Thus, although Koontz claims all Christians speak the same first language because they all share a common confession concerning Jesus Christ, when he articulates his Christology, it is strongly pacifist in a way with which most Christians would *not* agree.

From another angle, Koontz's implication that public policy actors are not Christians (since they cannot understand our first language) ignores the fact that the vast majority of U.S. presidents and legislators has been and continue to be professing Christians.

If we were to use the "two language" motif, might it not be more helpful to distinguish between those who speak the language of empire and those who speak the language of democracy? Or, those who speak the language of pacifism and those who speak the language of acceptable warfare? If we do so, however, we will have Christians on both sides of the distinction, and Koontz's use of his distinction will lose much of its relevance.

A second question arises from Koontz's assertion that "often our 'first language' of Christian theology will be unintelligible or unacceptable to our neighbors and our policymakers." Besides the problematic assumption that policymakers are not Christians, we also need to reflect on why (if Koontz is correct) our language of Christian theology will be "unintelligible."

Koontz seems to imply that there is something about Christian theology that people who are not Christians simply cannot understand. However, if Christians do indeed have problems making their convictions understood, perhaps this is due more to the fact that many Christians wrap their first language of Christian faith in jargon. Jargon creates an artificial divide that does not relate to the intelligibility of our convictions so much as our own inability to speak clearly and concretely about them.

The model of Jesus, who presented his core theology in concrete, accessible language, provides us with a different kind of challenge. Christian pacifists need not construct a first language/second language distinction that may have the effect of inhibiting our engagement in the much-needed conversation in our broader culture concerning issues of war and peace. Rather, we should learn better how to speak of our faith convictions in the same kind of concrete, accessible way that Jesus did—to anyone who will listen in any available context.

Koontz worries that if we do not make a careful distinction between our first language and our second language, and focus our energies on the former, we will run the risk of losing our first language. Let us grant his premise for a moment, in this case that Christian pacifists do commonly lose their first language, and (he appears to be implying) with it their pacifism. We still must wonder about the reasons for this loss.

Perhaps there are other reasons for the loss of pacifist convictions. One of these reasons may actually be that many people in power have corrupted what Koontz calls our second language, the language of public policy. Through the use of propaganda, public-policy actors often act in ways that actually contradict the stated values of the second language world itself.

That is, were public policy actors seriously to act according to values such as democracy, humanitarianism, or genuine national and global human interests, they would not lead the United States into the kind of hegemonic violence that has characterized foreign policy for most of our nation's history. It remains an interesting theoretical debate as to whether a nation-state is conceivable that does not use violence, but surely all Anabaptists should welcome movements that seek to make the state less violent.

The stated values of U.S. public policy are not all inherently antithetical to Christian pacifism. Most of the ideals reflected in the stated value system of U.S. public policy could easily support the thorough rejection of warfare. Christian pacifists should be speaking to the common ground they share with those ideals. However, the kind of self-imposed inhibitions for which Koontz seems to be calling would lessen the likelihood of that happening, insofar as they limit the involvement of voices that could support such a rejection.

Koontz argues that we cultivate our first language so that we will still have grounds to oppose war even when we do not have strong second language basis for doing so. He cites World War II as a case when surely "pragmatic and humanitarian considerations did not line up clearly in opposition to war." How viable will Christian pacifism ultimately be, however, when it grants that there are not strong real-world reasons for opposing war? Such an admission may lead to a kind of fideistic pacifism where our rejection of war becomes merely a "leap of faith." In fact, many people did oppose World War II on pragmatic and humanitarian grounds; to them the issue was clear even if they did not have Jesus's commands to fall back on.

To grant Koontz's point that we do not have strong second language reasons for opposing some wars may well lead to Christian pacifism becoming primarily a "vocational" matter for people who agree that their core convictions are not normative for the wider world. But this is not a position that will be very attractive, either for those who do feel a strong sense of responsibility for being a positive influence in that wider world or for those who seek to integrate their Christian convictions with their beliefs about social life.

Fortunately, many outside of Koontz's first language circle have been doing excellent work over the past century in articulating and implementing convictions that point toward pacifism and that have great relevance to the wider world in which we live. We may, most obviously, cite Mohandas Gandhi and those influenced by his work. But many others have also been working to understand the world in ways that are fully compatible with Christian pacifism, providing evidence that all wars are illegitimate on pragmatic and humanitarian grounds.

Koontz's argument seems to imply that Christian pacifists should not seek, to the full extent possible, to exorcize their call and utilize their opportunity to have an impact on public policy as citizens of the United States. Perhaps this is not his intent. Yet in his focus on the integrity of our first language he seems to be echoing Hauerwas's tendency to present the "church being the church" as our main social responsibility—and stop there.

Both Koontz and Hauerwas argue that we should hope to have an impact in our larger society on issues of war and peace; both would abhor the classic "two-kingdom" notion that the wars of the world are of no concern to followers of Jesus. Nonetheless, they seem quite ambivalent about taking up Jeffrey Stout's implied challenge to enter the public square actively as Christian pacifists and to challenge American foreign policy head on—with the language of citizenship and democracy.

If we take seriously the distinction I have been discussing between the Empire Story and the Democracy Story, however, and accept Stout's claim that the American democratic conversation *does* allow for us to remain fully committed to our faith convictions, and for us to express those convictions openly without watering them down, then we may affirm full and active participation in public debate as Anabaptist Christians.

SEEKING THE WELFARE OF THE CITY

If we were to combine a strong and overt commitment to our core Anabaptist convictions with a boldness to participate fully in the democratic conversation of the American civic nation, and if we joined this with a special concern to resist the supremacy of the Empire Story in our culture, what might we say and do to contribute to genuine national security?

Let us return to the four core sixteenth-century Anabaptist convictions noted earlier: the church as free from state control, refusal to fight in wars, affirmation of upside-down social power, and commitment to an alternative economics.

Understanding the community of faith to be free from state control in the sixteenth century did not lead only to institutional independence. It also signified the affirmation of a different worldview, centered on a different set of values. The way of Jesus took precedence over the way of Caesar. Rather than a rationale for withdrawal, the embrace of a free-church approach is best understood as a means for people of faith to have a more creative and profound impact on their wider world ("the nations").

As a free church we should be in a strong position to perceive the difference between the Empire Story and the Democracy Story. We should be in a position to discern how the best of the Democracy Story draws on the best of the biblical tradition and deserves our strong support. Likewise, we should also be in a position to offer penetrating critiques of the Empire Story and its inevitable commitment to the myth of redemptive violence—asserting that dependence upon militarism actually fosters *insecurity*.

Certainly we should also offer critiques of the Democracy Story itself insofar as it sometimes allows for the use of violence. Such critiques, however, need not lead to a rejection of the Democracy Story per se. Such critiques are an inherent part of the give and take that the Democracy Story affirms; it implicitly encourages us to make the case for a thoroughly nonviolent civic culture.

Our pacifism is not given to us merely so that our own children may remain safely behind when the servants of Mars send their children off to spend their lives in war. Rather, our pacifism should help us to join the *public* discussion and help our nonpacifist neighbors better see how the Empire Story so powerfully subverts the Democracy Story we all profess to affirm. Koontz's keeping the "first and second languages" distinct and Hauerwas's concern about "the church being the church" may be selling the potential power of our pacifist witness too short, at least insofar as these views inhibit direct engagement with public conversation.

The Anabaptists' convictions about upside-down social power pose a clear challenge to the top-down political and ecclesial patterns of domination that have characterized the modern era. A major global political dynamic in our postcolonial time is people throughout the world desiring freedom from the domination of outside powers. Anabaptists should support such movements, perceiving them as a sign of great hope that the Empire Story may be resisted.

To be sure, we are challenged to enter the discussion by insisting that these drives for self-determination dare not become merely new versions of the Empire Story. We certainly must draw upon our Anabaptist tradition in offering a theological critique of all domination. However, we also should consider offering this critique in conjunction with affirmations of the Democracy Story by providing a vision for self-determination that is humane and life-enhancing.

Finally, the Anabaptist commitment to share life together in practical ways as a means of sustaining a witness to the way of Jesus remains central to the possibilities of faithful living. As present-day Anabaptists, we must not simply allow ourselves to acculturate and be absorbed in the broader American culture. However, our task of fostering a sense of separation from "the world" (i.e., the "domination system") is for the sake of a constructive engagement with "the world" (as the object of God's love).

We may see continuity between core Anabaptist convictions and our potential today to contribute creatively to making the world a more peaceable, humane place. We must take seriously the potential we have through our nation's democratic processes to resist empire. Jeffrey Stout gives us hope that it is indeed possible for us to enter America's public conversation boldly as citizens *and* as Anabaptist Christians—recognizing that we would not be faithful to either calling were we to separate them.

FOR FURTHER READING

Berry, Wendell. "A Citizen's Response to the National Security Strategy of the United States of America." *Orion* 22, no. 2 (March/April 2003): 18–27.

Chomsky, Noam. *Hegemony or Survival: America's Quest for Global Dominance.* American Empire Project. New York: Henry Holt, 2004.

Hauerwas, Stanley. "A Response to Jeff Stout's *Tradition and Democracy.*" In *Performing the Faith: Bonhoeffer and the Practice of Nonviolence*, 215–42. Grand Rapids, Mich.: Brazos Press, 2004.

Karp, Walter. "The Two Americas." In *Buried Alive: Essays on Our Endangered Republic*, 13–26. New York: Franklin Square Press, 1992.

Koontz, Ted. "Thinking Theologically About War Against Iraq." *Mennonite Quarterly Review* 77, no. 1 (January 2003): 93–108.

Nichols, John, ed. *Against the Beast: An Anti-Imperialist Reader.* New York: Thunder's Mouth Press / Nation Books, 2003.

Schell, Jonathan. *The Unconquerable World: Power, Nonviolence, and the Will of the People.* New York: Metropolitan Books, 2003.

Stout, Jeffrey. *Democracy and Tradition.* New Forum Books. Princeton, N.J.: Princeton University Press, 2004.

Yoder, John Howard. "The Christian Case for Democracy." In *The Priestly Kingdom: Social Ethics as Gospel*, 151–71. Notre Dame, Ind.: University of Notre Dame Press, 1984.

PART II

SEEKING THE WELFARE OF THE CITY: ESSAYS ON PUBLIC PEACE, JUSTICE, AND ORDER

Conference Papers

_____

SECTION C

The Rule of Law, Public Order, and Human Rights

—15—

A MENNONITE HUMAN RIGHTS PARADIGM?

Timothy Wichert

Mennonites are uneasy about human rights. They have not ignored human rights entirely, and they occasionally use rights language when convenient. But human rights language tends to be a "second language." Their preferred language is that of compassion, care, and community.

Yet human rights have become an integral part of the international legal system. What's more, they have offered one of the most significant, nonviolent, "political" contributions to public peace, justice, and order in the past fifty years. They play an important role in moderating conflicts. Human rights institutions have ensured that there is a systematic international response to torture, unlawful detention, and violence against women and refugees. At a national level, legal instruments like the Canadian Charter of Rights and Freedoms, or the American Bill of Rights, provide the basis for a rule of law that has largely ensured public peace, justice, and order.

Human rights do present a significant challenge to peace theology, which has been the primary tool for Mennonites to respond to conflict and victimization, especially through the preferred options of forgiveness, mercy, and reconciliation. But despite the challenges, developing a human rights discourse that is rooted in peace theology—as well as restorative justice—could prove to be a more universally helpful response to conflict.

HISTORY OF HUMAN RIGHTS

Human rights in the modern political era are primarily rooted in the United Nations. The charter that created the United Nations in 1945 wanted to "reaffirm faith in fundamental human rights, in the dignity and worth of the human person, in the equal rights of men and women," and to "promote social progress and better standards of life."[1] Governments meeting at the UN have also adopted treaties or conventions to address specific issues and vulnerable groups: the Genocide Convention (1948), the Refugee Convention (1951), the Convention to Eliminate Discrimination against Women (1979), the Convention against Torture (1984), and the Convention on the Rights of the Child (1991).

The modern human rights era emerged in the aftermath of World War II as a response to the evils of Nazi Germany and the massacre of six million Jews, along with homosexuals, Gypsies, Marxists, and other nationalities. It was also a response to other totalitarian regimes of the early twentieth century, including the Soviet Union under Stalin, and Imperialist Japan. The international human rights regime, under the umbrella of the UN, was an attempt to create a new world order that could avoid violent conflict through greater respect for all people and their "human dignity."

But human rights go back much further. The Old Testament prophet Isaiah wrote: "Woe to those who enact evil statutes, and to those who constantly record unjust decisions, so as to deprive the needy of justice, and rob the poor of my people of their rights, so that widows may be their spoil, and that they may plunder the orphans" (Isa 10:1-2 NASB).

In his book *Crowned with Glory and Honor: Human Rights in the Biblical Tradition*, Christopher Marshall provides a helpful analysis of human rights from a Christian perspective.[2] He places human rights directly in the biblical tradition, suggesting that it offers the best justification for ascribing dignity and rights to human beings, who have been made in the image of God, occupying a place a "little lower than God" (Ps 8:5, Heb 2:7). Rights represent the justice of God, in whose image human beings are made; they are expressions of what God is like.

Martin Shupack, a Mennonite pastor and lawyer, demonstrates in his article, "The Demands of Dignity and Community: An Ecumenical and Mennonite Account of Human Rights," that churches have been at the forefront of human rights advocacy.[3] In 1891 the first modern Catholic social encyclical, *Rerum Novarum*, highlighted the primacy of rights inherent in human nature. In 1963 Pope John XXIII placed human rights at the center of Catholic social teaching. The World Council of Churches, at its first assembly in 1948, proclaimed the responsibility of churches to "take a firm stand" against "violations of human rights."

Church support for human rights arguably goes back further. Glen Stassen, in his foreword to Marshall's book, recounts a story of human rights being developed during the 1645 movement for religious liberty among free church Puritans in England: "In 1645 Richard Overton originated the concept of human rights. Overton had been a member of the first Baptist church in history, which emigrated to Holland in search of religious liberty and joined with the Waterlander Mennonite Congregation." Overton eventually returned to England, and began publishing booklets arguing against religious persecution while promoting religious liberty and freedom of the press. He was thrown in jail for his writings but was not deterred. Soon he was calling attention not only to poor prison conditions, but was arguing for rights of housing and of care for poor orphans and widows, the aged and the handicapped, as well as the right to education and land.[4]

Historians might debate whether Richard Overton, an early Anabaptist/Baptist, actually articulated the first clear concept of human rights. But as a Christian prophet, he was clearly following in the footsteps of Isaiah, defending the rights of the poor and vulnerable, and stressing the dignity and worth of all people.

CONTENT OF HUMAN RIGHTS

Civil and political rights, which we hear about most often today, include the rights to "life, liberty, and security of the person"—the right to a fair trial, and the right not be tortured, arbitrarily arrested, or summarily executed (i.e. without any legal process). They also include freedom of thought, conscience, religion, and association. The core concept of these "first generation" rights is liberty, in particular the liberty of the individual from arbitrary and totalitarian state actions. On the one hand, they are often considered the classic human rights, yet at the same time are also viewed by some with suspicion because of their roots in "liberal individualism" in general, and the American and French revolutions in particular.

Economic, social, and cultural rights deal primarily with equality, and include the right to an adequate standard of living—to sufficient food, clothing, housing, and medical care, and to education. They primarily set out the requirements for human well-being, but they also imply a strong element of community well-being, in the sense that all should have enough. A presumption has also developed that these rights may require state intervention, and that governments have a duty to provide these rights as resources allow. Critics claim that they are rooted in socialism and Marxist revolution.

Human rights discourse has become rather complicated, with a "bewildering diversity of meanings," as Marshall says. There are tensions between individual and collective rights, liberal and socialist approaches, and religious and atheistic underpinnings. Terms like liberty, freedom, and equality are themselves ambiguous. Perhaps the most basic dispute is over the question of whether human rights are universal, or merely Western cultural values.

Natural law theory, which developed primarily within the Catholic Church tradition, gained particular prominence during the Enlightenment and formed the basis for both the French and American bills of rights. It suggested that human rights and dignity derive from our "human nature" and can be discovered by "rational intelligence." However, other

Christian traditions, including Evangelicals and some Protestant churches, generally opposed or disregarded this approach to human rights. In part they believed that natural law theory was not amenable to Christocentric theology, and that it lacked a Christian foundation.

Some Christians today have moved toward a "liberation theology" view of human rights, whereby the gospel calls them to respond to human oppression. Yet this too is opposed by others within the church as too radical.

Despite these ambiguities, the Bible still offers one of the best justifications for ascribing dignity and rights to human beings. Human beings have been made in the image of God, and human rights represent the justice of God. As such, human rights language is largely consistent with the language of faith.

MENNONITES AND HUMAN RIGHTS

There is no official Mennonite statement on human rights. Mennonite Central Committee (MCC) does not explicitly include human rights work in its mission statement. It states that MCC "seeks to demonstrate God's love by working among people suffering from poverty, conflict, oppression . . . serves as a channel for interchange by building relationships that are mutually transformative . . . strives for peace, justice, and dignity of all people."[5]

Yet MCC workers have been involved with human rights work in various places: supporting those suffering torture or disappearances in Central America; working with detainees in apartheid South Africa; helping victims of military oppression in Southeast Asia; supporting the rights of Palestinians in the Middle East. They have also supported broader Mennonite efforts for the legal recognition of conscientious objection, historically in Canada and the United States, and more recently in Colombia and Honduras. MCC programs in Canada have focused on the rights of refugees and Native Canadians. At the same time, some of this work has been sharply criticized within the Mennonite constituency, usually on the basis that the issues are too "political."

In a 1995 *MCC Peace Office Newsletter* focusing on "Christian Faith and Universal Human Rights," Bob Herr and Judy Zimmerman Herr suggested that the motivation for MCC work in these areas has been Christian faith—seeking to follow Christ's teaching to help those in need—rather than lengthy deliberations about the universality of human rights norms.[6] Writing in the same newsletter, Mennonite theologian Ted Koontz reckoned that "rights language is too flat and individualistic to direct us towards the good life," though it may be an important "second language." He expressed his belief that Christian compassion is actually our "first language," stressing mutual care, community well-being, and harmonious living within community.

The Mennonite Confession of Faith also reflects this approach.[7] For example, article six of the Confession of Faith, on "The Creation and Calling of Human Beings," states that "God has created human beings in the divine image," that God "gave them a special dignity among all the works of creation," and that "God's will from the beginning has been for women and men to live in loving and mutually helpful relationships with each other." These statements are very similar to Christopher Marshall's biblical account of human rights, and are also remarkably similar to the UN charter.

The more practical manifestations of these beliefs, however, are articulated in article twenty-two on "Peace, Justice, and Nonresistance": the "same Spirit that empowered Jesus also empowers us to love enemies, to forgive rather than to seek revenge, to practice right relationships . . . to resist evil without violence." And article twenty-three, on "The Church's Relation to Government and Society," calls on "the nations (and all persons and institutions) to move toward justice, peace, and compassion for all people."

How does this help us address injustice? Arguably the only Mennonite organization to be outspoken in the face of injustice is Christian Peacemaker Teams (CPT). CPT had its genesis in the Mennonite World Conference in France in 1984. Ron Sider challenged participants: "Unless we . . . are ready to start to die by the thousands in dramatic vigorous new exploits for peace and justice . . . we dare never whisper another word about pacifism to our sisters and brothers in those desperate lands filled with injustice."[8]

CPT was created on the premise that "ordinary people could stand in front of the guns and encourage less violent ways for change to happen." While it does not specifically call itself a human rights organization in its mission statement, it is for all intents and purposes a human rights organization. In fact, CPT received international media attention in spring 2004 because it had documented the abuse of Iraqi detainees at Abu Ghraib prison in Baghdad in January 2004, four months before news appeared in the mainstream media. The media referred to CPT as "a Chicago-based human rights group."

The Mennonite World Conference (MWC), which represents ninety member churches in fifty-four countries, has increasingly commented on human rights abuses, though without using rights language. Following its assembly in Bulawayo, Zimbabwe, in 2003, it issued a statement on the dire situation in that country, stating that "we grieve and deplore . . . the fear and brutality that result from political oppression and conflict, excess police powers, and arbitrary arrests. . . ." And in early 2004, MWC sent a letter of concern to Vietnamese authorities about the arrest of Mennonite church leaders in Ho Chi Minh City. This intervention followed a "letter of protest" signed by forty Vietnamese Mennonite Church leaders, which was sent to the Prime Minister condemning specific incidents against Mennonite leaders.

Meanwhile, an increasing number of Mennonites are pursuing human rights as a discipline and approach to identifying and resolving issues. But the dilemma for Mennonites is this: How to reconcile the pursuit of justice with Jesus's command to love enemies, to pray for those who persecute you, to forgive wrongdoers, and not to resist evildoers? In particular, how does one address injustice?

PEACE THEOLOGY AND HUMAN RIGHTS

Mennonite peace theology has created a conundrum with respect to human rights abuses. It has focused on enduring accusation and abuse without retaliating, in order to "turn the other cheek." Jesus's crucifixion represents an atonement for all past injustices and all future injustices; arguably it thus achieved great justice. But it also did so at enormous cost, for Jesus had to willingly submit to the abuse and violence of the crucifixion itself. The apostle Peter supports this approach: "If you endure [pain] when you do right and suffer for it, you have God's approval . . . you should follow in [Christ's] steps" (1 Pet 2:20-21).

Mennonite Peace theology has emphasized the healing and restoration of relationships where there has been abuse and harm. A "restorative" concept of justice has thus developed. Not wishing simply to seek revenge, practitioners of restorative justice try respectfully to call those who cause harm to account, encouraging them to fulfill their obligations to make things right. The goal is accountability and healing. But repentance and change are left up to the abuser; demanding or even requesting accountability is difficult. As a result, the abuser's assumption of responsibility for harm inflicted may never occur. Further harmful behavior is not necessarily prevented.

The limitations of this "voluntary" approach to justice are apparent in the continued prevalence of rape and other gender-based persecution in the context of war and conflict. Marlene Epp, in her book *Women Without Men: Mennonite Refugees of the Second World War*, has documented how extensive was the rape of Mennonite women in the context of that war.[9] Mennonite women refugees were part of a generation and a community that valued acquiescence, submission, and humility, especially on the part of women. Arguably, the "peace theology" that urged these abused women simply to forgive their abusers has ensured that the abusers are unlikely to be held accountable for their abusive behavior. This lack of accountability leads to a continuing cycle of violence that often legitimates the abusive behavior, or at the very least does not condemn it.

This fear of condemnation seems well-rooted in Mennonite theology. One is to love enemies and to endure accusation and abuse without retaliation, and preferably with acceptance and forgiveness. Evil will be overcome by good. Justice will be done in another time, and another place. But justice might not be—indeed is unlikely to be—accomplished now.

As a result, this concept of justice is arguably limited. And the claim that Mennonites seek justice, or strive for justice, as stated in various confessions of faith or mission statements, is rather disingenuous. Seeking justice has actually been postponed in favor of non-resistance, forgiveness, and compassion. Mennonites have been *too* careful—*too* kind perhaps—and have been unwilling to condemn wrongdoing or demand accountability.

Mennonites have taken some steps forward. MCC has developed a program in Canada called "Victims' Voice," which is a program of empowerment and healing for victims of homicide and other serious crime. It has focused greater understanding of, and support for, victims within the criminal justice system. It advocates specifically for victims' rights. This perspective has offered an extremely important and helpful contribution toward a fuller concept of "restorative" justice.

"Just peacemaking theory," which Glen Stassen and Duane Friesen developed in the mid-1990s, offers an example of deliberately using human rights language in peace theology.[10] Bringing together both idealist and realist schools of political science and international relations, they sought to link the idea of justice as an absolute ideal with actual practices that have successfully restored communities. Their list of ten "just peacemaking practices" includes greater support for the United Nations as an important international forum for cooperation and human rights. Another is to promote democracy and human rights through a network of people working together to raise public awareness of those suffering human rights violations.

The Quakers have developed an approach to human rights that is consistent with their peace theology. The Quaker United

Nations Office has been based in Geneva since 1926, and has become known for its independence and impartiality on important policy issues. Rather than singling out individual states for condemnation, they tend to focus on thematic issues that cross boundaries and involve particularly marginalized and vulnerable groups. Historically, they have advocated for the right to conscientious objection. More recently, they have advocated for the rights of children not to be forced or conscripted into armed forces. Their advocacy is generally done through education and persuasion, a combination of careful research and gathering information from their own experiences, together with deliberate dialogue with government officials and decision makers who can influence changes in policies. Because there is "something of God in everyone," they consider that wrong-doers (and others whose policies they disagree with) are capable of change. But first they must be confronted with the facts.

A (Mennonite) Human Rights Paradigm

There are three essential elements of human rights work that can contribute to a human rights paradigm based in peace theology, and that might assist in meeting the needs of vulnerable and abused people, addressing injustice, and holding wrong-doers accountable. These three elements are presence, protection, and persuasion.

1. Presence

Protecting the vulnerable involves presence. MCC is well-known for its deliberate approach of "working among" those who are suffering from poverty, conflict, oppression, or other difficulties. Apart from assisting those in need, their main concern is often to foster and maintain relationships. Presence or accompaniment can take many forms.

In the mid-1990s, MCC developed a program of civilian peacemaking in Burundi at the request of local Quakers.[11] They hoped that international volunteers could assist in reducing the level of violence and create space for positive developments. They would also accompany individuals who felt vulnerable so that they could carry on with their activities and daily lives. Inevitably, various issues and dilemmas arose. For example, it was difficult both to stand with people and to document human rights violations. Local authorities forced two international workers to leave immediately after reporting abuses in the community where they had been a presence.

The kind of presence is a regular subject of debate, especially among human rights and humanitarian organizations. One popular suggestion currently in vogue within many NGO, UN and government circles is an armed UN force, capable of rapid deployment, or a minimally armed international police force. Others prefer to promote the use of unarmed civilians and neutral non-governmental organizations. MCC has suggested that if NGOs had remained present in the region of Kosovo in 1998-99, and had insisted on other international monitors remaining, NATO bombing might have been forestalled.

In the midst of conflict, this kind of work is risky business. In Burundi, MCC workers faced increasing violence; insecurity increased, especially against expatriates. Who is willing to risk their own life to stand by those who are at risk of losing theirs? Robert Charles, a Mennonite political scientist, has noted that there is "growing interest throughout significant portions of the North American Mennonite constituency in this kind of international peace activism"; it taps into an ethic of "costly discipleship."[12] CPT was created as a response to this very challenge to be "ready to start to die by the thousands in dramatic vigorous new exploits for peace and justice."

Other presence initiatives have included local peace committees or peace sanctuaries (e.g. Mennonites in Colombia). Sometimes high profile, short-term fact-finding missions by church groups, pastoral delegations, or inter-religious groups have also been able to provide presence and visibility for the needs of the vulnerable in the midst of conflict.

Presence also involves building relationship, for example with those suffering abuse in the midst of conflict in Burundi or Colombia. Building relationships with the vulnerable is a practical means of uplifting their dignity as human beings, and is the first step toward achieving a sense of justice for them. There is more work to do to develop this latter notion of accompaniment of people within the justice system, including the victims of crime as well as those accused of crime. MCC programs in Canada include "Victims' Voice" and "Circles of Support and Accountability," which accompany people on opposite sides of the justice system.

2. Protection

While mere presence offers some protection or solace to those whose lives or liberty are in jeopardy, the notion of protection implies something more. Protection is more active than presence. It actively guards against the abuse of power. Human rights developed as a tool to protect individuals from arbitrary and totalitarian state actions. But protection not only involves uplifting and defending the civil and political rights of people; it involves their economic, social, and cultural rights as well.

When sufficient food, housing, medical care, and education are merely considered to be the compassionate response of NGOs or "socialist" governments, then we forgo the means to compel their provision to those in need. Using rights language to claim entitlement to these basic human needs provides a more compelling reason to provide them. Governments have rarely provided these willingly, and it usually requires the diligent efforts of individuals and other interest groups to ensure they are achieved.

There are a number of active steps that can be taken to develop a more compelling notion of protection:

a. Learn the language of human rights. Familiarity with international human rights documents is a start, especially the more practical and usable guides, e.g. the UN's "Guiding Principles on Internal Displacement."[13]

b. Develop mechanisms within organizations to deal with human rights violations when they are encountered. In situations of armed conflict, strategies can include partnerships with "presence" teams like CPT, or organizing short-term visits by church leaders. In addition, there must be a process for sharing this information with others, perhaps local authorities, government decision makers, human rights organizations, or the media.

c. Initiate programs that provide human rights education and training. For example, there are numerous opportunities for providing peace education and human rights education in refugee camps. Education is a key to ensuring that future generations understand there are viable alternatives.

d. Ensure a process is in place to address violence against women and children. There is ample documentation of violence against women, including Mennonite women, in the context of war, yet Mennonites rarely focus attention on the need to end this kind of violence. These atrocities continue to happen in almost every current conflict. Responses should include succor and treatment (e.g. trauma counseling), but must also focus on condemning the abuse.

e. Focus more attention on justice mechanisms. With their experience in restorative justice, Mennonites can assist governments to explore local justice alternatives which ensure appropriate accountability.

3. Persuasion

Finally, protecting the vulnerable involves putting pressure on those perpetrating the conflict and abuse. Mennonites have developed some expertise in engaging authorities, primarily at the national level. In the past, Mennonites were primarily concerned with their own needs, such as rights to conscientious objection or to manage their own education. Now, they do advocacy on behalf of many other groups of vulnerable people, usually rooted in practical programs and focused at a local or national level.

While advocacy at a national level is important, there should be greater attention to the international system. On the one hand, rights developed at the international level set standards for all to achieve. Because they are primarily the result of consensus decision making, they also acquire a universality that crosses borders and cultures. At the same time, these international standards simply remain goals unless they are incorporated into national policy. So there is a need to persuade governments that have agreed to international standards to put them into practice.

Governments can be pressured into complying with international obligations, through international human rights mechanisms and through political pressure. One example in which this occurs is the UN Commission on Human Rights, which meets each spring in Geneva to discuss the state of the world's human rights. Upwards of 500 people from around the globe—diplomats, UN officials, human rights activists, church representatives—gather to put forward their views. While the political nature of the process offers mixed results for policy making, it allows pressure to be brought to bear on offending states for their human rights violations. This commission has been an invaluable venue for achieving progress in recent decades in places like Chile, Argentina, and South Africa.

Another remarkable example of successful persuasion at the UN was the process of putting the issue of internally displaced people (IDPs) officially on the international agenda. Internally displaced people are those who are forcibly displaced for similar reasons as refugees, namely armed conflict and violations of human rights. But unlike refugees, they do not cross international borders, and so cannot rely on the international protection of the UN Refugee Convention.

Through careful advocacy of NGOs in Geneva, in particular the Quaker UN Office, the World Council of Churches, and Caritas Internationalis, the UN Commission on Human Rights in 1992 requested the Secretary-General to appoint a representative for IDPs. As a result of the work since then by the representative, Dr. Francis Deng, international awareness of the existence of IDPs has increased substantially. He has visited more than a dozen countries with acute IDP problems, including Sri Lanka, Burundi, and Colombia, to look at internal displacement. In 1996, Deng prepared a significant compilation and analysis of international legal norms relating to IDPs, which were eventually endorsed by the commission in 1998. These thirty "Guiding Principles" have now been published in a handbook, and set out key rights and obligations for IDPs as articulated in international humanitarian and human rights law.[14]

This example demonstrates the power of persuasion. NGOs, UN agencies, and governments now provide substantial assistance for IDPs. Governments understand that they can no longer ignore or abuse these vulnerable people in their midst. The facts have confronted them, and they have begun to change.

Conclusion

Although the complexities and ambiguities of human rights have evoked an ambivalent response among Mennonites, we should recognize and use human rights law as key tool in the pursuit of public peace, justice, and order. Given their consistency with biblical imperatives, and various Mennonite statements, appeals to human rights can enhance current work on behalf of oppressed and vulnerable people. While peace theology faces challenges in fully adopting the language of human rights, they need not be insurmountable, as Quakers and others have clearly demonstrated.

The challenge for Mennonites is to embrace the use of human rights to assist in the pursuit of justice now, not simply in some future heavenly realm. A traditional Mennonite focus on the dignity of all people, working among suffering people, and building relationships forms an excellent basis for developing a human rights paradigm that builds on the notions of presence and accompaniment. But this is just a first step, and must lead to a more complete pursuit of justice through protection and persuasion as well.

We must continue to find creative ways to ensure that we help those we are obliged to help, while also expanding our concepts of those in need. Ultimately, how we help those in need reflects our commitment to human rights.

NOTES

1. Charter of the United Nations, Preamble, signed on 26 June 1945 in San Francisco, and entered into force on 24 October 1945. (See: http://www.un.org/aboutun/charter).

2. Christopher D. Marshall, *Crowned with Glory & Honor: Human Rights in the Biblical Tradition*, Studies in Peace and Scripture Series, no. 6 (Telford, Pa.; Scottdale, Pa.; Auckland, N.Z.: Pandora Press U.S.; Herald Press; Lime Grove House, 2001). The book includes the Universal Declaration of Human Rights as an appendix.

3. Martin Shupack, "The Demands of Dignity and Community: An Ecumenical and Mennonite Account of Human Rights," *Conrad Grebel Review* 14, no. 3 (Fall 1996).

4. Marshall, *Crowned with Glory & Honor*, 13–14.

5. Mennonite Central Committee, MCC Mission Statement, http://www.mcc.org/about/whatis.html.

6. Robert Herr and Judy Zimmerman Herr, "Christian Faith and Universal Human Rights," *MCC Peace Office Newsletter* 25, no. 3 (July-September 1995).

7. Mennonite Church, *Confession of Faith in a Mennonite Perspective* (Scottdale, Pa.: Herald Press, 1995). Available at http://www.mennonitechurch.ca, http://www.mennolink.org, and other locations.

8. See http://www.cpt.org/publications/sider.php.

9. Marlene Epp, *Women Without Men: Mennonite Refugees of the Second World War*, Studies in Gender and History (Toronto; Buffalo: University of Toronto Press, 2000).

10. Duane K. Friesen and Glen H. Stassen, "Just Peacemaking," in *Transforming Violence: Linking Local and Global Peacemaking*, ed. Robert Herr and Judy Zimmerman Herr, foreword by Konrad Raiser (Scottdale, Pa.: Herald Press, 1998), 53–67.

11. Timothy Wichert, "Creating a Space for Peace-Making: Burundi and Beyond," *Refuge: Canada's Periodical on Refugees* 16, no. 6 (December 1997): 20–21.

12. J. Robert Charles, *Mennonite International Peacemaking During and After the Cold War*, MCC Occasional Paper, no. 21 (Akron, Pa.: Mennonite Central Committee, 1994), para. 4.2.1.

13. United Nations, *Guiding Principles on Internal Displacement*, Office for the Coordination of Humanitarian Assistance (OCHA), Geneva, 2000.

14. Ibid.

FOR FURTHER READING

Charles, J. Robert. *Mennonite International Peacemaking During and After the Cold War*. MCC Occasional Paper, no. 21. Akron, Pa.: Mennonite Central Committee, 1994.

Epp, Marlene. *Women Without Men: Mennonite Refugees of the Second World War*. Studies in Gender and History. Toronto; Buffalo: University of Toronto Press, 2000.

Friesen, Duane K., and Glen H. Stassen. "Just Peacemaking." In *Transforming Violence: Linking Local and Global Peacemaking*, edited by Robert Herr and Judy Zimmerman Herr, with a foreword by Konrad Raiser. Scottdale, Pa.: Herald Press, 1998.

Herr, Robert, and Judy Zimmerman Herr. "Christian Faith and Universal Human Rights." *MCC Peace Office Newsletter* 25, no. 3 (July-September 1995).

Marshall, Christopher D. *Crowned with Glory & Honor: Human Rights in the Biblical Tradition*. Studies in Peace and Scripture Series, no. 6. Telford, Pa.; Scottdale, Pa.; Auckland, N.Z.: Pandora Press U.S.; Herald Press; Lime Grove House, 2001.

Mennonite Church. *Confession of Faith in a Mennonite Perspective*. Scottdale, Pa.: Herald Press, 1995.

Shupack, Martin. "The Demands of Dignity and Community: An Ecumenical and Mennonite Account of Human Rights." *Conrad Grebel Review* 14, no. 3 (Fall 1996).

Wichert, Timothy. "Creating a Space for Peace-Making: Burundi and Beyond." *Refuge: Canada's Periodical on Refugees* 16, no. 6 (December 1997).

—16—

AMBIGUOUS LEGACY: THE PEACE TEACHING, SPEAKING TRUTH TO POWER, AND MENNONITE ASSIMILATION THROUGH THE CENTURIES

John D. Rempel

Peacemaking is always controversial. It involves a daring move from retaliation to restoration.

I lived in New York at the time of the terrorist attacks and saw such a daring move. Immediately after September 11 hundreds of public gatherings sprang up all around New York City for people to pour out their grief, rage, and confusion. Not surprisingly, most citizens turned their anger against the terrorists. Many called for war. From where I was standing in Union Square, I saw only one sign that called for another response: "Our grief is not a cry for war." Some New Yorkers took this as a betrayal of the victims. But others saw these words as the only response worthy of the dead.

Few realities have determined the course of history more than the choices by which individuals, social groups, and nations have responded to aggression and hatred. What made it possible for people in New York, surrounded by slaughter, to seek a response other than revenge? What enabled them to resist the cry for war?

The Anabaptist answer was that nonviolence is possible only for those who "walk in the resurrection" of Jesus. At the other end of the peace continuum are groups like the World Federalists who believe that the collective human will to create structures of peace can lead to the abolition of war.

Most of us, individuals and institutions, find ourselves somewhere between these extremes. When I was the Mennonite Central Committee representative to the United Nations there were days when I blessed that institution because it provided mechanisms for countries to negotiate crises with each other rather than resort to war. There were also days when I was tempted to curse the organization because its members still cling to naked self-interest and spurn the larger good. So, on Mondays, Wednesdays, and Fridays I believed that it was possible for political institutions to move from retaliation to restoration. On Tuesdays, Thursdays, and Saturdays I was convinced that only remnant movements willing to renounce all violence, even when such renunciation brings suffering, can bring the world healing. You will notice this ambivalence in the samples of Mennonite peacemaking that I assess.

I come to the subject as someone who has supported Mennonite participation in structures of peacemaking. The UN office of Mennonite Central Committee (MCC) cooperated with institutions of power and, in very modest ways, spoke truth to them. I was always in search of wisdom for that precarious undertaking so I looked for precedents to guide me, like the internationalism that arose after World War I, but also incidents from Mennonite and Quaker history.

From a survey of Mennonite peace tradition I observed what I would describe as an "inherent instability" in the movement, pulling it toward the extremes of separatism or assimilation. It seems, to use Yeats' phrase, that, "the center will not hold." In this essay I make the case that Pilgram Marpeck's thought and practice represent the "center" of the

Anabaptist–Mennonite tradition. But the Marpeck circle did not have staying power. It is important for us to ask why, because of all the sixteenth-century radical reformers Marpeck has the most in common with socially engaged Mennonite churches around the globe today.

A comparison of Mennonites and Quakers yields an instructive contrast as well as a likeness. Quakers see "that of God in everyone"; they see the Spirit of God at work in all creation. This has led them to try to replicate in the world what the Spirit can do in the church. Mennonites have focused primarily on the work of the Spirit in the church. Yet, when one studies the history of both movements the same three tendencies are evident: First comes a high view of the church as the "new humanity" (Eph 2), the bearer of the kingdom, the faithful dissenter. Both movements were missionary in character; the mission was to live as a vanguard of the kingdom. After each movement had become a settled institution two impulses arose that vied with each other for dominance. One of them softened the separatist edge by spiritualizing the church. Thus, a second tendency: The Christian could be a good citizen because church and society were distinct realms in which distinct norms apply. A third impulse universalized the call to peace and, with it, relativized the uniqueness of the church's mission. Thus, the Christian could be a good citizen because the church shares a vision of the common good with all peace-seeking institutions.

The Issues

For the sake of the larger conversation that this volume represents I will venture generalizations, particularly about the spiritualizing of the church and its assimilation into the dominant order. Those are the dangers I see, after all, among mainstream Mennonites on both the political left and political right, for whom I intend this study. My intention is to be faithful to the historical record. But the interpretation I offer needs testing.

I turn first to my theological models and then to historical case studies. What have Mennonites believed over the centuries about the possibility of peace? Historically, I see four responses to that question. Two of them have taken the posture of a remnant—"Christ against culture." And two of them have made common cause with the society around them—with elements of "Christ transforming culture" and "Christ within culture," to use H. Richard Niebuhr's categories.

First-generation Anabaptists and many after them stood as a remnant, the "wheat" that has been separated from the "tares," willing to renounce all violence and all direct responsibility for order in society. One form of this stance has been *separatist*: the church is called to put away the sword even though it affirms that the state has a limited calling to take the sword to keep order.

Another form of the remnant stance is that of the dissenter, or *prophet*. The church is called to put away the sword and to warn the state against the folly and idolatry of violence as a way to keep order. Here the emphasis is on an engaged non-conformity in the hope of changing the world.

Understanding the mission of the church as making common cause with society also has two forms. Both of them are accompanied by a sense that the church, like the world, is made up of "wheat" and "tares." One form of this stance is to call the church to a *priestly* role within the world, to share responsibility with public institutions in moving society from retribution to restoration. The current MCC Peace Project calls on the church to support institutions that provide order and security with the least violent methods. For some advocates of this view it includes Christian participation in policing. The priestly view argues that most Mennonites live their lives within institutions of power that make life safe and prosperous for them. Therefore, they cannot escape responsibility for those institutions. This view insists that the separatist and prophetic stances have integrity only for people willing to live outside the benefits that institutions of power offer.

The other form of the "Christ within culture" stance is often called *realist*. It holds that the world is fallen. Christians should follow the Sermon on the Mount as individuals. But according to this view, trying to make the Sermon on the Mount applicable to the public sphere is irresponsible because only force is ultimately able to preserve justice in an evil world.

One can find Quakers alongside Mennonites in each of the above categories. But Quakers are also different from Mennonites in instructive ways. I will occasionally introduce their peace stances as a foil for Mennonite positions on the issues I raise.

THE MISSING LINK: WHAT IS THE CHURCH?

Mennonite approaches to the world have long been more diverse than the popular picture of the "quiet in the land" (Ps 35:20) suggests. They have not always taken a separatist or prophetic stance toward society. Without ever developing an adequate theology for a priestly or realist stance in the world, some Mennonite groups in certain eras have understood their mission in those terms. There has never been a full theological accounting for this diversity. Mennonite understandings of "world" and "church" have been more ambiguous and fluid than is commonly assumed.

How one understands the church's place in the world determines its role in peacemaking. That is my thesis. Let me illustrate it with reference to each of my models—separatist, prophetic, priestly, and realist. To begin with, Hutterites were the most consistent of the Anabaptist groups in understanding the church as an alternate society to that of the world. They championed a distinct economic as well as spiritual community. Worldly institutions had only the most marginal relevance to the mission of the church, made it thinkable for them to refuse the payment of war taxes, unlike Anabaptist groups that were still tied economically to society. In the mind of the separatists the church is the "wheat" and the world is the "tares." The strength of this position is that it embodies a new order of things; its weakness is that it limits that order to the church.

In contrast, the prophetic stance believes that the kingdom is present in the church to the extent that the church seeks to realize God's reign in the world. In the prophetic mind "wheat" has been sown everywhere in the creation. The church is where the "wheat" has already sprouted but its calling is to tend "wheat" wherever it has been sown. The church is bound to the world but different from it. The strength of this position is the solidarity of the church with the world; its weakness is its tendency toward utopianism.

The priestly stance sees the fallenness of the church as well as the world. It emphasizes our common humanity: The line of the kingdom runs not between church and world but through every individual and institution. The strength of this position is the solidarity of the church with the world; its weakness is that it has lost the tension between them.

For the realist, the true believer in her prayer closet is a grain of "wheat" waiting to be harvested into eternity. But all institutions, including the church, are a mixture of "wheat" and "tares." The strength of this position is its clarity about the self-interestedness of all human institutions; its weakness is that it holds that there is no fundamental tension between the Christian as a member of the church and the Christian as responsible in the world; that same Christian is simply accountable to two different realms and standards.

HISTORIC CASE STUDIES

Sixteenth Century

How closely does reality fit the above typology? Anabaptist thought as a whole has conceived of the church as a historical, "public" institution and not only a spiritual one; it is an alternative community to that of society at large. Beyond that single commonality, there has been considerable disagreement about what it meant to be an "alternative community." Did the church's structures replace those of the world? The Schleitheim Confession came close to answering this question with a yes insofar as it distinguished between being inside or outside the "perfection of Christ." The Hutterites took this principle to its logical conclusion. All these separatists believed that God used the ban in the church and the sword in the world to restrain evil. The Christian was bound to nonviolent responses to evil. And since the role of politician, policeman, or soldier depended on the threat and use of lethal force, a Christian could not fill these roles.

At the other end of the Anabaptist spectrum were movements that claimed government could be constructed in conformity with biblical norms. Balthasar Hubmaier believed that a community of true Christians could create a just social order and that it was right to defend it with the sword. The Münsterites, with an opposite understanding of social responsibility to that of Hubmaier, believed in holy revolution and were prepared to overthrow an unjust social order violently to make way for a just one.

Anabaptism as a whole rejected both of these attempts to legitimize the use of lethal force for Christians. In between the extremes of just war and revolution, on the one hand, and Hutterian communalism, on the other, were Menno Simons and Pilgram Marpeck. Even though he was a separatist in his emphasis on a disciplined church, Menno developed Christian norms for a "just society" and "just rulers," holding those norms before the magistrates of his day. A magistrate who acted justly, and, for example, did not take human life, could be counted a Christian. Menno's life was under constant threat from magistrates he considered unjust, however. So, while a bare bones theory is present in his thought, the practice of Christians participating nonviolently in the creation of a just society remained untested.

Two factors make Marpeck, to my view, the most rewarding Anabaptist to study on the question of Christian participation in structures of power. The first is that for most of his adult life he was a career civil servant as well as a minister. He lived out his vocation in the world. That in itself would not be noteworthy without a second factor. Marpeck's mindset was clearly Anabaptist (believers baptism, a disciplined church, nonresistance) but not separatist and perfectionist. Before Marpeck became an Anabaptist he had been a mining engineer and magistrate in the Tyrol. In the process of his conversion to the left wing of the Reformation, he was ordered by mandate of the emperor to prosecute religious dissidents. After a long inner struggle he refused to do so, resigned from his office, and joined the radicals instead. Nonetheless, he did not remove himself from public institutions.

Marpeck moved to Strasbourg because of the ferment in radical circles there and quickly became a church leader. To support himself financially he took a position as forestry engineer for the city. I think there was more to this decision than money. A fortunate coming together occurred here: Strasbourg was a city more tolerant than any other in Europe; Marpeck was a person who saw the structures of civil society as an appropriate setting for confessing Christians. Although he had strong convictions he could not have assumed that everyone he worked with shared them. He argued with but did not condemn either radicals or leaders of the established church who took a different path from his.

Marpeck taught that in the incarnation, "Christ became a natural man for natural man" (with reference to Heb 2:10–18). He believed that creatures of flesh and blood are not so spiritual that they do not need outward signs of divine reality. One implication of these thoughts is that Christians share a common "flesh and blood" with all humanity. Here was the priestly impulse in Marpeck. His life and thought make the case that Christians ought to take positions of social responsibility in civil society for the sake of the gospel, except where institutions demand absolute loyalty, such as in the command to use violence. At the same time, Marpeck preserved the tension between church and world found in separatist and prophetic stances in Anabaptism.

Marpeck did not let go of the calling to follow Christ perfectly but saw it as the task of a lifetime, not the state one reaches upon conversion. For example, he urged the Swiss Brethren to be patient with one another, and to remember that love is the end of the law, rather than banning people who fall short in their striving for holiness of life. At the same time, he was convinced of the truth of believers baptism and of pacifism as inseparable parts of imitating Christ.

In the heat of debate one of Marpeck's opponents, Caspar Schwenckfeld, accused Marpeck of being an anarchist because of his claim that the use of the sword was forbidden to Christians. Marpeck squirmed under the weight of that accusation. In the end, he allowed for the possibility that a Christian could wield power (which he himself did in a modest way) in accordance with the Sermon on the Mount. Such a ruler, Marpeck argued, would resign his office rather than take up the sword. (Was he thinking of his own crisis years ago as a magistrate in the Tyrol?)

Although his writings are occasional and not systematic, in practice Marpeck held together faithfulness and responsibility. Marpeck saw to it that the "wheat" of the kingdom was planted in the world by Christians there. But ultimately, he held that only pacifist soil was fertile enough to sustain it. His vision sustained the congregations for whom he wrote and Swiss Brethren took it up a generation later in their search for a moderating theology.

The story of Pilgram Marpeck and the congregations he inspired ends in a sad irony, however. The tension of being in-but-not-of the world proved too hard to sustain. Within two generations of Marpeck's death the movement he shepherded was to disappear. Even his writings fell into disuse until the twentieth century. His golden mean did not have staying power. In the end, it was the separatists and the realists who were to shape Mennonite history.

Seventeenth Century

These opposite trends, separatism and realism, gained momentum in the course of the seventeenth century. Mennonites who were persecuted and isolated tended toward the Schleitheim model, in which the church represents the new age and the state the old age. The Amish division in the late seventeenth century would decisively reinforce this understanding of the church. Although it was not as ethically rigorous as Amish society, the early Russian Mennonite commonwealth was a more comprehensive separate order of things, with its own school system and municipal government, for instance, with a judiciary presided over by ministers.

The other model, realism, emerged among Mennonites who achieved toleration in the Netherlands and North Germany. After a long period of conflict that led to church splits, a new paradigm emerged: The church is a spiritual community of a different order than the civil or political community and not in contention with it.

What accounted for this remarkable shift to a benign view of Christian participation in the structures of power? Part of the answer lies in the fact that the state was no longer persecuting Dutch Mennonites. It safeguarded freedom of religion; its economic and cultural institutions brought Mennonites prosperity. They began to believe that pluralist, republican, and capitalist values were biblical. Thus, the Christian in the public sphere was to be governed by those attributes.

Take the example of merchant shipping. Urban Mennonites became prosperous traders. Dutch and foreign commerce was competing fiercely, increasing to the point of armed duels on the high seas. In a typical example, from 1619, one Amsterdam congregation forbade its members to arm their vessels. Most members withdrew as stockholders from trading companies that sanctioned such armed aggression. But this "Marpeckian" solution of nonviolent participation in civil society did not hold. The Netherlands was the richest trading country in the West. By mid-century prohibitions by Mennonite congregations against members who armed their fleets were unable to withstand the lure of profit. A minority of Dutch Mennonites, like Old Order groups today, turned further in the direction of Schleitheim; the vast majority traded in their Anabaptist understanding of the church for an Enlightenment one. They concluded that spiritual community was of a different order from civil community; one provided guidance for the soul, the other for the body. "Realism" about how the world is ruled had triumphed.

A comparison with the Religious Society of Friends is instructive here. Quakers faced similar dilemmas and sometimes made similar choices. But their relationship to the world was different. They had a more positive view of human nature than did Mennonites. They believed that there is "that of God in everyone," which the presence of God's Spirit everywhere evokes. Their "holy experiment" was to replicate the church's nonviolent structures in society at large. For example, when William Penn was governor of Pennsylvania, order was kept for two generations without a standing militia.

The point here is the greater Quaker optimism concerning the power of love in the conduct of human affairs, coupled with a certain pragmatism. Thus they were willing to make compromises that moved in a peaceful direction toward realizing the goal of a loving human society because they believed that ultimately it would win the day. Mennonites might say that Friends underestimated the stubbornness of evil: for Mennonites the sanctified life could be expected only from the sanctified community. Once their public frame of reference was the world at large, Mennonites increasingly adopted the pessimistic estimate of love's power shared by their "unsanctified" neighbors. This was the calculation behind the Mennonite decision to arm ships. By contrast, the Quakers pursued alternatives to lethal force, in particular in their relationship with Indians. Mennonites did the opposite: when they sanctioned aggressive commerce—and with it, the armed defense of property—they were replicating society's violent structures within the church!

Nineteenth Century

At the beginning of the nineteenth century the Napoleonic Code imposed upon Europe a secular legal order with universal rights and obligations. Based on an argument that there can be no minority privileges in a society of equals, the code also denied all rights to conscientious objection. This drove Schleitheim Mennonites further from engagement with structures of governance and renewed the role of conscientious objection as the litmus test of faithfulness. For assimilating Mennonites, in contrast, universal rights became the door to citizenship and equality before the law. With this change in status assimilationists completed their shift in ecclesiology: the church belonged to a private sphere whereas public life was regulated by institutions according to the norm of reason. So it happened that the two Mennonite deputies in the German parliament of 1848 were among the most vociferous opponents of a provision in the new constitution for conscientious objection!

This confinement of the Sermon on the Mount to the private sphere is a key reason, in my judgment, why there were virtually no German Mennonite public voices of dissent from Nazism. They had ended up with the worst of both worlds, a toxic mixture of separatism and realism. I venture the hypothesis that they borrowed their view of institutions of power without understanding the provisions in mainline Protestant ethics that set limits to institutional power. Assimilating Mennonites spiritualized the church and blessed worldly institutions as an autonomous realm, unaccountable to the gospel. Mennonites had so superficially legitimized the state (e.g., with their assent to war but without the tools of the just war tradition) that they were blind to the state's self-deification and its anti-Semitism.

TENTATIVE CONCLUSIONS

Many activist Mennonites would join me in finding the "prophetic" stance closest to the moral heights of the Old and New Testaments (Acts 17:6-7). Yet as a norm for Mennonites this claim has three strikes against it. First among them is the fact that few parts of the Anabaptist movement lived it. This was due in part to the fierce persecution that made them "strangers and foreigners on the earth" (Heb 11:13). But second, it is also the case that the Anabaptists never had more than fragments of a belief in the redeemability of creation. Finally, mainstream Mennonites today are not strangers and foreigners to the world around them. In the United States they have increasingly adopted the partisan political rhetoric (both Republican and Democratic) of the society in which they have such a great stake. They are bewildered by the power, and therefore the responsibility, they have to figure out what it means to "walk in the resurrection" among people who do not believe it is possible.

Marpeck can help us in that pursuit so long as we remember that he lived in a world that was different from ours. People like myself do well not to make him into a mouthpiece for twenty-first-century activist ideals. Yet his incarnational thought and practice did balance Anabaptist motifs such as a disciplined but not separatist church. Severing these motifs from each other leads Mennonites to the extremes of separatism and assimilation.

But what was it in the balanced life of the Marpeck congregations, which occupied the theological center point in Anabaptism, that lacked staying power? Is it really not possible to be in-but-not-of the world? Is the problem pacifism, something so "strange and foreign" to the present age that those who seek to live by it are driven either to separatism or assimilation? Is there an inherent instability in the Mennonite understanding of the gospel that needs elements out of other Christian traditions in order to graciously hold together faithfulness and responsibility?

The distinctive charism of Mennonitism is its combination of two convictions: that the church, most fully a believers church, is already the bearer of the kingdom and that one of the most astonishing evidences of this new reality is the possibility of loving one's enemy. It is this at once audacious and trembling confession that Mennonites have to offer the body of Christ.

Still, our sampling of the Anabaptist tradition suggests that this claim cannot be sustained by itself. Even within the tradition, the prophetic stance has been viable only by augmenting it with elements of the separatist, priestly, and realist stances. This is a humbling reality but that reality in itself is not a sign of unfaithfulness to the gospel. Unfaithfulness threatens when one of the augmenting elements takes over the prophetic one.

For mainstream Mennonites in North America historic forms of separatism are not our danger. Yet another kind of separatism lurks within our current ferment. In the priestly and realist positions it takes the form of spiritualizing the church, assigning it to the private realm, while taking norms for Christian participation in the public realm from institutions of power and the cultures they represent. Mennonites on the left and the right are adopting the view that the institutions of society and the state are the primary agents of God's will in the world, and that the mission of the church depends on an alliance with them.

Holding on to the distinctive Mennonite charism depends, above all, on two factors. One of them is a prophetic ecclesiology in which the church is *not* separate but *is* nonconformed. History has shown us that in and of itself this is an inherently unstable and unsustainable position. Therefore, it needs to be grounded in the universal body of Christ, somewhat like a monastic order. The parallel is not exact but it is suggestive. It is paradoxical but true that without the larger wisdom of the whole body of Christ—spiritual, liturgical, ethical, doctrinal— the vision of an eschatological body of believers, one of whose defining marks is nonviolence, will never realize its potential, never have staying power. But if that prophetic part is placed within the whole, the time for this distinctive charism is only now at hand.

FOR FURTHER READING

Blough, Neal. "The Holy Spirit and Discipleship in Pilgram Marpeck's Theology." In *Essays in Anabaptist Theology*, edited by H. Wayne Pipkin. Text Reader Series, vol. 5, 133–46. Elkhart, Ind.: Institute of Mennonite Studies, 1994.

Brock, Peter. *Pacifism in the United States: From the Colonial Era to the First World War*. Princeton, N.J.: Princeton University Press, 1968.

Hamilton, Alastair, S. Voolstra, and Piet Visser, eds. *From Martyr to Muppy (Mennonite Urban Professionals): A Historical Introduction to Cultural Assimilation Processes of a Religious Minority in the Netherlands, the Mennonites*. Amsterdam, Netherlands: Amsterdam University Press, 1994.

Jantzen, Mark A. "At Home in Germany?: The Mennonites of the Vistula Delta and the Construction of a German National Identity, 1772–1880." PhD dissertation. Notre Dame, Ind.: University of Notre Dame, 2002.

Klassen, William. "The Limits of Political Authority as Seen by Pilgram Marpeck." *Mennonite Quarterly Review* 56, no. 4 (October 1982): 342–64.

———. "Pilgram Marpeck and Our Use of Power." *Conrad Grebel Review*, no. 17 (Winter 1999): 42–50.

Koshy, Ninan. *Churches in the World of Nations: International Politics and the Mission and Ministry of the Church.* Geneva: WCC Publications, 1994.

Lichti, James Irvin. "Religious Identity Vs. 'Aryan' Identity: German Mennonites and Hutterites Under the Third Reich." MA Thesis, 187 pp. San Francisco: San Francisco State University, 1989.

GETTING STUCK IN:
ANABAPTIST INVOLVEMENT IN
LOCAL POLITICS

Judith A. Gardiner

Should Christians be involved in party politics and the structures of local government? You might assume that my answer would be a more or less qualified no. I am, after all, an Anabaptist schooled in the Swiss tradition of the Schleitheim Confession and its modern reclaimings by Mennonites such as Harold S. Bender and John Howard Yoder. According to this tradition, the work of government, even for worthy ends, frequently relies on coercion, retribution, and violence. Such means are "outside the perfection of Christ" and are incompatible with the ethics of the Sermon on the Mount. The work of politics and government, therefore, should be left to those who have not accepted Christ's yoke of obedience. The church's task is not to participate in the sub-Christian task of government, but to be a gathered community witnessing to the higher values of the kingdom.[1]

In the sixteenth century bitter experience forced this separatist stance upon Anabaptists. As Stuart Murray points out, the early Anabaptists were initially a socially engaged movement— making common cause with the peasants of central Europe and their demands for social justice, and for economic and religious reform. They advocated the cause of religious liberty for all, including Jews and Muslims. Within their own communities they developed distinctively radical ways of organizing, relating, and sharing based on a voluntary commitment to Christ. They undergirded such practices with an interpretation of the Scriptures that prioritized the interests of the poor and powerless. Their renewal efforts began within the existing political and religious structures; where authorities were prepared to assist them in realizing their vision of remaking the church and establishing a more just society, some Anabaptists were prepared to involve themselves in the process of government to varying degrees.[2]

Most, however, especially following the crushing of the Peasant's Revolt and the debacle of Münster, were clear that obedience to Christ precluded them from either taking up arms to defend themselves or swearing allegiance to the state. This, together with their radical social stance and their championing of a model of church that was not territorial but relational and voluntary, led to their reputation as dangerous subversives. State-sponsored opposition and persecution then drove them out of the established church and onto the social and political margins. This further reinforced their self-identity as an alternative society and their conviction that, although government has a God-ordained mandate to keep order, it was not an enterprise in which true followers of Christ could faithfully involve themselves.[3]

At the time, the Anabaptist stance of separation represented both a survival strategy, and a profound theological and political challenge to the structures of Christendom. It led them to reject attempts to identify God's kingdom with any particular national or political interest. It also reflected their biblical conviction that God's purposes of justice for the powerless could be worked out without violence, even when the rich and powerful stood in opposition.

Is Separation Relevant Today?

So can the Anabaptist model of separation from the political process carry the same force today? In some situations it clearly does. Anabaptists and other radical Christians—in trying to witness to kingdom values in the face of political and economic repression in Ethiopia, Indonesia, Colombia, and elsewhere—have often had little option but to withdraw from the public realm. Even so they have demonstrated that when a Christian community commits itself to an alternative way of living and questions society's accepted values toward wealth, power, and the use of force, it can have real political impact even in the most unpromising surroundings.[4]

Although critics continue to caricature the Anabaptist tradition as socially irrelevant and irresponsible, plentiful evidence disproves the thesis that disengagement from worldly power structures means giving up on the struggle to bring "principalities and powers" under subjection to the Lordship of Christ. Indeed, suggested Yoder, such separation allows the church to undertake the struggle more effectively because it maintains its critical distance from society, enabling believers to more clearly discern the "spirits of the age."[5] As Anglican Bishop John Gladwin has noted, "the Mennonite record of compassionate work in the world for the victims of power and oppression will stand comparison with any other and leaves the work of more established churches far behind in radical *commitment*."[6]

Drawing on this service experience, Mennonites have also influenced public policy and development practice by modeling imaginative and effective ways of addressing problems. These practices embody Jesus's ethics and example of love, reconciliation, and humble service. Pioneering Mennonite initiatives in Victim-Offender Reconciliation, for example, have sparked real interest in restorative justice methods, which criminal and youth justice systems are now incorporating worldwide.[7] Christian Peacemaker Teams and Anabaptist mediators such as John Paul Lederach, Ron Kraybill, and Joe Campbell are involved in efforts to foster reconciliation in international conflicts. And on a local and personal level, Anabaptist individuals and communities are developing myriad innovative ways of demonstrating the possibilities of a life cut free from the grip of the powers—living simply, refusing war taxes, befriending outcasts, supporting community development projects, and creating structures for mutual aid.[8]

So far, however, the Anabaptist tradition has tended to contribute to the political process from the outside. As Mark Charlton comments, we lack a coherent political philosophy to address in any systematic and structural way public policy issues such as the environment, abortion, homosexuality, reproductive technology, or my current preoccupations of local government: financing, housing, and planning law.[9] But, in our relatively open and democratic society, is there an argument for modern Anabaptists to allow themselves to get stuck more directly into the earthy tasks of decision making, practical government and political structures?

WHY I AM INVOLVED

This is a question with which I have struggled since becoming a Mennonite in 1983. I have lived in the inner city all my life—since 1982 in Tower Hamlets in East London, possibly the most deprived and certainly one of the most diverse boroughs in the United Kingdom. I have been actively involved in many local and national campaigns for peace and justice, and became a Labour Party member in 1983. I am now an elected local councilor. So what inspired me to get stuck in?

They say that your theology is shaped by where you sit. I sit thirteen floors up in the heart of inner city London. So almost all the physical landscape I see—the park, streets, public housing, school, motorway, and the derelict land earmarked as a potential London Olympic site—is shaped for good or ill by decisions made in the political realm. My neighbors' mental and spiritual landscapes are also shaped, often negatively, by their daily engagement with the powers that inhabit offices of the housing department, immigration service, Social Services, etc. Here, you are involved in politics whether you acknowledge it or not. Your theology, discipleship, and mission strategy must all take account of the positive and negative impact of these realities.

Every day we take advantage of the good and necessary outcomes of politics—a decent home, public transport, the health service, street lighting, etc. To a greater or lesser degree these all reflect a joint commitment to the common good and to the dignity and value of each individual, especially the most vulnerable, realized by practical organization and financial resources. (Taxes are society's common purse!) These good things do not just appear by chance. They are the product of a long process of communal decision making—with dialogue, conflict resolution, and sheer hard work involving individuals, community organizations, faith groups, politicians, and paid public servants—and are maintained by continuing such processes. This is the essence of politics: identifying social needs and problems, exploring their causes, educating and redirecting social policy and public opinion, and organizing structural and practical change.[10]

Some Anabaptist thinkers are negative or skeptical about this work. They see it, at best, as creating and maintaining structures to keep order in a fallen world.[11] I believe however that this work, however imperfectly, contributes positively to God's creative purposes by enabling human beings to live together. It also reflects God's will that we shape society's structures and our stewardship of the earth to reflect the kingdom's characteristics. So why would I not want to be involved?

I do not believe that we ought to restrict application of Sermon on the Mount ethics, or biblical teaching on servant leadership, peacemaking, and sexual, racial, or economic equality, to the Christian community. These *shalom* principles express God's best intentions for the whole community. Hebrew prophets applied such principles to Israel and pagan nations (Amos 1-2; Isa 10:12-19). When society's structures did not protect and liberate the poor or powerless, God intervened directly in judgment. God's people should join God in transforming society so that his will "may be done on earth as it is in heaven."

On the negative side, in the inner city we all know what happens when politics goes wrong. In the early 1980s I lived in

Manchester near one of the biggest, worst planned, and worst executed housing projects in Europe. It suffered all the problems you would expect. Drug dealing and taking were rife, and violence was frequent. Even by the standards of the northern cities, which Thatcherite policies had economically pulverized, unemployment was high, especially among black young people. Most community services had closed down or pulled out, with one exception. We saw the police frequently and excessively surrounding community events in the park with dogs and staves, or routinely harassing and humiliating kids on the street. This was not an aberration; it was direct policy ordered by the evangelical Christian Chief Constable. Urban riots were breaking out across the country, so we did not need much prophetic genius to see that we would be next. We "told it to the church" we belonged to and met a wall of incomprehension and anger from people who did not see the problem or recognize that the church (despite being the one of the few agencies still present) had any responsibility to address the issues beyond continuing its evangelism and meeting individual needs as they presented.

Three weeks later the neighborhood burned.

This was a formative experience for me. It is not often I get to be a prophet. I was particularly struck when local churches, including ours, then rushed to try to be part of the solution and often met with rebuff because "you weren't here before." Meanwhile the work of peacemaking, reconciliation, and community rebuilding was being done by the residents themselves—youth workers on the streets, local housing and community organizations, and politicians who had identified and tried to deal with the problems for years. Only now had they gained the attention and resources to act.

In situations like this, a mission strategy that forbids direct engagement with the political decision-making process seriously limits the church's ability to speak hope into people's lives. By leaving the political structures untouched, such a stance also risks perpetuating the suffering that they can inflict.

Seeing God's intentions for *shalom* modeled in secular

movements for peace, equality, ecological responsibility, and economic justice has also inspired my political involvement. Such movements have often called the church back to core biblical values. In the inner city, where the body of Christ is more noted for its absence than its presence, it is humbling to learn what hunger for justice, sacrificial love, integrity, and compassionate service means as one sees people of other faiths and no faith practicing *shalom*. Among those who "labored in the vineyard" long before we arrived were

- Bangladeshi parents who created and staffed a respite care service for their severely disabled children;
- a local council that sponsored a micro-credit union for people to whom the banks would not lend, but who can now borrow in need or to invest in their future;
- trades unionists, Labour Party members and other local citizens, who put their bodies on the line to protect terrified Bangladeshi families facing racial harassment, and to safeguard their right to vote in the face of intimidation and aggression from neo-fascists.

These are all signs of God's presence and activity working for the *shalom* of the city.

This last example of solidarity, hospitality, and concern for outsiders offers a modern parable of the Good Samaritan, which many local churches thankfully have heeded. Their members joined an umbrella organization coordinating election monitoring and safe election debates, with twenty-four-hour teams watching the homes of Asian families moving into previously white estates in order to avert the threat of fire-bombing. The effort has helped shape the council's approach to housing, employment, and education issues. Now our borough is regarded as a model of good practice on promoting community cohesion.

Such examples teach me as much about love and community as I learn, theologically and practically, in a strong and committed Mennonite church. They witness to the commitment "to the least of these," that Matthew 25 recognizes as service to Christ himself. And, in the unglamorous day-to-day dedication and compassion of social workers, council officers, health service employees, community activists, and politicians—many of whom choose to stay and work to improve the quality of this community's life rather than earning greater rewards and status by enjoying an easier life elsewhere—I believe I see something of the image of the Suffering Servant.

So as a Mennonite seeking to "follow Christ in life" in the inner city, I am involved in local politics because I believe Christ is here already, at the margins, with those who suffer from oppression by the domination system. I now expect to find him not only in the church, but also on the front line, with all who, whether they acknowledge it or not, do Christ's will by working for peace and justice. Where *shalom*-shaped things are happening, I want to be present to learn, to witness, and to celebrate.

The Risks of Getting Involved

Still, I appreciate the fact that involvement in organized politics poses challenges and risks. Anabaptists, who uphold demanding standards of discipleship and tend to be reflexive critics of the existing order, may find the transition from a politics of opposition to the responsibilities of government particularly challenging.

Politics can be uncertain and morally ambiguous. It requires willingness to compromise, to accommodate differing interests and values that may conflict with one's own, and to accept collective responsibility for supporting and implementing pragmatic and provisional solutions that may fail to realize the fullness of one's ideological vision. It may also require a willingness to accept powerlessness or to risk commitment to a course of action without knowing whether, in the long run, it will deliver as intended or prove to be a mistake.[12]

The processes of local governance are extremely complex, and can be frustrating for any impatient idealist who wants "Jerusalem builded here" overnight. A decision to approve a Foyer scheme (halfway house) to provide housing, support, and training to young offenders, for example, involved five years of lobbying, consciousness raising, feasibility studies, capital and revenue fundraising, scheme development, land-swapping, planning approvals, public consultations, tendering, and implementation planning. Even then this project might have failed had my colleagues not had the courage to face down hostile press coverage and public flak.

Significant political activity makes demands on leisure and family time, money, and emotional energy. For instance, I spend sixty-to-eighty hours a month, and considerable portions of leave from my full-time job, to fulfill my Council duties. It requires patience, resilience, and a long attention span. Achieving success for individuals or shifting major policy often takes a long time. Personal and political defeats or disappointments are all too common.

In an imperfect world awaiting redemption, however, such costs and risks are inherent in all activity.[13] Christians cannot expect to be exempt from pain, moral ambiguity, confusion, or defeat. Still, we who profess a commitment to Christ's way of loving, vulnerable service should not let the risks daunt us. As Anabaptists we have rich resources of story and spirituality to sustain us when facing opposition or suffering, and to inspire us to endurance and hope. Jim Wallis defines such hope as "believing in spite of the evidence and then waiting to see the evidence change!"[14]

One of my personal role models is Conservative Christian MP William Wilberforce, who drove the legislative campaign for the abolition of slavery through the British Parliament. He campaigned for over forty years, facing public hostility, ridicule, and political and private betrayals, all with grace and forbearance. He suffered defeat after defeat after defeat in the House, but never gave up lobbying, building alliances, and skillfully using the moral force of public campaign groups to exert pressure. Finally he "changed the wind," as Jim Wallis would say,[15] and votes were carried for the abolition of the slave trade (1807) and the abolition of slavery itself in all British dominions (1833).

Wilberforce could have given up many times and retreated to safer Christian campaigns for public morality.[16] But justice and morality went together in his understanding of gospel and discipleship, and so he persevered in hope and faith. As one commentator has noted, "there seems no reasonable ground for believing that without [his and the Clapham Sect's] leadership, their concerted labors, their infectious passion, their unwearying persistence, the abolition campaign could have been carried, at least in their generation, to its successful finish."[17] But, as John Gladwin notes, there can be no successes for those absent themselves from the struggle.[18]

So What Can Anabaptists Contribute to the Political Process?

Here, for the reasons given, I am tentative. Anabaptists certainly do not have a monopoly on virtue and values. In culturally diverse areas like mine, we may not have the contacts or the local credibility necessary to understand issues and make things happen. Still, the distinctive elements we bring could breathe life into the political culture, helping move it toward nonviolence, cooperation, and welfare.[19]

A Lack of Fascination with Power

As Anabaptists, we rightly suspect politicians' attempts to co-opt the influence of religion in order to legitimize their own status and policies. We recognize the idolatry involved in confusing any national or partisan identity and loyalty with our ultimate identity and loyalty to the transnational body of Christ and to the kingdom. We are equally suspicious of Christians tempting us to use our influence, or create power blocks, to pursue our interests or impose our morality. As Jonathan Bartley points out, such tactics merely reflect the agenda and values of the domination system that we battle against.[20]

We follow Jesus "who came not to be served but to serve and give his life," and who taught that leadership means "the greatest among you must become like the youngest, and the leader like one who serves" (Luke 22:26-27). Anabaptists insist therefore that the criteria for leadership are not wealth, education, status, charisma, or sheer power, but rather maturity, discipline, integrity, and persistence in service. Our structures for corporate discernment and decision making aim to be non-hierarchical and inclusive, enabling all members to offer their contribution.

How might this perspective inform our political involvement? It should lead us to combat the tendency to centralize and concentrate power, and instead seek ways to enable as many people as possible to contribute to public dialogue and political discernment rather than make decisions on their behalf. This could involve developing more imaginative ways of consulting local people, or, as in my borough, bringing other service providers, faith groups, businesses, community organizations, and individuals together in strategic partnerships to pool experience, ideas, and resources, thus enabling a more integrated approach to tackling local problems.

We could also encourage greater devolution of decision-making control and budgets to local communities, enabling them to direct, own, and manage their public services. Such devolution feels threatening if one assumes that only professionals and elected officials should exercise power. But, on the housing project where my husband works, a shift from council control to a tenant management organization is providing new opportunities for servant leadership. He and other professionals now offer their expertise to empower and support local people who do not suffer the limitations of a traditional governmental mindset. They often generate alternatives and options that professionals miss. Anabaptists should be better suited than most to offer this humble style of community leadership, and to advocate and support such initiatives.

We know that power is not an end in itself, but a trust and a gift from God that humans should exercise in the spirit of servanthood. This understanding should help us sit loose to the seductive and addictive aspects of politics—the aura of importance and celebrity, financial rewards, and pressure to climb the power ladder that tempt all politicians. Such detachment can be enormously freeing. If our motivation is service, rather than seeking or clinging to power and status, it is easier to resist the populist compulsion to tailor one's words and actions to the polls and power brokers. Such a compulsion fosters short-term thinking and militates against making difficult decisions. It also makes it easier, though not less painful, to take a stand and to be ready, if required, to relinquish ambition or position when conscience demands.

Jesus-like leadership emphasizes humility that does not parade our achievements, claim authoritative judgment on every issue, or indulge in arrogant control freakery. Such humility may inspire us to reconsider our day-to-day priorities—ensuring we spend rather more time working hard and sacrificially with local people, and rather less with the "movers and shakers." It also calls us to remember that, like the Roman centurion, we serve as "people under authority" and this authority is God's alone. We will therefore want to be conscientious in our service and hold our commitments, judgments, and performance open to dialogue and criticism in the light of Christ. Yet precisely because we "pray as if everything depended on God" we know that we do not need to act as if everything depended upon us. We can therefore resist, and help others resist, the occupational hazard of the "messiah complex" that easily afflicts conscientious politicians, leading them to take on too much and internalize too much responsibility for outcomes. This, in itself, would help humanize the political process!

Orientation to the Margins

Anabaptists have long historical experience of social and theological marginalization. Our vision for our common life emphasizes God's "preferential option for the poor" and God's active will that the faithful community reflect his justice and *shalom*. We have tried to incarnate that vision in various forms of compassionate service and mutual aid. This marginal perspective could help shape our political analysis and policy decisions.

We could question political programs and processes that prioritize the interests and voices of the comfortable, articulate, and privileged above those of the more vulnerable, incoherent, and needy. Suburban home owners have an interest in property values and countryside views; the homeless, the overcrowded, and the families of poorly paid public workers have a need for low-cost homes. But, when Planning decisions about new developments on the city outskirts are debated, we might want to question why the interests of the former seem invariably to carry greater weight than those of the latter and try to redress the balance.

We could also usefully advocate for those whose voices are not popular or may not get heard, and scrutinize the impact that policies and procedures may have on vulnerable groups. I recently initiated and chaired an investigation, for instance, into the problems that newly accepted refugees have in accessing housing and healthcare in our borough. This exercise helped raise the political profile of emerging minority ethnic communities and should help ensure that future planning recognizes their needs. In the short term, this has resulted in funding for a project to which health and other professionals can refer clients in need of support, advice, and social contact, as well as the production of a multilingual "welcome pack" giving information to help new entrants obtain the services to which they are entitled. Not a great vote catcher. But with follow through, this initiative could make a significant difference to people struggling to live with their traumatic past and to build a future. I hope it may also help shift public attitudes on these issues.

Commitment to Truth-Telling and Personal Integrity

Following the Iraq war, we know how impoverished the political process becomes when press, public, and politicians collude to create an atmosphere in which honest discussion, investigation of truth, and the ability to admit and learn from mistakes are subservient to the partisan imperatives of oppositional politics. Even in local politics, it is hard to avoid a "them and us" culture in which opponents become enemies, where debates and attitudes are polarized, and where "truth" too easily equates with arguments that buttress our position and undermine theirs. Clever statistics, euphemistic language, and technological obfuscation then tend to obscure problems, while critical examination of the system becomes difficult.

Christians are not immune to this. We have seen many examples of Christian lobbying groups from right and left, using the tactics of ridicule, personal attack, emotional overstatement, and exaggeration to make points or defend their own self-interest on issues such as sexuality or religious education. As Anabaptists, however, our commitment to truth telling and mutual admonition could inform our political strategies and tactics and help us contribute to changing the prevailing political ethos.

We could begin by being personally honest, acknowledging our failings or ignorance, and accepting criticism with humility. Such humility is not easy for politicians. Hence the shock when Estelle Morris, the British Education minister, resigned acknowledging that she was not doing her job well enough. Still, as reaction to her showed, such honesty can be disarming and create space for others to reconsider their expectations of politicians. We could also be honest about what we can achieve—not, for instance, selling false hope to constituents desperate for rehousing. When 20,000 applicants are chasing 2,000 social housing vacancies annually in my borough, I realistically help them consider their options.

We could try to work across party and other divisions, affirming the positive in our opponents' views and speaking our truth with gentleness and without exaggeration or distortion. Such an approach is not easy in a charged environment, where any sign of weakness or ambivalence about the party line provokes derision. But it can create a healthier atmosphere for discussion and investigation, enabling people to leave entrenched positions and focus constructively on the task or problem. As Jesus demonstrated and Walter Wink has explained, such forbearance may also reinforce our impact when more robust truth-telling in the sense of prophetic naming and exposure of social, political, and economic injustice is required.[21] We usually think of this latter task as belonging to outside pressure groups. But brave politicians, unafraid of ridicule and unconcerned about personal advancement, can effectively speak uncomfortable truths to their colleagues. Jonathan Blakeborough, my Anabaptist friend, showed this as the only councilor in York who opposed a motion supporting British troops in Iraq.[22]

Commitment to Peacemaking

Anabaptists have a long tradition of embodying our peace commitment in a variety of practical initiatives, ranging from small-scale mediation projects and peace tax campaigns, to assisting in mediation efforts to resolve national or international conflicts, such as the one in Northern Ireland. Our experience helping individuals and communities reach across divides and develop ways to break cycles of injury, rage, and vengeance could be invaluable in local government.

In the United Kingdom, most housing authorities have independent mediation schemes to help residents resolve neighbor disputes. New multi-agency structures working with high risk and sex offenders now draw from restorative justice models, including family group conferencing and circles of accountability. Such initiatives are often greeted with suspicion by the public, whose anxieties about crime and anti-social behavior can express themselves in attitudes of punitive hostility and rejection toward those feared to be different. Anabaptist politicians however could help promote these initiatives and develop the public understanding that is essential to their success. Mediation and conflict resolution methods might also prove useful for the conduct of political and public discussions, by assisting people with opposing views to work together on developing consensual and practical approaches to hot issues like school admission policies or reconfiguring elderly people's services. The process can be difficult and time-consuming, tempting politicians to avoid such debates or to try to railroad one position through. But decisions made this way are stronger and have a better chance of successful implementation because they are understood and owned.

Commitment to Community

Anabaptists have a strong ethos of community. We express this, albeit often fallibly, in various practical arrangements for mutual aid and decision making, as well as in organizational structures that value each member's contributions to the common life. Our sense of community also underpins our global work for justice and peace as we recognize and celebrate our common humanity and seek to ensure that our lifestyles, our wider socio-political structures, and our economic relationships reflect our accountability to God, the earth, and each other.

Principles of equality, equity, and community should guide our approach to local politics. As Anabaptists we could foster and nurture community relationships, and encourage understanding of difference and cultural diversity. One way to do this is to promote symbolic initiatives like community festivals or twinning arrangements; another is to challenge policies of housing allocation or schools admissions that may reinforce racial and economic separation. We will want to combat all forms of discrimination and to support efforts to ensure the civic and political workforce reflects the community, thus increasing the proportion of women and ethnic minorities at all levels so their perspectives will help reshape future processes and outcomes.

We could promote investment in the community's social capital—encouraging financial institutions to give money and staff time to support local schools, housing, and community organizations, or to work with the council to promote training, childcare, and employment schemes that enhance local people's skills and economic opportunities. We could support changes to the planning system to require developers to contribute a proportion of their properties for social renting or low-cost home ownership (35 percent is the figure my borough uses). They could also be required to contribute toward new roads, schools, and community centers. We could encourage sustainable development—promoting reuse of brownfield sites, energy conservant construction and heating methods, car-free estates, and other environmental initiatives such as recycling schemes and cycle routes. Such initiatives encourage healthier lifestyles and contribute to stewardship of God's creation.

We could also promote policies and initiatives that utilize the abilities of local communities to identify and meet their own needs. My council has developed schemes supporting and training local health, social care, youth workers, teachers, craftsmen, and business people whose skills will help maintain the physical and social environment. We want local community organizations more involved in planning and delivering services—to improve the appropriateness and responsiveness of services to local needs and to increase local employment opportunities.

Local demands for change often drive these initiatives; community organizations and faith groups often inspire them with their innovative work. Many would be unsustainable, however, without continued pressure and support from local politicians committed to reshaping budgets, policies and services to better meet the needs of a changing population. As Anabaptists, willing the *ends* of greater social justice, it would help if more of us got stuck into the difficult political process of setting priorities and securing the financial and practical *means* of delivery.

A Long Vision

As Anabaptists, perhaps our most valuable contribution to the political process would be an irrepressible sense of hope. True hope sees beyond the inevitabilities of the present to a future pregnant with possibilities for change. For us, this is not blind optimism; Jesus's experience and our own history reveal the likely costs of struggling against the powers of evil and injustice. Rather, it is a quality of patient perseverance and resistance grounded in a conviction that, however overwhelming the odds, the power of the current powers is not absolute and God's purposes for justice will prevail. Such hope sustained our forebears through persecution and exile. More recent examples from South Africa, Eastern Europe, Latin America, and our own cities show such hope being nurtured and kept alive by faith communities, oppressed peoples, and awkward dissenters. Choosing to live imaginatively, they have opened the door to social transformation and change in seemingly impossible situations.[23]

Local politics is rarely this dramatic. Yet the same hope could still be a vital asset to Anabaptist politicians, offering us the spiritual resources we need to keep going, to maintain our principles, and to endure discouragements and defeats with courage and grace. It could help us support and mobilize colleagues, opponents, constituents, and council officers, whose own energy and enthusiasm may be sapped by cynicism or the sheer relentlessness of it all. As people of hope we could be catalysts for creativity, bringing fresh energy and perspectives to the political process and shaking up the structural status quo.

Most importantly, this hope frees us from the compulsive need for results, which causes so much disappointment and disillusion in politics. The future we hope for will have the shape and character of God's just and peaceable kingdom; the defeat of the powers is not ultimately due to our striving but results from God's action within and beyond history. This freedom enables us to concentrate on the value and rightness of our present task knowing that, in God's economy, none of our efforts to serve others or to contribute to the arduous, repetitive, and routine work required to maintain the "walls of the city" will be wasted. In ways we cannot even envisage, they will find their redemption and fulfillment in the *shalom* order of God.

NOTES

1. Even the Schleitheim Confession, however, is phrased in such a way as to indicate that these issues were matters of considerable debate within the Anabaptist movements of the day. See Nigel Wright, *Disavowing Constantine: Mission, Church and the Social Order in the Theologies of John Howard Yoder and Jürgen Moltmann*, Paternoster Biblical and Theological Monographs (Carlisle, Cumbria, U.K.: Paternoster Press, 2000), 199–203.

2. Some Anabaptist groups, notably those around Balthasar Hubmaier, maintained more positive views about the possibilities of working with the state even if it meant some acceptance of the use of coercive force to support reform. Others, like Pilgram Marpeck and Menno Simons, opposed the use of coercive force in religious matters, yet nevertheless were not doctrinaire about the need to withdraw from civil society. They could even concede a positive function for Christians in wielding the sword of justice to protect the vulnerable, though not the sword of war. This tradition, though largely overtaken by the radical apoliticism of Schleitheim, did survive in later years in the Dutch and North German Communities and has remerged at times, notably in the Prussian and Russian contexts. For a summary of these developments, see chapter 3 of Wright, *Disavowing Constantine.*

3. Stuart Murray, *Post-Christendom: Church and Mission in a Strange New World*; After Christendom (Carlisle [England]: Paternoster, 2004), 170–74; J. Denny Weaver, *Becoming Anabaptist: The Origin and Significance of Sixteenth-Century Anabaptism* (Scottdale, Pa.: Herald Press, 1987), 119–22.

4. See Sisay Beshe, "Taking on the Powers," *Anabaptism Today*, no. 7 (October 1994), as well as contributions by Alix Lozano and Paulus Widjaja in the present volume.

5. How well Anabaptist churches, especially in the West have used that space is of course variable. Recent histories have highlighted some uncomfortable truths in relation to Mennonite/Anabaptist collusion with or acquiescence in Nazi and Communist oppression. Recent pictures of Amish campaigners for President Bush also suggest some narrowing of the critical distance occurring even in the most conservative communities!

6. John W. Gladwin, *God's People in God's World: Biblical Motives for Social Involvement* (Downers Grove, Ill.: InterVarsity Press, 1979), 19.

7. See Howard Zehr, *Changing Lenses: A New Focus for Crime and Justice*, Christian Peace Shelf Selection (Scottdale, Pa.: Herald Press, 1990).

8. John D. Roth, *Choosing Against War: A Christian View: A Love Stronger Than Our Fears* (Intercourse, Pa.: Good Books, 2002); Jim Wallis, *The Soul of Politics: A Practical and Prophetic Vision for Change* (New York; Maryknoll, N.Y.: New Press; Orbis Books, 1994); and

Jim Wallis, *Faith Works: Lessons from the Life of an Activist Preacher* (New York: Random House, 2000) for some inspiring examples.

9. Mark Charlton, "Where's the Political Science Department?" in *Minding the Church: Scholarship in the Anabaptist Tradition: Essays in Honor of E. Morris Sider*, ed. David Weaver-Zercher (Telford, Pa.; Scottdale, Pa.: Pandora Press, U.S.; Herald Press, 2002), 150.

10. Wallis, *Faith Works*; 133-38, 145-55; Gladwin, *God's People in God's World*, 184-85.

11. See for example Guy F. Hershberger, *War, Peace, and Nonresistance*, 3d ed., Christian Peace Shelf Selection (Scottdale, Pa.: Herald Press, 1969), chap. 8, p. 242f. and appendices; and John Howard Yoder, *Discipleship as Political Responsibility* (Scottdale, Pa.: Herald Press, 2003).

12. Gladwin, *God's People in God's World*, 184–86. Also see chapter 7 of Jonathan Bartley, *The Subversive Manifesto: Lifting the Lid on God's Political Agenda* (Oxford: Bible Reading Fellowship, 2003), on "political pitfalls."

13. Gladwin, *God's People in God's World*, 188.

14. Wallis, *Faith Works*, 324.

15. Ibid., 306–24.

16. Gladwin, *God's People in God's World*, 31. See Ernest Marshall Howse, *Saints in Politics: The "Clapham Sect" and the Growth of Freedom* (Toronto: University of Toronto, 1952) for a full account and appreciation of the amazing range of religious, moral, philanthropic, and social causes that Wilberforce and his evangelical colleagues successfully pursued, along with their impact on political campaigning and legislative progress in subsequent generations.

17. Howse, *Saints in Politics*, 64.

18. Gladwin, *God's People in God's World*, 31.

19. See chapter seven of Duane K. Friesen, *Artists, Citizens, Philosophers: Seeking the Peace of the City: An Anabaptist Theology of Culture* (Scottdale, Pa.; Waterloo, Ont.: Herald Press, 2000). Friesen's insightful reflections on the "Dynamics of Dual Citizenship" underlie much of my thinking in this chapter, and his proposals on "Guidelines for Christian Citizenship" have provided a jumping off point for the suggestions that follow. Like he, I offer my suggestions in the spirit of ongoing conversation rather than definitive statements. Also see Murray, *Post-Christendom*, 245–50, and both books by Jim Wallis that I have cited above.

20. Bartley, *The Subversive Manifesto*, chap. 4.

21. Walter Wink, *Engaging the Powers: Discernment and Resistance in a World of Domination* (Minneapolis: Fortress Press, 1992), 227–28, 271–77 and chap. 9.

22. Jonathan Blakeborough, "Walter Klaassen, John Woolman and

a Pair of Gloves: Reflections on Anabaptist Political Involvement," *Anabaptism Today*, no. 35 (February 2004).

23. Wallis, *Faith Works*, 238–324; Wallis, *The Soul of Politics*, chap. 8.

FOR FURTHER READING

Bartley, Jonathan. *The Subversive Manifesto: Lifting the Lid on God's Political Agenda*. Oxford: Bible Reading Fellowship, 2003.

Charlton, Mark. "Where's the Political Science Department?" In *Minding the Church: Scholarship in the Anabaptist Tradition: Essays in Honor of E. Morris Sider*, edited by David Weaver-Zercher, 140–51. Telford, Pa.; Scottdale, Pa.: Pandora Press, U.S.; Herald Press, 2002.

Friesen, Duane K. *Artists, Citizens, Philosophers: Seeking the Peace of the City: An Anabaptist Theology of Culture*. Scottdale, Pa.; Waterloo, Ont.: Herald Press, 2000.

Gladwin, John W. *God's People in God's World: Biblical Motives for Social Involvement*. Downers Grove, Ill.: InterVarsity Press, 1979.

Murray, Stuart. *Post-Christendom: Church and Mission in a Strange New World*. After Christendom. Carlisle [England]: Paternoster, 2004.

Roth, John D. *Choosing Against War: A Christian View: A Love Stronger Than Our Fears*. Intercourse, Pa.: Good Books, 2002.

Wallis, Jim. *Faith Works: Lessons from the Life of an Activist Preacher*. New York: Random House, 2000.

———. *The Soul of Politics: A Practical and Prophetic Vision for Change*. New York; Maryknoll, NY: New Press; Orbis Books, 1994.

Wink, Walter. *Engaging the Powers: Discernment and Resistance in a World of Domination*. Minneapolis: Fortress Press, 1992.

PART II

SEEKING THE WELFARE OF THE CITY: ESSAYS ON PUBLIC PEACE, JUSTICE, AND ORDER

Conference Papers

_____

SECTION D

Practicing Wisdom in Public Systems

—18—

BREAKING THE UNEASY SILENCE: POLICING AND THE PEACE MOVEMENT IN DIALOGUE

Jeff Gingerich

Since the September 11, 2001, terrorist attacks on U.S. soil, people of peace and nonviolence have been questioning the role of police and peacekeeping forces on an international level. This challenge has stretched former assumptions about safety and security in a world that now feels less certain, and along with other factors resulting from America's "culture of fear," is moving many in the historic peace tradition closer toward just war thought, or at least just policing. Yet the questions that surround policing have been strangely ignored for some time, even at the level of local domestic jurisdictions.

The peace church in particular has allowed itself to lapse into an uneasy silence on the issue of domestic policing, yet now the church must confront a series of difficult questions. Is it hypocritical for the peace church to take a strong stance against international warfare while at the same time ignoring the issue of local police, or even calling upon an armed local police force frequently? Is it morally acceptable for nonviolent members of the church to utilize the civil police if they are not willing to join the same police force because of their pacifist views? Of course the answers to these questions will rely on a response to a broader set of factors, such as the relationship between the church and a legal state, the degree of pacifism that church people espouse, the manner by which individuals define and expect security, and the social and economic conditions that fertilize conditions that lead to crime.

Why has the peace church been so hesitant to discuss and challenge the issue of domestic policing despite the basic fact that nearly every police force in the United States relies on the ultimate threat of violence to maintain security in communities? Is the issue too close to home? When we consider the protection of our families and our loved ones do we think differently from when the potential attacker is on the other side of the ocean? Perhaps it is because we are more likely to know police officers in a personal way, see them every day, and be helped by them on the street, while we rarely are able to personalize the military officer on duty in a combat zone.

The peace church and other nonviolent practitioners have more fully accepted the paradigm of restorative justice as an alternative to the more punitive, retributive, and violent system of justice that exists in the modern criminal justice system. But except for the involvement of police officers in victim-offender conferencing, restorative justice has done very little to address the larger issues of police force and violence. To put it simply, we acknowledge how important it is to prevent crime, and we believe that restorative justice is a good way to deal with offenders after they have been caught and admit to their crime, but we do not acknowledge the force that it may take to apprehend offenders and bring them to the restorative justice table.

How *should* the peace church think about and relate to the formal police system? On a simple, but practical level, we might say that the church has four possible options that move beyond the uneasy silence on the issue of an armed police force:

> 1. Actively resist all forms of community social control that utilize the threat of violent force.
> 2. Not resist, but not actively call upon forms of

community social control that utilize the threat of violent force.

3. Utilize but not participate in community social control that relies upon the threat of violent force.

4. Actively participate in community social control that utilizes the threat of violent force, but only use violent force in "just" situations.

The theories and tactics of nonviolence have served well in the struggle to confront oppressive dominant structures. The restorative justice movement has provided an alternative to punitive models in corrections. But a need to bring offenders to the restorative justice table remains, and armed police forces provide this function most often. A need for consistent safety assurance in communities also remains. Might nonviolence be a tactic that is suitable for daily crime control and policing? While many in the field of nonviolence are distraught over the current brutality and military-like style of domestic police, their distress should actually press the question: what *would* an acceptably nonviolent policing system look like? The purpose of this chapter is to begin a discussion on the possibilities for a nonviolent community order that relies less upon a traditional armed police force.

WHO ARE THE POLICE?

The issue of policing first began to draw my attention while working with the Resolving Conflict Creatively Program in New Orleans, Louisiana. We were known as the conflict resolution people in the city. New Orleans was known at the time for a corrupt police department and for police brutality. We were asked to work with the department to develop appropriate ways to better train police officers in nonviolent methods of conflict resolution. Over a period of six months we worked with members of the police academy to put together a conflict resolution curriculum there. We knew that many police consider the real training of law enforcement to begin after the academy, when "field training officers" take the new recruits, tell them to forget everything they have learned in the academy, and promise to tell them about "real" policing. As we pieced together a workshop, therefore, our focus was on those field training officers.

Among the police officers I encountered there was a palpable tension in the culture of policing. On the one hand, many officers shattered my stereotypes. At the academy I met fresh young recruits whose genuine motivation for becoming police officers was to make a difference, and to do something good with their lives. I also met seasoned officers who were sensitive to social justice, hated racism, and were deeply bothered by stereotypes of New Orleans police officers in the public that portrayed them as uncaring and brutal.

On the other hand, I encountered aspects of the police culture that were deeply troubling. Some field training officers saw basic communication as a weak approach to law enforcement. An atmosphere of machismo and violence enjoyed higher status than upholding the law. Loyalty and cohesion among the police often required that they defend officer actions no matter how unethical or illegal.

Breaking into such a police culture is difficult. Still, police departments across the country have been working to incorporate new methods into their training. In St. Paul, Minnesota, a field training officer has built upon the concept of restorative conferencing to incorporate "restorative language" into officers' everyday interactions. Michigan, New York, Florida, and Maine have all implemented small steps toward nonviolence training based on a Kingian philosophy of nonviolence.

In Canada, Mennonite police officers have begun meeting with each other and with Mennonite academics to explore whether one can be both Mennonite and an armed police officer. Within this discussion, it has been clear that the eight individuals involved feel a calling to their jobs in law enforcement. It is also clear that their religious communities push them to think about what their sense of vocation might mean for the historic pacifist tradition of the Mennonite church. The officers have stressed their correlation with the Mennonite peace position;

they want to be called "peace officers" and believe that their actions most often help to stop future violence and conflict. "We're not fighting the enemy," one officer told the group. "These are good people that we're trying to help. We're just trying to keep good guys from hurting other good guys."

The function of policing, of course, varies greatly according to the organizational and cultural context of any local force. In ancient times, individuals were expected to follow the rules of the majority, and policing was conducted informally. The tribe, clan, and family had responsibility to guide the individual's behavior and to enforce the informal rules or customs that the tribe or clan had established. Eventually, rules became laws, and rule breaking was formalized as an act committed against the state.

It was not until the eighteenth century that the term "police" began to be used, and not until the early nineteenth century when the British Parliament received a recommendation to appoint a paid civilian police force to maintain order in London. This police force was unarmed and instructed by Sir Robert Peel, in his legislative appeal,

> To use physical force only when the exercise of persuasion, advice, and warning is found to be insufficient to obtain public cooperation to an extent necessary to secure observance of law or to restore order; and to use only the minimum degree of physical force which is necessary on any particular occasion for achieving a police objective.

American cities adopted the British model of policing in the eighteenth century, but these cities felt a need to adapt new strategies in reaction to the larger social dynamics at the time. Modern policing developed in America during a period marked by disorder and violence. Most American cities experienced mob disorder. A variety of factors appear to have contributed, including ethnic and racial conflict as well as economic disasters. This led to the more formalized organization of policing, resulting in uniformed and armed police forces in the 1850s.

This brief history underscores the initial progression of U.S. police systems toward what some would call a "paramilitary" style of police today, despite its origins in nonviolent, peacekeeping efforts. Mark Taylor, author of *The Executed God*, argues for dismantling the police force as we know it:

> Across the United States today, there is a vigorous movement to end police brutality, the use of excessive force against residents that results in injury and often death. The movement is anchored in urban experiences of police violence in communities of color. . . . Every region of the United States now shows police violence to have reached problematic levels.[1]

The peace church must realize that to deal with the issue of policing is to tread into dangerous waters. Perhaps this is an additional reason why Mennonites and others have avoided the subject for so long. Yet, much of police work has little to do with violence, and actually parallels much of the peacemaking work of the church.

USE OF FORCE AMONG POLICE OFFICERS

In assessing the role of peace officers, or police officers, people of nonviolence must first assess just how much violence individual officers typically use on a daily basis. Here, I will use the term "force" to refer to this potential violence, since this is the general terminology used in policing. Legally, use of force among police officers relies heavily upon the "reasonable officer" rule, with many court decisions hinging on whether the jury or judges accept that officers have acted in a reasonable manner—a morally ambiguous judgment to be sure. Fortunately, the data as seen in the box below shows that, while the potential for violence may be a constant threat for police officers, the actual use of force is not an issue that police officers face on a daily basis.

Such statistics are mostly positive. Police are indeed spending most of their time serving the community, all of which they could accomplish without any weapons at their side. In char-

What do we know about the police use of force in the United States?

- Police use force infrequently—a 1996 study by the Bureau of Justice Statistics indicates that police force was used in less than 1% of the contacts that police officers made.
- Police use of force typically occurs at the lower end of the force spectrum, involving grabbing, pushing, shoving.
- Police use of force often takes place in poor neighborhoods where the relationship between police and local residents is strained.
- 17.1% of arrests involved use of force.
- Weapons were used in 2.1% of arrests.
- Severe restraints were used in 1.3% of arrests.
- Most use-of-force involved the use of weaponless tactics (15.8% of arrests).
- Police "justifiably" kill on average nearly 400 offenders each year.
- From 1976 to 1998, the U.S. population age 13 and older grew by about 47 million and the size of the police force grew by over 200,000 police officers, but the number of citizens justifiably killed by police did not generally rise.
- The rates at which African-Americans were killed by police in 1998 are 4 times higher that of whites (as compared to 8 times higher in 1978).

(Data from "Police Use of Force: Collection of National Data," Bureau of Justice Statistics and "Characteristics Associated With the Prevalence and Severity of Force Used by Police," Garner, Maxwell, and Heraux, *Justice Quarterly* (December 2002).

acterizing police use of force as infrequent, I do not mean to minimize the problem or to suggest that the issue is unworthy of serious attention. However it is important to put the use of force into context in order to understand the potential magnitude of use-of-force issues. The data does not support the notion that we have a national epidemic of police violence. Yet, the final statistics do provide a strong warning: police do kill, and they are not immune to the social ills of racism and class-ism. Poor people of color are likely to be the most likely victims of police abuse. The ugly head of police brutality continues to emerge consistently in the United States and the least-privi-leged in society are most likely to experience it. It will not be easy for these disenfranchised communities to regain trust in the current state police system.

The Canadian Mennonite police officers mentioned above emphasized their role as peacemakers, and their role as com-munity mediators. We need to recognize that much of the police role is as a third-party intervener and we need to build on these skills. Police officers act as mediators much more often than do even the most experienced of our professional com-munity mediators. They could serve a valuable role in the peace community.

Despite the individual officer's reluctance to use force, a common cultural attitude prevails, and in some cases is a legal requirement. Police officers believe that the use of force is required not only for their personal safety, but also for the safety of their colleagues and of the state itself. Such a situation leads to the perceived need for a high degree of personal loyalty within the police force. Regardless of the individual officer's philosophy on the use of force, other officers must know that their col-leagues "have their back" when they face violent situations, and are willing to use lethal force if necessary to save the lives of fellow officers or other citizens. The situation has not changed much since 1973, when Rubenstein made the follow-ing observation in his book, *City Police*:

> Very few policemen use physical force gratuitously. A man will cajole, joke, advise, threaten, and counsel rather than hit, but once his right to act is questioned, once his autonomy is threatened, he is prepared to respond with whatever force is necessary. And once his power is contested, he can do no wrong. The legitimacy of this authority allows him to do whatever he must to preserve it. An attack on him is treated as an attack on the state. A man resisting a policeman is suddenly an

alleged criminal, and although he has not been convicted, the policeman knows he can treat him in a manner in which he cannot treat others.[2]

COMMUNITY POLICING: A LESS VIOLENT ALTERNATIVE

One of the ways that the government has tried to shift away from a reliance on force to the use of community relationships is the community policing model, a trend that has become increasingly popular within the last few decades, but has yet to become any sort of dominant mode of policing.

Community policing is a collaborative effort between the police and the community, whereby police officers become embedded in the community, utilizing more foot patrol than car patrol. The philosophy institutes an intentional focus on reducing crime and fear of crime by involving the same officer in a community for the long term so that he or she can form personal links with residents. These relationships become proactive crime prevention tools, replacing guns as the ultimate force for maintaining community safety. In community policing, officers focus on crime prevention by working as problem-solvers before crime is committed. Problem-solving supports peacekeeping.

Although no currently available research definitively proves that community policing reduces the amount of force that police officers employ, the philosophy closely relates to theories of nonviolence and restorative justice in a number of ways. First, the focus of community policing is on the building of relationships rather than the breaking of laws—one of the central foundations of restorative justice. Second, community policing seeks to hold accountable the wrongs that individuals have done while at the same time building community support and cohesion with as little violent threat as possible. Finally, community police should be willing to think at a structural level, examining the root causes of crime, including racism and economic victimization.

Should the advocacy of community policing by people of nonviolence be considered within the same parameters as "just war" theory? Both just policing and community policing is active engagement in community-building that goes beyond traditional law enforcement. I do not seek to present here a theological justification for community policing. We should consider that community policing, on a local level, does still fall short of the peace church ideal because its officers continue to carry firearms, and ultimately rely on the use of violent force to carry out their otherwise peaceful duties.

ENVISIONING THE FUTURE

Community policing is an appropriate model from which to begin, but the peace church will need to envision a broader, more nonviolent, type of policing if it hopes to remain true to its pacifist traditions. As long as local communities continue to rely on the professional model of policing, we will need to be content with an approach to community policing that is backed by the potential use of force, even if it is not used excessively. An initial step would be to begin to conceptualize the nonviolent alternative to policing as community order rather than policing, moving us toward a more restorative response to public safety while at the same time adhering to nonviolent ideals.

How can we use what we have learned to allow us to envision a domestic policing agent who relies on the impending threat of nonviolent love rather than the ultimate threat of violence? While we are a long ways from approaching the idea of a nonviolent police force politically (both within the government and church, I might add), we might borrow from Howard Zehr's suggestion that "changing the lenses" by which we view the function and nature of policing would be a useful step.[3] I would like to suggest four possible ways in which this might be considered:

1. *Participatory, grassroots community-building.* This approach would *not* rely on the police to do community policing. Community policing as currently understood still relies too much on the officers (and government) to do the community

building, particularly with those offenders who are on the edges of sustainable communities. We are talking about active community building that is consistently engaging the "edges" of the community, or those who are not following the order that has been prescribed by law. We cannot expect our professional police force to become nonviolent if the community itself is not constantly involved with those whom force may be required to apprehend. This will require that we radically reduce the social distance between ourselves and sections of the community that commit the most crime. Social distance is the degree to which people do not identify with other community members or do not feel connected by common interests or a sense of common fate. This is obviously a factor in crime prevention, but also in criminal apprehension. Community police officers are able to find the offenders more quickly and easily than those who are not building relationships within communities. Middle-class, white Mennonites have failed to adequately reduce the social (and spiritual?) distance between their communities and poor communities.

2. Redistribution of power and accountability in community order. The history of U.S. reliance on lethal force for maintaining security and the ease by which the peace church and others of nonviolent persuasion can abdicate their duty to the government might suggest that the most appropriate move toward nonviolent policing would be a radical shift from professional power to citizen power. This would be a very difficult shift for government and local officials who are called upon to protect and serve. Will the government be willing to give up its power in order to allow citizens actively to engage crime through community relationships? Such a shift would allow a move toward a restorative response that revolves more around people than laws, that works to satisfy crime victims as much as court judges and public officials, and that is radically forward-thinking and preventative rather than reactionary and violent. Such a shift would allow additional accountability to enter into policing procedures, both in the secular and spiritual realms.

3. Reconsider "police" training. Traditionally, police officers are trained in police academies through a regimented instructional venue and then turned over to "field training officers" for mentoring on how to survive the streets in the real world. This not only perpetuates the professional status of police officers but it also cements the "us versus them" mentality that will more likely lead to the need to use violent force. Active nonviolent engagement may require thorough nonviolence training by all church members, rather than relegating the role to a few dedicated professionals in uniforms. Christian Peacemaker Teams have begun to model this type of nonviolent strategy in Cleveland, Ohio, where team members organized and attended public vigils to pray for justice and peace while also walking each month to examine street activity during evening hours. Even though the church may not replace civil law enforcement with its own "peace forces," individual church members could be trained more thoroughly in nonviolent responses to crime in order to minimize the number of times that they need to call upon the armed police force. Staying mindful of the current mediating function of most police, officers themselves might partner with community members to provide such training, so as not to alienate the relationship between community and church bodies. Finally, all training, whether for civil servants or for civilians, should include a strong understanding of the root causes for why people commit crime in the first place, with a particular emphasis on the structural conditions that effect decisions regarding law and order.

4. *Lay down weapons.* Would police officers be willing to patrol their beats without lethal weapons at their side, as many British "bobbies" continue to do today? The public may be surprised at the number of officers who would be open to leaving their weapons behind in the station while performing daily activities. What might be the long-term safety implications of such a radical strategy? How does the presence of police guns in neighborhoods add to the level of violence in neighborhoods? Social science research, combined with theological inquiry, would appropriately consider such questions. Crime

victims should also be fully involved in such a discussion since those who are victims of violent crime might perceive a law enforcement environment that is devoid of weapons most negatively. Perhaps churches in smaller communities with less crime could be the first to call upon their local jurisdictions to consider such possibilities. Since non-lethal weapons are becoming more popular, police officers may feel safer if they have the available resources to protect themselves without the violent reaction that guns may generate. Are pacifist theologians willing to consider a theology of pepper-spray and taser guns?

CONCLUSION

Should individuals who wish to follow a nonviolent or pacifist lifestyle become police officers who carry lethal weapons? Or should such individuals call and support police officers who may use violent force to apprehend the offender? The answers are not easy to discern, but it is imperative that people of nonviolence engage the question and not continue to lapse into the uneasy silence on this peacekeeping issue. We must begin to construct new paradigms that build upon the current peacemaking models of policing, as well as the history of successful nonviolent reform.

We must acknowledge that, for the time being, even the sacred cow of restorative justice relies heavily on the threat of violence that exists within the criminal justice system, even while we move forward toward a nonviolent way of doing justice. To move just policing toward nonviolent, restorative policing will require active, participatory involvement with community order by the entire community and will not come about if we simply wait for the system to change.

Perhaps the ideal of a nonviolent police force is far too utopian. But thirty years ago, much of the public would have considered it ridiculous to try to bring together victims and offenders to talk about the harm that was done in crime. Today we have a restorative justice movement that is effectively growing in leaps and bounds. Perhaps such a paradigm-shift in policing is more within our reach than we might imagine, and quite possibly we can envision a future in which the police force is an integral part of the peace movement.

NOTES

1. Mark L. Taylor, *The Executed God: The Way of the Cross in Lockdown America* (Minneapolis, Minn.: Fortress Press, 2001), 137.

2. Jonathan Rubinstein, *City Police* (New York: Farrar, Straus and Giroux, 1973), 327. Cited in Michael Palmiotto, *Community Policing: A Policing Strategy for the 21st Century* (Gaithersburg, Md.: Aspen, 1999), 48.

3. Howard Zehr, *Changing Lenses: A New Focus for Crime and Justice*, Christian Peace Shelf Selection (Scottdale, Pa.: Herald Press, 1990).

FOR FURTHER READING

Alpert, Geoffrey P., and Roger G. Dunham. *Understanding Police Use of Force: Officers, Suspects, and Reciprocity.* New York: Cambridge University Press, 2004.

Germann, A. C., Frank D. Day, and Robert R. J. Gallati. *Introduction to Law Enforcement and Criminal Justice.* Springfield, Ill.: Thomas, 1973.

Jackson, Dave. *Dial 911: Peaceful Christians and Urban Violence.* Scottdale, Pa.: Herald Press, 1981.

Kauffman, Ivan J., ed. *Just Policing: Mennonite-Catholic Theological Colloquium 2002.* Bridgefolk Series, no. 2. Kitchener, Ontario: Pandora Press, 2004.

Nicholl, Caroline G. *Community Policing, Community Justice, and Restorative Justice: Exploring the Links for the Delivery of a Balanced Approach to Public Safety.* COPS Publication. Washington, D.C.: U.S. Department of Justice, Office of Community Oriented Policing Services, 1999.

Taylor, Mark L. *The Executed God: The Way of the Cross in Lockdown America.* Minneapolis, Minn.: Fortress Press, 2001.

Winright, Tobias. "From Police Officers to Peace Officers." In *The Wisdom of the Cross: Essays in Honor of John Howard*

Yoder, eds. Stanley Hauerwas, et al., 84–114. Grand Rapids, Mich: Wm. B. Eerdmans Publishing Co., 1999.

Zehr, Howard. *Changing Lenses: A New Focus for Crime and Justice*. Christian Peace Shelf Selection. Scottdale, Pa.: Herald Press, 1990.

19

JUST POLICING AND THE CHRISTIAN CALL TO NONVIOLENCE*

Gerald W. Schlabach

A remarkable historical convergence is occurring in Christian thinking about war and peace. Pacifist and just war thinkers find that they agree on far more of the conditions for peace and the ethics of peacemaking than they disagree. Prominent examples are the Roman Catholic Church, which has long been custodian of the just war tradition, as well as Protestant ecumenical representatives who gathered with others to work carefully on initiatives such as the Just Peacemaking project of the 1990s, and historic peace churches such as Mennonites. Perhaps Christians will never be able to agree on whether their ethic allows killing in exceptional circumstances or whether they should participate in police functions, where social dynamics and the rule of law stand a reasonable chance of limiting lethal violence to last resort. But it is now possible to imagine that war, at least, might cease to be a church-dividing issue.

The fact that the ethics of war and policing do not present themselves in exactly the same way, however, requires

---

* While other chapters I have written for this book articulate the consensus of the entire research team for the MCC Peace Theology Project, this chapter represents my own scholarly initiative alone. —Gerald W. Schlabach

Christian pacifists to think carefully about the nature of their calling and their practices of vocational discernment.

BROAD STROKES AND CRUCIAL DETAILS

The big picture is visible in representative features such as these:

Mennonite peace theology has increasingly turned to the biblical concept of *shalom* in order to account for the interrelationship between peace and justice, and has acknowledged the role that "structures" play in creating conditions of justice or injustice. Debate continues over whether and how Mennonites ought to participate in those structures when work for peace and justice actually issues in some kind of response and opportunities arise to help correct injustice.

During the same time period in which Mennonites were becoming more socially and politically engaged, the Roman Catholic Church has been moving toward them from the opposite direction: The Second Vatican Council called for a thoroughgoing reevaluation of Christian approaches toward war (*Gaudium et spes* §80), and church teaching under subsequent papacies has encouraged a tighter and tighter narrowing of what might qualify as a just war in the modern era. Pope John Paul II has insisted firmly that war is always a failure of humanity. Though bedrock Catholic commitments to protect the innocent have kept open the possibility of "humanitarian intervention" in the face of egregious human rights abuses, the Vatican recently clarified that this primarily means relief aid, which might secondarily require an armed escort—and does not simply mean war with humanitarian intentions.

Meanwhile, and reflecting broader ecumenical and Protestant thought, developers of Just Peacemaking theory have argued persuasively for ten peacemaking practices that are normative for Christians in both pacifist and just war streams.

When an artist paints a "big picture," of course, the overall pattern and broad strokes come into view early; it is the execution of details that determines its stunning quality, yawning mediocrity, or embarrassing failure. Much of what has made it possible to imagine war ceasing to divide Christians would be *un*imaginable without hundreds of thousands of smaller examples of grassroots collaboration between once-divided Christians, and of course many others besides. But then, there are other "details" to fill in. The catechetical gap between official church pronouncements and support in the pews for recent wars is a reminder of how many Christians are working within what sometimes looks like another frame altogether— America as their church, civil religion as their guide, and "redemptive violence" as their sacrament.

Another example: even within the consensus of the Just Peacemaking project, disagreement remains over whether humanitarian military intervention might fit within one of its ten normative practices for peacemaking. So whether it is ever right to use or threaten lethal violence in order to protect the innocent, under limited exceptional circumstances, remains *and should remain* a point of debate. To some this might seem a small detail within the big picture of historic Christian convergence around peace and war. But even if they are right, it is not just a niggling detail. If Leonardo da Vinci had, with only a few slightly different strokes, rendered Mona Lisa's smile in an utterly unremarkable rather than subtly mysterious way, she would not be the crown jewel in the Louvre.

The concept of just policing—which I first introduced in a background paper made available to the international dialogue between representatives of Mennonite World Conference and the Vatican—calls attention to missing or muddled details in this broad historic Christian convergence around "the things that make for peace." What "just policing" especially highlights is twofold: If the best intentions of the just war theorists were operational, they could only allow for just policing, not warfare at all. If Christian pacifists can in any way support, participate, or at least not object to operations with recourse to limited but potentially lethal force, that will only be true for just policing.

Just policing—and *just* just policing.

What just policing proposes is not a grand convergence

right now, or a mere and premature compromise between just war and pacifist traditions at any point. Rather, what it proposes is an agenda for mutual, mutually challenging, and respectively self-critical conversation that explores the conditions for the possibility of further convergence. It notes that in the long-standing Christian debate between pacifist and just war positions, the moral status of policing has received surprisingly little attention. It holds out some hope that joint attention to this unmapped territory might open up a new horizon in which the possibility of agreement concerning war might come into view. Just as importantly, it calls forth greater faithfulness and coherence on both sides, whether or not further convergence becomes possible.

So while the pursuit of convergence is only a suggested possibility, what the just policing proposal insists is that both sides come clean about their respective views on policing. This agenda requires more than theoretical rigor. The just policing conversation cannot move very far forward unless both sides embody their arguments through lived communal practices. Churches that have traditionally affirmed the possibility of just war have no chance of moving pacifists with their arguments unless they do a far better job of showing *in practice* that they can render their "exceptional" use of lethal violence truly exceptional—in effect turning just war into just policing alone. Churches that have traditionally affirmed the moral requirement of nonviolence even in the face of grave injustice have no chance of moving just war folks unless they do a far better job of showing *in practice* that they have ways to participate in governance that can be as effective as they claim to be faithful.

One new point of convergence should show up on the horizon quite quickly, therefore. Even to make their respective arguments, both sides will need to strengthen their practices of vocational discernment and counseling. What might first look like a minor detail against the backdrop of huge historical developments about momentous matters of war and peace turns out to be as crucial for filling in the big picture as the defining brush strokes on Mona Lisa's smile.

JUST POLICING, AND *JUST* JUST POLICING

Virtually every Christian tradition is trying to have it both ways on war. Twenty years ago *The Challenge of Peace*, a book-length "pastoral letter" by U.S. Catholic bishops, explicitly paired just war and pacifism as legitimate Christian responses to war. Three years later, Methodist bishops in the United States made a similar affirmation. Although "historic peace churches" such as Mennonites and Quakers can hardly be expected to reciprocate by embracing just war thinking, the events of September 11, 2001, did prompt some of their leaders, ethicists, and peacemaking practitioners to affirm international rule of law as the best framework for responding to terrorism. And that implies international enforcement mechanisms—policing.

Surprisingly, policing has received far less attention in Christian ethical thought than warfare. In crucial ways, war and policing follow very different dynamics, which neither just war thinkers nor pacifists have quite faced. To do so together and honestly, however, could help point a way through the long impasse between pacifism and just war—for the good of both Christian unity and international peacemaking. War and policing are significantly different in the following ways:

• Political leaders draw on the rhetoric of national pride, honor, and crusading to marshal the political will and sustain the sacrifices necessary to fight wars. This routinely produces the phenomena we call "war fever" and "rallying around the flag," which undermine moral deliberation. Police officials by contrast appeal to the common good of the community to justify their actions, and do so in less feverish ways.

• Even circumscribed warfare that meets the standards of the just war theory is too blunt of a tool to serve the police officer's task of identifying and apprehending criminals. Police officers are expected to use the minimum force possible to achieve their objective, and are judged harshly if there is collateral damage of the kind that routinely occurs in warfare.

• War can never be subject to the rule of law in the way that policing is. As Stanley Hauerwas notes, in good policing the "arresting agent is not the same as the judging agent," but in war "those two are the same." If the development of democratic processes since the ancient Greeks teaches us anything it is that no rule of law is possible without separating the roles of judge and arresting agent.

• We have words like "frenzy" and "berserk" in our vocabulary because European ancestors noticed that in the heat of battle, irrationality sets in. In this volatile psychological situation soldiers can strike indiscriminately and draw on every emotion that Augustine's theory of "right intention" would rule out. Police officials by contrast go to great lengths to prevent this phenomenon, and when it occurs we condemn it as police brutality.

What most distinguishes good policing from warfare are the relationships police forces have with the populations they are sworn to protect. "Community policing" is a new name for an old strategy that gets police out of their patrol cars, onto the street, into town meetings, and integrated into neighborhoods. Writing in *The Christian Century* in 1994, Christopher Freeman Adams described it as a shift from military-inspired responses to crime

> to one that relies on forming partnerships with constituents. It employs health and human service programs as well as more traditional law enforcement, with an emphasis on crime prevention. It represents a change from a reactive model of law enforcement to one dedicated to developing the moral structure of communities.

But this is how leading peace practitioners from the historic peace churches, such as John Paul Lederach, urge us to respond to terrorism. Terrorism is not located in any one territory, he notes. It instead uses "the power of a free and open system" for its own benefit. Its threat is like a virus, which uses the host system's resources to destroy the host. "And you do not fight this kind of enemy by shooting at it," Lederach observes. "You respond by strengthening the capacity of the system to prevent the virus and strengthen its immunity."

What Just Policing Asks of Just-War-Affirming Churches

Ours is a world that suffers from crime, unjust aggression, exploitation, and wholesale abuse of human rights. In such a world, love of neighbor and protection of the innocent seem at times to require the judicious use of violent force. It thus appears to be mere "common sense" that war may sometimes be necessary to protect innocent third parties and maintain order between nations, just as police force does within a given community.

The just war theory has gained much of its credibility by imagining war to be like police action, without facing up to how different the dynamics of warfare can be from policing. But if war is justified through an appeal to the virtually irrefutable need for policing, it consistently becomes something quite different from policing, and just war reasoning itself all too often devolves into propaganda. It becomes permissive rather than stringent—and it sometimes becomes permissive precisely through the reassuring guise of having been stringent. Historically it proves to be a very small step from believing *some* wars are just, to believing the war in which one's own nation is involved is *necessarily* just.

Just-war-affirming churches must recognize, however, what actually happens to their words of counsel. In the context of 9/11 terrorism, U.S. Catholic bishops urged relatively more attention to nonmilitary work addressing the causes of terrorism—so that even as they reaffirmed the principle of a right of national self-defense, what they intended most to emphasize was not unlike the policy recommendations of peace churches. Media recounting of the bishops' post-9/11 declaration, however, skipped past their extensive recommendations calling for redoubled work for economic development and diplomacy in the region, while ignoring the "heavy moral obligation to see that the full range of nonviolent means is employed" before resorting to military force.

In the context of Saddam Hussein's tyranny the bishops' recommendations did remain largely within a just war framework. Yet even here, the bishops' consistent warning against unilateral, preemptive action by the United States carried forward a bottom-line concern to uphold and strengthen the rule of international law. This too is a concern that pacifist and just war Christians share. Still, if the United States actually had gone to war against Iraq within the framework of United Nations resolutions, it would have done so in letter only—working within the UN structure only after domineering its deliberations precisely by threatening to ignore them. This capricious version of accountability is a species of what worries critics of just war thinking, even when they recognize it as a noble attempt to bring the rule of law to bear on international conflict.

In any case, what is to happen when a war is not just? Who decides? What moral obligation is there to suffer—even surrender—when the only apparent alternative is to wage an unjust war, thus committing murder? And if churches declare a war unjust but the state has members of those churches under its military command, what obligation do church institutions have to aid or even require their conscientious objection, and to join them in public conscientious resistance?

Neither just war theorists nor the Catholic Church that has long championed the theory have fully faced these questions. The just war *theory* is not really even an operative just war *tradition* so long as the churches that affirm it fail to answer these questions in practice—with the resources that ordinary Christians throughout the church need to evaluate wars conscientiously rather than nationalistically. As a Catholic pacifist I am committed to the hope and indeed the faith that the church is moving determinately in this direction. But I will feel no obligation even to consider subscribing to the just war theory until the church does far more to create the pastoral and catechetical conditions for its actual application. Much less would I ask my brothers and sisters in the historic peace churches to reconsider their rejection of all war unless just-war-affirming churches can show that claiming recourse to the exceptional use of violence will no longer tend in fact to make violence unexceptional.

The good news is that even to rectify the just war approach so that it does what it claims—reducing violence to the bare minimum that seems necessary to order society and protect the innocent in a fallen world—will so have to transform the just war theory that it becomes what it should have been all along, just policing and *just* just policing. To apply the model of "community policing" in the international arena opens up a way for Catholics finally to fulfill the Second Vatican Council's mandate to "undertake an evaluation of war with an entirely new attitude." It is also a way to respond faithfully and practically to the increasingly critical approach toward warfare that Pope John Paul II initiated.

Not that it will be easy. For all of this to become a political reality the world's Christian community will need to take leadership in applying already-proven strategies for nonviolent action to the defense of whole populations—what we currently refer to as national defense. U.S. Catholic bishops pointed in this direction in their 1993 pastoral letter, *The Harvest of Justice is Sown in Peace*, by declaring that "the vocation of peacemaking [is] mandatory" for all the faithful. They also recognized that "the Church must seek to foster communities where peaceable virtues can take root and be nourished." When they turned to policy recommendations, however, the bishops were far more specific about steps the nation-state should take than steps the Church itself should take. To be faithful to its peacemaking vocation, the Catholic Church needs practices that are church-wide and parish-deep. It needs institutions that correspond to the magisterium's teaching that the just war tradition begins with a strong presumption against violence, allows wars only as an exception, and does so only in last resort.

Perhaps in this time of great change the international church should explore doing nothing less than developing a nonviolent peace force of its own. This is something in which pacifists and just war Christians could cooperate, and it would provide a model for national governments in making the transition to new forms of conflict prevention and civilian-based defense. The church is history's archetypical transnational society, along with Diaspora Judaism. When Vatican II described the church as a transnational "Pilgrim People of God" while simultaneously renouncing direct political control, it created the conceptual space for a nonviolent "army" to achieve the political goals of the people of God.

The just policing proposal calls upon the Catholic Church to begin this process by forming strategic think tanks and pilot projects for the nonviolent defense of peoples, building on parish experience throughout the world, diocesan social justice offices, and its college and university justice and peace studies programs. Without such efforts Catholics serving in the military and in international police forces stand little chance of fulfilling the just war criterion of last resort.

Just as Mennonites must now contemplate a historic reversal to their rejection of governmental responsibilities, the just policing proposal would require Catholics to contemplate an equivalent transformation in political theology and pastoral practice. To institutionalize practices involved in just policing, after all, Catholics will need to act in ways that may be uncomfortably counter-cultural for them at first. But in the context of what Pope John Paul II has called the modern "culture of death," there may in fact be no other way to be pro-cultural in the best and most human sense, than to be counter-cultural at strategic points.

What Just Policing Asks of Historic Peace Churches

If just-war-affirming churches have found they must have it both ways, so too have historic peace churches. They have had to acknowledge the need for someone, somewhere, to use potentially lethal violence to preserve order in a fallen world. The case of Mennonites is especially instructive here. Historically they have been more reticent than Quakers to participate in local police forces, much less international policing. Yet after September 11 the best alternative to military retaliation many pacifists could advocate was treating the attacks as a crime and trying the terrorists in international law courts.

A Mennonite Central Committee statement upheld "the

call of Jesus to love enemies and live as peacemakers," but it also called on "governments to exercise restraint and respect for the process of international law and diplomacy." Veteran Mennonite peacemaker John Paul Lederach called for a multi-faceted response to September 11 that would address root causes and strengthen the international system. He also recommended recourse to the United Nations and Islamic courts of law, as well as to "domestic and international policing." What appeals such as this generally did not do was specify who would apprehend the criminals, how the arresting agents would operate, and whether the political bodies that conduct international policing would have the support of pacifist churches.

Jim Wallis, editor of *Sojourners* magazine, stated the problem clearly. He had advocated "the most extensive international and diplomatic pressure the world has ever seen against bin Laden and his networks of terror focusing the world's political will, intelligence, security, legal action, and police enforcement against terrorism." But, he acknowledged, "when the international community has spoken, tried, and found them guilty, . . . we will still have to confront the ethical dilemmas involved in enforcing those measures. The terrorists must be found, captured, and stopped. This involves using some kind of force." Wallis's primary focus remained on the conditions of global inequity and superpower hubris that breed resentment and terrorism. Nonetheless, he was acknowledging that even if society did everything he and other peace activists called for it would still require a police function.

When asked why Mennonites have traditionally not served as police officers, one answer has been that Christians simply have more important things to do. At mid-twentieth century, Guy F. Hershberger wrote that "the Christian is called to live a life on a higher level than" being involved in police work. Later his student John Howard Yoder wrote, "The question, 'May a Christian be a policeman?' is posed in legalistic terms. The answer is to pose the question on the Christian level: 'Is the Christian *called* to be a policeman?'"

The development of politically effective nonviolent action in the twentieth century has caused many pacifists to identify themselves as adherents of Gandhian nonviolent resistance. Catholic moral theologian Tobias Winright, a student of Yoder and one ethicist who has not neglected policing, has pointed out that with the demonstrated effectiveness of Gandhian techniques, "the efficacy of violence in policing, generally assumed by nearly everyone, is called into question." The result is that "policing itself can be envisioned in a completely different way."

There are precedents both in Mennonite practice and among leading Mennonite thinkers for seeing policing as a different question than warfare. Mennonites have been leaders in developing nonviolent alternatives to the criminal justice system and have created programs for victim-offender reconciliation, with restitution rather than retributive punishment as the judicially recognized consequence of crime. Viewing the enforcement of international law as "just policing" would allow pacifists to integrate the contributions they have been making to international peacemaking into a process of "just policing," without requiring them to condone warfare even in exceptional cases.

The big-picture challenge Mennonites face, along with others in the historic peace churches, is to articulate what they will do when civil authority institutionalizes the approaches they have been advocating. Just war Christians may legitimately ask, *Are you willing to help implement the changes you have called for? Can participation in governance not be legitimate for Christians?* This research project and conference represents a serious Mennonite effort to grapple with such challenges. But if there are some appropriate ways for pacifist Christians to participate in governance, Mennonites must still help fill in a crucial set of details in practice.

VOCATION AS A PASTORAL TASK

In response to the question of policing, Hershberger and Yoder implicitly recognized that war and policing are recognizably different phenomena, presenting notably different moral challenges to the pacifist. What is so suggestive here is the implication that while a Mennonite response to war and militarism is a matter of principle, a Mennonite response to policing *might* be a matter of vocation.

But the concept of vocation can be dicey for Mennonites. To put pacifism itself into the category of vocation is especially problematic if it means the wider Christian church accepts their pacifism as legitimate only because it is relegated to the status of vocation. Mennonites have already encountered the patronizing attitude by which the twentieth-century Protestant thinker Reinhold Niebuhr said they were not heretics, and had a place in the Christian tradition, so long as they accepted their marginal and socially irresponsible role as living reminders of the rigorous but impracticable standards of Jesus's ethic. Mennonites will not be wrong to reject gentler offers of recognition for their vocation too, if that is what vocation means.

The work of philosopher Alasdair MacIntyre suggests how an ethical position can be true and binding for all, however, even though in the course of historical development a particular community may bear a special responsibility to represent that truth. As a viable community extended through time, a tradition is itself a socially embodied argument about the true good of human beings. It is this need to embody our arguments through communal practices that suggests the sense in which it *is* proper to speak of a pacifist vocation.

In a divided Christian church, we must presume that history has made some gifts, lessons, and words from the Lord relatively inaccessible to some Christians—though intended by God for all. In this situation, the very vocation of Christian pacifist communities may well be to offer a living, socially embodied argument that nonviolence is normative for all. To call this a vocation is not to compromise the integrity of that very argument, but to name the urgent sense of responsibility that some community must take upon itself in order to do what will first make that argument intelligible, then imaginable, then credible to other Christian communities and ultimately to the whole, catholic, body.

Relative to their size, Mennonites already have a remarkable record of witness. They have sent their people to work among the poor around the world, built relationships in nations labeled "enemy," returned home with lessons for addressing the root causes of injustice, worked behind the scenes at international mediation, launched pilot projects for the unarmed defense of populations, and created alternatives to retributive criminal justice. The challenge Mennonites face is to articulate what they are doing or will do when their very witness leads to wider institutionalization of their initiatives, in some cases by civil authority. Mennonites have faced this question with varying degrees of consistency when their own ministries have positioned them to take governmental roles in health systems, welfare programs, international development agencies, and so on. Yet these state functions already assume the rule of law, made possible in part through policing. What if Mennonites now advocate alternative forms of policing itself?

In order to work at this challenge for other functions of state, Mennonites have increasingly seen themselves in the role of Jeremiah's exiles, whom the prophet exhorted to "seek the *shalom* of the city" where they find themselves while remembering that their primary loyalty was to God and God's covenant people. Yoder increasingly explained his understanding of how Christians should serve the world within the rubric of this "Jeremianic" model for being a Diaspora people, which needs neither territory to maintain its identity nor control of state to render its service "for the nations."

What Mennonites must show in practice in order to embody their argument, is whether and how the Jeremianic model provides a convincing response to the legitimate challenge of governance. Some of Jeremiah's exiles were civil officials, after all. If this is a model for critical engagement with the tasks of structuring and governing society without Christian officials losing their ethical moorings within the master narrative of Israel, Jesus, and the church, how will modern Mennonites guide their members and hold them accountable? What will happen if society's need for some kind of policing meets the possibility of non- or less-violent policing—precisely because Mennonites have advocated for just policing, perhaps?

For many of us, the baseline for many of these discussions

remains Yoder's *Christian Witness to the State*. First drafted in the late 1950s, the book can read as either an exercise in rigorous ethical logic or as a mandate for Mennonite social activism, but it also sets forth a pastoral agenda that has largely been neglected. There and in a later speech to the nascent Evangelicals for Social Action entitled "The Biblical Mandate," Yoder insisted that Christians in positions "of relative power in the wider society" will need the support and the discipline of congregational accountability groups. Given the widespread entrance of Mennonites into positions of governance—professional and corporate *as well as* civil and political—such groups would now have to be quite widespread, would have to test and sometimes conscientiously object to the bounds of increasingly rigid codes of professional confidentiality, and would in other ways deliberately grate against our deepening modern habit of separating "personal" and "public" spheres of life. They must become standard practice not only for the few Mennonites who hold administrative positions in government bureaucracies or the even fewer who hold elected office, but just as surely for Mennonites in corporations, the academy, journalism, law, and other professions.

For now, Mennonites need not respond to the just policing agenda by actually commissioning their members to become police officers. Direct responsibility for showing how Christians can "just" participate in "just policing," domestic or international, without once again rationalizing war, falls first upon Christians who have historically affirmed the possibility of justifiable war. What Mennonites must instead do is broadly implement the kinds of accountability groups that Yoder encouraged—before their own acculturation makes the practice even more difficult.

In the end, I cannot predict how much more convergence will prove possible between divided Christians over issues of peace and war. I am realistic enough to recognize that Mennonites are not usually among the Christians most scandalized by division in Christ's church. My plea is that Mennonites not reject the just policing agenda simply to protect their pacifist identity for its own sake. Whether through conscientious collaboration with other Christians who are trying to be faithful, or conscientious objection to the ways that other Christian traditions have been unfaithful, Mennonite pacifist identity has limited value unless it contributes to the global witness of the entire church to Jesus Christ.

But have it either way. Focus on how the just policing agenda contributes to church unity. Or focus on how historic peace churches must take it up in order for their own witness to cohere. Vocational discernment, counsel, and discipline for "Jeremianic" exiles seeking the *shalom* of the civic orders in which they find themselves is critical for any new and more unified Christian witness; we need such a witness if we are to break out of the just war/pacifist impasse that leaves Christians squabbling while tribes and empires burn each other down. That case can be made from either side of the just war/pacifist impasse. Whether Mennonites feel the need for Christian unity little or deeply, however, they must greatly extend the practice of vocational testing and counsel just to be faithful according to the nonviolent calling they have already heard.

BIBLIOGRAPHY

Kauffman, Ivan J., ed. *Just Policing: Mennonite-Catholic Theological Colloquium 2002.* Bridgefolk Series, no. 2. Kitchener, Ont.: Pandora Press, 2004.

Mennonite World Conference, and Pontifical Council for Promoting Church Unity. "Called Together to be Peacemakers: Report of the International Dialogue Between the Catholic Church and Mennonite World Conference, 1998–2003." *Information Service* 03-II/III, no. 113 (2004).

Stassen, Glen, ed. *Just Peacemaking: Ten Practices for Abolishing War.* Cleveland: Pilgrim Press, 1998.

Wallis, Jim. "Hard Questions for Peacemakers." *Sojourners,* January-February 2002, 29–33.

Winright, Tobias. "From Police Officers to Peace Officers." In *The Wisdom of the Cross: Essays in Honor of John Howard Yoder*, eds. Stanley Hauerwas, et al., 84–114. Grand Rapids, Mich.: Wm. B. Eerdmans Publishing Co., 1999.

Yoder, John Howard. "The Biblical Mandate for Evangelical Social Action." In *For the Nations: Essays Public and Evangelical*, 180–98. Grand Rapids, Mich.: Eerdmans, 1997.

20

EFFECTIVE AND FAITHFUL
SECURITY STRATEGIES

Lisa Schirch and J. Daryl Byler

Government officials are telling the people of the United States to prepare for the next terrorist attack. They warn of biological, chemical, or nuclear attacks, of airplanes used as weapons again, of attacks on places of worship, schools, shopping centers, and other places of comfort in our lives. In cities and small towns across the country, healthcare providers, police, fire fighters, and city officials are developing rapid response teams and procedures in case of an attack.

What is the church doing to prepare for and prevent future attacks? How would Jesus respond to September 11? What guidance can we find from our Anabaptist heritage to tell us what to do practically today? How do we bridge our faith with concrete, practical responses to security?

In chapter six we offered a conceptual framework for understanding the war on terror and an alternative, Anabaptist approach to thinking about security. In this chapter, we offer a ten-point set of strategies for American citizens and their political leaders. We believe that these biblically-rooted approaches are more likely than many current U.S. policies to lead to human and global security.

These strategies grow from the work we do at the Mennonite Central Committee (MCC) Washington Office and at Eastern Mennonite University's Center for Justice and Peacebuilding (CJP). We and our colleagues met together on several occasions to analyze the global context and discuss how we can be "strategic doves" who are innocent of harming others, yet, in the words of Matthew, "wise as serpents" in thinking about global security issues. Our conversation resulted in a set of ideas for alternative security strategies with our Anabaptist lens. This chapter is a result of those discussions and a synthesis of previous publications by people at both organizations on the topic of alternative security. Our strategies stem from the following assumptions and principles.

First, we believe that religious actors play powerful roles in supporting peace or calling for violence. While religion has long been seen as irrelevant to the secular world of government and foreign policy, there is increasing awareness of its potential to build peace. We see ourselves as religious actors working with other civilian and state actors to increase global security. This set of strategies, then, is for people in our churches, throughout civil society, and government leaders. We do not intend this chapter to be a comprehensive list of strategies for alternative security. Rather, the strategies below are a starting point based on MCC's and CJP's domestic and international work, and on the voices of our partners. This list needs testing in the church for consistency with biblical-Anabaptist thought, in the expectation that additional ideas will emerge from this conversation of discernment.

Second, we too often assume that faithful or moral strategies are ineffective, or else we simply fail even to care whether the particular faithful responses we choose are effective. We should aim to be both faithful *and* effective. Human security delivered through relationships is faithful and it is more secure and sustainable than national security delivered through military hardware. Let us leave behind the image of the naïve pacifist who critiques war yet offers no alternatives in a complex and dangerous world. Let us instead embrace the call to be what we described in our earlier chapter as "strategic doves."

Peace does not just happen. While prayer is a powerful

component of peacebuilding, God gives us many more tools to help bring about peace. Many see the failure to quickly establish order, much less peace, in Afghanistan and Iraq as instigating a new-found openness to nonviolent conflict resolution and peacebuilding. Anabaptists helped to found these fields of practice and study, which seek practical, effective ways of preventing and transforming violent conflict. Peace is built when people take great care in their decision making by planning for the long term, anticipating potential problems, and engaging in ongoing analysis of conflicts. This implies coordinating resources, actors, and approaches to accomplish multiple goals and to address multiple issues in all stages of conflict and at all levels of society. The field of peacebuilding fosters right relationships that form an architecture of peacebuilding networks, which allow people to cooperate and coordinate to constructively address conflict.

Third, in keeping with Anabaptist pacifist traditions, we assume that an important role of government is to maintain order, but do not assume that the New Testament supports the lethal use of force. Efforts to apprehend and bring to justice those who engage in criminal activities such as terrorism should always seek to preserve human life and, therefore, should increasingly rely on non-lethal methods.

Fourth, we believe that strengthening U.S. security will require work both within the U.S. (internal capacities) and between the U.S. and the rest of the world (external capacities). We believe this must happen in the short term and long term at all levels—from the individual and community to society and global community. Current attention to U.S. security provides an opportunity to re-envision larger questions of U.S. domestic and foreign policy. U.S. security is intimately bound together with global security. Crisis events are inevitably embedded within a "nest" of relationships and systems. We must respond to crises and incidents but also to the root causes in systems and relationships. The best antidotes to militant religious extremists and anti-Western frustration and hatred are democracy, human rights, and economic hope. Greater human security will be found in U.S. policies and practices that emphasize diplomacy, mutuality, and consistency. These are principles found both in the biblical tradition and in the U.S. Constitution.

The strategies we offer below seek to transform relationships both within the United States and between the United States and the rest of the world. We offer these approaches in a confessional spirit, acknowledging our complicity as U.S. Christians in consuming a disproportionate share of the world's resources and recognizing that no alternative security approaches can succeed without a commitment to act justly to change the underlying structures that gave birth to a world full of conflict. Ultimately, true security is rooted in trusting God to give us the wisdom and strength to create a more peaceful and just world.

BUILDING INTERNAL CAPACITY

1. Address trauma within the United States resulting from 9/11 and the war on terror.

> But let justice roll down like waters, and right-eousness like an ever-flowing stream (Amos 5:24).

Many Americans support the "war on terror" at least in part out of their own sense of trauma and insecurity. Many U.S. citizens continue to feel a sense of trauma in reaction to ongoing security threats against the United States. In order to build a secure and just world, Americans first need to turn inward to address their own trauma. Preventing aggressive acts and stopping a cycle of violence is an essential first step in securing the United States. This includes not only preventing others from attacking its territory, but also preventing the United States from attacking other countries in response to American trauma. Understanding and healing trauma within U.S. society and offering new ways of understanding justice are key components in moving Americans toward more effective security strategies.

Trauma is an event, a series of events, or the threat of an event that causes and results in lasting physical, emotional, or spiritual injury. People have different ways of responding to trauma, but there are some patterns. Trauma begins with physiological effects as stress hormones flood the body and people experience feelings of shock and pain. They then move to asking questions such as "Why me?" and often experience feelings of shame or humiliation about their victimization. As they begin to process the violence, they may move to an inward depression, a strong desire for a justice based on revenge, or both, feeling that the revenge will alleviate the depression.

Seeking justice is a central concept in the post-9/11 U.S. worldview. Without healing, trauma can turn into a "justice" that attacks others; it is no accident that so many victimizers have themselves been—or perceive themselves still to be— victims. The U.S. government, however, has offered its citizens only one type of justice—hunting down and killing the terrorists. Trauma healing and recovery processes are an essential part of creating a sustainable, smart security based on a restorative understanding of justice. Trauma healing programs help victims identify themselves as survivors capable of being active peace builders to change their situation and prevent future trauma.

For example, after 9/11 Church World Service and Eastern Mennonite University partnered to create a training program aimed at building the capacity of faith leaders to respond to trauma and conflict in times of crisis with the skills of dialogue and conflict analysis. Many communities across the United States have organized community dialogues to address the trauma of being a targeted nation at war while preparing for and discussing options for future responses to terror.

Trauma healing also includes an accurate self-perception that reflects both self-esteem and respect for others. One can promote patriotism and love for the positive attributes of the United States when one pairs this with humble acknowledgment of ways that the United States has failed to live up to its mandate to protect human rights and democracy for all people. Approaching American citizens and leaders with a lens toward their trauma can provide pathways for challenging our communities to consider other ways of understanding U.S. security and the array of options we have in responding to it. It can also lead to efforts to show compassion and ask for forgiveness from people living in areas affected by the war on terror. For example, an organization called Faithful America rallied American religious people to contribute money toward an apology aired on Arab television programs for U.S. aggression in Iraq and, in particular, the Abu Ghraib torture abuses.

2. Start a civilian-based defense program in the United States.

> Keep alert, stand firm in your faith, be courageous,
> be strong (1 Cor 16:13).

In traditional warfare, fighting between armed groups takes place at specific places and times between clearly identified soldiers. In today's world, groups who conduct surprise attacks against civilians in restaurants, office buildings, and shopping malls are challenging the rules of war. It is impossible for the U.S. military or homeland defense police to defend against such diverse attacks.

An active civic education program within the United States could educate its citizens about the nature and responsibilities of living in a democracy as well as civilian-based defense. Civilian-based defense uses unarmed civilians in conjunction with or instead of an armed military to defend against attack by outside forces. During the Second World War, unarmed citizens of Denmark successfully saved a majority of their Jewish population and actively resisted Nazi occupation. The night before the Nazis were to begin taking Jewish people to the death camps, Danish civilians coordinated a massive strategy to hide Jewish people and move them out of the country on fishing boats.

U.S. citizens need training in how to defend nonviolently their own homes, communities, institutions, and neighbors of all ethnic backgrounds. On 9/11, the only plane that did not reach its target, either the White House or the Capitol, was the one that crashed in Pennsylvania because civilians on the hijacked airplane organized themselves to resist the hijackers.

Civilian-based defense does not mean vigilante-style law enforcement using lethal weapons. Civilian-based defense is premised on the idea that citizen networking is the best way to resist aggression. The Department for Homeland Defense, with the assistance of civil society groups, could offer trainings in nonviolent defense in communities across the country. These trainings would help people identify what is worth protecting in their communities (e.g. their families, neighbors, values, parks, etc.) and would help move beyond the paralysis of color-coded warning systems toward a sense of empowerment. Preparing communities to defend themselves nonviolently in the face of a terrorist attack offers all citizens an opportunity to enhance the quality of democracy by forging new and deeper relationships in our communities. The church can provide moral and structural leadership for citizen-based security, both sounding the call to prepare nonviolent responses in the face of the next crisis, and creating training and dialogue programs where people meet with their neighbors now to learn how to strengthen the American democratic tradition.

3. Build rapid-response networks to prepare for internal crises following an attack.

> Blessed are the peacemakers, for they will be called children of God (Matt 5:9).

God clearly calls human beings to reach out to their neighbors, and even their enemies, in times of crisis. In the days after September 11, many Americans worried for the safety of their Muslims neighbors in towns and cities across the nation. They offered to accompany Muslim women, provide a protective presence at local mosques, or be on-call in case of threats. Many churches also invited local Muslim leaders to provide forums to learn more about Islam so that people would understand that terrorism is not part of the true Islamic faith. For many churches, this was the first time they reached out to the Muslim community. Religious groups and other civil society actors need to prepare relationships across the lines of faith so that we can better coordinate our responses in a time of crisis.

In preparing for the next crisis, we need to take these relationships another step. In war zones, peace builders help organize "rapid response networks" that meet together to create plans for how community leaders might best react in times of crisis. Churches, temples, mosques, and other religious centers can begin to build rapid response networks of faith-based peace builders who will be able to react immediately after a crisis and jointly provide public forums for helping communities deal with the emotional, physical, and spiritual trauma that results from the crisis. The networks can also implement plans for keeping people safe in their community, including people who may share some aspect of their identity with those responsible for the crisis. Faith-based peace builders can prepare to speak out with a spirit of care and dialogue against theological calls for violence or bigotry against others and confront religious leaders or followers who advocate for violent policies that would hurt others. The development of these rapid response networks of people from religious, civil society, and government sectors should begin immediately, and can begin by training community leaders in trauma healing and recovery, human rights values, conflict analysis, relational skills such as mediation and facilitating dialogue, and the design of peacebuilding processes.

4. Uphold American values and the integrity of diverse American communities.

> Let each of you look not to your own interests, but
> to the interests of others (Phil 2:4).

The security of the United States depends on the strength of society to hold itself together, to protect everyone within its borders, to protect its basic values in human rights, democracy, and liberty. It requires the self-confidence to invite others from around the world to visit and experience a democratic, welcoming society. However, current security strategies offer safety, ironically, at the expense of that which we wish to maintain.

In the name of furthering U.S. security, the nation has experienced a severe rollback of civil liberties since September 11. These result from the policies in the USA Patriot Act, an acronym for "Uniting and Strengthening America by Providing Appropriate Tools Required to Intercept and Obstruct Terrorism" Act. The Act has created new laws that authorize secret searches and the indefinite detention of both citizens and non-citizens. In addition it creates a new broadly-defined crime of domestic terrorism that could include acts of civil disobedience and nonviolent dissent (previously protected by the right to assemble in the First Amendment). The Patriot Act also restricts greatly the number of people from other countries who are able to visit or come to the United States for educational purposes. In essence, the Patriot Act curtails democratic freedoms in the name of protecting them.

True security requires the building of communities where everyone is welcome and ready to work together to defend their shared lives. Hospitality and reaching out to strangers is a strategy that Jesus clearly put into practice in his own life and advised others to use. Government policies like the Patriot Act arbitrarily inspire fear of strangers and have inadequate mechanisms for ensuring accountability and oversight. It offers a false sense of security with little thought to the insecurity it actually breeds by instilling resentment and fear among immigrants already in the United States. It hinders the building of true security by preventing people from Muslim and other countries from visiting or being educated within the United States. It attacks the very values that we want to defend.

Building domestic capacity for security within the United States will depend on supporting just immigration policies as well as respectful and equal treatment of all U.S. citizens regardless of ethnic or religious background. We need more efforts by government and community to foster respect, mutuality, and accountability to one another, and to build welcoming and peaceable communities at home and abroad. We secure our own liberty and freedom when we demand due legal processes and equality before the law for all people, and when we oppose the abuses of racial profiling, surveillance, and detention. Government can do this by providing legal channels for immigrants and refugees, guaranteeing workplace protections, allowing for family reunification, and offering a path to citizenship for all newcomers to the U.S. These domestic policies relate closely to foreign policy and trade agreements that undermine stability in immigrants' home countries. Within civil society, we strengthen U.S. security when we welcome immigrants and refugees among us by inviting them into our homes and churches. In keeping with a commitment to challenge racism and transform relationships, we need to continue to foster self-reflection to examine unacknowledged privileges and assumptions based on race and ethnicity.

Other domestic policies also need to reflect the values that build a strong, caring society. The war on terror takes resources away from programs that strengthen American communities through education, healthcare, and poverty-reduction. As funding decreases for domestic programs, the fabric of American society weakens. Policies that support strong education programs, affordable housing, universal healthcare, a living wage, drug abuse programs that focus on treatment rather than punishment, and a reduction of guns within the civilian population for purposes other than hunting all foster the kind of environment that creates strong, responsible communities. Such communities actively care for the weak, sick, young, and old members in their midst. Strong communities with active support programs for the vulnerable have been shown statistically to have less violent crime and happier citizens. They are more likely to be able to prepare for, prevent, and respond to acts of terrorism.

5. Develop renewable energy, reduce dependence on oil, and live in a sustainable way.

> You put us in charge of everything you made, giving us authority over all things (Ps 8:6 NLT).

The United States is the world's largest polluter and also its biggest consumer of global energy supplies. These habits go directly against biblical directions for stewardship of the earth. Many called the attacks of September 11 an "attack on the Western way of life." The World Trade Center and the Pentagon are symbols of American life, and that is precisely why they were attacked. There is a perception around the world that the United States perpetuates unfair trade policies through both economic policy and military force that benefit Western countries at the expense of millions of lives in Latin America, Africa, Asia, and the Middle East. As U.S. citizens we have a choice. We can continue to protect our own very high standard of living and continue to center our economy on consumption. Or we can take steps to use less of the world's resources, and to develop economic policies and institutions that focus on a global living wage, sustainable environments, and a reduced focus on consumption. We have an opportunity now to rebuild and reconstruct these American monuments in a way that addresses global perceptions and criticisms.

Many reasons have been given to explain the wars in Afghanistan and Iraq. Some have justified the wars as necessary to track down and stop terrorists or weapons of mass destruction. Others have understood the war as an exercise to broaden human rights and democracy in these regions. Still others have argued that these wars are essentially about ensuring U.S. access to oil.

There is in fact wide documentation in the field of international relations that U.S. administrations have made many foreign policy decisions primarily for economic considerations based on protecting U.S. access to oil and other material resources. One-tenth of the world's population living in North America and Western Europe account for 60 percent of the world's material consumption. One-third of the world's people live in South Asia and sub-Saharan Africa and they account for only 3.2 percent of material consumption. Securing access to oil and material resources seems necessary if people in the United States want to continue to live at their current level of material consumption, especially if they want to consume as much oil as they currently do. Various U.S. administrations have actively supported dictators "friendly" to U.S. oil-interests in the Middle East region, including Iraq's Saddam Hussein. Supporting dictators to ensure access to resources such as oil is a dangerous risk, as dictators often violate the human rights of their own citizens, develop extensive weapons programs, and switch political sides depending upon their own interests. Thus, efforts to lessen dependence on oil help disentangle our relationships with abusive dictatorships.

Investing in proven renewable energy sources such as wind and solar power can lessen oil dependence. Supporting advanced technology to develop a sustainable, renewable energy policy will meet energy needs without compromising environmental protection, despoiling pristine lands, or putting future generations at risk. Keeping our own environment clean through the enforcement of tight environmental controls, recycling of waste products where possible, limiting the amount of trash produced, and reducing our consumption also contribute to our security. We need to continue to foster appreciation and knowledge of how to live in a way that equitably shares the world's finite supply of energy and resources.

6. Provide training in peacebuilding to all levels of society.

> You … have not asked for … riches, or for the life of your enemies, … but have asked for yourself understanding to discern what is right (1 Kings 3:11).

If we are to create a secure society, we will need to equip ourselves with the skills to interact in a world of conflicting interests. U.S. citizens and leaders lack information about how development programs abroad create environments of hope and health that deter violence and terrorism and create a more secure world and thus greater American security. We need training programs at all levels and in all sectors of our society in the new social technologies of restorative justice, conflict resolution, principled negotiation, mediation, and collaborative problem solving. As a society, we need broad-based media programs that help people understand the relevance of trauma, development, conflict resolution, and human rights work to U.S. security. These approaches to preventing violent conflict have grown immensely in the last twenty years, and have proven effective. Yet most government officials and bureaucrats have not had training in these skills and processes. Capacity-building trainings and ongoing education programs for U.S. military and government officials in these relationship-building skills will begin to address the roots rather than the expressions of terror.

BUILDING EXTERNAL CAPACITY

7. Dismantle terrorist networks.

> Hate evil, love good; maintain justice in the courts (Amos 5:15 NIV).

Anabaptists are uncomfortable with the coercive nature of law and order, although generally we do recognize the need to hold people accountable for their crimes. Analysts used different metaphors to describe the attacks committed on September 11. Some labeled the attacks a criminal act while others called them an act of war. Metaphors matter. The crime metaphor leads to the pursuit of legal justice while use of the war metaphor leads to a justification for counteracts of war. Media and government news sources predominantly labeled 9/11 with the act of war metaphor and justified invasions of both Afghanistan and Iraq based on this metaphor. The war metaphor places emphasis on the struggle to demonstrate power over others. The West has inadvertently set up bin Laden as a war hero and a symbol of the struggle against the West. His picture now appears on street corners in impoverished parts of the world where people are already disenchanted with Western economic and political policies. The imprudent focus on bin Laden also incorrectly assumes that the organization will not survive without him.

The crime metaphor, however, can serve to guide smarter, more effective, security strategies. Treating terrorism as crime highlights the use of violence against innocent civilians as a violation of international law. Governments can dismantle terrorist networks and the perpetrators of terrorism through international law. For example, an international tribunal could be set up to address justice questions relating to 9/11, including the ways powerful Middle Eastern governments considered U.S. allies continue to support terrorist groups. Using the principles and strategies of restorative justice, they could involve victims of both terrorism and the war on terror in identifying their needs in the justice process. Governments could use specialized multinational police units equipped and trained with the sophisticated new generation of non-lethal weapons to capture operatives and gain information on terrorist cells. They can continue to dismantle the financial support system of terrorist networks, and use incentives rather than threats or military force to gain information and cooperation on a legal approach to terrorism. Once multinational police have captured terrorists, international monitors from a variety of impartial, nongovernmental groups could ensure that prisoners are treated according to international law standards.

This approach to terrorism, based on the "crime" metaphor rather than the "act of war" metaphor, would prevent future terrorist acts by containing those who conduct terrorism while also demonstrating restraint and respect for the international rule of law. Modeling restraint against vengeful strategies and support for law and order would do more to de-legitimize strategies that use terrorism to pursue change than does the current war on terror. That war both legitimizes violence as a tool for change and fuels hatred against the West through its blatant obstruction of international law and its high levels of civilian casualties in places like Afghanistan and Iraq.

8. Address the roots of conflict and violence, including legitimate concerns of groups that commit terrorist acts.

> Peacemakers who sow in peace raise a harvest of righteousness (James 3:18 NIV).

Terrorism is a tactic for addressing conflict. We need to separate the legitimate concerns of people from the illegitimate tactic of terror. The war on terror should be an effort to find better ways of addressing conflict, such as creating forums that address these legitimate concerns and by eliminating the tactic of terror rather than aiming to kill the people who use methods of terror. If we really want to prevent terrorism we will need to take seriously the calls for change that fuel anger toward the West and understand that U.S. security is tied to global security. We must respond to specific complaints about U.S. policy in the Middle East, since these policies have been named as a motivating factor for terrorists. Palestinians condemn U.S. support for Israeli occupation. Some Arabs fear an ongoing U.S. military presence in the Middle East even after the current war in Iraq is over.

We can create nonviolent channels of communication that encourage groups using terror to engage in political and diplomatic methods of addressing their concerns. We need to invest major diplomatic resources in negotiating issues that fuel the current support for terrorist actions—e.g., removal of U.S. troops from Saudi Arabia, an end to the U.S. military occupation of Iraq and Afghanistan, a more even-handed approach to the Israel-Palestine problems, and support for negotiations in Kashmir and other conflicted areas. The international community can put major resources toward negotiating issues fueling the current support for terrorist actions by sending teams of highly skilled peacebuilding consultants to conflicts around the world. These teams of consultants could be made up of high and low-level diplomats, religious leaders, and scholar-practitioners in the field of conflict resolution from the local regions and from the international community. In addition, it may be necessary to establish an international civilian peace-keeping presence in Israel/Palestine in order to back recommendations to stop all new Israeli settlements in the West Bank and scale back the existing settlements.

On a regional level, we can craft and support long-term multilateral arrangements and organizations, honor our commitment to work through multilateral bodies including the World Court of Justice, and thereby indicate our willingness to be part of the "family of nations" rather than the one nation exempt from rules that govern everyone else. American security ultimately rests on the quality of its relationships with other groups and nations around the world.

9. Make human rights and democracy the central guiding principles of Western foreign policy.

> Violence shall no more be heard in your land, devastation or destruction within your borders; you shall call your walls Salvation, and your gates Praise (Isa 60:18).

The United States does not have a coherent foreign policy. Critics point to the contradictory policies of supporting some dictators and overthrowing others, of upholding human rights in some cases and ignoring them in others. Both conservative and progressive analysts point to a "double-speak" that uses human rights language to cover for policies based on national economic and geopolitical interests instead of human rights and democracy. In order to be accountable to its own guiding principles and to win the support of others around the world, the United States must be consistent.

American security depends on transforming U.S. military policy in and military aid to other countries. Many experts within the military have openly disagreed with U.S. attacks on Afghanistan and Iraq. They understand that dropping bombs and killing more innocent people will plant more seeds of hatred toward the United States and create more potential for future terrorism. We need to support the training of military personnel to protect against terrorist attacks through nonviolent and human rights—respecting intelligence gathering, arrest, and use of new and effective non-lethal weapons.

In addition, we can continue to advocate for a transformation of the mission and methods of the current military toward the nonviolent defense of human security. This includes the reduction and elimination of lethal military weapons, particularly nuclear, chemical, and biological weapons both in the United States and in regions like Colombia, Iran, and North Korea. We can also advocate restructuring military aid, particularly in the Middle East, to support joint confidence- and security-building measures along with peacebuilding processes by and for Israelis and Palestinians.

The international community can support internal democratic movements in other countries in a variety of ways, including financial aid, training in overthrowing dictators through nonviolent strategies, and the use of international media to gain sympathy and support for democratic movements around the world, including the Islamic world. Twentieth-century revolutions in South Africa, Chile, Poland, India, and El Salvador, for example, give proof that even ruthless, repressive dictatorial regimes can and have been brought down through nonviolent revolutions.

Dictators are vulnerable to democratic movements. Dictators depend on the cooperation and complicity of vast numbers of people. Their authority rests on fear rather than public legitimacy. The international community needs to provide both "carrots" to lead dictators to step down and "sticks" that pressure them to step down. Both persuasion and coercion bring about change. Dictators can be given "retirement" packages that make their exits more tempting. While paying off dictators to leave office does not foster accountability or set a good precedent, it can be the most inexpensive solution to some complex problems. It also takes into consideration the psychological dimension of international conflicts; dictators look for ways of "saving face" that allow them to step down peacefully.

In Iraq, the international community could have offered "carrots" in return for demobilizing, demilitarizing, and creating an Iraqi democracy. A combination of internal and external pressure on dictatorial regimes can persuade and coerce leaders either to step down or to allow democratic elections. All Arab countries have key groups seeking to bring an "Arab democracy" to their countries. Of course Arab or Islamic democracy might look different from Western democracy, since democracy takes different forms in different cultures.

10. Build global justice and restructure international relationships.

> If your enemy is hungry, give him food to eat; if he is thirsty, give him water to drink (Prov 25:21 NIV).

We need to begin to examine our broader relationships with people around the world, along with the economic and political policies that guide these relationships. Creating new relationships between nations in the northern and southern hemisphere could begin by committing funds, resources, and personnel to building better cultural understanding between the United States and the southern hemisphere, particularly the Muslim world. It can include stopping the cultural imposition of Western values and institutions onto other countries.

We can also support a transformation in global economic and political decision-making processes that foster a sense of justice. People who are unable to meet their own human needs often engage in conflict and violence to achieve their needs. Their own struggle with poverty is all the more grating when vast inequities of economic distribution confront them daily— as they see how rich people live in their own communities and as media images display those gross inequities. When people have an ability to meet their own needs, they are less likely to fall prey to calls for them to use violence to gain power, respect, or material wealth at the expense of others.

On an economic level, perceptions of justice and fairness would increase if the West would cancel the debts of the most impoverished countries, and would implement just and equitable global trade relationships. Canceling debt and supporting just trade policies can be coupled with massive funding for schools, universities, healthcare facilities, food and shelter programs, ending the global HIV/AIDS pandemic, and fostering democratic infrastructures around the world.

Ensuring the health and education of people around the world would likely inhibit terrorism far more than our military strategies. Many Arab and Islamic countries are underdeveloped in terms of education and employment. It is widely recognized that a lack of access to free education has driven large numbers of destitute Muslim parents to send their children to schools sponsored by religious fundamentalists. This has strengthened the influence of formerly marginal elements in the Muslim world. UN-sponsored international schools throughout the Islamic world could provide an Arabic-based liberal arts education. Adult training programs teaching computer and technology skills as well as a full range of peace-building trainings and programs could strengthen the economy and the capacity for democratic leadership within civil society. Free interdisciplinary education would strengthen and empower civilians to participate in democratic movements. It would also contribute to economic development and improve relationships with Western countries.

Creating global conditions to prevent terrorism and violent conflict depend, therefore, on creating societies that provide access to jobs, affordable education, healthcare, and respect for the full human dignity of all. These lofty goals are not out of our reach. Each year the UN Development Program releases statistics on development around the world. The price for healthcare, education, and employment opportunities for everyone is not cheap, but it is not out of reach. The problem is that the political will to create societies that offer such opportunities is missing. Each year the United States alone spends far more on its own military capacity than the cost of providing basic universal healthcare and education to people around the world.

CONCLUSION

Security is on the minds of many Americans. Yet Jesus prompts us to have bigger dreams than simply staying safe: we are commissioned to help build and enter into the Kingdom of God. While U.S. Christians face great challenges in changing the direction of their nation's domestic and foreign policy, we also live in a nation with great opportunities to help build a world where people of different faiths and cultures live together and share the resources God provided for humanity.

When a dove returned to Noah with an olive branch in its beak, it symbolized God's promise to let humanity shift its course. What would it mean to be a flock of doves in a land of hawks? God gave humanity the creativity and passion to create the change we need. The solutions to the world's security problems and the hope for building the kingdom of God are the same: They both rely on loving our enemies, doing good to those who hurt us, examining the log in our own eye before we pick at the speck of dust in our neighbor's, and finding new and ever more creative ways to love our neighbors around the world. These acts, concretized in the strategies above and discovered every day when we pray for wisdom, will enable us to be the flock of doves following the Holy Spirit—the Dove of peace.

FOR FURTHER READING

Friesen, Duane K. *Christian Peacemaking & International Conflict: A Realist Pacifist Perspective*. With a foreword by Stanley Hauerwas. Christian Peace Shelf Selection. Scottdale, Pa.: Herald Press, 1986.

Sampson, Cynthia, and John Paul Lederach, eds. *From the Ground Up: Mennonite Contributions to International Peacebuilding*. Oxford New York: Oxford University Press, 2000.

[Scheuer, Michael]. *Imperial Hubris: Why the West Is Losing the War on Terror*. Washington, D.C.: Brassey's, 2004.

Schirch, Lisa. *The Little Book of Strategic Peacebuilding*. Intercourse, Pa.: Good Books, 2004.

CONCLUSION

21

CONTINUING LINES OF INQUIRY

by Gerald W. Schlabach
on behalf of MCC Peace Theology Project team

To conduct a theological research project in the believers church tradition is to expect and invite further testing. Certainly that is true when the discerning Christian community faces a new or particularly challenging issue as it engages the needs of the world and converses with other Christians. Such is the question of ordering and security for the Anabaptist-Mennonite tradition. In concluding this book, therefore, the research team for the Mennonite Central Committee (MCC) Peace Theology Project encourages further theological conversation and practical work in at least seven areas:

1. *More empirical evidence.* Pamela Leach has provided an extended case study examining the conditions and practices that favor true human security. Duane Friesen, Lisa Schirch and Daryl Byler, Pam Nath, Alain Epp Weaver, Jeff Gingerich, and others have inquired further into "what works," in some cases offering extensive policy proposals. Still, we could use a further project combining the folk methods of Doris Janzen Longacre[1] and the scholarly methods of Gene Sharp[2] to gather far more examples of nonviolent "best practices" that are contributing to human security.

2. *"Nonviolent coercion"—will it communicate?* The project team has found unexpectedly wide consensus in favor of a

definition of "coercion" that distinguishes it from violence and thus opens up the possibility of nonviolent coercion (Friesen, pp. 53-54). But will this be understood within the MCC constituency? Will it communicate to non-pacifist critics who have a stake in conflating coercion and violence in order to keep pacifists in an "apolitical," "sectarian" box? This is especially a tendency among Protestant thinkers in the United States who have been influenced by leading twentieth-century Christian ethicist Reinhold Niebuhr. But a few of the European theologians with whom Fernando Enns has been in ecumenical conversation also show signs of the same attitude.

In any case, the anxieties that John Rempel has voiced about accelerating Mennonite acculturation, even through well-meaning efforts to contribute to the ordering of society, do call for care. Is there a danger that a finely tuned concept such as "nonviolent coercion" could contribute to rationales for violent coercion that mark the erosion of Anabaptist-Mennonite peace commitments?

3. *Dangers in contesting the language of "security" and "order."* If there is an "underside" of silenced, marginalized, and oppressed people in history there is also what one might call an "overside"—the broad opposite of the underside that includes both those who exercise and those who are glad to benefit from current power configurations. Those in the overside have often exercised a near-monopoly on the language of "security," "governance," "realism," "law," and "order."

Our research team strongly advocates that the historic peace churches contest such language, and the "ontology of violence" behind them. The concepts of human security and just ordering are too important—and too biblical—to abandon or neglect. From Colombia, Alix Lozano illustrates why. For the United States, Ted Grimsrud argues why. Many other authors here join in attempting to take back the language of security and ordering. Still, what are the possibilities and dangers of miscommunication when we attempt to crack the monopoly?

4. *What about "exceptions"?* We must recognize that in any advocacy of international law, community policing, and other

improvements in human governance, a thorny question continues to lurk: In a fallen world, are there any legitimate exceptions to the Christian moral norm of nonviolence? Gingerich and Gerald Schlabach inevitably evoke this issue by exploring the neglected area of policing. Friesen walks carefully through situations in which pacifists struggle to love their neighbors in social and political settings that have developed to the point that policymakers find it hard to imagine nonviolent solutions. Carol Penner tells of working with parole officers in order to include sexual offenders in congregational life while protecting children; thus she reminds us that Friesen's difficult cases are not so distant as we might like to believe.

Schlabach does argue that pacifists should not feel compelled to consider the legitimacy of "exceptions" to the moral norm of nonviolence until non-pacifist Christians demonstrate that these can be kept truly exceptional. But pacifists must be honest enough about the dilemmas of human fallenness (even within the church) that they allow the question to continue goading them to help develop nonviolent alternatives.

5. *Two-kingdom theology vis-à-vis human solidarity?* Pamela Leach's analysis demonstrates that multilateralism, solidarity, interconnection, and resourcefulness provide a more promising basis for human security than policies so often carried out in the name of national security. Numerous other contributors echo and extend such analysis in their policy discussions, and Mary Schertz suggests a deeply rooted biblical basis for such thought. Meanwhile, Enns reports great receptivity to multilateralist conceptions of security in ecumenical circles.

Still, if Mennonites are glad to emphasize the promise of interconnected human solidarity when they argue against the ideologies of "national security," they continue to employ modified versions of Anabaptist-Mennonite "two-kingdom theology." John Howard Yoder's early notion of "middle axioms" and later notion of multilingual translation across markedly different ethical systems are less rigid, more supple, versions of two-kingdom theology. With Duane Friesen and Lydia Harder, our research team affirms that some such "middle discourse" remains valuable and necessary if Mennonites are to engage God's world while clearly naming what of "the world" runs counter to the ethic of Jesus.

And yet we must ask: Does the continued use of modified "two-kingdom" language, even its more sophisticated forms, risk redisconnecting Mennonites from wider networks of human solidarity? Judith Gardiner and Paulus Widjaja demonstrate why it dare not. Grimsrud argues that it need not. But lines that mark the boundaries between communities are not lines that connect them in webs of solidarity.

6. *Develop congregational accountability groups?* One can read John Howard Yoder's *Christian Witness to the State* as an exercise in rigorous ethical logic or as a mandate for Mennonite social activism. But in its insistence that those in positions of authority can only carry out their tasks as faithfully Christian vocations if they are accountable to their local congregations, Yoder's book also set forth a pastoral agenda. Unfortunately, that agenda has often gone unnoticed and largely been neglected—though Alfred Neufeld informs us that Paraguayan Mennonites have discovered it for themselves. Is there still time for North American Mennonites to encourage the widespread development of congregational accountability groups for people in positions of governance?

Governance is not just the task of civil and political authorities. Professional, corporate, and indeed church leaders also govern. Schlabach argues most forcefully that practices for vocational testing and accountability are key to any peace church witness that hopes to convince Christians in other traditions as they face security challenges. Meanwhile Penner shows most poignantly that deliberate accountability processes are crucial if congregations themselves are to be both inclusive for offenders and secure for the innocent. Between the extreme challenges of global terrorism and sexual abuse, however, lies a vast sphere of life in which social workers, lawyers, teachers, entrepreneurs, and many others need the support and guidance of their Christian communities if their vocations are truly to be Christian ones.

7. An inter-church, inter-religious, or in-group conversation? Probably this question is settled already. Enns, Leach, and Schlabach write from explicitly inter-church contexts. Epp Weaver and Widjaja write from explicitly inter-religious contexts. Wichert explicitly opens a conversation with the global community of human rights activists and the philosophical positions encoded in international law. Every author here, in fact, converses with a wide range of theological or interdisciplinary sources from well beyond the Anabaptist-Mennonite tradition alone.

If some Mennonites or Brethren in Christ, including some participants in our project consultations, find that such wide-ranging exchange is itself a source of insecurity, their anxiety ought not to be dismissed. Such anxiety is of a species with the anxieties that many peoples in our globalizing world are experiencing as they—as we—find our identities threatened by forces we sometimes welcome, sometimes feel imposed, and sometimes have welcomed to unforeseen effect.

Though exchange and interconnection certainly can corrode the identity of a community, a culture, or a church, this is not an inevitable fate. Enns's report on interchurch conversations concerning peace and security indicates that long years of debate have produced an ecumenical culture in which no position will dominate if it "clearly [conflicts] with the ecclesiological identity" of a member church, even a small one representing a minority tradition. Ecumenists have found that progress toward authentic Christian unity comes not when they flatten out communal identities and confessional differences but when they honestly throw them into relief. Similar hopes for civil society emerge from Grimsrud's chapter. Drawing on recent work by religion professor and political philosopher Jeffrey Stout, Grimsrud argues that authentic democratic conversation will not simply tolerate the arguments that citizens make from out of their particular religious communities, but will welcome them. Civil debate among diverse traditions may be difficult, but the discipline required to articulate deeply held convictions in conversation with others may as well strengthen communal identities as corrode them.

Perhaps this is only a hope, itself insecure and risky. If so it is of a piece with the hope that the church offers to the world as an Abrahamic people, called and blessed to live in service as a blessing amid all other peoples. If so it resonates across centuries and cultures with the exhortation of Jeremiah to the exiles he knew—urging them to remain loyal to their God precisely by finding their peace in seeking the peace of the city that had both captured and hosted them.

For in a globalizing world, everyone and every people now lives in Diaspora, recognize it or not. The disconcerting strangeness of life in Diaspora is much the source of insecurity in our world, prompting some to lash out with terror, others to erect walls against the cultural sieges they fear, and others to attempt illusory empire. In such a world the only remaining path to peace and security may be to find ways for distinctive communities and cultures to live together without the homogenization—the pressing out of local and religious identities—that is itself so threatening.

The transnational people that is the church should be learning to do this in its own life, as it practices the blessing of Abraham, the service of Jeremiah, and the peace of Christ. In the very measure that it learns to do so, it offers such life to the world, without threat to the integrity of any people or nation. To do this not just to say this, of course, is our ultimate challenge.

NOTES

1. Doris Janzen Longacre, *More-with-Less Cookbook*, 25th anniversary edition (Scottdale, Pa.: Herald Press, 2000).

2. Gene Sharp, *The Politics of Nonviolent Action*, 3 vols., ed. Marina Finkelstein (Boston: Extending Horizons, 1973).

CONTRIBUTORS

J. Daryl Byler is director of the MCC's Washington Office and monitors U.S. militarism and Middle East policy. He is an ordained Mennonite minister and an attorney. He is married to Cynthia Lehman Byler. They have three children.

Fernando Enns was born in 1964 in Curitiba, Brazil, and is married to Renate Enns. He is Director of Studies at the Ecumenical Institute, University of Heidelberg, Germany, and represents Mennonite Church Germany on the Central Committee of the World Council of Churches. Enns is co-editor of *Seeking Cultures of Peace: A Peace Church Conversation* (Cascadia and WCC Publications, 2004).

Judith A. Gardiner has been a member of the Wood Green Mennonite Church in London for twenty-two years. A published poet, she works as a probation officer, specializing in delivering cognitive behavioral programs to offenders. A member of the Labour Party since 1983, Gardiner has twice been elected as a councilor for the London borough of Tower Hamlets. With her husband, Sean, she is a parent to two adult children.

Jeff Gingerich is associate professor of sociology at Cabrini College in Radnor, Pennsylvania, where he teaches both criminology and sociology courses. He received his PhD in sociology from the University of Pennsylvania. His research interests include prisoner re-entry initiatives, the intersection of nonviolence and policing, and racial segregation within religious organizations.

Ted Grimsrud lives in Harrisonburg, Virginia. He has served as Associate Professor of Theology and Peace Studies at Eastern Mennonite University since 1996. Prior to his work at EMU, he served for ten years as a pastor in Mennonite churches in Oregon, Arizona, and South Dakota.

Lydia Harder earned her ThD from Emmanuel College at the Toronto School of Theology in 1993 and is presently adjunct faculty member at Conrad Grebel University College and the Toronto School of Theology. Her teaching experience includes short-term assignments in schools in Paraguay, Egypt, and Winnipeg. In 2000 and again in 2004 she visited Iran as part of a theological exchange sponsored by MCC.

Robert Herr and **Judy Zimmerman Herr** are Co-Directors of the International Peace Office for MCC. They co-edited the book *Transforming Violence: Linking Local and Global Peacemaking* (Herald Press/Pandora Press, 1998), and have contributed to a number of other publications on peacemaking. They serve on the planning committee for a series of Historic Peace Church theological conversations related to the Decade to Overcome Violence, and were the main staff persons for the MCC Peace Theology Project.

Pamela Leach is a Quaker and teaches Political Studies and Human Rights at Canadian Mennonite University in Winnipeg, Canada. She has been an MCC volunteer in Burkina Faso and has also lived in Ghana. Her articles include "Citizen Policing as Civic Activism: An International Inquiry" *International Journal of the Sociology of Law*, 31 (2003) 267-94 and "Rwanda: para deconstruir un genocidio 'evitable'" *Estudios de Asia y Africa*, Vol XXXVIII, 2003 (2) 321-44. She welcomes correspondence: pleach@cmu.ca.

Alix Lozano was born in Bucaramanga, Colombia. She holds a MTh and serves as director of the Seminario Bíblico Menonita de Colombia in Bogotá. She has participated in various areas of ministry in the Mennonite Church of Colombia, including pastoring, teaching, and working with women who suffer violence. She writes for Colombian religious journals on women and violence, and family violence.

Pamela S. Nath is Professor of Psychology at Bluffton University, where she has taught since 1996. After earning her doctoral degree from the University of Notre Dame, Nath worked as a licensed psychologist in community mental health and private practice settings before returning to academia. Recent research projects have included such diverse topics as faith development in college students, women in pastoral ministry, peace psychology, and peacemaking in post-conflict societies.

Alfred Neufeld holds a Doctor in Missiology degree from Basel and currently is Dean of the School of Theology of the Protestant University of Paraguay (Universidad Evangélica del Paraguay), an academic confederation of Mennonite, Mennonite Brethren, and Baptist theological institutions. He has authored a book on systematic theology from an Anabaptist perspective, entitled *Vivir desde el futuro de Dios*, to be published at Kairos, Buenos Aires.

Carol Penner lives in Vineland, Ontario, with her husband Eugene and two children. She is a pastor at First Mennonite Church in Vineland. She has worked as a chaplain, a freelance writer, and a sessional lecturer. She has a PhD in systematic theology from Toronto School of Theology.

John D. Rempel teaches historical theology at Associated Mennonite Biblical Seminary in Elkhart, Indiana, where he is also the assistant director of the Institute of Mennonite Studies. He served as minister of the Manhattan Mennonite Fellowship in New York for ten years and in 1991 became the first Mennonite Central Committee representative at the United Nations. He is author of *The Lord's Supper in Anabaptism* (Herald Press, 1993). With Jeffrey Gros he edited *The Fragmentation of the Church and Its Unity in Peacemaking* (Eerdmans, 2001).

Mary H. Schertz is happily employed teaching gospels, Sermon on the Mount, and other sundry aspects of the New Testament, including Greek, at Associated Mennonite Biblical Seminary. She is a member at Assembly Mennonite Church and participates in a lively extended family as well as an affectionate neighborhood. In all these settings, she is enjoying moving into the more curmudgeonly stages of life.

Lisa Schirch is an associate professor of peacebuilding in Eastern Mennonite University's Conflict Transformation Program. A former Fulbright fellow, Schirch has fifteen years of experience consulting with a network of strategic partner organizations around the world in the fields of conflict resolution and peacebuilding. She is the author of three books: *Ritual and Symbol in Peacebuilding*, *The Little Book of Strategic Peacebuilding*, and *Keeping the Peace: Exploring Civilian Alternatives in Conflict Prevention*. Schirch holds MS and PhD degrees in Conflict Analysis and Resolution from George Mason University.

Alain Epp Weaver is MCC co-representative for Palestine, Jordan, and Iraq. Together with his wife, Sonia, with whom he has two children, he has worked with MCC in the Middle East for over a decade. Weaver co-authored, with Sonia, a history of MCC's work in Palestine. He has also published articles in a wide variety of journals, including *Journal of Religious Ethics*, *Review of Politics*, *Jerusalem Quarterly File*, and *Mennonite Quarterly Review*.

Timothy Wichert is a lawyer with the firm of Jackman and Associates in Toronto, focusing on refugees, immigration, and human rights. He spent seven years with MCC in Nairobi, Geneva, and New York, and another six years as refugee program coordinator for MCC Canada. He obtained his law degree from Queen's University in Kingston, Ontario in 1984.

Paulus S. Widjaja is on the faculty of Theology at Duta Wacana Christian University in Jogjakarta, Indonesia, where he earned a Sarjana Theologia degree in 1987. He later earned a Master of Arts in Peace Studies (MAPS) from the Associated Mennonite Biblical Seminary in Elkhart, Indiana, in 1997 and a PhD from Fuller Theological Seminary, School of Theology, Pasadena in 2002.

About the Editors

Duane K. Friesen is Edmund G. Kaufman Professor Emeritus of Bible and Religion, Bethel College, N. Newton, Kansas, and on the faculty of Associated Mennonite Biblical Seminary Great Plains Extension. He holds a BA from Bethel College, a BD from Mennonite Biblical Seminary, and a ThD in Christian Social Ethics from Harvard Divinity School, and is the author of *Christian Peacemaking and International Conflict: A Realist Pacifist Perspective* (Herald Press, 1986) and *Artists, Citizens, Philosophers: Seeking the Peace of the City* (Herald Press, 2000). He has collaborated with Glen Stassen and other scholars in developing just peacemaking theory. He served on the MCC Peace Committee from 1996 to 2005. Friesen is a member of the Bethel College Mennonite Church, where he currently serves on the Peace and Justice Commission. He is married to Elizabeth Voth Friesen; they have two married daughters and four grandchildren.

Gerald W. Schlabach is Associate Professor of Theology at the University of St. Thomas, in St. Paul, Minnesota, where he teaches courses in social ethics and Christian morality. He has written books and journal articles on topics ranging widely from peace, social justice, and nonviolence in Latin America, to the thought of St.

Augustine, Benedictine spirituality, and the Eucharist. A Roman Catholic, Schlabach serves on the MCC Peace Committee and is Executive Director of Bridgefolk, a grassroots movement of Mennonites and Catholics seeking to exchange the gifts of one another's traditions. He is the author of *And Who Is My Neighbor?: Poverty, Privilege and the Gospel of Christ* (Herald Press, 1990) and *To Bless All Peoples: Serving with Abraham and Jesus* (Herald Press, 1991). Schlabach and his wife, Joetta, are the parents of two sons. He is a member of St. Peter Claver Catholic Church in St. Paul, and an associate member of Faith Mennonite Church in Minneapolis.